HOME

HOME

HOW *Heaven* AND THE *New Earth*
Satisfy OUR *Deepest* LONGINGS

ELYSE M.
FITZPATRICK

BETHANYHOUSE
a division of Baker Publishing Group
Minneapolis, Minnesota

© 2016 by Elyse M. Fitzpatrick

Published by Bethany House Publishers
11400 Hampshire Avenue South
Bloomington, Minnesota 55438
www.bethanyhouse.com

Bethany House Publishers is a division of
Baker Publishing Group, Grand Rapids, Michigan

Printed in the United States of America

Library of Congress Control Number: 2016938456

ISBN 978-0-7642-1802-6

Unless otherwise noted, Scripture quotations are from The Holy Bible, English Standard Version® (ESV®), copyright © 2001 by Crossway, a publishing ministry of Good News Publishers. Used by permission. All rights reserved. ESV Text Edition: 2011

Scripture quotations marked NASB are from the New American Standard Bible®, copyright © 1960, 1962, 1963, 1968, 1971, 1972, 1973, 1975, 1977, 1995 by The Lockman Foundation. Used by permission. (www.Lockman.org)

Scripture quotations marked NIV are from the Holy Bible, New International Version®. NIV®. Copyright © 1973, 1978, 1984, 2011 by Biblica, Inc.™ Used by permission of Zondervan. All rights reserved worldwide. www.zondervan.com

All emphasis in Scripture and other quotations indicated by italics is the author's.

Cover design by Rob Williams, InsideOutCreativeArts

16 17 18 19 20 21 22   7 6 5 4 3 2 1

To Phil,
dearest, kindest, most loving friend
and husband.

Contents

Foreword

Have you ever been camping? I don't know how much you appreciate the outdoor activity, but I've always thought that one of the fundamental purposes of camping is to make you long for home.

If you've been camping, you know what it's like. It all starts with giving in to the romantic notion of wilderness living with your friends and family in the great outdoors. You have visions of sleeping under the stars and cooking over an open fire. You pack up, filled with the positive vibes of adventure, and travel to what you think will be the ideal site to experience your camping dream. You set up your tent and collect firewood, and with feelings of pioneer accomplishment, you prepare that first meal over the campfire. Food tastes different when it's been cooked over an open flame. (Is that ash?)

By the third day, your back hurts from sleeping on an air mattress that slowly deflates, your tent has taken on smells that seem subhuman, and all the available dry wood within a half-mile radius has been used. At this point, something begins to happen inside of you: *You begin to think about home.* But you still have hope for the rest of the trip. That is, until you go to the cooler and find your special roast—the one you knew would just "wow" your family—is now a sickly gray color, floating in stomach-turning bloody water.

It's happened: You're hit with a deep longing for home—the comfort of a soft mattress, the ease of a stove where you turn a knob and get an instant flame, and the convenience of a refrigerator that does such an amazing job of keeping food cool and fresh. You long for the sights, sounds, smells, and luxuries that only home can provide, and you begin to listen for comments from friends and family about being homesick so you can say, "Hey, let's just pack up and go home."

But, if you decide to go "camping" in a sixty-foot Winnebago with a fifty-inch flat-screen TV, high-speed Internet, the kitchen of Gordon Ramsay, and beds from the Ritz-Carlton, you probably won't be homesick, and you won't be as grateful for your home. Why? Because you've done everything in your power to make camping just as good as, or better than, your actual home.

Perhaps one of the reasons why God chooses to leave us in this terribly broken world with its various disappointments is to create in our souls a certain dissatisfaction, an insatiable hunger for home. In his sovereign plan, this world is not meant to be our final destination; we're not meant to live with a right-here, right-now mentality, where we expend our physical, emotional, spiritual, financial, and relational energies trying to turn this temporal home into the eternal home it will never be.

We try to numb our homesickness with an endless cycle of remodeling, hoping that each renovation we make will get us closer to satisfying our longing for home. We jump from house to house, from job to job, from church to church, from accomplishment to accomplishment, from marriage to marriage, hoping the next move will give us what we long for. But we only become more distracted, more cynical, more discouraged, and more fearful because nowhere we've been and nothing we've done can turn this brokenness into the home we long for. The trying will simply make you crazy.

But there's another dynamic operating here. Allow me to refer back to my camping illustration. Imagine getting to the point where you recognize that camping is not as wonderful as it's cracked up to be, but you have no clear idea of what home is like. Now you're stuck between what you've found to be disappointing and what you don't really understand. What I have described is not a pleasant place to be, but I'm convinced it's where many Christians find themselves.

It's nearly impossible to be homesick for a place that you have little or no real understanding about. When you're away from home, you long for home because you know what's there. You recall the welcoming smells, the warmth of the family room, where you can kick back and not be disturbed, the dinner table that always seems to deliver familiar and comforting meals, your bedroom that is yours alone or that you lovingly share, the backyard that carries the memories of many childhood adventures. But more than anything else, you long for home because of the people that are there—people who love you and accept you as you are. I am aware that some of you sadly do not have this experience of home.

You see, we're all homesick, but many of us don't know we're homesick because we're too busy giving ourselves to the impossible task of turning where we are into home, and many more of us don't know we're homesick because we simply don't know what home is like. Whether we know it or not, we long for home:

Every sad moment in marriage is a longing for home.
Every moment of hurt and concern as a parent is a longing for home.
Every cry in the midst of loneliness is a longing for home.

Every complaint in a moment of physical pain is a longing for home.

Every loss of physical or mental vitality is a longing for home.

Every frustration with corrupt government is a longing for home.

Every urban fear in the dark of night is a longing for home.

Every "if only" that interrupts our sleep is a longing for home.

Every loss of a friend or family member is a longing for home.

Every discouragement at the loss of a job is a longing for home.

Every sadness at the failure of a pastor is a longing for home.

Every disappointment with ourselves is a longing for home.

Every frustration with a lost opportunity is a longing for home.

Every day we hit our heads against the reality that this is not our home—that it is, in fact, a far cry from what we long for home to be. This is why I love the book that you're about to read. It brilliantly accomplishes two very important things— things that I confess I need, and things I'm sure you need, too. These two things only accomplish their purpose when they work together.

First, Elyse does a wonderful job of helping us recognize and own our homesickness. She also lifts the burden of feeling guilty that we're homesick. Like a tender friend, she stands with us and says, "Of course you're homesick; so am I, and here's why." It's hard to understand in a few words the spiritual importance of recognizing your homesickness and being comfortable with it, but if you carefully read Elyse's words, you will understand the balance.

There's another thing this book does better than any book I have ever read: It does an excellent job of describing the stunning glories of what home will be like. As I read Elyse's descriptions of home, it brought tears of longing to my eyes. One of the most important things this book did for me is stimulate a healthy homesickness. Embedded in the DNA of homesickness is surrendering to the reality that this is not home. And once you surrender to that reality, you quit asking people, places, possessions, and experiences to be what they will never be. You become liberated from unrealistic expectations and the resultant disappointments. You are freed from being overly critical and unrealistically judgmental. You are progressively freed from a life of grumbling and complaining. You are freed from asking your spouse or children to be the messiahs they will never be.

Homesickness is a tool the Savior uses to free us right here, right now. He frees us by confronting us with the universal brokenness of the here and now and by comforting us with the assurance that we are on the road to a home that is wonderful in every way, glorious beyond the scope of our wildest dreams. And he assures us that no matter how completely messed up we have been and continue to be, the glories of home are ours by grace and grace alone. We don't have to mortgage our lives away for this home, because it's already been paid for in full by our Savior King, and there's a special place waiting for each one of his children.

Allow yourself to luxuriate in the portrait this book puts before you. Its words have been painted by a seasoned and skilled gospel artist. Take time to respond to the questions that follow each chapter; they are worth your effort. Then, go out and live in the painful joy of homesickness, while you enjoy the freedom of being comfortable with a longing that nothing or no one in all creation right now can satisfy.

Paul David Tripp
March 11, 2016

Acknowledgments

Nothing of any value is ever constructed in isolation, this book included. I am deeply thankful for all the friends on social media who responded with prayers when I sent out the distress call. Thanks again!

I am also thankful for my friends at church who continually told me they were praying for me, and especially for my pastors and elders, David Wojnicki, Tony Suitor, Jon Walters, Paul Behneman, and Jason Smith, and their dear wives, who never failed to encourage me.

I'm grateful for Andy McGuire and the folks at Bethany House who allowed me to write this book out of order . . . and for their kind suggestions, and for Ellen Chalifoux's careful editing.

I could not (I really mean that) have done this if it were not for the help of my dear friend Scott Lindsey and Logos Bible Software. Seriously. Logos has been such an immense help, allowing me to finish this project on time. Thank you to all the folks in Bellingham, Washington, who spend their days making this sort of thing possible. Amazing.

And, of course, I remain sincerely grateful for my family. For my mother, Rosemary, and my brother, Richard, who prayed for me and patiently waited for me to be available to them. My children and their spouses and children are foretastes of heaven to me. Thank you, my dearests.

And especially, I am thankful to Phil, who has been the primary conduit of love to me throughout our lives. He has loved me, and I am grateful.

Introduction

Bright overhead lights in the cabin rouse drowsy passengers. Children rudely awakened from restless sleep cry, while harried moms and dads try to soothe them with words about "almost there" and home. Like automatons, wearied business travelers stow their laptops and grab their jackets. Tray tables are locked in place. The seat that has been both my private space and instrument of torture is again in its full upright position. I lean forward to look out the window. . . . *There's Balboa Park and the bridge. . . . There goes Interstate 5. . . . Any moment now. . . .* "Thank you, Lord," I whisper. With a jolt the jet's tires make contact with concrete and the flight attendant tiredly welcomes us to San Diego.

I text one word to Phil, "Home."

He texts back, "I'm here and waiting for you."

"Thank you, Lord," I whisper again.

"Please remain in your seat with your seat belt fastened until the captain has turned off the seat belt sign and we're safely parked at the terminal. Only then will it be safe for you to move about the cabin. Remember to be careful when opening overhead bins, because items may have shifted during the flight and could fall out and . . . blah . . . blah . . . blah. . . ." I don't have any more room in my brain for words other than home. So I wait. It seems like another hour before the cabin door is opened.

Home. Finally freed from this marvel of modern technology, and torment, I grab my carry-on, check again in that seat pocket, and deplane as fast as the struggling families ahead of me will allow. I make my way out of the terminal and onto the street. Our car approaches, and Phil automatically opens the trunk. I throw my suitcase in the back and jump in the front seat. He's got water and snacks waiting for me.

"Hello, dear."

"Hello." We kiss like old friends who have been married for over four decades, and he gets us back on the road.

"Just relax, honey," he says. "I'll get us home soon."

"Thank you, dear," I reply. *Thank you, Lord,* I pray.

For the first time in days I can relax. I know what awaits me at home. My bed. My shower. Quiet and warmth. No trying to listen to people who want desperately to talk with me. No shoes that pinch. No struggling to remember the right word or the name of the pastor I've just met. And best of all, no pretending . . . no hoping that I'm being a faithful witness . . . no censuring every thought and word so that I don't offend. None of that now. I'm finally home.

"Home." As Dorothy famously quipped, "There's no place like home." That's so true, isn't it? Not only is there no place like it, there is no other place that wields more power in our lives. Home can be the source of immense joys and crushing disappointments. It can engender thoughts of deep relationship, love, and family, but it can also tie you up in knots with memories of anger, conflict, regret, abuse, or shame. There's not a place in our lives that has more power to shape us, to build us up, or to destroy us than home. How we answer questions like "Where were you born?" and "Where did you grow up?"

not only reveals facts about our history but also communicates considerable unspoken information. If I said to you, "I have lived my entire life in Southern California," you would immediately draw some conclusions about me. If, on the other hand, someone said, "I don't know where I was born," or "I lived in twenty different foster homes growing up," what would you have learned about them? In many ways, how we define home defines nearly everything about us.

Home can be a source of great pain. To have a home, to be in relationships, to love, and to trust, is to know loss, brokenness, and hopelessness. That's what it means to live here, this side of heaven. Strong relationships grow weak; people we've trusted desert us. The eggs we've carefully placed in *that* basket get scrambled on the floor. At the bottom of our hearts, when we are being brutally honest, even the happiest among us wouldn't say that our homes here are completely satisfying. And even in those deeply satisfying homes, everyone still has to say good-bye.

Loss: My Lifelong Companion

Loss of relationship, family, and home started for me before my fourth birthday. Although I was too young when it happened to retain a clear memory of it now, it was about that time when my mother and father divorced. I do remember the sadness I felt every summer when my brother and I had to leave my dad and head back home. And though my mother tried valiantly to provide for us and to build a home where we were loved and cared for, I distinctly remember the feeling of desertion, emptiness, and loss. I was longing for life as I thought it should be. I longed for unchanging, secure, satisfying relationships. In some way, even then as a child, I knew things weren't as they ought to be. Something wasn't right. I pined for the home that I thought I would have if only my father were present.

19

Don't misunderstand. In some ways, especially considering my tumultuous childhood, my adult life has been surprisingly stable. After a short and disastrous marriage and divorce, the Lord saved me, and then, in 1974, Phil and I were married. We've been together ever since then—which, I jokingly say, "proves that there is a God." We've got a lovely family here in San Diego, with three married adult children and six delightful grandchildren. We've made our home and put roots down deep in the sandy Southern California soil. This is home. And I'm thankful.

Even so, I find within myself a longing that no family gathering, party, or reunion can alleviate. No matter how I fuss with my home, trying to fashion it into my ideal, it never quite satisfies. And no matter how much time I spend with my kids and grandkids . . . no matter how many lunches we have together or waves we ride down in unison, it's never quite what I'm craving. Christmas can be beautiful, the Fourth of July a blast . . . and still, I always walk away knowing that although it was indeed wonderful, I still want something more. Isn't there anything here that will ultimately satisfy my deepest longings?

After one Christmas celebration, I asked my daughter Jessica, "How was it for you? Did you feel like something was missing?" "It was really nice, Mom," she said. "But you know you will never be satisfied here, right? You are not supposed to be."

I Am Homesick

What is this emptiness I feel? What is it that I'm hoping to find when I finally return home after a trip? Even deeper, what is this longing that makes me reminisce over forgotten yesterdays, why this current of nostalgia running through my every desire? It feels as though I've lost something, but I'm not quite sure what.

Does this feeling have a name? I think so. I think it is called homesickness. These moods of nostalgia and this longing for some just-out-of-reach settledness are actually just symptoms of homesickness. I sense that something important is missing, and though I anxiously search for it, it remains elusive, like a word I'm trying to recall that hides until my desire for it passes out of my memory.

I'm homesick for a place . . . for *the* place I was created to live, for my true home with my Father. How many times have I heard people say, "He went home to be with the Lord," and I know exactly what they mean. Yes, home is here, but it is also there, with the Lord. I am homesick; I'm pining for Jesus. I am an exile here. I feel it every day. I am a wanderer, never quite settling in, never quite satisfied, never really rooted in this world. I am homesick for heaven.

Is *Heaven* Really What I'm Pining For?

I've finally come to realize that this place of peace I'm longing for is called heaven; but I also know that word carries unfortunate negative baggage with it. It really is woefully inadequate and profoundly misunderstood by most everyone, both believers and unbelievers. Sure, unbelievers can scoff at cartoon angels playing harps on clouds, and actors like Jimmy Stewart in *It's a Wonderful Life* can opine about angels getting their wings, but they're not the only ones who are mistaken.

Believers are confused, too. We're confused about what heaven will be like, and our misconceptions don't help us identify what's actually missing. I don't believe my homesickness will be satisfied by life without a body, strumming a harp with see-through fingers while perched on a puffy cloud. I'm not longing for less of life. I'm longing for more, for deeper, stronger, sharper life and a glorified body that will actually function the way it was created to. I am not hoping for eternity on a cruise ship where I'll lie around by the pool while the angels wait on me. No, that isn't what I'm wanting. Nor am I longing for a never-ending church service while I float around as a disembodied soul. No, that's not home either, though perhaps it is a bit closer to what I long for.

And so, because most of us have failed to understand heaven and the New Earth, where we are headed, and the satisfaction we will ultimately experience there, we try to scratch this itchy homesickness by refashioning this wasteland into a true home. Of course, once the renovation project is complete, we discover that it isn't quite right, but that doesn't stop us from trying again . . . and again . . . and again.

The answer to much of our worldliness—our love and commitment to make the here and now into heaven—is to obtain as clear a picture as possible of what our coming life will be like. What will heaven be like? When we read the Bible closely, we discover that it will be a life more concrete than anything we've ever known. We will live in a physical body, a body as it was meant to be, and we will live here on the earth as the Lord created it. We want to be delivered from suffering here, of course, but we wouldn't want our eternity to be completely disconnected from life as we know it now.

Where We Are Headed

Over the next twelve chapters, I will do my best to sketch a portrait for you of the home we are journeying toward. It is my goal to make you thirst for it like you never have before and to prepare you, by the work of the Holy Spirit, to live your life *here* keeping your life *there* in view, understanding that much of the discontent you experience now flows out of homesickness and will only be answered when you are truly Home.

Your Eschatology (or What You Believe About Last Things)

I recognize that there is a wide divergence of opinion among true Christians about the events of the last days or what theologians generally call *eschatology*. This is not a book about the different strains of Christian thought regarding who goes up when or comes down or witnesses or rules for a thousand years. I have my own views on the topic, but they are not the subject of this book. Rather, this book will focus on life *after* the last day, wherever you want to place that day on your personal time line. I've known folks who, seeking to be humorous, have said that they are pan-millennialists, meaning that they believe everything will pan out in the end. For the sake of this book, I will join them. We all want very much to be able to figure out all the particulars of every event of the last day (or days). I won't help you do that in this book. Instead, we're going to be looking at life afterward, which actually is far more satisfying to our souls and really will help with our homesickness.

My Hermeneutics (or How I Interpret Scripture)

I also admit that I am making an assumption in the way that I use and interpret verses about the future. I assume that all the glories of any future time, say of the millennium, for instance, will certainly be more than dwarfed by the glories of the New Heaven and New Earth. So, I will use Scripture, especially prophetic and apocalyptic Scripture, as though it were plainly written in reference to the days after the last day, even though these might be verses that you have usually heard applied to another epoch. So if, for instance, you've always believed that the lion will curl up with the lamb (and not for dinner) during the millennium, then I think it is surely acceptable to press that reality out into the New Heaven and New Earth, too. Certainly what is a blessing in a temporary time like the millennium will remain a blessing in eternity.

23

Our Shared Faith

I am also making one more assumption: I am assuming that you have already come to a saving faith in Jesus Christ. (If you haven't, or aren't sure what "saving faith" means, please turn to the appendix at the back of the book.) Because of that assumption, I won't encumber you with if-you-have-come-to-faith language whenever I speak of the blessings that will be given solely to believers. The Bible is clear that the blessings of heaven and the New Earth are only for those who believe that God is good enough and loving enough to bestow them on sinners by faith.

The Antidote for Homesickness

When you send your sixth grader off to camp, you usually pack her suitcase with reminders of home—tangible items that she can actually hang on to while she's trying not to be a crybaby in front of her classmates. Perhaps you send along a little stuffed animal or write a note expressing your love for her. I trust this book will be like that for you: a reminder of your true home that you can hold on to when the days get dark and you feel like you are going to die from longing. Come back here often. Revisit these pages, and then someday, and probably sooner than we know, we'll all sit around and have a great laugh about what we thought home would be like and how we didn't even begin to scratch the surface of how wonderful it actually is. "Well," we will say, "at least we tried." And then, perhaps, as we're having that lovely chat, the King of Glory, Jesus himself, might come walking up and join in the revelry. "Lord, I tried," I will say. And he'll say, "Yes, I know, daughter," maybe with a twinkle in his eye, and we'll all burst out laughing again.

1

On Loss and Homesickness
and Baking Bread

It was not my plan to write this book . . . at least not yet. I apologize if that seems like an inauspicious start to your read, but I need to be up front with you. I want you to trust me and your trust demands my honesty. You rely on me to give you something worth your while. But what exactly are you investing in? Only this: Words. Black lines on a white page arranged in a way that enriches you. Black squiggles . . . letters and words in sentences that assure you that, as the movie *Shadowlands* claimed, you are not alone.

C. S. Lewis knew that one of the reasons we read is to recognize our shared human experience. We are not alone, and what you and I are walking through now we walk through together, as fellow sojourners in a world where there is nothing unshared, nothing uncommon, and nothing new. We have each other and our communal experience of life where "what has been is what will be . . . and there is nothing new under the sun" (Ecclesiastes 1:9). The path we are walking on is well trod.

We are walking with women and men of faith who have gone before us, believers who felt a gnawing sense of isolation and exile and needed to know that this isolation and exile weren't as absolute as they feared they might be. We read to hear our own voice of faith whispered in the storm of doubt, to hear another's voice calling back to us from somewhere on the road up ahead. We read to find our way to rest, to family, to home.

But knowing that we are not alone is not all we need. We also need these black lines, these words, to impart a strength that will enable us to keep on, to keep walking by faith through the dark. Have others gone before us? Did they make it home? Was God faithful? Can we actually hear their voices? We need assurance that there is a God who is sovereignly ruling over our journeys and will one day put everything right. In essence, you are trusting me to arrange words in such a way that they miraculously spring to life, that inanimate black ink turns into living golden light, infusing your soul with strength. I trust that they will, but as I said, arranging them like this at this time really wasn't my idea.

I also realize that what I want to do is far beyond my ability to accomplish. In part, that's because although I have written a lot, I am not really what I would call a writer . . . not like those artists who construct sentences that are so beautiful they make you want to cry. But I am also going to struggle because I will be writing about a place I have never seen or experienced. Yes, I will use the words of the faithful witnesses from Scripture and I will pray for the Spirit's enabling, but I am quite sure that there are no earthly words for what we will ultimately see there.

Even the apostle Paul himself, after he had visited the "third heaven" (or Paradise, where God actually dwells), said that he had "heard things that cannot be told, which man may not utter" (2 Corinthians 12:4). So, some of the pictures I will sketch will undoubtedly stretch your imagination; they certainly did mine. When I am speculating (and know it), I will tell you. But the truth is that much of what we're going to investigate together will necessitate the use of "devout imagination"; while seeking to be true to the Bible, we will push our imagination out past its normal moorings. So, please join me in praying, as I have throughout this entire writing process, *"Lord, grant us all grace to see the unseen and to be satisfied to live by faith, not sight, in what we cannot see right now."*

My Journey Here to You

The book you're holding right now is the result of the Lord's work in and through me at a very dark time in my life. On some days during this season I was aware of the fact that he was leading me here to write these words. On other days, I admit to being oblivious, apathetic, or angry. I struggled to ignore his gentle direction. During these days I discovered deeply troubling truths about myself (and this world in which we live)—truths that I would have said I was aware of but really hadn't a clue about.

It was also during this time that he taught me how to define what was at the center of my longing. I ultimately realized it was centered on one word, *Home*.[1] Isn't there something about that word that evokes desire and emotion in you? I have longed for Home. I longed for something more than this devil-filled, sin-cursed world. I wanted a place where love overruled every event, where joy infused every word. I wanted holiness to infiltrate, to make right all I saw. I longed for rest from the battering. I wanted Home . . . to go there, yes . . . but not just for a visit. No heavenly two-hour church service would ever satiate me now. I wanted heaven, to live there, to never be alone again, to be with Jesus forever.

A friend once told me that her longing for heaven was like walking by a bakery and being drawn in by the fragrance of the bread baking inside. I was beginning to smell heaven . . . but I was stuck outside. Smelling it. Longing for it. I yearned for it and this yearning created homesickness in me. I was starving for the most delicious-smelling bread but just couldn't get to it. I needed a better map, enhanced trail markers, a more accurate vision of the door.

I had to write this book because it helped me read the map and see the door. It gave me sight and it temporarily allayed my homesickness. I wrote it because I was pining away and needed to find the remedy that would both quiet and strengthen my desire for something that remained beyond my reach. I needed to get as close as I could to that bakery so that I really believed that what was coming was as good as I needed it to be, so my soul would be quieted. So I could wait. But I also needed my imagination to be set ablaze so that I wouldn't lose sight of my Home in the midst of the darkness I was stumbling through. I had to run toward a vision, a lovely smell (if you will), a homing beacon. Little squiggles needed to be infused with the smell of bread baking and the sight of a place where all would ultimately be as it should be. Home: a place for everything where everything had its place . . . including me.

This book we've titled *Home* . . . this is the Lord's idea. I am trusting him to speak through it to you and to use it however he wishes. But I am mostly glad for it because I needed it. It has kept me from sliding off a perilous road into the quicksand at the bottom of the valley of the shadow of death. Home is in the distance. The lighthouse is burning brightly in the night. Words help me see what my eyes are too weak to perceive . . . and yet I'm continuing this walk in the dark.

I Got This!

Like most independent, self-directed, and self-deceived mortals, I recently thought I knew what my immediate future held.

28

Everything was planned out, tidy, even exciting. I could smile and quip, "I got this!" without a second thought. I thought I knew what to expect from my family, my church, my ministry, my day-to-day life. But then I began to sense that something was amiss; life wasn't proceeding along the tracks I had so carefully laid out.

A ministry that I had recently aligned myself with was falling apart and events that had been completely unthinkable a few months prior were headlines in Christian magazines. Friends were wounded terribly. Many simply vanished from the landscape of faith. I hugged a dear friend who sobbed and sobbed over the losses in her life as she questioned everything she had ever believed, and feared that all her work was for naught.

"Lord," I wondered. "We prayed about this . . . You opened this door . . . I don't understand." Plans that had been carefully arranged and prayed over evaporated overnight. Relationships shattered. Bridges burned. I began to feel like I was caught up in a raging torrent headed unavoidably toward destruction. The harder I paddled to get out of that treacherous current, the more ground I lost. I was headed for the falls and was completely powerless to change my course. But that was just the beginning.

Just when it seemed that we had weathered that storm and could see those shiny train tracks laid out in front of us again, another distressing event occurred. My church went through difficult changes. My head was spinning. My heart was broken. "O Lord, God . . . What are you doing?" The waterfall's roar was deafening.

While I was struggling to cope with this loss, I became aware of the fact that I was being misrepresented and maligned by people I had assumed were friends. I offered an olive branch to them and suggested that rather than attacking and counterattacking one another on the Internet, it would be a good idea for us to try to come to some understandings by phone. The day was set for our conversation and it quickly went downhill. It was one of the most hurtful conversations I had ever been party to.

And then . . . less than thirty minutes after that conversation ended, I received the news that a dear friend was leaving his pastorate. The ministry he had built was being shut down. From that sadness there was born grief after grief as people struck out in pain, responded in misunderstanding, and assumed the worst about one another. Friends savaged friends. Accusations flew back and forth. Efforts to help blew up in my face. This went on for months and consumed every waking hour and many hours during sleepless nights. The ramifications continue to this day.

A few months later, my sweet daughter's pastor resigned. The church plant she had labored in for six years was on the brink of extinction.

And finally, my dear uncle died. This was a man who had, for all intents and purposes, functioned as a father to me. As a child I had spent sweet weeks during the summer playing with my cousins at his house. I had such fond memories of splashing in the pool with them. As I became an adult, he was always there for me: someone I could call on, someone I could count on. During the last decade of his life we became even closer; his wife became a dear friend, and we loved attending their birthday parties. His death felt like another devastating blow to me. Of course, he had been ailing for some time, but his death seemed so sudden. It wasn't supposed to happen yet, was it? On one hand, I was thankful because I had visited with him the week prior and was as convinced as I could be that he had come to faith; on the other hand, it seemed too soon. I experienced a year bookended by the loss of a beloved pastor on the front end and the loss of a beloved father on the other. Over the falls I went.

All Right, Already! Isn't This Enough?

I don't mean to sound blasphemous, but sometimes I wonder if God doesn't have a tendency to be heavy-handed. You don't need to tell me about how wise he is. I know and believe that. But I also know that the writers of the Psalms felt this same impulse: "How long, O Lord?" was their ancient refrain. Yeah. How long? Isn't this a little much? Of course, it's nice to know that my experience was also theirs, but, seriously, *Can't a gal get a break?*

It was about this time that I leaned over to my husband during church one Sunday morning and said, "I have no idea what I'm doing here." I knew then that I was a step away from leaving everything I had once held dear and that, if I didn't head in another direction, I was in danger of denying the faith . . . or at least leaving the church.

It was then I also knew I had to write this book. I began reading. A book I had been slated to write was set aside for a later time. I kept reading. I began talking about heaven and the New Earth to friends. I talked about it with everyone who would listen. I listened for it everywhere. These conversations were a God thing. He was directing my thoughts. He was forcing me to think more deeply. I hiked with friends at Torrey Pines State Park and asked them if we would be hiking like this on the New Earth. We watched the waves and wondered if we would ride them in eternity. I read and read and took pages and pages and pages of notes. I prayed.

What will heaven be like? What about the New Earth? What do I have wrong? Exactly what happens when I die? Where will I go? How is that different from where I will spend eternity? What are my loved ones who have already died doing now? Will we work? Will we learn? How will the answers to these questions help me now? These were the questions I asked over and over again while God was untethering me from the here and now. I kept reading and praying and asking.

What Is This Longing I Feel?

I began to try to define the pain I felt. Yes, it was sorrow, but it was something more, something infinitely deeper. I felt it all the time, even when I was happy. It wasn't just sorrow. It was a longing: a pining for a better place and time . . . no, not just a better place and time, a *perfect* place and time; a different reality. It felt like longing for home, but not for a home I had ever been to. I began to see that it was something like homesickness, so I began to study that, too.

The word *homesickness* was coined in the 1700s. Homesickness is defined as "distress . . . caused by an actual or anticipated separation from home."[2] The word *nostalgia*, which we commonly use when we talk about a longing for the way things used to be, was also coined around 1700. Since there was no word in medicine for this sense of sadness, Johannes Hofer, a Swiss scholar, combined two Greek words, "*nostos,* meaning 'return home,' and *algia*, the word for 'pain.'"[3] This pain I was feeling felt like nostalgia. I was suffering because I wanted to return home. But I didn't want to return to any place I had already been. I was living in San Diego, where I had lived practically my entire life. I wasn't longing for San Diego or a log cabin on a prairie—Lord, no! I was still living with my dear family. I wasn't longing for them, but they were involved in this longing, too. Yes, I wanted to be with them, but with them in a different way. And yet this longing was something deeper . . . something, I began to see, I had felt for years but had been too busy, too "in control" to notice. I had been trying to silence this cry in my heart my entire life in all sorts of foolish ways. I realized that I had actually been homeless, but kept trying to build a home out of pretty matchsticks I found on the street.

There is a passage from an unpublished novel by Walker Percy that captures the homelessness of humanity. Percy imagines this dialogue between two men in a tuberculosis sanitarium:

"What's the matter, Willy?"
"I don't know, Scanlon. I'm homesick."
"How long have you been homesick?"
"All my life."

Percy's dialogue captures the restlessness of the soul that wanders through this world until it finds a home with God.[4]

I related to those words: I realized I had been homesick *all my life*. But even though I had indeed found a home with God, the answer to my restlessness hadn't been completely quieted. I'm not saying that coming to faith wasn't a homecoming. It was. But it was also true that my faith didn't instantaneously translate me out of here to there; it didn't change me from being an exile to living life by the hearth at home. In fact, perhaps in some ways it made my nostalgia worse because it had enabled me to see that there was something more than this life, something infinitely better. Perhaps Christians are the most consistently homesick people in the world because they know this world (as it is) isn't their true home. Yes, I was home, but I was still homesick.

An Inn on the Side of the Road

I longed for home but not just any home anywhere. I was looking for a capital *H* home, a real, tangible, flesh-and-blood, Home-on-Earth-With-Him Home. I wanted a Home where my Father lived, and if he was going to be there, then it had to be a home filled with righteousness; a capital *H* home that was crammed to bursting with capital *H* holiness. I wanted, no, actually *needed* a Holy Place where I would finally say, "Oh, yeah! This is it! This is the place I've been looking for my whole life! This is what solid holiness feels like! It's this face I've needed to see! This is Home!"

33

This Home was what I was looking for all those times I rearranged the furniture, went on vacation, watched palm fronds dance in the breeze out my window and wished I understood what they were saying. This is the look I saw in my dog's eyes when I knew she knew that I wanted something more for her than this ending we had finally come to. This is the place I wanted to live when I struggled to communicate my heart to Phil and it came out all wrong and I cried into my pillow like a child. This is the peace between brothers, the quiet of soul when, for just a few seconds, you can search your mind and find nothing amiss.

That! That! But more than that! This is the momentary joy when families hug and laugh and wine flows and the food is shockingly delicious. This is the excitement of discovery, the experiencing of fulfilled anticipation; this is what I feel when a great movie tells the story of redemption all over again and I'm stunned by the gifts God has given unbelievers.

It's all that and yet, none of these shadows, no matter how hard they struggle for substance, were solid enough to cure my homesickness. I remained homeless. I am an exile. They were merely reminders . . . inns on the road to the real place, to the Home I'm pining for. But just inns, not Home.

Cheer *Up*! After All, You're a Christian!

When you talk about longing for Home a lot, people start thinking you're being morose. They think they ought to pat you gently or kindly offer to pray that you will be happier. They think that you ought to buck up and smile and work hard at bettering your lot. They think you should take a pill. They think that in time you will feel better, once you get free from this briar patch of despondency you have fallen into.

They might suggest a list of things you should do so you could smile like the ubiquitous televangelist. "Read your Bible!"

they advise. "Pray more! Go to church!" they counsel. And yes, they're right, sort of, but I also respond, "No. Sorry. Those things don't quite scratch where I am itching right now." They are only inns on the side of the road. And, yes, a good church is the best inn of all. But everything I can do here, even those things I do by faith, are merely the Motel 6s where I'm checking in for the evening and hoping for a halfway decent rest. Maybe a biblical church is like a really gorgeous Hilton with a bed that promises deep sleep. I don't know. But all these things remain just inns on the road, after all. They let me rest a bit on this weary road; they give me a bit of refreshment, but they don't get me off this road. They are not Home.

Those of us who are Americans tend to think we can solve any problem. We can build a better mousetrap or mobile device, perform laparoscopic surgery, develop GMO corn, or create a selfie stick for our GoPro. Got a problem with drought? Hang on, and we'll think of a fix for that. Just give us time and money. We are an overconfident nation of fixers. Of course, that doesn't mean we are the happiest people on earth, just that we think there is a solution to every ill and we can find it if we just buck up and press on. It's un-American to say, "I can't . . . and neither can you!" We believe in capital *P* progress. I used to. I used to think that there was some secret key to living life without homesickness. I don't believe that anymore.

Please don't misunderstand. I do believe that we should read and pray and work hard here and that joy is possible now. I even believe something more radical: I believe that our faith and good works will somehow make a difference in our Home to come (see chapter 11), but as best I can now, I'm shipping that basket of eggs—trust in real deliverance from longing—Home. I'll bet we could invent some way of shipping boxes from one dimension into another. It's just a matter of logistics, right? No, probably not. Eventually everything will be better. I will finally be Home.

That's what I'm trusting for while I pine away here. I'm no longer expecting to find Home in the here and now.

Strangers and Exiles All

Freedom from this longing for Home is impossible for us in the same way it was for the people of faith who have gone before us. On one of his best days, a day when he was rejoicing in all the good things God had given him and done for him, King David acknowledged, "For we are strangers before you and sojourners, as all our fathers were. Our days on the earth are like a shadow, and there is no abiding" (1 Chronicles 29:15).

King David, with all his faith, at the height of his power, knew that he was merely a foreigner here. He confessed that he was a sojourner, a "temporary, landless wage earner."[5] We would call these kinds of people alien day laborers. Got a lawn that needs mowing? They're here for you. They are without land; they live from job to job. Many of them take what they earn and send it back home. They're not building a home here. They're not abiding. They know that. I admit that until recently I rarely saw myself as a sojourner, a temporary, landless wage earner. Not because it was a wrong way of thinking, but because I was so invested in my home in the here and now. In Psalm 39, King David again refers to himself as a sojourner. He calls himself a "guest, like all [his] fathers" (v. 12). We are landless wage earners, guests in a land that is not our Home.

> These all died in faith, not having received the things promised, but having seen them and greeted them from afar, and having acknowledged that they were strangers and exiles on the earth. For people who speak thus make it clear that they are seeking a homeland.
>
> Hebrews 11:13–14

36

No amount of faith in God will change the fact that we are homesick exiles, pining for another place, a place where he is. *Jesus is our Homeland.*

The Jewish exiles experienced this longing, too: "By the waters of Babylon, there we sat down and wept, when we remembered Zion. On the willows there we hung up our lyres" (Psalm 137:1–2). Their homesickness silenced their song. "How shall we sing the Lord's song in a foreign land?" (v. 4). How indeed?

Home Is Where He Is

We can't put our hope in our own progress, either. Inns along the road won't answer this longing. Not even great faith will satisfy our seeking. Even when the Jewish exiles were finally able to return to Jerusalem, they still longed for something more. This alone is our hope: That at the very moment of our death we are finally at Home with the Lord. When the church's first martyr, Stephen, was being stoned to death, his eyes were finally opened and he was able to see his Homeland: "But he, full of the Holy Spirit, gazed into heaven and saw the glory of God, and Jesus standing at the right hand of God" (Acts 7:55).

When Stephen saw the doors of the heavenly dimension open, what did he see? The glory of God and Jesus standing there, awaiting his arrival. He saw Home. Death would usher him instantly into the presence of the Lord.

The apostle Paul puts it this way: "We know that while we are at home in the body we are away from the Lord. . . . We would rather be away from the body and at home with the Lord" (2 Corinthians 5:6–8).

Did you notice how he talks about our home here, "in the body," and our Home there, "with the Lord"? Did you hear him say he'd rather be with the Lord? Sounds like homesickness to me. Paul recognized that we are traversing a road between two homes, leaving one behind, heading toward another. Home in the place to come will truly be *Home* for us because it is where the Lord is. We miss him. We feel so homesick because we are "away from the Lord" right now. But a time is coming when we will be with him and his presence will make it Home for us. Yes, that place will be heaven; it will be Paradise. Because we were made for him, any place where he isn't will never satisfy us.

In another letter Paul writes,

> For to me to live is Christ, and to die is gain. If I am to live in the flesh, that means fruitful labor for me. Yet which I shall choose I cannot tell. I am hard pressed between the two. My desire is to depart and be with Christ, for that is far better.
>
> Philippians 1:21–23

What was his desire? To die. To depart this life and be with Christ. He felt hard pressed because he didn't want to leave his fruitful work *here* in this home, but he also really wanted to be *there* in that Home. His mind was pulling him in two directions; his heart was speaking two different words to him:[6] Work for others here or rest with Christ there? He admitted that he wanted to be there because it was "far better."

Do you think about Home in that way? Is it just better or is it *far* better? How much better do you think it will be? A hundred thousand times better? A million times better? Little black squiggles could never describe better? Yes, that much better and then some. Paul defined his homesickness as an overwhelming ache to be at Home with the Lord. It will be *that much better.* And though he counsels us to continually rejoice in the Lord, he was also filled with an unending longing for a different life. Together with him, we both pine and rejoice.

The trials of Paul's life in ministry made him long to be with the Lord (2 Corinthians 11:23–29). The dangers and hardships he faced are inconceivable. Most of us have never faced much persecution at all—perhaps aside from a snide remark or being passed over for a promotion. But the dangers he faced actually worked to sweeten his longing for heaven. They gave him the ability to smell the bread baking. In addition, aside from perils from persecution, he wrote, "And, apart from other things, there is the daily pressure on me of my anxiety for all the churches" (v. 28). Daily pressure and anxiety coupled with his longing for the Lord were tearing him apart. It's easy to understand why the thought of dying and being with the Lord was much better. Though the difficulties I've faced are nothing in comparison to what he went through, they have accomplished the same work in me. Home, with Jesus, does seem *very much better.*

Here's one more passage from Paul in which he admitted to "groaning." Have you ever been in such deep distress that words won't come and all you can do is sigh or moan? That was Paul's experience, too. He was longing, pining, even moaning for his true dwelling. "For in this tent [our earthly home] we groan, longing to put on our heavenly dwelling. . . . For while we are still in this tent, we groan, being burdened" (2 Corinthians 5:2–4). In chapters to come we'll talk more specifically about our physical resurrection, what Paul refers to as our "heavenly dwelling," but for now I would simply like you to see that Paul himself felt this homesickness, too. He was burdened. He groaned. Me too. How about you?

Our Journey Home

Like Paul, like you, I'm longing to go Home. Sure, the last few years have been hard, and they have pressed me into a place where I'm groaning for my Savior. I'd like to see his face, to rest in that garden Paradise, to let him heal my homesickness. I don't know what the future years will hold. If I am to live on,

I am sure there will be days of both sunshine and deep pain. And then, one day, I'll take one step over into the heavenly dimension, and all will be at rest. I'm longing for it . . . and yet, I know that while I still have work to do, God will sustain me here. I am hard pressed. I am groaning. I long for Home. Can you smell the bread baking? Are the tiny black lines starting to glow a little?

———— FIXING OUR EYES ON HOME ————

1. Have you ever gone through a difficult time when your desire for Home grew stronger? Describe it.

2. Have you gone through an extended time away from home where you experienced homesickness? What was that like? How did you quell your longings?

3. Have you ever thought about your desire for the life to come as homesickness? Philip Yancey wrote, "Faith is, in the end, a kind of homesickness—for a home we have never visited but have never stopped longing for."[7] Respond.

4. Are you beginning to smell the bread baking? If so, describe it. If not, that's fine.

5. Summarize what you've learned in this chapter in four or five sentences.

2

Let Not Your Hearts Be Troubled

When Jesus said, "Let not your hearts be troubled. Believe in God; believe also in me" (John 14:1), he knew all too well the darkness that would soon invade his friends' world. He had told them he was heading to a place they could not go, and although they were bewildered and confused by his statement, they could not have even imagined the disaster looming on their doorstep. How could anything that bad happen to them now? Hadn't he just been hailed as the returning King into the royal city? Didn't all the people love him? Weren't there shouts of "Hosanna!" with cloaks and palm branches spread at his feet? What could possibly go wrong now?

I know what it's like to assume my future is secure. I'm sure you do, too. My husband once owned his own business, and it had been our plan to ultimately sell the business to partially fund our retirement. But through a series of events, many of them completely out of our control, the business was taken from us. Phil and I were completely shocked, devastated. Although Phil was employed for a few years until he was old enough to retire, the nest egg that we had been banking on was gone in an instant. We thought we knew what the future held. We were wrong. God had something else in mind, and although the Lord has taken care of us during the ensuing years, those events eventuated in the loss of a house and much of our retirement money. It was easy for us to look at circumstances and assume we knew what the future held. We were wrong to assume that the good times we were enjoying would never end. We thought they meant that we knew God's ultimate plan for us. We were wrong. Yes, God was faithful, but that didn't mean his faithfulness wouldn't lead us into unexpected trouble.

Like Phil and I, the disciples looked at the palm branches and heard the shouts of "Hosanna!" and thought that meant their future was secure. But the Lord knew the truth and sought to warn and comfort his beloved friends at the Last Supper. In a few short hours, this band of men who had boldly left all to follow the Messiah would flee for their lives under the cover of darkness and pray for anonymity. Simply put, their lives as they had come to know and love them were over.

Yes, he was about to be glorified, but his definition of glorification and theirs were poles apart. They expected vindication. He awaited humiliation. They expected fame and glory. He anticipated the mocking and the lash. And there would be blood: enough blood, in fact, to fill the whole world with both guilt and forgiveness. Tomorrow would be his coronation day, but not the one they had envisioned. Sure, there would be a royal robe, a presentation before the masses, the proclamation of his reign over the nation, and a carefully crafted crown, but none of it was what they'd thought it would be.

Jesus knew what to expect, so he warned them, "Let not your hearts be troubled. Believe in God; believe also in me" (John 14:1). In a few short hours all you will have left is your faith . . .

so believe. Believe even though what you see happening around you will tear you apart; keep believing that I've got this and will take care of you. "I will come again and will take you to myself" (14:3). *Believe.*

He was calling them to believe even though he knew that he would soon feel the fangs of that ancient Serpent striking his heel while he crushed his head (Genesis 3:15 NIV). He knew that his Father would inflict upon him the punishment that our disobedience deserved. He heard the tomb mock all his words about eternal life.

But he also knew that, through the tomb, hope would be reborn, never to die again; the gateway to our Homeland would reopen. The cherubim's flaming sword that once blocked Adam's reentrance into Eden would be doused by holy blood as it plunged into the flesh of the Son. The curtain emblazoned with cherubim that separated sinful man from the holiness of God would be torn in half from top to bottom. The Son would open the way back into God's presence, into fellowship with him in a garden in the cool of the day, to Home.

But how could he die? How could death have mastery over him? Hadn't the disciples seen him overcome it? Hadn't they watched him raise the widow's son and his friend Lazarus from death? How could it be that he was now powerless before it? Had death reclaimed its throne? To the disciples' eyes it seemed that it had; it seemed that death, that ultimate destroyer of every possibility, the inevitable end of every hope, was still king. "He saved others; he cannot save himself" (Matthew 27:42), death's cynical slaves jeered. And at Jesus' death, the disciples saw only utter failure and an endless refrain of futility, hopes crushed, and meaningless lives snuffed out without so much as a whimper from heaven. "There's no escaping me," death mocked over and over for thousands of years.

43

I've heard that mocking, too . . . in the death of our dreams, in the death of a beloved ministry, in the death of beloved parents, in the death of my uncle. I've heard death's mocking voice, "There is no escaping me." But like the disciples, like you, I'm being called to believe.

Though Jesus had told them on several occasions about his crucifixion and resurrection, the disciples weren't even close to understanding what he meant (Matthew 12:40; 17:22–23; Mark 8:31). I've known about the wisdom, power, and love of God and yet I haven't understood, either. What they didn't know was that everything was about to change. All the old axioms would shortly become untrue. The course of the world was about to reverse itself. Death would finally have died, and though death had previously reigned from Adam forward, "those who receive the abundance of grace and the free gift of righteousness [would now] reign in life through the one man Jesus Christ" (Romans 5:17). Death would no longer be king. King Jesus would arrive Home with his queen on his arm. And though I know this . . . and I do believe it, "Help, me Lord," I have to pray. "Help my unbelief!" (see Mark 9:24).

I believe Jesus ended death's dark rule, and that could only happen as he went through death as the only Man who didn't deserve it. He would end our hopelessness through his resurrection. Cold, dead flesh came to life again. And with his enlivened flesh he carried in his bosom all of our hopes and dreams and a valid expectation of a future freed from sin's dark curse. Death's dark rule ended when that stone was rolled away. Hope was reborn. "I do believe, Lord. Help me."

"Death [had] been conquered, bound hand and foot at the cross,"[1] and with that conquering we are welcomed back Home again. We've been freed from our exile. We've been invited to hope again. He's asked us to believe that we will again see the good land from whence we have been expelled. As the writer of Hebrews said,

> We who have fled for refuge might have strong encouragement to *hold fast to the hope set before us.* [For] we have this as *a sure and steadfast anchor of the soul, a hope that enters into* the inner place behind the curtain, where Jesus has gone as a forerunner on our behalf.
>
> Hebrews 6:18–20

We who have known only futility, decay, homesickness, and exile, have strong encouragement to hold fast to our hope because we are no longer helpless and alone. He's already gone before us, trail blazing straight through exile and death into life as our Captain. Yes, I know this is true. I can hope even in the midst of doubt.

Through his death and resurrection, he has flung open the gate, torn the curtain that divided us from God's presence, and done it all as the incarnate Son of Man. God has not forever abandoned his creation. Mankind is still his good work. In the body of Jesus, Man has gone into the presence of God, to his throne room, to the company of myriads of angels dressed for a party (see Hebrews 12:22). I'm in a form of exile now, but exile doesn't mean abandonment. Jesus has made sure of that.

A Place for You

Let's look more closely at what he said to his disciples on his last night with them before his death:

> Let not your hearts be troubled. Believe in God; believe also in me. In my Father's house are many rooms. If it were not so, would I have told you that I go to prepare a place for you? And if I go and prepare a place for you, I will come again and will take you to myself, that where I am you may be also.
>
> John 14:1–3

Jesus knew that the coming events would be troubling. His disciples would feel abandoned. Like orphans, like exiles. Their hearts would be torn apart from deep emotional distress and turmoil.[2] They would be overcome with a painful nostalgia; they would long to see him. And what does he do? He tells them that though he is physically leaving them for now, in his heart he could never abandon them. Yes, he was leaving, but he was going so that their Home would be ready for their arrival. His goal was to take them to himself, so that they would be with him forever. What is this dwelling place that he has prepared for us? Is it heaven? Well, yes, it's heaven . . . but perhaps heaven won't be what you're expecting.

I'm Really Longing for Heaven . . . But Not *That* Heaven

Like the disciples, I am longing for the Lord. I am homesick for a place of peace and rest, a place where I, even I, will never wound or disappoint those I love. In the past, I would have identified that place as heaven, but now I know that *heaven* isn't quite the right word. Sure, we can go ahead and call this place *heaven*, if by "heaven" we mean life in a coming world where we go when we die. But we should not call it heaven (or worse yet, scoff at it), if by the word we mean an existence forever unhinged from this earth where we do that absurd cloud-floating thing. As C. S. Lewis wryly quipped,

> There is no need to be worried by facetious people who try to make the Christian hope of "Heaven" ridiculous by saying they do not want "to spend eternity playing harps." The answer to such people is that if they cannot understand books written for grown-ups, they should not talk about them. . . . People who take these symbols literally might as well think that when Christ told us to be like doves, He meant that we were to lay eggs.[3]

(I love C. S. Lewis, don't you? Someday we will sit down with him and have a proper British chat with tea and biscuits. Won't that be lovely?)

So many people have really wrongheaded ideas about heaven. Perhaps it would be better to refer to the place we are longing for, the place where we go immediately after death, as "Paradise" rather than "heaven" because, after all, that's what Jesus called it when he comforted his fellow sufferer on Calvary. "Truly, I say to you, today you will be with me in Paradise" (Luke 23:43). *Paradise* isn't a word we use much, but we should. In Jesus' day it meant a garden park surrounded by a wall.[4] In that thief's pain, Jesus knew what words would relieve his suffering. "You're going to a garden of exquisite joy, freedom from pain, and rest with me . . . today."

The thought of the paradise awaiting me gives me hope today. So maybe it would be better to say that we Christians go to Paradise when we die. I know that seems odd; it is not the way we usually speak. Maybe the word *Paradise* might seem a little too Middle Eastern to us, but then, Jesus was a Middle Easterner, wasn't he? We would have to get used to using that kind of language if we wanted to be more precise. Or, we can say, as millions of believers have, that we "go to heaven when we die," as long as we know that *going to heaven* actually means going to a beautiful garden in another dimension and not floating around on clouds in the sky.

Hair-Splitting Land . . . Just for a Moment

I know this might seem like splitting hairs, but getting our definitions right really is important because words carry meanings that can make the difference in our expectations. I need a real hope about a real place to dispel my fear and discouragement, so I want to be as precise as I can be. I'm hoping that this understanding of the truth will give me the strength I need so that I can keep on believing.

47

So please indulge me for a few moments while we take a brief excursion into Hair-Splitting Land. In the Bible, the word *heaven* can have two different meanings. First, it can mean the physical place above us where the atmosphere and planets are. That's the place Moses was talking about in Genesis 1:1: "In the beginning, God created the heavens and the earth." The word *heavens* here means all that is above the earth, not the eternal dimension where God lives. Of course, once we think about it, this makes sense because we know that God wasn't homeless before the first day of creation. That's the first use of the word *heaven* in the Bible.

To be mistaken about this makes our faith seem really silly. Here's an example of how someone attempted to use that silliness to attack Christianity: In the early 1960s, at the beginning of the space race, Russian premier Khrushchev said, "Why should you clutch at God? Look, Gagarin [the first cosmonaut] flew in space and saw no God."⁵ Khrushchev had a faulty definition of the word *heaven*. He thought that because Yuri Gagarin flew into space and didn't see him, it meant that God didn't exist. In 1971, when Khrushchev died, he no doubt discovered his error.

God's immediate presence isn't in *that* heaven. We aren't hoping that the Hubble Telescope will photograph God's throne or the resting place of the millions of believers who have gone before us. That's because our *heavenly Home* isn't *up there* in the clouds or even in the farthest solar system. So when Christians use the term *heaven*, they should be clear (at least in their own thinking) that we don't mean some place "up there" in what we call outer space. The heavens (everything that is not the earth) is not where God lives.⁶

Okay, now that we've got that clear. Ready? The heavens can also refer to the place or dimension where God does dwell, as in Psalm 2:4: "He who sits in the heavens laughs" or "He will send from heaven and save me" (Psalm 57:3). I know this might seem confusing, but when we use the word *heaven* in this way, we are actually talking about a different dimension . . . the place where God resides. So, if Christians use *heaven* in this way, meaning that when they die they are going to the place *where the Lord is*, then that's great. This is the place where Jesus is right now, the dwelling place he has been preparing for us for thousands of years.

Both . . . And

Heaven is *both* part of God's material creation *and* the uncreated, immaterial place where God is enthroned. Both . . . and. You know, there are actually loads of words in the English language that have different meanings even though they are spelled and pronounced the same way . . . like bear (to carry) and bear (a scary animal). So, there's heaven (the sky and the stars) and heaven (God's Home). Two different places. One word.

About now you might be wondering why I'm talking about heaven being heaven in one way but not in another. It's because these definitions will influence the way we think and long for our eternal Home. I'm not longing to float around on the Horsehead Nebula (though I would like to see it sometime). I am, however, longing for Paradise, to be with the Lord. Maybe it would just be best to say that when we die we "go Home to be with the Lord."

I'm not homesick for a cloud to float on. My guess is that you aren't either. I'm looking forward to a lovely rest in a beautiful park. But even that Paradise won't be our final Home.

Home . . . Sort Of

I live in a home. It's in Southern California. This place with the lovely pepper tree branches swaying outside my window is what I think of when my iPhone tells me I'm eight minutes from home. (How does it know?) I have an address, and could

49

tell you what color the walls in my office are. It's the only place on the street where my garage door opener works. This place is my home . . . and yet it's not.

My body, this quirky sixty-five-year-old breathing bag of skin and bones (made of dust) is also my home. No matter where I go, this home comes along with me. I think I used to be happier about that than I am now. Gravity has taken its toll. When I go for a swim, I have to drag my body along. When I want to dance, my body would rather watch. Frequently I want to go places and do things that my body objects to. "Not so fast," it scolds. Sometimes it simply won't cooperate at all. This body is me, sort of. My mind, my soul, the real me resides in this home. This body is my home . . . and yet it's not.

On the day I die, I will leave both of these homes (the one in SoCal and the one typing these words) and be welcomed to another. Obviously, I won't take any of my belongings with me. I didn't come into this world owning anything. I'll be leaving it the same way (Job 1:21). I won't even take my body. At the time of my death, I will be "un-bodied." My soul, my consciousness, my mind will leave these cells here to dissolve back into dust (what they are already trying to do), and the real me will be in Paradise with Jesus. Paradise will be Home . . . but even then, that won't be my final Home.

Being un-bodied in Paradise after my death is not the Home I'm really longing for, either, so it's fortunate that it won't be my permanent address. Paradise (as great as it will be) is not our eternal Home. It won't completely satisfy this longing we feel. I like parks, but parks don't quite fit the bill, either. We will still have one more journey to make.

Theologians call this in-between, un-bodied life the "intermediate state." It's a stopping-off place, like a rest stop on a freeway, only a hundred thousand times better! It is the place where we will be until Jesus wraps everything up on earth. It's Paradise, a beautiful, secure park, where we will pray for the church on earth,[7] rest, and wait with joyous patience for our "re-bodying" day, the day when we will be given a new, glorious resurrection body that will be fit for our new, glorious resurrected earth.

That day will begin with the *Parousia,* or the revealing of Jesus Christ (Titus 2:13) as he returns to the earth to reunite the remnant of his church that is alive at his coming with those who have gone on before them (Matthew 24:30–31; 1 Thessalonians 4:15–17).[8] On that day all of us, those who are at rest in Paradise and those who are still laboring on the earth, will be instantly changed into perfect flesh-and-blood men and women, boys and girls (1 Corinthians 15:23, 49, 51–52; Philippians 3:21). We will populate and reign on this globe we call Earth (Matthew 19:28–30; 2 Timothy 2:11–13; Revelation 2:26)

Of course, that day will also be the King's Scrubbing-Up Day, when he will wash the earth with fire and rearrange the universe to be exactly what he wants it to be for his Home (2 Peter 3:10, 12–13). He will paint this old manse, rearrange all the furniture, and get it ready for the arrival of his Bride and the rockin' party to come. Heaven and earth will be joined together in a way that is beyond our understanding, and we will finally be Home: We will live in a place where "righteousness dwells" (3:13). No more sorrow. No more suffering. No more homesickness. Ever. I need to know this. I need to think about it every day. I need to keep trying to smell the bread baking so that I don't wander off the path . . . or just lie down and give in to my sadness. The *Parousia* is coming! He will be revealed! Hurrah!

I'm So Very Thirsty

As great as all this will be (and it will be great!), I'm not there yet. I'm filled with homesickness. This homesickness in me is a thirst . . . a thirst for the Lord, a thirst for my Home. I'm

51

thirsting for Jesus, and no matter how much I try to satisfy that thirst here with refreshments both spiritual and material, there really isn't anything that quite quenches it. I always walk away dry, thirsting for more. Perhaps part of what it means to believe in an unseen God is to thirst. Sure, there is a partial slaking of our thirst as Jesus promised there would be (Matthew 5:6; John 4), and yet . . . there is an intensifying of it, too. The psalmist wrote,

> As a deer pants for flowing streams, so pants my soul
>   for you, O God.
> My soul thirsts for God, for the living God.
> When shall I come and appear before God?
> My tears have been my food day and night,
>   while they say to me all the day long, "Where is your
>   God?"
>
> Psalm 42:1–3

Yes . . . yes. My soul resonates with those words. Where is my God? Where is he in the middle of all this longing? In the middle of this mess? Why doesn't he "rend the heavens and come down" (Isaiah 64:1)? Why does he wait? Why does he create this thirst within me for himself and then withhold himself from me? I'm panting for him, longing for him. I'm homesick for him. Yes, a day is coming when I'll be un-bodied and will rest in Paradise with him; and yes, I know I need to stay here and accomplish what he has for me . . . but still, I'm so thirsty. This marathon I'm running has left me panting for a drink not found here.

The only hope I have is that he promised to come again and take me to himself. That's the hope I have to keep before me. Yes, I have come to him. I know he is the living God who loves me. But I want to appear before him . . . I want to see him and be comforted by him. Perhaps for some it would be scary to appear before him, but I know that when I stand there I won't be naked. I won't be on my own. I'll be clothed with the royal robes of his Son and will be welcomed as his bride, on his arm. When will my faith finally become sight?

"Hope in God; for I shall again praise him, my salvation and my God. My soul is cast down within me; therefore I remember you" (Psalm 42:5–6). The psalmist seeks to comfort himself. But then he falls back into despair: "I say to God, my rock: 'Why have you forgotten me?'" (v. 9), and again he says, "Hope in God; for I shall again praise him, my salvation and my God" (v. 11).

This life of faith that we are all living is not static. It's anything but. That's because we're not Home yet. Things here aren't settled. We're still walking by faith. Sometimes I see clearly. Other times I wonder how much of what I believe will actually be found true. Yes, there are days when I seek to comfort myself: "You will again praise him, Elyse," I say. "He is your salvation." And I do believe it. And yet, there are days when I say, "Why have you forgotten me?"

Here's another homesickness psalm:

My soul longs, yes, faints for the courts of the Lord; my heart and flesh sing for joy to the living God. Even the sparrow finds a home, and the swallow a nest for herself, where she may lay her young, at your altars, O Lord of hosts, my King and my God. . . . Blessed are those whose strength is in you, in whose heart are the highways to Zion.

Psalm 84:2–5

Longing. Fainting. That's our experience here. I'm like the sparrow who finds a place to build her nest at God's altars, building a home near him . . . and yet, I still need to be strengthened by him, I still need that map. *O God, help me not lose my way to Zion, your dwelling place.*

Jesus' Homesickness

On the night he was betrayed, Jesus, too, was homesick. Of course he was also burdened for his friends. They were about to enter into terrible suffering. But he was looking forward to the reunion with his Father he had waited for all his earthly life. "Let not your hearts be troubled, neither let them be afraid," he said for the second time. "You heard me say to you, 'I am going away, and I will come to you.' If you loved me, you would have rejoiced, because I am going to the Father, for the Father is greater than I" (John 14:27–28).

All his disciples could see was impending doom. If they had really loved him, they would have been happy for him, because he was finally getting to go Home. So many times my own self-love and unbelief blind me to the real joys that our Lord knows now. I want to be with him there, or at least have him here with me. But it is far better that he is there, with his Father. I admit that's a hard pill for me to swallow. "I am going to my Father," he was telling them, "and if you think I'm something, you should see him!" I should rejoice for him. I should rejoice for all those who are with him in Paradise. But I miss him and I miss them. Home will be the place of great reunion.

Later on that evening Jesus told his Father, "I am coming to you" (John 17:11). You can almost sense his excitement. "I'm finally coming home! I finally get to see you again!" What does he want? What is he longing for? To be with his Father. Just like us. In verse 13, he reiterates, "I am coming to you." Perhaps you can even see his smile. For thirty-three lengthy and excruciating years he's longed to be Home again. He was the Man of Sorrows from the day of his birth. He's wanted to see that face that out-shines all other faces. And yet, he waited, willingly laying down his prerogatives, his rights, his desires. Why? Out of love for us.

So for all of us who are still earthbound, still thirsting and longing for him, here's his prayer for us: "Father, I desire that they also, whom you have given me, may be with me where I am, to see my glory that you have given me because you loved me before the foundation of the world" (John 17:24).

He knows our homesickness. Here's the shocking truth: He's missing us, too. For now. He's preparing a place for us, a place where we can rest in his embrace and see his glory. A place that will satisfy all our desires. A place of unmitigated love and welcome.

Even when I'm struggling to believe, even when it seems that the days are getting darker and darker, there is one thing I can believe: the prayer of the Son has been heard and it will be answered. I have been given to him by his Father. I am a bride cherished and beautified by love, and the Father will see to it that I will be with him where he is. And so will you.

Finally on the Inside

And what will I see there? Glory. The glory of the Son and the glory of the Father and their mutual love for each other and for me. I love the way C. S. Lewis describes our shared glory:

> For glory means good report with God, acceptance by God, response, acknowledgement, and welcome into the heart of things. The door on which we have been knocking all our lives will open at last.[9]

We'll be welcomed into the heart of things. No longer on the outside. But right there, right in the middle of everything that is good and holy and delightful. There won't be anything hurtful there. No jostling for position. No wishing things could be better. Listen to what Lewis says about our homesickness, our nostalgia:

> Apparently, then, our lifelong nostalgia, our longing to be reunited with something in the universe from which we now feel

cut off, to be on the inside of some door which we have always seen from the outside, is no mere neurotic fancy, but the truest index of our real situation. And to be at last summoned inside would be both glory and honour beyond all our merits and also the healing of that old ache.[10]

My dear sisters and brothers, this is where we're headed: to Paradise, to heaven, to his presence, to indescribable joy. We will no longer be exiles, on the outside, always looking forward, wishing for a way to transform our faith into sight. "Let not your hearts be troubled" (John 14:27). *Father, please grant us faith to believe this today, we pray. I do believe . . . help my unbelief! Amen.*

––––– FIXING OUR EYES ON HOME –––––

1. Have you ever thought about where believers go after they die as Paradise? Does this change your perspective on life after death at all?

2. What is the "intermediate" state, and why is understanding it important?

3. Do you long or thirst for God? Have you ever thought about these desires as "homesickness"? Would thinking in that way change your daily experience at all? How?

4. There is confusion among some Christians about the word *heaven*. What are the two ways we may use this word, and why is it important to have a clear understanding of both definitions?

5. French philosopher Blaise Pascal wrote, "What does this craving, and this helplessness, proclaim but that there was once in man a true happiness, of which all that now remains is the empty print and trace? This he tries in vain to

fill with everything around him, seeking in things that are not there the help he cannot find in those that are, though none can help, since this infinite abyss can be filled only with an infinite and immutable object; in other words by God himself."[11] Respond.

6. Summarize what you have learned in this chapter in four or five sentences.

3

Surprises in the Garden of New Life

A few years ago, I was in conversation with a sweet relative who asked me what I did for a living. As I explained to her what I write and speak about, she asked me to tell her what the word *gospel* meant (what an opportunity!), so I sought to explain concepts like incarnation, sin, substitutionary death, and resurrection.

"Wait," she said. "You're saying that you actually *believe* that Jesus rose from the dead? I've never heard that before!"

After I recovered from my shock that an adult American woman had never even heard the resurrection story, I told her that, in fact, I did believe that the physical body of the man who was called Jesus of Nazareth had been raised from the dead and eventually ascended into heaven. She was stunned.

Then she said, "That sounds crazy, but I know you're not crazy . . . so it must be true."

As we continued our conversation, I told her why the resurrection is so important to the Christian faith and what it means about God's welcome and the promise of the forgiveness of sins. I trust that the Lord brought her to faith that day.

While it's certainly true that most Christians celebrate Easter in some form every year (at least with bunnies and egg hunts), I'm not convinced that we all know why the resurrection is so vital to our faith or even what it might have to do with our eternal destiny. As I've been forced to think more deeply about my eternal Home and how it is the only answer to my homesickness, truths about the resurrection of Jesus have become more and more important to me. I'm learning to push my hope out . . . even past my death and rest in Paradise to the resurrection, and this learning is in many ways something new for me, even though I've been a Christian for nearly half a century. Theologian N. T. Wright agrees when he says, "Most people have little or no idea what the word *resurrection* actually means or why Christians say they believe it."[1] I have been right there with those people with "little or no idea."

Much to the shock of the disciples, Jesus was executed and then, even more surprisingly, he was resurrected after being entombed for three days. The fact that the disciples had real trouble believing the women's testimony proves that they weren't expecting this turn of events. No one in the Ancient Near East believed in bodily resurrection. It was simply not on their grid. They would have thought it repulsive that the physical body might live again after death. So when the disciples heard the testimony of the empty tomb from the women who had gone to embalm Jesus' body, they automatically assumed they were delirious and refused to believe their story (Mark 16:11; Luke 24:11). But Jesus was intent on proving he was physical beyond a shadow of a doubt. So, as Paul writes,

> He appeared to Cephas, then to the twelve. Then he appeared to more than five hundred brothers at one time, most of whom are still alive. Then he appeared to James, then to all the apostles. Last of all . . . he appeared also to me.
>
> 1 Corinthians 15:5–8

Someone might rightfully ask, "So what if God raised Jesus from the dead? What does that have to do with me?" Here's one way to think about it: If someone tells you that he's going to go prepare a place for those who love him and then he comes back from the dead, it's reasonable to believe that his words are reliable. People have promised all sorts of things to me, but none of them has come back from their execution yet . . . so what he said is certainly trustworthy. He's coming back for us. He's preparing a place for us. I believe it.

The resurrection also proves that God has accepted the work of his Son Jesus on our behalf. In other words, it proves that everything Jesus said and did, including his death, completed all that his Father had sent him to do. He was the perfectly obedient Son who stood in for us disobedient children and took the punishment we rightly deserved. But then his Father demonstrated his satisfaction with Jesus' work on our behalf by resurrecting him, raising him bodily from the dead. *The resurrection proves that all who believe in him are justified,* which means not only that our record of sin has been washed away but also that all the good works he did, all the obedience he displayed, is now credited to our account. We are not only forgiven, we're also counted obedient, righteous. How do we know this is true about us? Because of the resurrection. Here's how Paul put it when talking about the righteousness (perfect record of obedience) that has been given to us: "[Righteousness] will be counted to us who believe in him who raised from the dead Jesus our Lord, who was delivered up for our trespasses and raised for our justification" (Romans 4:24–25).

So the resurrection proves that we who believe are forgiven, loved, and welcomed by our heavenly Father, who not only sees our (sometimes) pious outward behavior but also reads every thought and intent of our hearts. We no longer have to question whether we are loved and welcomed by God or question whether he's angry with us or not, no matter how our lives might be falling apart. The resurrection settles all those issues once and for all. We are justified, forgiven, and righteous in his sight. Everything he said about loving us and taking us to himself in our eternal Home is true!

Our Incarnate King, the Man Christ Jesus

But that's not all Jesus' physical resurrection tells us. It also says that life in our Home to come might not be quite what we're expecting. It means that it is far more physical than we might assume. Now, I realize that this may mean a change in your thinking, so let me assure you, I'm just like you. I've had to wrestle through my presuppositions and expectations to see what the Bible actually says.

In order for us to begin to see forward to our eternal Home, we'll first have to look back about two thousand years to that very first Christmas. In fact, we've got to go back even further to behold the Son, as he existed before he came to earth as part of the Trinity: Father, Son, and Holy Spirit. The Son has always existed eternally as God, as spirit, and in immortality, in perfect fellowship and love within the Trinity. The Son was "the Word," who was "in the beginning with God." In fact, he was God himself: "and the Word was God" (John 1:1).

But then, the inexplicable occurred. At his Father's will, and in the power of the Spirit, the Son willingly humbled himself and entered the Virgin Mary's womb, taking her DNA, blood, oxygen, and life. He took on himself humanity and became a Jewish baby boy, Jesus, son of Mary. In that form he grew through childhood and into an adult just like you and me.

Jesus took on our humanity for two reasons: First, so that he could perfectly obey all God's rules in our place (as our stand-in), and second, so that he would be able to die (as our stand-in). He was, and always will be, our representative Brother. And like all our brothers, he is truly human. He looked like any other Middle Eastern man, completely like us in every way, except that he never sinned. Most Christians know and celebrate the incarnation at Christmas.

But now here comes the astounding part of the story we aren't generally acquainted with: Jesus didn't stop being human after he died and was raised from the dead. In fact, on several different occasions he took pains to prove his humanity by saying things like, "Touch me and see; a ghost does not have flesh and bones, as you see I have" (Luke 24:39; see also John 20:27 NIV). After the resurrection, he looked so human that Mary mistook him for the gardener (we'll talk more about this in a bit). He wasn't shiny or sparkly or see-through. And while it is true that he was able to suddenly appear in locked rooms, the only thing unique about him was his wounded hands and side. His bodily resurrection communicates an intensely important message, a message not only of forgiveness and welcome but also of the *continuity of our physical bodies and ultimately this planet we live on.* Because he lived in his resurrected body on the earth, we can see that resurrection life and this physical world are not ultimately at odds with each other. This is how Randy Alcorn puts it:

> Jesus walked on earth in his resurrection body for forty days, showing us how we would live as resurrected human beings. In effect, he also demonstrated *where* we would live as resurrected human beings—on Earth. Christ's resurrection body was suited for life on Earth. . . . As Jesus was raised to come back to live on Earth, so we will be raised to come back to live on Earth (1 Thessalonians 4:14).[2]

Our Incarnate King in His Cloud Chariot

But there is even more astounding news. Ready? Not only was Jesus raised in his physical body, *he was also taken into heaven in his physical body.* He's still a Man, even though he's no longer on earth. He's in heaven. I know that's hard to wrap your mind around, but that is what the Bible teaches, so let me try to help you out a bit.

After staying with the disciples for forty days, proving that he was as alive as ever, teaching them how to read the Scriptures, and all about his kingdom (Acts 1:1–3), Jesus, "as they were looking on . . . was lifted up, and a cloud took him out of their sight" (Acts 1:9). Here's the surprise: He didn't change from a man into an angel or a ghost or some other sort of spirit being before returning to heaven. Nor did he just disappear or go shooting up into the air like a magic rocket or dissolve down into the ground. He was surrounded by a supernatural mist, probably very similar to the "bright cloud" that the disciples saw when he had been transfigured before them (Matthew 17:5).³ And so he was taken into heaven, while they stood there gawking.

Get the picture: The disciples had been standing with him, asking about when God would restore Israel's kingdom. After telling them that the answer to that question was really none of their business, he suddenly arose from the ground and took a "cloud chariot" into heaven (Psalm 104:3). I can't imagine the shock the disciples felt in that moment, can you? There he was, as normal and physical as he could be, and then a cloud enveloped him and he was gone. It's kind of humorous that the angels chided them, "Why do you stand [around] looking into heaven?" (Acts 1:11). The answer to that question seems a bit obvious, doesn't it? "Er . . . We're trying to figure out where Jesus just went—" The angels said that he had been taken from them into heaven and that in the same way he would return. When he left, he did so as a physical (though glorified) Man. When he returns, he'll come back as a physical (though glorified) Man.

While all this is more than a little strange to us earthbound creatures, the important truth is that he took that journey as a Man. Yes, a God Man for sure, but yet still human. Think of it, he took Mary's DNA into the heavenly dimension. That should shock you a little—it shocks me. It certainly shocked his disciples.

And now, two millennia later, Jesus, the Son, is still a Man, awaiting our arrival and looking forward to the day when he will return (as a Man with Mary's DNA) to reclaim the earth and establish his kingdom here forever. Is he glorified? Yes, of course. But that doesn't mean his essence has changed. If he walked into your room right now, you wouldn't mistake him for a light bulb or a ghost. When he took on our humanity, he took it on forever, as Stephen testified when he "gazed into heaven" and "saw the glory of God, and Jesus standing at the right hand of God" as he was about to become the first Christian martyr.

Notice how Stephen describes him: He calls him "the Son of *Man*" (Acts 7:55–56). Scripture teaches that he is the Word made flesh (see John 1:14) and will be so forever because it is impossible for him to change (see Hebrews 13:8). The apostle Paul twice refers to the ascended Jesus as a Man (not a spirit). He does so once when calling him the mediator between God and man in 1 Timothy 2:5, and another time while preaching in Athens, as the man through whom God will judge the world (Acts 17:31). What would Jesus look like today if we could see him? He'd look like a normal man. As Randy Alcorn puts it, "A fundamental article of the Christian faith is that the resurrected Christ now dwells in Heaven."[4]

Too earthy for you? Yes, I get that . . . and yet, it's that very earthiness, that very humanity, that's so crucial to understanding our eternal destiny. Our DNA gets taken into heaven. Man walks through a door made of mist right into the presence of God.

Why All This Earthiness Is Crucial

All this incarnation-DNA-in-heaven talk tells us that God isn't finished with the physical world yet. It's not his plan to do away with the material or bodily cosmos he has created. He's not getting rid of the elements or jettisoning the dust of which we are all made. Yes, of course, there will be changes, and drastic ones, but they will not be fundamental to what we are at the core of our beings.[5] It means that I'll somehow be reunited with my DNA at my resurrection, even if my body disintegrates or "sees corruption," something Jesus' body didn't do (Psalm 16:10; Acts 13:35).

These changes will definitely be transformational, but they won't be a change from what we are now to a different sort of being. They will be deep and real, but not so much so that there won't be anything recognizable left. We're not changing from humans into angels or ghosts. We're still going to be human, but gloriously so, without sin. Our sin nature will be fully eradicated and we'll finally be what we had always hoped to be: fully ourselves, fully freed from sin. Yes, he's going to cleanse humanity and the entire world with fire, much like he did with water in the time of Noah, but just as the world remained after the cleansing flood, so the world will remain after his return and the cleansing fire. Satan's plans to spoil God's good creation won't succeed. God could never be forced to start over again by some fallen angel. His pronouncement that his creation is "very good" will again ring true in the ears of the entire universe.

But . . . But . . .

My guess is that some of you are stumbling over those last thoughts a bit. Let me suggest some reasons why that might be true.

A Man Ruling in Heaven?

First of all, not many of us have been taught much about Jesus' ascension. I admit that for many years I sort of pictured Jesus up in heaven, somewhere "in outer space," as it said in a children's song we taught at my church. I thought about him as being in sort of a spiritual form, floating around near his Father's throne, if I thought about his present state of being at all. Honestly, it never would have occurred to me to think of him as having a beating heart or blinking eyes up there . . . wherever "up there" was. So I'm right with you. The thought of Jesus' ongoing incarnation didn't become central to my faith until I wrote about it a few years ago.[6]

The Greek Philosophers Would Disagree!

The second reason we feel uncomfortable with the thought of a Man ruling in heaven is that most of us have unwittingly bought into the old Greek philosophical lie that everything that is physical or material is evil and everything that is immaterial or spiritual is good. We demonstrate our underlying belief in Greek philosophy when we say things that make it sound as though earthiness is undesirable, like when we talk about shedding our earthly bodies so that our spirits can finally be free and pure. This way of thinking is so inbred into us that we hardly bat an eye when someone talks about how great it will be to finally be freed from our physical bodies or when we sing about soaring "to worlds unknown."[7]

That's not to say that our physical bodies (and souls) don't need to be cleansed, redeemed, and glorified. It's just that we think that physicality is somehow a lower form of life than spirituality, and in that we're deeply mistaken. Contrary to popular belief, Greek philosophy is completely wrong when it comes to the innate wickedness of the world—apart, of course, from sin.

"Flesh" ≠ "Fleshly"

I know that part of our problem with thinking in this way is because some verses in the Bible speak negatively about our "fleshly" or "flesh"[8] nature, and so we automatically think that *fleshly* means our physical body. But *flesh* or *fleshly* doesn't necessarily mean actual "flesh" like "flesh and blood." It stands for the old Adam, the "unregenerate former life of those who now believe."[9] Apart from sin, our flesh is not evil in itself. It was created by God from the dust of the ground that he had created and pronounced to be very good.

So, primarily because the evangelical church has bought into Greek philosophy, which actually has more in common with Buddhism than Christianity, we assume that this world and all that's in it is evil or on a lesser plane and completely doomed. But the Bible teaches us that we couldn't be more wrong. It's because of this basic miscue that most of us gloss over passages about the physical ascension of Jesus and instead enjoy thinking about zipping around like sprites in some sort of vaporous heavenly realm. In other words, we have a hard time reconciling the human earthiness of a physical Jesus who has flesh, blood, hair, bones, and actual solidness with the pristine holiness of the place we normally call heaven where the Father dwells. Why? Simply because Plato or Aristotle would be horrified by it.

Why am I spending so much time talking about the resurrection and the ascension in a book about our eternal destiny? Simply because Jesus is the pattern, the firstfruits, the example of what the Father has decreed will inevitably come next. The resurrection means that everything that once was true about the futility of life and the reign of death is now over. Here's C. S. Lewis on the importance of the resurrection:

> The New Testament writers speak as if Christ's achievement in rising from the dead was the first event of its kind in the whole

history of the universe. He is the "firstfruits," the "pioneer of life." He has forced open a door that has been locked since the death of the first man. He has met, fought, and beaten the King of Death. Everything is different because He has done so. This is the beginning of the New Creation: a new chapter in cosmic history has opened.[10]

Gardens From Beginning to End

Let's think now about some clues about our Home on the New Earth that the gospel writers have left for us. Here's one: "Now in the place where he was crucified there was a garden, and in the garden a new tomb in which no one had yet been laid" (John 19:41).

Jesus' body was laid in a tomb in a garden. Why would that be important for us to know? Because even in this, the interment of his body, his Father was continuing to work his plan to reclaim the earth. His body was laid to rest in a garden.

I'll be honest here. I'm not a gardener. I appreciate a pretty garden . . . sort of. Truth is that my allergies are so bad that I've often told Phil that if I didn't have a family, friends, or church obligations, I'd like to live on a little spit of sand in the middle of the ocean (with no vegetation) or in a concrete bunker on the twenty-fifth floor of some high-rise. Pollen and Elyse aren't friends. I'm assuming that once I get to the New Earth all my allergies will be gone and I'll be able to stick my nose into a beautiful flower without my face blowing up. But in the meantime, I take allergy medicine daily and try to enjoy the days when I don't get high pollen alerts sent to my phone.

Even so, gardens are everywhere in the Scriptures. Remember that it was in a garden called Eden that man first fell after demanding his own will, but it was also in a garden named Gethsemane that the Second Man yielded his will to obey his

Father's (Matthew 26:36ff.), and it was in another garden that his body was laid (John 19:41). And as we've already discovered, our "rest stop" after death will also be a garden park. Gardens are everywhere!

In her grief and to anoint her Friend's body, Mary had gone to the tomb that first Easter morn. You remember the scene: She was overcome with anguish, weeping as she approached the garden tomb. Then she saw it—insult upon insult—someone had taken his body! Mary had been anxious to honor him by covering him with spices, thereby sparing him the final indignity of the odor of decay, but now his body was gone! Dear Mary. She was on a mission to take care of him. She had no idea what had already happened, or what was about to happen. Here's John's account:

> Now on the first day of the week Mary Magdalene came to the tomb early, while it was still dark, and saw that the stone had been taken away from the tomb. . . . But Mary stood weeping outside the tomb, and as she wept she stooped to look into the tomb. And she saw two angels in white, sitting where the body of Jesus had lain, one at the head and one at the feet. They said to her, "Woman, why are you weeping?" She said to them, "They have taken away my Lord, and I do not know where they have laid him." Having said this, she turned around and saw Jesus standing, but she did not know it was Jesus. Jesus said to her, "Woman, why are you weeping? Whom are you seeking?" Supposing him to be the gardener, she said to him, "Sir, if you have carried him away, tell me where you have laid him, and I will take him away." Jesus said to her, "Mary."
>
> John 20:1, 11–16

In this touching scene of both loss and reunion, John wants us to notice that Mary mistook Jesus for the gardener. Interesting mistake, to be sure. Without making too much of it, let's just say that though she was ultimately mistaken in his identity, she wasn't that far off the mark. You see, Jesus *is* the Master Gardener. He's the Second Adam, the true and obedient Son of God, tasked with caring for God's garden and protecting it from evil, fulfilling the mandates God had given in the beginning, mandates Adam failed to complete (Genesis 1:28).[11] And then her Adam, her perfect Husband (and ours), spoke her name, "Mary," and everything changed. As the Master Gardener, he was tasked with reopening the garden for his people, refitting it, cleansing it, redeeming it, so that he could live there with his bride (the church) forever.

Do you see? The Lord was in charge even of her mistaking the Son for a mere gardener because he wants us to realize who the Son really is and what he has done for us. He is the Second Adam, succeeding in the garden where the first Adam had failed (Romans 5). The garden he will ultimately open on the New Earth isn't some cramped little plot of land. It will also be much more than the wayside Paradise garden where we await the New Earth. It will be a magnificent garden city where all the resurrected redeemed will dwell together (Revelation 22)! A beautifully planned urban area where with all of his people we'll be gathered together to worship, explore, plant, nurture, and develop the world he's made. And like your Savior, you will eventually walk through this garden city in a renewed body.

Paul wrote that our present bodies are like seeds that are planted into the ground and are raised into imperishable, glorious, powerful, spiritual bodies. Our bodies on the New Earth will be like Jesus' body after his resurrection: whole, perfect, eternal. We will be immortal (1 Corinthians 15:54). "We shall also bear the image of the man of heaven" (1 Corinthians 15:49). You will be *you* and yet so much more you than you've ever been. We will walk with each other through a beautiful garden in bodies that will never wear out or betray us. The garden city is coming; it will be Home. Think of it. Let your imagination soar.

Why Are You Weeping?

Let's allow Jesus' counsel to sink into our hopeless hearts, take root, and grow into full faith. "Let not your hearts be troubled" (John 14:27). "Whoever believes in me, though he die, yet shall he live (John 11:25). When someone comes back from the dead, his words are trustworthy. He's strong enough to do something that no one else has been able to do. He knows what he's talking about. Of course, Lazarus was raised from the dead, but he eventually died again. Only Jesus' resurrection was an eternal resurrection. He continues to live as the incarnate God Man today. We can trust him. Our plans may fall apart . . . we may not see everything (or anything!) he's promised in this life, but we do know who he is and what he's done. So we shouldn't be deeply troubled by what's happening around us.

Yes, things do look dark, but joy comes in the morning; at dawn, when we're looking for him in the tomb, he's opening up the New Earth for us. As C. S. Lewis assures us, "The bad dream will be over: it will be morning."[12] Circumstances could not have looked worse for Mary and the disciples, but at dawn the light of heaven broke through. "Why are you weeping?" was Jesus' question to her and to us. Believe in God. Believe also in the God Man. Yes, Lord, we believe. Help our unbelief. Confess along with Martin Luther, "He has given heaven to us; it belongs to me."[13]

--- FIXING OUR EYES ON HOME ---

1. Easter, the church's commemoration of the resurrection of Jesus, means more than a fun family celebration or new clothes for the kids. In fact, it means everything to us as

Christians. What does the resurrection teach us about who we are? What does it teach us about our life to come?

2. What does the ascension of Jesus tell us? Why is it important that he went into heaven still as a Man? Have you ever thought about him in this way before? Is there anything that troubles you about it? If so, what?

3. "The Christian church looks upon the worst setbacks . . . and declares . . . 'Christ Jesus reigns in heaven, and so, at the deepest level, all is well. What of my circumstance? I am in Christ and he has triumphed. In him, by the Holy Spirit, I am kept in heaven.' The ascension provides . . . for our peace in every circumstance."[14] Why is the ascension necessary for our peace?

4. Gardens seem to be important places in the Bible. We discussed three of them in this chapter. Name them and talk about why they are important, especially in understanding our eternal destiny.

5. Why is it important to know that we will be physical and not immaterial beings in the New Earth?

6. Summarize what you've learned in this chapter in four or five sentences.

4

A Glimpse of Our Garden Home

I'm a California girl. I've lived here in what we locals call SoCal for practically my entire life. Everything about San Diego—the roads, the stores, the restaurants, and especially the beaches—is home to me. In fact, I've been going to the same beach to ride waves, catch rays, and listen to the Beach Boys sing about California girls (me!) for over half a century. (Yikes! That sounds really old!)

Everything of any import to my life has happened here. I was saved here, I was married here, and all my children and their children were born here. I understand the weather patterns and know what to expect when a Santa Ana is forecast. I've lived through numbers of earthquakes (without any fear) and through major fires, quaking in my boots. I know what it means when someone says, "The 15 is a parking lot," and why people put "Life's a Beach" bumper stickers on their cars, or cheer if they think they've seen the green flash. Phil's a native, too, and he loves both the Chargers and, especially, the Padres dearly. The kids even bought him a commemorative brick at Petco Park with his name on it. San Diego is home, but it isn't Home. We like to say, "It's not heaven, but you can see it from here."

Yes, San Diego is home . . . and yet it's not. Sure, it is close, but when I look out over the ocean, dancing in golden jewel-light, or stare off into an endless azure sky while I enjoy a mild warm sun and cooling breeze, there's still something wrong . . . something's not quite perfect. I hear the ticking of the clock, and I know that if I don't get on the road soon, I'll be stuck in traffic, or that in just a few short minutes that ubiquitous marine layer of clouds will show up again and turn everything gray.

Even when you live as close to paradise as I do, you sense it's not quite right. So it doesn't stop me from longing for a perfect place to live or from trying to make this place into paradise for Phil and me. No matter how hard I work on it, though, rearranging this, painting that, every day I continue to long for that *something more* that is just beyond my reach, right out there and yet not there. C. S. Lewis recognized this desire within himself, too:

> Creatures are not born with desires unless satisfaction for those desires exists. . . . [So] if I find in myself a desire which no experience in this world can satisfy, the most probable explanation is that I was made for another world. . . . I must keep alive in myself the desire for my true country, which I shall not find till after death.[1]

Yes, I find within myself an unsatisfied desire for something like Home. And that's a desire that never seems to abate. It's unending homesickness.

Back Home in the Garden

In the last chapter we were introduced to Jesus as the Master Gardener. As you know, God's original gardener, Adam, failed to complete the work his Creator had assigned to him, so he and his wife were banished from their perfect home and sent out into a land filled with thorns, thistles, and pain, not only in work and childbearing but also in every relationship. Their firstborn son, Cain, the one they had assumed would crush the head of the serpent, murdered their next born, Abel. Can you imagine their heartache? In addition, although the world was certainly more resplendent then than it is right now, they still had to toil for their food, and the earth resisted every step of the way. They had chosen independence from God, demanded to taste the forbidden, and now they were reaping the consequences of their foolish choices.

The worst curse of all was that they had been blocked from reentering the Garden, where their relationship with God was unhindered and the Tree of Life grew. No longer would they be able to walk in the Garden with the Lord. Now they would fear, even cringe at his presence. They knew that if they saw his holiness now they would be obliterated. They slunk away in the shadows. The Garden was gone . . . a thing of the past. Men and women would never taste that fruit again. It was over . . . or so it seemed.

Thousands of years passed, and still the way to the Garden remained closed. Prophets had foretold a coming King, a Rescuer who would set everything right again and bring them Home, but he was nowhere to be found. The earth had been washed with water, but still folly reigned. A man from Ur had been chosen, but he wasn't the Deliverer men and women were longing for. A nation was delivered from the hand of Pharaoh, and yet even for those who outlasted the wilderness wandering, the Promised Land that was supposed to be home wasn't. "Flowing with milk and honey"? (Exodus 3:8). Didn't seem to be. Sure, they had the tabernacle and then the temple where God's presence dwelt, but his dwelling place certainly wasn't their Home. They were told not to go in there uninvited or unprepared or they would surely die. Hardly sounds like Home, not a place for pj's and a visit with a beloved Father.

Even after the miraculous crossing of the Jordan River and great military victories, there were still enemies all around, and for a season the people continued to follow in Adam's footsteps, doing "what was right in [their] own eyes" (Judges 21:25). Then God gave them a king, and their hopes for deliverance and a true home was reborn. But their king was a failure. In fact, all of Israel's kings were. Even the good ones eventually died and left the kingdom to sons who were scoundrels. Israel's first king, Saul, was deposed and committed suicide. The second one, the greatest of all of Israel's kings, David, committed adultery and murder and failed to train his sons in the ways of God. His son Solomon, the wisest man on earth, regularly acted like a fool. And the cavalcade of folly continued on and on until their exile from the land and Israel's loss of independence as a nation. After the nation's king's eyes were gouged out, her people were taken away in chains to Babylon. Even after resettling back in the land, Israel remained under the boot of one conqueror after another. But still the prophets prophesied of a coming King, and then for four hundred years (similar to their time in Egypt), God went dark. He stopped speaking and seemed to be ignoring them. But he wasn't.

Onto the scene walked Jesus . . . the true King of Kings and Lord of Lords. No, better yet, onto the scene the King was carried by his mother (of questionable morals). Wait. This isn't the kind of King the nation needed. Hadn't God seen Rome's atrocities? Didn't he see what kind of ruler Herod was? Was his answer to their desperate need really a squalling baby? And an illegitimate one at that! Really?

But their King matured in obscurity for thirty years, sawing wood and hammering nails. Then he was baptized by his very strange cousin, John, and went on a fast in the desert and fought evil. Very odd. Upon his return, he gathered to himself twelve thickheaded nobodies and spent the next three years "doing good and healing all who were oppressed by the devil" (Acts 10:38). Well, okay, maybe things were beginning to look up. Events seemed to be really progressing along now, especially once he was welcomed like a second King Solomon, riding a donkey into Jerusalem. Maybe this was the King who would bring them back home again. Maybe a King had finally come! A kingdom, a home was within their reach! Or not . . . Within a few short days of his triumphal entry, he was bleeding out on a cursed tree under his Father's wrath, while his enemies jeered. Down came the King's body, hurriedly placed into a tomb so as not to break God's rules about the Sabbath. The earth had gobbled up another captive; a garden would imprison him. And the desire for a King who would conquer our enemies and reopen Paradise to us would lie decaying in a borrowed cave.

But then, surprise! Jesus' Father shouted an amen in response to his Son's "It is finished," and he drew the breath of life again. But this time he breathed in the air of a new world, a world on the other side of decay, exile, and homelessness. Everything that we had longed for, everything that had been missing, the King had earned the right to restore. Everything. In creation, he had rested from all his labors on the seventh day. Now he inaugurated an eighth-day celebration . . . a time of jubilee, of return to our true Home, a brand-new age of freedom from condemnation and futility.

> The Bible thus tells one comprehensive and ultimately coherent story of God's purposes for the flourishing of earthly life. Although the world has been in the grip of terrible evil . . . God has been at work throughout history—through a series of redemptive agents and ultimately through Jesus—to overcome all that impedes his purposes from being fulfilled.[2]

Jesus' bodily resurrection proved that the kingdom he was sent to establish had been successfully planted and would continue to grow until that tiny seed finally filled God's entire garden world with a tree big enough for birds to nest in (Matthew 13:32). God's kingdom had come to the earth (Acts 17:31). His will had been done. Life and holiness had conquered death and sin. In his resurrection and ascension everything had changed, and heaven and earth were now reconciled through the body of the God from heaven who was also the Man of earth. The die had been cast and the ultimate reconciliation and re-creation was just a matter of time. The reclamation of God's good creation had begun.

Earth would be Home once again! "The one thing we can be sure of is that this redeeming of creation will not mean that God will say . . . 'Oh, well, nice try, it was good while it lasted.'"[3] God isn't finished with what he originally created. It's still his creation. His Son spoke it into being. There's no way (in this world!) that he would let Satan have the last word about what he's made or that he would leave it in ruins and try to make something better in its place.

So what will our new home be like? In order to answer that question, let's think about what the original garden was like. It was, after all, the place we were created to live, and we are headed back there once again. God isn't finished with his garden world. In fact, he's blasted open the doors and emblazoned a banner that reads *Welcome home, sons and daughters!* on its gates.

A Very Good Home

In describing all that the Son had originally made, the Lord pronounced his work "very good." Here's how Moses described those beginning scenes:

And the Lord God planted a garden in Eden, in the east, and there he put the man whom he had formed. And out of the ground the Lord God made to spring up every tree that is pleasant to the sight and good for food. . . . A river flowed out of Eden to water the garden. . . . The Lord God took the man and put him in the garden of Eden to work it and keep it. And the Lord God commanded the man, saying, "You may surely eat of every tree of the garden. . . ." Now out of the ground the Lord God had formed every beast of the field and every bird of the heavens and brought them to the man to see what he would call them. . . . The Lord God . . . made . . . a woman and brought her to the man. . . . And the man and his wife were both naked and were not ashamed. . . . And they heard the sound of the Lord God walking in the garden in the cool of the day.

Genesis 2:8–10, 15–16, 19, 22, 25; 3:8

What do these passages tell us about the Home we were meant to occupy? First of all, it was created specifically for us, for humanity. It was perfectly suited to us, beautiful, and "pleasant to the sight." In fact, it was mind-blowingly exquisite. But it wasn't only beautiful. It was also filled with everything necessary for our survival. There was abundant food and water there, and there were animals for us to enjoy and shepherd. There was unrestricted communion with its Creator, who strolled there in the "cool of the day." Remember that in his presence is "the path of life," "fullness of joy" and those "pleasures" were at his right hand "forevermore" (Psalm 16:11).

Imagine a place where everything was as it should be, all relationships completely open, all conversation honest and loving, every view in every direction more splendid than the last. Imagine a place where righteousness actually dwells (2 Peter 3:13), a place infused with holiness, where "joy and gladness will be . . . thanksgiving and the voice of song" (Isaiah 51:3). Imagine being able to trust everyone around you as you walk together through a garden filled with delights. Friendship unhindered, unashamed communion between the man and his wife. Nothing being held back, no shame, no regrets . . . just love and beauty, peace and song. All work completed without frustration or grumbling, in the right time; the earth gladly yielding her bounty. All rest deep and fully satisfying. All touches pure and generous; all the animals our friends; never hiding in fear.

It's nearly impossible for us to imagine such a place. Lewis gets at this a bit when he says, "The good things even of this world are far too good ever to be reached by imagination. Even the common orange, you know: no one could have imagined it before he tasted it. How much less Heaven."[4] Now, that's a place I want to call Home.

Where will this heavenly garden be? Where would it be? Why, here, on this earth, of course. That's the whole point! Our ancient foe who assumed he had won a victory by forcing God's sons and daughters out of his beautiful temple garden still has some setbacks in store for him. God isn't going to give his good world over to loss and ultimate decay. Do things need to change on this planet? Yes, of course! If we die before his return, will there be an intermediate resting place? Yes, but the events still to come will not ultimately separate us from the world the Son spoke into existence and died to reclaim. Trash the glorious work it took him six days to complete? Unthinkable!

> In fact, so positive a view did [God] take of what he had created that he refused to scrap it when mankind spoiled it, but determined instead, at the cost of his Son's life, to make it new and good again. God does not make junk, and he does not junk what he has made.[5]

The Creation Mandate

Let's think a little more about what life will be like in the earth garden we'll inhabit. To do that, let's once again go back to Genesis for clues. You remember that after the Lord had placed the man and the woman in the garden he gave them, he commanded about the work they were to do. We call this command about their mission the Creation, or cultural, Mandate. This is what humanity was to accomplish as the vice-regents in the Son's kingdom:

> And God blessed them. And God said to them, "Be fruitful and multiply and fill the earth and subdue it, and have dominion over the fish of the sea and over the birds of the heavens and over every living thing that moves on the earth." . . . The Lord God took the man and put him in the garden of Eden to work it and keep it.
>
> Genesis 1:28; 2:15

Adam and Eve were given specific instructions even aside from the command not to eat of the Tree of Knowledge of Good and Evil. They were to raise faithful children who would populate the earth and serve God wisely. They were also to "subdue" the earth, which means that they were "to bring . . . [the] land into subjection so that it will yield service to the one subduing it."[6] They were to "develop the earth's resources to make them useful for human beings."[7] Adam's role to work and keep the Garden meant that he would prepare, tend, and also guard it.

You know, when you think about it, this is what people, even unbelievers, still spend their entire lives doing. They seek to make their world a pleasant place to live; they develop the world and bring order to it. They file things alphabetically, they fold clothes . . . they write books (and posts, tweets, and blogs). They work, even on their days off, to tend the resources they have and guard them from loss. God's creational design wasn't lost, even in the fall, though, of course, it was twisted. It makes sense, then, doesn't it, that once we're back on the New Earth, where we will once again inhabit God's beautiful garden, his commands to us will remain the same. What will we do on the New Earth? We will tend it, explore, and develop it, foster ways to use its resources wisely, and care for one another. We will work and we will rest, and it will all be glorious.

Again! Again!

For the last few years my husband and I have been vacationing with our lifelong friends, Phil and Julie. A few years ago, we explored Zion National Park together and discovered a hike called "The Narrows." Basically this is a hike up the Virgin River in Zion Canyon. In order to do the hike in the fall, when we vacation, you need to rent a dry suit because the water can get pretty cold. The rock walls tower over a thousand feet on both sides of the gorge, and in some places they narrow to only thirty feet. The year we discovered the hike, we didn't have time to complete it, but planned to return to it the following year. But the next year, on the night before our drive out to Zion, I got the stomach flu, and although we went ahead and drove out (might as well throw up in a wastebasket in the car), by the time we got there, I didn't have the strength to attempt it. As I lay in bed in the lodge, I comforted myself with this thought: *This will just have to be something I do on the New Earth.* And the more I thought about it, the more that thought became a mantra for my life . . . for all the things I long to do but just can't seem to get done: "That'll just have to be something I'll do on the New Earth."

Think a bit about that with me. Have you ever longed to explore towering mountains or swim into deep water and see what the Lord has hidden there? I was having a discussion about this with my eldest grandson, Wesley, when he said, "But . . .

Mimi . . . in order to do that you have to . . . er . . . die." Sweet thing. "Right!" I said. Then he said, "But that won't happen even if you die right now. Won't you have to wait till Jesus comes back?" "Right again!" I said. Smarty. "If I die before Jesus' return, I will rest in Paradise while I await my new resurrected body and the new resurrected earth . . . but then we'll explore, dear boy, then we'll explore! And guess what? We'll never feel too tired or get sick. And here's the best part of all: We'll never get bored! Think of it: We could hike the Narrows, and then when we were finished, we could say, 'Again! Again!' and do it all over again, seeing things we didn't see the first time and laughing all the way. We could be like toddlers who are so filled with life and joy that they can say, 'Again! Again!' to some song you've already bounced them on your knee fifteen times to and can't wait to stop."[8]

Toddlers don't get bored; they're unaware of deadlines and the end of playtime and the serious adult business of getting on to the next serious adult thing. Sound like fun? Of course it does. I personally plan on doing a lot of exploring of nebulae and riding of waves.[9] Imagine . . . life without boredom. Or deadlines. Or endings. Imagine a life full of learning and exploration and dominion and strength and life. Imagine work that's satisfying and meaningful and offered gladly for the benefit of others. That's it . . . life on the New Earth!

The Missing Command

Take a second and go back to look over the Creation Mandate a couple of pages back. Can you see anything that's missing? Think about the one activity of heaven that is our default setting. What is it? Worship, of course! Whenever we think of heaven, we almost always think that we'll spend all of our time there worshiping. Don't you find it fascinating that Adam and Eve were never commanded to worship God? Do you know why? Because before sin entered the world, everything they did was worship. Naming animals, tending the trees, walking together in loving harmony, trying a new fruit, sleeping—everything was worship! It was only after we became bent in on ourselves that we had to be commanded to remember our Creator and give thanks. We've been so marred by sin that we can't rule properly or remember to worship God. Rather than remembering to give thanks and worship the Lord, we habitually worship ourselves.

I don't think we will have to be commanded to worship on the New Earth, because all of life will be worship. Every trip up The Narrows will be filled with God-glorifying joy and delight. Every conversation will find its nexus in the Son, who might just come strolling up to join us. "Why, we were just talking about you!" we will exclaim, and he'll laugh, and we'll walk over to the throne of God together, where we'll sing and rejoice for days. Will we spend time worshiping? Yes, of course. Sometimes before the throne, but other times, our worship will take the form of hiking up the Narrows, exploring caves, describing Saturn's rings (will they still be there?), learning how DNA actually works or why the universe is made up of spirals. What will we do in the New Earth? How much time do you have for me to get your imagination going?

A new day is coming. In fact, it's been dawning ever since the first Easter. Jesus did everything Adam had failed to do. He fulfilled the Creation Mandate completely. The creation is back on track again. Are you beginning to sense that there's a change in the air?

Resting on the Seventh Day

As we bring this chapter to a close, let's think again about the creation account, and the resurrection of our Lord, and how these events intersect in another surprising way. This is how Genesis 1:1, 5; 2:2 reads:

> In the beginning, God created the heavens and the earth. . . . And there was evening and there was morning, the first day. . . . And on the seventh day God finished his work that he had done, and he rested on the seventh day from all his work that he had done.

And so, like the Father, we will enter into rest, too. We won't only learn, explore, and subdue the earth; we'll also rest, but not on just one day in seven, because the era of the seventh-day Sabbath is over. In the creation account in Genesis, we read that after God finished all his work, he rested on the seventh day, the Sabbath. But never does it say, "there was evening, and there was morning, the seventh day" like it does for all the other days. "It's like there's a missing verse in the creation account. Why? It's as if this day never ended. It seems like it's waiting for something—or someone—to bring it to a close." Jesus is the One who ultimately brought the unending seventh day of creation to a close by resting in the garden tomb all that day . . . and then ushering in the glorious new eighth day. On that first Easter "he began the eighth day, after which there is no other."[10] The eighth day of creation, the day of restoration, reconciliation, and full life has already begun!

All of us are on a journey, looking for Home, searching for a place of true welcome and joy and rest. And though we can't quite see it yet, we're beginning to get a hint of what might be waiting for us, up around the bend. Yes, I love SoCal . . . but I also know it's not my true Home. San Diego is great, but in comparison to the New Earth . . . it's not even a contest. The eighth day has dawned . . . we're just awaiting our turn to enjoy it. We will live on in that day, worshiping in ways we've never even considered, and joy and gladness will fill our hearts forever.

———— FIXING OUR EYES ON HOME ————

1. C. S. Lewis said, "I must keep alive in myself the desire for my true country, which I shall not find till after death."[11] Do you see in yourself a desire for your "true country"? How does that feel? How might we keep that desire alive within ourselves?

2. Have you ever thought about God re-creating the Garden of Eden in the New Earth before? What do you find challenging or exciting about the thought?

3. Why is the resurrection of Jesus so important when we consider the New Earth? What did he do to fulfill the Creation Mandate? How does that enable us to do the same?

4. The psalmist wrote of Jesus, the God-Man, "Yet you have made him a little lower than the heavenly beings and crowned him with glory and honor. You have given him dominion over the works of your hands; you have put all things under his feet" (Psalm 8:5–6; see also Hebrews 2:8–9). Jesus earned the right to have dominion over all the earth through his perfect obedience and substitutionary death. What that means for us is that in the New Earth we, too, will have dominion over creation and explore and enjoy it to the glory of God. Respond.

5. Summarize what you've learned in this chapter in four or five sentences.

5

Seeing the City Abraham Saw

If I were to ask you to try to imagine where you see your daily life after you die, my guess is that you wouldn't automatically shout out, "New York!" "Beijing!" "London!" or even "San Diego!"

My guess is that you'd imagine it being something more like an idyllic emerald pasture, with a sparkling brook, clear blue skies, and lush trees, or even the garden parks we've been talking about . . . that is, if you imagined it as having physical form at all. If you didn't envision yourself floating around on a cloud, you'd probably think it would look like something that just materialized out of a Thomas Kinkade painting. You probably wouldn't picture it teeming with all sorts of people who look, think, and act quite differently from you. You might envision a little cottage with glowing lights and a beautiful picket fence, where you and one or two like-you others lived . . . but New York? High-rises? No. Hardly.

As someone who's been to all four of those cities I mentioned above, I admit that although I found visiting them very interesting and frequently even exhilarating, I never walked down their streets thinking, *Wow! This reminds me of heaven!* No, in the past, when I've thought of heaven, I've thought of solitary beauty and the quiet of coming "to the garden alone, while the dew is still on the roses."[1] I would have thought of a place where the Lord and I would have quiet, personal talks or maybe where I'd excel at singing in a choir. But Scripture teaches that perspective is pretty wrongheaded. When I think like that I'm thinking more like Plato than Paul.

Everyone knows that their life here ends. Christians believe that a day is coming when our lives here will cease and we will then transition to another reality, but we rarely imagine that reality to be shaped like Tokyo. If I were to ask you what you thought you would be doing for the next trillion years, would you say, "Exploring a city," "Meeting new people," or "Learning about why every snowflake is different"? Probably not. Most of us would piously answer, "Worshiping God," and although that isn't wrong, it isn't nearly all that we can expect.

We all recognize that we're on a journey, but we're confused about where that journey is taking us. In part, this is because no one we know has ever been there and back again to tell us about it, aside from John the Revelator, of course, but the words he used to describe what he saw seem pretty incomprehensible in places.[2] We're also confused because most of us haven't spent a lot of time thinking about our ultimate destination, which is kind of silly when you really consider it. I mean, how much time do you spend thinking about, researching, and planning your summer vacation? We know we're headed somewhere, but we're not quite sure where. But this heading out into the great unknown really isn't anything new for the community of believers.

The faithful believers spoken of in Hebrews 11 acknowledged that they were "strangers and exiles on the earth" (v. 13). Like us, they knew that life here was temporary. No matter where we live right now, whether in a high-rise in Mexico City, a family farm in Iowa, or a beach cottage in Ireland, all Christians are like Abraham, who lived in "tents" (that is, temporary dwelling places) while he journeyed toward his more permanent home. And just like him we have set out "not knowing where [we are] going" (Hebrews 11:8). That's an interesting statement. Abraham didn't know exactly where he was going, but he knew that he would eventually get there.

Are we going somewhere after we die? Yes! Do we know where? Sure, we're headed toward heaven, right? But do we realize that we will eventually end up in a city? Not so sure. Although we don't have as many details as we might want, the Bible clearly teaches that at our death we go from earth to Paradise, and then come back to the renewed earth in our new resurrected bodies as citizens of the New Jerusalem (Revelation 21). It's then that heaven and earth will be joined together and we'll be residents of one really grand city. Is that how you would answer if I were to ask you, "What happens when you die?" No. Me either.

Let's take some time to look again at where we're headed and why our final destination might just be a bigger city than any of us could ever imagine.

Heading to the New Jerusalem

Here's an obvious point that hardly bears expressing: Cities are called cities, at least in part, because of the number of people that live in them. In fact, even the word *city* comes from a Latin term that means "citizen." So when you think of the word *city*, rather than thinking "locale" (like East Coast), first think "citizens" or "people." A city is properly defined as a large group of citizens sharing membership in a community, in a particular location. This might be a little confusing, because the word *city* has gradually changed in sense from focusing on the citizens or inhabitants of the city almost exclusively to a particular place or location.³ So when I say, "New York City," most of us picture the Statue of Liberty or the Empire State Building rather than the millions of people who reside near those landmarks. But when John refers to a particular city that comes "down out of heaven from God" (Revelation 21:2), he's using the word *city* in its original way. He primarily means people rather than landmarks or boroughs. That's not to say that John doesn't spend time talking about the architecture in the city, it's just that the buildings aren't his primary focus.

When John says we're heading toward a city, what he's describing is not a quaint little town or village. Villages are quiet . . . idyllic . . . peaceful. They certainly aren't teeming with millions of strangers. Cities, on the other hand, are full of people; they are bustling with activity. They're anything but quiet! Have you ever been to Manhattan? Or Paris? Or Hong Kong? *Quiet* would not be a word that would come to mind. But the Bible says that a city is exactly what our eternal destiny will be like: It will be a place with way too many people even to number. John describes the population in this way: "After this I looked, and behold, a great multitude that *no one could number*, from every nation, from all tribes and peoples and languages" (Revelation 7:9). This city that comes down out of heaven from God will be anything but quiet.

Consider those words again: "a great multitude that no one could number." Think about that. Let me try to put it into context by considering a city whose multitude we *can* number. In 2014, Shanghai, China, was the world's most populated city with over 24 million people. By comparison, the most populated city in the United States is New York, which boasts over 8 million people (as does London). Los Angeles has less than 4 million.⁴ Think of that. You would never say that Los Angeles is a quaint little village . . . or would you?

The New Jerusalem, God's city, will make Shanghai look like a town and New York a hamlet. Los Angeles wouldn't even get mentioned. And the city will be so amazingly cosmopolitan that you could spend all day every day for thousands of years meeting people from different countries, discovering what their earthly life was like, learning how they heard about Jesus and what they love about him, sharing their favorite foods, enjoying their culture, observing how they demonstrate the many-faceted glory of God in their own unique way. Bustling? Well, yes! Quiet? Never! Diverse? Of course . . . that's quite the understatement. The New Jerusalem is a God-sized city. Of course it is! It's where he will dwell forever! When we look at the zillions of snowflakes or the immeasurable number of stars he created, we shouldn't be surprised at the size and diversity of his city, should we? Here's the Lord shouting, "Again! Again!" over and over again, and this time doing it with *his* redeemed in *his* city!

Many of us have already recognized that in our eternal home there will be people from every nation because we've read that in the Bible. But since we don't often consider that we'll have real physical bodies in the afterlife, we usually don't think about actually rubbing shoulders with different kinds of people, especially not those outside our ethnic group, do we? Of course, you trust that your family members will be there (at least the ones that you get along with), but those folks two doors down or from that "other" country where they eat *what*? They'll be there? What about those strange people from that even stranger land who lived three thousand years ago? That kind of diversity? That many people? Can you hear the Lord shouting, "Again! Again!"?

A City Marries a Lamb?

I admit that it's hard for me to get my mind wrapped around this concept because John refers to this gargantuan city as the Bride of the Lamb (Revelation 21:2, 9). Here he presents us with three seemingly incompatible entities being linked together in a way that bends our imaginations. Cities don't usually get married. Sure, people get married in cities, but I've never heard of an entire city getting married . . . and especially not to one man! I've also never seen an actual lamb stand in a church awaiting his bride's arrival. It's obvious that these words are meant to stretch our imaginations, to help us understand something we've never seen by comparing it to something we have seen. We are to think of the city itself as meaning actual people, in fact, a great host of them beyond numbering, and those people (both men and women) are going to be presented as a bride, a community, a gift from the Father to the Son, who is the Lamb upon whom was placed all our sin and who purchased us and to whom we will pledge our mutual love and fidelity forever. Think about it again, *This city, who is a bride, is marrying a Lamb, who is her husband*. Okay, that about sums it up.

But a City? Really?

It seems to me that it is easier to think about our eternal home being like Eden than it is to think about it being a big city. One reason for this is that we look at cities and see crime and decay and sanitation workers striking . . . and we automatically assume that places that are more solitary have to be closer to what God designed. And while it's true that God originally put just two people on the earth, he also told them to fill the world with loads of kids, and their kids and their kids. God never meant for the world to stay an isolated garden paradise. He meant for it to be a garden city, filled with an innumerable number of people. As Pastor Tim Keller says,

> If you want to understand the narrative arc of the whole Bible, what you actually have in history begins in a garden, but it ends in a city. When God has the world the way he wants it, it's urban. . . . Notice it's a garden city. . . . When I say it's a

94

garden city, the word *city* means dense population, lots and lots of people. But this city is filled with rivers and water and trees.[5]

Here's how John described the city he saw: He called it "the city of my God," the "new Jerusalem," that "comes down from my God out of heaven" (Revelation 3:12). He called it a "holy city . . . prepared as a bride adorned for her husband" (Revelation 21:2). John also wrote:

> And he carried me away in the Spirit to a great, high mountain, and showed me the holy city Jerusalem coming down out of heaven from God, having the glory of God, its radiance like the most rare jewel, like a jasper, clear as crystal.
>
> Revelation 21:10–11

Amazing words, aren't they? What a sight that will be! Wherever you want to put that event in your eschatological timeline, it doesn't ultimately matter. The salient point is that there will be millions and millions and millions (and millions?) of blood-bought people who have been awaiting their new bodies and life on the New Earth, who will come as the one unified visible church from Paradise to this planet. They will be radiant and take up residence here on the New Earth, once again.

What does it mean for this unified group of people, this city of citizens, to be dressed like a bride? It means the city is beautiful, holy, and pure. He's made her that way! What does it mean that together we will be radiant, shining like a rare jewel? It means that the transformation process we'll go through at our physical resurrection will make us glorious, and the light of God will somehow radiate from us. The one who said, "I am the light of the world" (John 8:12) will actually light our Home.

What does a "holy city" even look like? Everyone loving God? Yes, of course! But also, everyone loving each other, too! And millions of friends! And tons of parties! More friends than you can imagine . . . and all of them remade into the loving image of their Savior Husband . . . and every one of them happy to meet you!

I realize that if you would call yourself an introvert, the thought of being thrust into a crowd like what I've just described doesn't sound much like heaven. It might be giving you hives. I get that. I've finally come to realize that the reason public speaking and even counseling are so exhausting to me is that I'm really an introvert at heart. When I speak at a weekend conference, the hardest thing for me is to have to be "on," to have to interact with strangers, which is why I can't wait to get home. Please don't misunderstand: I do have friends and I do like being around them, it's just that crowds of people that I am obligated to interact with absolutely wear me out.

So if you're an introvert, I get that. Let me reassure you, I don't anticipate that the Lord will completely transform our personalities so that what we once were is completely unrecognizable in what we are there. I don't imagine that I'll become an extrovert like my husband, Phil. But . . . I do believe that I will be strengthened and purified and given an overpowering love for people that I presently don't possess, so that I'll actually really want to be around others. To think that I will love people the way I have been loved overwhelms me with gratitude. And perhaps, as the days and years go on there, I'll find myself more and more at ease, and more and more in love with people, even those I've never met before. And I'll be stronger physically, too, so that being with many friends won't wear me out like it does now. So, my dear introverted sisters and brothers, don't be afraid. You'll be transformed, and aside from that, I don't think you'll be obligated to spend all your time in the city . . . but more about that later.

The City's Dimensions

John goes to great lengths to describe just how big this city, the New Jerusalem, is. Now, whether you want to say that the measurements that John gives us are to be interpreted literally or not, his point is that it's a really massive place. The city itself is a cube measuring 12,000 stadia in length, breadth and height, which means that it extends about fourteen hundred miles (1,380 to be exact) in every direction (Revelation 21:16).

Need help thinking about how big that is? First of all, that city would stretch from the United States' border with Mexico all the way to Canada. It also means that if the western edge of the city started in Southern California, where I live, its eastern edge would reach Dallas, Texas.

But that's not all. It would also be 1,380 miles in height. Now . . . that's even harder to imagine. It will reach way up, beyond the outer reaches of the present earth's atmosphere, though nowhere near the moon (which, of course, may or may not be where it is right now). By the way, John is careful to say that the angel who is measuring the city is using a "human measurement" (Revelation 21:17), so we're probably safe in assuming that we're supposed to take these measurements at least somewhat literally. (It might be interesting for you to figure out where a 1,380-mile cube would take you, if you don't live in the United States, or in Southern California, where I live.)

If these measurements were of an actual building, it couldn't support its own weight. But remember, we're talking primarily about the circumference of a group of people who are being transferred from heaven (and their intermediate state) to earth in their resurrected bodies. But, on the other hand, John is careful to give us measurements with the size of walls, number of gates, and even the construction materials of the foundation, so we've got to conclude that it at least appeared to be some sort of massive structure to him. This is how John described what he saw:

97

"Come here. I'll show you the Bride, the Wife of the Lamb."
He took me away in the Spirit to an enormous, high mountain
and showed me Holy Jerusalem descending out of Heaven from
God, resplendent in the bright glory of God.

The City shimmered like a precious gem, light-filled, pulsing
light. She had a wall majestic and high with twelve gates. At
each gate stood an Angel, and on the gates were inscribed the
names of the Twelve Tribes of the sons of Israel: three gates
on the east, three gates on the north, three gates on the south,
three gates on the west. The wall was set on twelve foundations,
the names of the Twelve Apostles of the Lamb inscribed on
them.

The Angel speaking with me had a gold measuring stick to
measure the City, its gates, and its wall. The City was laid out
in a perfect square. He measured the City with the measuring
stick: twelve thousand stadia [1,380 miles], its length, width,
and height all equal. Using the standard measure, the Angel
measured the thickness of its wall: 144 cubits [216 feet]. The
wall was jasper, the color of Glory, and the City was pure gold,
translucent as glass. The foundations of the City walls were gar-
nished with every precious gem imaginable: the first foundation
jasper, the second sapphire, the third agate, the fourth emerald,
the fifth onyx, the sixth carnelian, the seventh chrysolite, the
eighth beryl, the ninth topaz, the tenth chrysoprase, the elev-
enth jacinth, the twelfth amethyst. The twelve gates were twelve
pearls, each gate a single pearl.

The main street of the City was pure gold, translucent as
glass.[6]

What John saw was an immense pulsating cube of golden
light supported by stones every color of the rainbow. This cube
city was filled with people, who collectively are called the Bride—
radiant, pure, holy . . . us! It was guarded by twelve massive
beings, angels who stood by the gates of the city to protect it.
The city was placed upon the New Earth, for the "first heaven
and the first earth had passed away" (Revelation 21:1).

Is it impossible to conceive of a city so beautiful, so massive? Nearly so. But we've been given John's eyewitness report, as well as these words from Isaiah:

> For behold, I create new heavens and a new earth,
> and the former things shall not be remembered or
>   come into mind.
> But be glad and rejoice forever in that which I create;
> for behold, I create Jerusalem to be a joy,
> and her people to be a gladness.
>
> Isaiah 65:17–18

And this is where we have to confront our Greek philosophy again and perhaps our Star Wars theology, too, and proclaim that this beautiful city is not going to be like Lando Calrissian's Cloud City from *The Empire Strikes Back,* nor will we be strumming harps on puffy clouds. No, this city is going to be right here on terra firma. At the end of history, we don't see "individual souls escaping the earth and going to heaven. What you have is heaven coming down and transforming the earth."[7] What earth? This earth that was created by God, of course, the earth we're all familiar with.

My supposition is that this earth, as beautiful as it is, is merely the shadow of what is coming. Even here on this fallen planet, we know that one thing can be surprisingly transformed into another thing, seemingly ignoring everything we might expect. Just by looking at it, would you have ever said that a fuzzy worm could fly with azure wings? Would you think that an acorn could grow into a beautiful oak? What do we know of the laws of nature (more properly called "God's providential care") on that New Earth? What do we know even of what the earth was like before its first scrubbing with water in Noah's time? We've been told that there will be a cataclysmic restructuring of heaven and the earth, with the darkening of the sun and moon, and stars falling from heaven. "Whether these events are to be understood as being primarily literal or primarily figurative, it is clear that these will be 'earth-shattering' events, through which all creation will be radically transformed at the return of Christ."[8] After all, if death and sorrow and decay are gone, then it certainly is a new and different sort of place. Certainly, it will have some things that we'll recognize—like trees and streets and parks and rivers—but there will be many other things that we'll stutter trying to describe.

Remember that what we're trying to understand now is something none of us has ever seen, though we have some good signposts in Scripture. Signposts? Yes! Videotape? No. Again, in Hebrews 11, we learn that like us, Abraham was looking forward to "the city that has foundations, whose designer [architect] and builder is God" (Hebrews 11:10). So, if God designs and builds the city, we don't have to worry about whether it will be able to support itself or what might happen if it's taller than our present atmosphere. We know that the atmosphere as it was originally created was changed after the flood, so why couldn't God change it again? "On the holy mount stands the city he founded. . . . Glorious things of you are spoken, O city of God"! (Psalm 87:1, 3).

Of Course It Had to Be a City!

But does the metaphor of a city really work when we think about our eternal Home? Is there something about cities that speaks to our true nature? Or conversely, is there anything about cities that is antithetical to God's perfection? Let's think about what cities might tell us about ourselves and what the Lord has in store for us.

My sister lives in New York City, where she has a high-pressure job in the publishing industry. Aside from the fact that her life is completely consumed by her job, she loves living in the city. She thrives on the energy, intensity, and vitality there. As New York pastor Tim Keller says,

> The city creates an explosion of human creativity . . . an explosion of human achievement. It's in the city where our talents are brought together and the best is brought out of us. That's what the city does. . . . It brings out what God has locked in the deepest recesses of the heart—the giftedness, the talents, and the brilliance of the human being.[9]

So, on one hand, cities are marvelously creative places with seemingly unstoppable human achievement. Think what a city would be like if there were billions of people there all working for the common good of others! Is there anything in that thought that we could say was intrinsically evil or something that should be excluded from a sinless earth? Of course, people do use their creativity and talents to devise wrong, but what if they consistently used their gifts to create beauty and to serve others? What if this new city was the center of human achievement, a place where mankind finally had dominion over the earth, where we had discovered and shared ways to make the earth yield her bounty? Would that be wrong in any way?

The Best Schools

One of my favorite activities is attending classes at Westminster Theological Seminary, which is less than five minutes from my home in Escondido. I love auditing classes there from time to time and getting to listen to smart people answer questions I've never even thought of. It's a real joy. In fact, as I think back on some of the greatest joys in my life, they've always involved conversations with interesting people who challenged and broadened my thinking. For instance, I can recall a number of conversations I had with my family, especially my daughter, Jessica, and other friends when we were in the process of writing *Give Them Grace*. It was those conversations and being with others that actually pulled out of me thoughts that had been rumbling around in my brain but hadn't taken shape yet. Sometimes I've heard myself saying things that I hadn't realized I understood. Conversing with people can be ever so rewarding. Think about what those New Jerusalem conversations will be like!

Now . . . imagine for a moment what it will be like to be a citizen there. I can imagine myself saying, "I'm going up to the city tomorrow for a class being taught by the Inklings and friends on imagination. Wanna come?" What joy to hear Lewis, Tolkien, or Dorothy Sayers talk about what it is like to allow your imagination to take flight without sinning! And the great thing about the class will be that even though I probably won't immediately understand everything they say, I'll have literally all the time in the world to try to grasp it . . . and I'll never get bored or feel frustrated, embarrassed, or ostracized. And maybe they'll even hold a writing clinic. Think about that!

The Glory of This City

Of course, the primary glory of this city will be the presence of our God (we will talk more about this later), as he will be with us and heaven will have come to earth in ways that we presently cannot fathom. But for now, let's continue to consider how glorious the city will be. We'll borrow some thoughts from nineteenth-century British preacher Charles Spurgeon.

Spurgeon, who lived in London, proposed that a city is a fitting description for our eternal Home because it is "a place of fellowship," where people can meet one another. It is not a solitary, lonely place.

Heaven is not like . . . lonely places; we look upon heaven, not as a spot where there will be half-a-dozen people of our own views and sentiments, but as a great city where there will be a wide fellowship among a multitude that no man can number.[10]

Even though I am a writer who craves solitude, hours and hours of uninterrupted thought, I also know that if I force myself out into company, to get together with people, I discover that rather than being depleted of thought, my mind becomes more alive, more fertile. Sure, there are times when quiet is necessary for creativity, but I have also found that being with others to whom I have to explain my thoughts and from whom I receive insight, is extraordinarily helpful. No wonder the Inklings loved getting together every Tuesday morning! Consider the amazing literature they produced!

If you were to research any country on earth, you'd see pictures of its main metropolises. Frequently, what we know about a country is embodied in photographs of its cities. It's almost as though each nation were saying, "Look how great we are!" Check out Times Square, or the Burj Khalifa in Dubai, or the miles and miles of apartments in São Paulo, Brazil. Cities display all the best and worst—a country has to offer. But in the New City, there won't be any "worst"—just glory and beauty and immense creativity and joy. Cities show off all the great wealth and accumulations of useful things that can never be found in villages. "We can learn a lot about people by walking through their houses. The whole universe will be God's house—and the New Jerusalem will be his living room. God will delight to share with us the glories of his capital city—and ours."[11] The wealth of the universe is there. Of course it is; that's where the people and their King are! Here's how Bruce Milne captures this thought:

Nothing of ultimate worth from the long history of the nations will be omitted from the heavenly community. Everything

which authentically reflects the God of truth, all that is of
abiding worth from within the national stories and the cultural inheritance of the world's peoples, will find its place in
the New Jerusalem.[12]

Here's one more thought that hopefully will make you long
for the New Jerusalem and not shy away from it: *There won't
be any discrimination.* There won't be any "Sorry, but you don't
belong here," only open access, welcome, and love for everyone.
As an older woman, I've felt the sting of being discriminated
against. Don't misunderstand, that sting I've felt is nothing
compared to what so many other people go through. But still,
I've known what it is to feel invisible, to be passed over, to feel
unwelcome. Maybe that unwelcomeness has something more to
do with my faults and failures than anything else, but still . . .
to live in a city where the welcome mat is always out, the gates
are *always* open, where everyone is excited that you're there,
where every conversation is open and trusting and full of love.
Can you imagine?

> There's no elitism in Heaven; everyone will have access because
> of Christ's blood. . . . All people will have access to the city's
> parks, museums, restaurants, libraries, concerts—anything and
> everything the city has to offer. Nobody will have to peek over
> the fence or look longingly through the windows.[13]

It's no wonder the ancient martyrs who really understood
these truths were able to sing while they were burned as torches
to light a party they would never have been invited to (not that
they would have wanted to be). They knew they were going
to shine again in a land where there would be no discrimination, no persecution, no snubbing, no gossip, no slander . . .
and rather than a place with no people, it would be absolutely
overflowing with people of faith who would bring all their love
and relationships there to share with everyone else.

World's Greatest Padre

At Petco Park, the baseball stadium of the San Diego Padres, there is a plaza surfaced with commemorative bricks. In 2004, when the ballpark was being built, our kids donated a brick in honor of their dad, the quintessential fan. The brick reads *World's Greatest Padre*. It was such a kind gift, one that we revisit almost every time we go to a game. Of course, we know the brick wasn't a necessary part of the park. It didn't need to be there for the park to be built. It's just that for our family, that special brick makes the park special. It makes it *our* park. It's not the brick itself that's so great, but the love behind the brick. The New Jerusalem will be filled with commemorative bricks—symbols of the love God has placed in us—that we enjoy now, but that will also be transferred over to the great City to come. (Revelation 21:26; Isaiah 60:5).

Where are we headed? To a New City filled with gardens and billions of people, to a city like nothing we've ever seen before, and I can hardly wait! What about you?

———— FIXING OUR EYES ON HOME ————

1. Seminary professor Dennis E. Johnson writes, "You are living between two worlds: the first heaven and earth, which are destined for destruction; and the new creation, to which you already belong as God's Holy City, the bride now being beautified for her Husband."[14] What are some of the difficulties that you're experiencing now, as you await the New City? How does knowing that we're living a transitory experience between two worlds help you as you face your daily trials?

2. What God has prepared for us in heaven comes down to the earth. Although we may "go to heaven" for that

intermediate season, heaven is not our eternal Home; the earth is. How does this change how you experience the world around you and your hope of the afterlife?

3. The New Jerusalem is not merely buildings, but actually God's people en masse. In fact, the people of God make up the city of God . . . where he dwells. What will it mean to be part of the city where the Lord will permanently dwell with us, his people? Does that change your experience of isolation in any way? See Revelation 21:3: "The dwelling place of God is with man."

4. What did you find most intriguing about the description of the New Jerusalem? How might these thoughts encourage you today as you struggle with opportunities lost (or never presented)? What do you think about having millions of friends? How does this encourage/challenge you?

5. Have you ever been discriminated against or felt yourself to be an outsider? Describe one situation like that. How does the thought of the New Jerusalem help with that? How does it help you not to discriminate against others?

6. Summarize what you have learned in this chapter in four or five sentences.

6

His Kingdom Has Come

You and I are on our way to a new and glorious capital city where the Great King is always in residence, always holding court and, best of all, always happy to receive us. It's a city where the innumerable masses whose names are "written in the Lamb's book of life" (Revelation 21:27) will have free access to him, get to know him, and spend days in glorious worship and fellowship with him. It's a city so perfectly pure that sinless angelic beings cover their faces and feet because his person in the middle of it is so magnificent, and yet, it is a place where we will walk openly and freely.

None of us can even begin to imagine what that will be like because none of us have ever encountered a being with such unadulterated majesty and holiness. Even if you've been so fortunate as to have had audience with a great world leader, that is nothing in comparison to the audience you'll have with the King of Kings. Those who are great and mighty now will one day have to hide themselves from the "face of him who is seated on the throne" (Revelation 6:16).

In the throne room, where the Father is both seen and sees, we who have been both known and embraced will have free, open, joyful access to his person and will respond in wholehearted worship. We won't cringe or hide. We won't beg for death . . . or even pardon. We will be fully loved and fully welcomed into this, our Father's home, because the Lion who will defeat all his foes is also the Lamb who died for us. This is another one of those places where our imagination fails us, no matter how we try to expand it. Welcomed into the presence of the Great King of All? Really?

What will it mean to stand in his presence with unfettered access, to look upon his beautiful holiness and to do so without any fear at all? What would it be like to live with anyone, even someone as inauspicious as you or me, without any masks, in complete honesty? None of us can answer because all of us are far too acquainted with our shame and hypocrisy. In the entire history of the world, only three people have been able to stand before God openly and unselfconsciously: Adam, Eve, and the Lord Jesus. Of course, you know that Adam and his wife were eventually exiled. No one else, aside from the Son, ever had unmediated access to the Father.

Ever since the cherubim received the command to guard the Garden of Eden from the intrusion of man, we've longed for yet been prevented from open fellowship with our Lord, who once walked with our father and mother in the cool of the day. Even when Moses constructed the wilderness tabernacle or Solomon built his glorious temple in Jerusalem, the order was heard: *Don't let the people, not even the faithful priests, get too near. They can't have unrestricted access or they will be vaporized. Don't forget who he is! Don't forget who you are!* The curtain had to divide the people from the "most holy place" because no matter how hard the people worked to be holy, they'd never be holy enough. Slaughter every lamb in the nation and there wouldn't be enough blood to give you confidence before the face that instantaneously incinerates every excuse, where "no creature is hidden from his sight, but all are naked and exposed to the eyes of him to whom we must give account" (Hebrews 4:13).

And even now, even though that temple curtain was torn in two at Jesus' death (Matthew 27:51), and even though we have a "great high priest who has passed through the heavens, Jesus, the Son of God" (Hebrews 4:14), we continue to experience separation from him because of the curtain of this earthly life. We still must walk by faith rather than by sight. But a day is coming . . . a day is coming when that earthly shroud will be torn apart, and we'll step into our Father's presence without any fear at all.

You Are Welcome Into the Holy of Holies

As we discussed in chapter 5, the New Jerusalem was described by John as a 12,000-stadia-cube city (1,380 miles in every direction). The city's shape is not insignificant because the place where the glory of God dwelt both in the wilderness tabernacle and in Solomon's temple was also a cube (10 x 10 x 10 cubits). The message implicit in this perfect cube shape is meant to both describe and to warn. This cube shape tells us that the God who chooses to put his name there is perfection itself. The name put there was the four-letter name YHWH, the Tetragrammaton, the I AM, the self-existent one. It was a name so holy that it couldn't even be spoken by the pious Jew. The I AM isn't an amorphous blob, some sort of willy-nilly spirit that gives no thought to form or shape. Nor does he choose to indwell a circle. He creates and chooses a cube as a perfectly balanced shape, a complete square in every direction because he is perfection.

That the New Jerusalem has the same shape as the Most Holy Place also gives us a warning: "Nothing unclean will ever enter it, nor anyone who does what is detestable or false" (Revelation 21:27). In the Old Testament, two of the sons of Aaron the high priest died because they didn't respect God (see Leviticus 10). In addition, once a year on the Day of Atonement, one person, the high priest, was allowed to enter into the Most Holy Place in order to offer blood that would temporarily atone for his sins and the sins of the people. The message was clear: No one is holy enough to enter in. No mere human is welcome; you'd better not even say his name aloud. Sinners need not apply. No one reading this book right now would have been holy enough to walk into that cube-shaped space where YHWH, or as we say, Yahweh or Jehovah, resided. What was the punishment if you did? Was it a slap on the wrist or a time-out? No. It was annihilation, complete and utter destruction.

The Book Written by the Lamb

And yet . . . not only is there a group of people who are barred from entrance there, there is also a people for whom the doors are thrown wide open. Who are they? "Those who are written in the Lamb's book of life" (Revelation 21:27). Think of that: He has placed our names in the cube sanctified by YHWH. I'll be honest with you: On my own, I know I would never be welcomed in that city. I haven't perfectly kept every commandment, not by a long shot. I've sinned enough today, even as I've worked on this chapter, to have my name blotted out forever. I've sullied my soul with daily disobedience, every day since I first believed. In God's sight, I've done what is detestable . . . and most certainly been false with him and with others. On my own, I would be utterly barred from that city. On my own.

110

Because we are not on our own, we won't be cast out. Why? Our names are there. Not only does God's holy name dwell there in that perfect space, but our names are inscribed there, too. My name is there, and so is yours, written in the Lamb's Book of Life. Who owns this book? Why, Jesus, of course. It's the Book of Life, belonging to the Lamb that was slain from the foundation of the world (see Revelation 13:8). Jesus owns this book. He bought it and inscribed it with his blood.

Perhaps it might be helpful to think of the list of names in the Lamb's Book of Life as a guest list for a really exclusive party. You know how it goes . . . you bring your invitation and hope that whoever was in charge of inviting you received your RSVP and didn't neglect to put your name on the welcome list. I regularly experience something similar when I've been invited to join speakers in what's most commonly known as the greenroom. The door to the greenroom is usually guarded by security personnel who hold the all-important clipboard that lists the all-important people. I walk up, give my name, and hope that I won't suffer the indignity of being sent away (without any goodies). Sometimes I've gained admission to these protected spaces by being with someone who actually is important. "I'm with him," I mumble, and hope that's enough. Happily, it usually is.

This concept of a book wherein are listed those who belong to the Lord is mentioned frequently in Scripture. One such place is in Luke, where we find the disciples rejoicing in their great success in ministry. Jesus counseled them that they shouldn't find joy in their accomplishments but rather should rejoice that their "names are written in heaven" (10:20). His point was that although it is wonderful to be used by God to accomplish work for him, the real surprise is that their names are written where YHWH has signed his. Jesus wasn't impressed that they had power over Satan . . . after all, he had seen Satan's fall and knew his destiny. Power over spirits? That's really nothing worth rejoicing about. But a welcome into the presence of God in his glorious city? Now, that's something truly amazing! Here's how the pastor writing to the Hebrews captured this same thought:

> But you have come to Mount Zion and to the city of the living God, the heavenly Jerusalem, and to innumerable angels in festal gathering, and to the assembly of the firstborn who are *enrolled in heaven*, and to God, the judge of all, and to the spirits of the righteous made perfect, and to Jesus, the mediator of a new covenant, and to the sprinkled blood that speaks a better word than the blood of Abel.
>
> Hebrews 12:22–24

Did you see yourself referenced in that passage? *You* have come, *you* are the welcomed into the "city of the living God," where a party with innumerable angels is going on. (Let your mind imagine what that might be like!) *You* are part of the church where the firstborn is your Shepherd, your Pastor. What does *firstborn* mean? Simply this: Jesus is qualified to lead you because he is the first man born from the dead. Humanity was shrouded in death . . . but he walked through that death into life, and he's brought his church right along with him. You're in Jesus' church now.[1] You are "the righteous made perfect" because of him; he's the mediator of a new covenant by his sprinkled blood. Rejoice!

Think of this: You're on your way to a church party with more wealth, richness, food, music, beauty, and delight than you can imagine. The Lord has already signed you in. Your name is on the list. You're registered in the book. It's guaranteed because you have a living hope, "an inheritance that is imperishable, undefiled, and unfading, kept in heaven for you, who by God's power are being guarded through faith"

112

(1 Peter 1:4–5). God's power is guarding your inheritance, and he's guarding you, too. Forever. Why? Because your name is written where his is.

Theologian N. T. Wright proposes that one way to think of this is by imagining a situation where you know your parent has already purchased your Christmas present but is keeping it safely "in the cupboard for you."[2] Do you have an inheritance in that city? Yes! Just because you can't see it right now doesn't mean it's not there. It's hidden from your sight right now, but that's not how it's always going to be. You *will* be welcomed into his presence. He *is* your inheritance. You *will* go to that party, on his arm. I wonder what it will be like to see angels dance.

But I'm Such a No-Name!

How is it that *our* names have been written there, especially in light of the fact that our works are never perfect enough for us to be welcomed into that flawless city? Well, of course, it's because it's the *Lamb's* book. It isn't the Book of the Law, which would expose our every failure. Nor is it the Book of the Accuser, who delights in flogging our souls with reminders of our sin (Revelation 12:10). No, it's the Lamb's book. What do we know about this Lamb? When his cousin John saw him walking toward him, he said, "Behold, the Lamb of God, who takes away the sin of the world!" (John 1:29). This man, this Jesus, was God's Lamb, God's sacrifice sent to remove from us and to place upon him the sins of the world. How is it that our names are written there, ensuring our admission into that city? Is it because we've finally been completely faithful and obedient? No! It's because all, and I really mean *all*, of our sins have been borne away, carried away, transferred, sent off into the depths of the sea, by that "Lamb who was slain from the creation of the world" (Revelation 13:8 NIV).

Here's the point: You . . . yes, *you* . . . are a welcome guest in this perfect city. Your name is listed there among all the great Christians of the ages . . . and there isn't an asterisk by your name. It's written there just like everyone else's name:

St. Paul ✔

St. John ✔

Augustine ✔

Luther ✔

Spurgeon ✔

Elyse ✔

Your name ✔ . . . Wait! What?

How is it written? Indelibly. In blood. Forever. And who has attested to its authenticity? The King, of course. Who would have the audacity to argue with him? "Who is to condemn? Christ Jesus is the one who died—more than that, who was raised—who is at the right hand of God, who indeed is interceding for us" (Romans 8:34). If he puts your name there, no one . . . and I mean not even you, can erase what he has written.

(write your name)

Check. Your name is there!

The Dwelling Place of God Is With Man

There was no light in the Most Holy Place in the wilderness tabernacle. It was covered with a four-layer removable roof. The first two layers were animal skins (the outer one brown, the next one dyed red); the next was woven white goat hair. The fourth and innermost was a beautiful tapestry woven in red, blue, and purple representations of cherubim. From the outside, the

114

structure seemed mundane, nondescript, common. But from the inside, everything in the room was gold, cloaked in artistically woven draperies on every side. Inside the Most Holy Place, God's presence resided in what was called the Ark of the Covenant. (Yes, the same sort of thing that you may have seen in *Raiders of the Lost Ark*). The Ark of the Covenant was a rectangular chest containing the Ten Commandments, a branch that demonstrated the high priest's authority, and a pot full of manna. Over the ark was a slab of gold called the mercy seat, where atoning blood was sprinkled once a year. On top of that were two golden cherubim facing each other, their wings touching.

But none of this beauty would ever be seen by anyone but God, and also dimly by the high priest once a year. Even if you managed to get a glimpse into the wilderness tabernacle itself, you would never see into that room. It was dark, hidden, foreboding, and dangerous. In fact, the only light in all the Most Holy Place was from the golden candlestick, but it remained on the other side of a thick curtain. Was the room beautiful? Yes, beyond imagination. But you and I would never have seen it. It was off-limits to the likes of us. Did the Israelites know that God's presence was there? Yes, they did. Was he dwelling with his people? Yes, but he had separated himself from them. In essence, there were No Trespassing signs posted all around. And unless you were the one in 5 million, the high priest, you would always be separated from the Lord. Even if you were a Levite, among God's family of priests, your chances of seeing that beauty were practically nil. Imagine the tears you would have shed knowing that you were forever separated from the God you loved and longed to know.

That's why the description of the New Jerusalem is such shockingly great news:

> And I heard a loud voice from the throne saying, "Behold, the dwelling place of God is with man. He will dwell with them,

and they will be his people, and God himself will be with them as their God. He will wipe away every tear from their eyes, and death shall be no more, neither shall there be mourning, nor crying, nor pain anymore, for the former things have passed away."

Revelation 21:3–4

I've heard it said that the entire message of the Bible could be summed up in these words: "Behold, the dwelling place of God is with man." From the Garden, to the wilderness tabernacle, to the Man who was God, who lived, died, arose, and ascended, to the returning King, the sum of the message is "The dwelling place of God is with man." And yet . . . we've never really seen him, have we? Sure, he's there in the Word and the sacraments,³ but all we know right now is the walk of faith; we only know the "former things." He says he's with me by the Spirit, and I believe it. But . . . my eyes have always been too weak to see through the shroud that blurs my vision. Sadly, the words of the hymn are still true: "Holy, Holy, Holy . . . Though the eye of sinful man Thy glory may not see."⁴ He's too holy. We're too sinful; we're simply not able to see him . . . *yet*.

Don't be confused. Even if we would have lived when Jesus, our Immanuel (God with us) did, seeing him as he walked on earth, there would have been nothing about him that would have attracted our gaze. Like that outer covering on the Holy Place, his appearance was nondescript, common, earthy (Isaiah 53:2–3). He was veiling his deity, the beauty that resided within him, as he walked through this world being our Perfect Representative. He was the Ark of the Covenant personified: The Law was in his heart; all authority had been given to him (Matthew 28:18), and he was the Bread that had come down from heaven (John 6:32). His very life was an answer to his own prayer that his kingdom would come on earth as in heaven. Heaven and earth were united in him. God had come to earth and was throwing open the door to God's presence for all his children.

What we can see with our eyes now is not all we will ever know; it's not all we will ever see. In an instant our entire orientation, the way we habitually think, will be transformed, and we *will* see him. Just like that. Right now our view of him is like looking at a reflection in a shattered mirror by dimly flickering candlelight. But then . . . but then, it will be face-to-face. Now I only see glimpses of him (and distorted ones at that); then I will know him the way he already knows me. (See 1 Corinthians 13:12.) Heaven will indeed be Home because he'll be there and we will experience him in a way that is utterly beyond our imagination. "God's re-creation is more than just a better heaven and earth, or a new setting for the people of God; it is the unmediated and unrestricted dwelling place of God."⁵ And we'll be there. You are welcomed into his presence! Forever!

Are you beginning to understand what's so great about this oddly shaped city? It's his Home! And downtown will be his living room! He will be there with us, his people, forever, in sheer joy and delight. Of course, there won't be any more pain, tears, or death. How could there be? He's the source of life and joy and pleasures forevermore. All this sadness . . . all our crying and longing is part of the "former things," our former lives spent in separation from him, in exile and alienation. The former things will have completely vanished. "Welcome home!" he'll say. And we will cheer and worship and dance like little calves set free to romp in a grassy pasture. Dad's home; dinner's ready. You've already been washed up, so pull up a chair at his table and have a banquet.

Let There Be Light!

When we experience "the dwelling place of God" in its fullness, when all of the hiddenness and darkness has been chased away, our eyes will open and we'll be able to see, at last. On that day, the shroud that envelopes our sight will be unwrapped and our dim eyes will grow strong . . . strong enough to see light: golden, radiant, dense light. And from where will this light emanate? His presence among his people, the church, of course.

> And I saw no temple in the city, for its temple is the Lord God the Almighty and the Lamb. And the city has no need of sun or moon to shine on it, for the glory of God gives it light, and its lamp is the Lamb. By its light will the nations walk . . . and its gates will never be shut by day—and there will be no night there.
>
> Revelation 21:22–25

> And night will be no more. They will need no light of lamp or sun, for the Lord God will be their light.
>
> Revelation 22:5

We will walk into pure light and we won't be afraid! The darkness that our sin occasioned will be banished. The new world will be filled with light, and we will finally see him as he is. We will see what Isaiah saw, the "Lord sitting upon a throne, high and lifted up," with the train of his robe filling the temple. But we won't cry out as he did, "Woe is me! For I am lost; for I am a man of unclean lips, and I dwell in the midst of a people of unclean lips; for my eyes have seen the King, the Lord of hosts!" (6:1, 5). No, instead we will say, "My eyes have actually seen the King, the Lord of hosts! Hooray for our King! Hallelujah to our Savior!" The darkness that our sin brought about will finally be gone and we'll know nothing but light—glorious, golden, brilliant light.

There have been times in my life when I've seen golden light. I've seen it when the sun is setting and it pierces a cloud bank, sending a shaft of golden brilliance to the sea. I've seen it illumine the curve of a puffy cloud or dance on the ripples of the ocean. But I've never seen it emanating from a throne in a

118

city filled with people. But I will. All the darkness and disguising will be over. The city will be filled with Light . . . and so
will we. We will be radiant. We will reflect his splendor as his
emissaries. Glorious, unending day.

The King and His Kingdom

Think of this: In the city where God is the temple and we have
unfettered access to him, we are referred to as a kingdom of
priests. We are a "royal priesthood" (1 Peter 2:9), sons and
daughters, princes and princesses of his imperial house, like
the children in THE CHRONICLES OF NARNIA. This means that
as his priestly representatives, we will share our experience of
his goodness, sing to him, and rule over the earth as those who
carry out his commands in the universe. We will be vice-regents,
ruling for him in our particular areas of influence. Queen Lucy,
King Peter . . . and us! We, you and I, will be both members of
the royal family and priests. We will have authority over his
creation, and we will humbly offer up all our devotion to him.
We will finally fulfill the Creation Mandate to rule the earth
and subdue it. The kingdom that he promised us will be ours
(Luke 22:29–30). We "will administer the Father's rule along
with the Lamb,"[6] our shepherd, in his kingdom (Revelation
2:26–27).

Daniel, the Old Testament saint, wrote that a time would
come when believers, "shall receive the kingdom and possess the
kingdom forever, forever and ever" (Daniel 7:18). I think there's
a reason he said, "forever, forever and ever." He wants us to
know that once that kingdom begins, there will be no stopping
it. We can't mess this kingdom up. We will rule righteously and
worship wholeheartedly. I know that stretches credulity, but
Paul told even the Corinthians (of all people!) that they were
going to judge not only the world but also angels (1 Corinthians

6:2–3). And Jesus promised the lukewarm Laodiceans that if they would simply repent of their apathy and love him more than they loved the world, he would grant them to actually *sit with him on his throne*, as he "conquered and sat down with [his] Father on his throne" (Revelation 3:21). Sit with him on his throne? I'm glad he said that and I didn't.

The fact that the New Jerusalem will be the capital city of God's kingdom means that it will be from there, from within and through all the redeemed, that the Lord will exercise sovereignty and dominion over the entire created universe. He will rule through us. And his kingdom will expand through us, in the same way that the earthly kingdom of Israel expanded through the Israelites, with "every place on which the sole of your foot treads" becoming ours (Deuteronomy 11:24). In the same way that Adam failed to expand the garden and rule the earth, national Israel failed, as well. But the heavenly Israel, the New Jerusalem, his church, will never fail. Every place where our feet will tread he will give to us. All for his glory and our eternal pleasure!

You Are a Citizen of Heaven *Now*

I was not raised in what you might call a Christian home. It's not that my mom didn't believe in God, it's just that belief in Christ was not something that was emphasized there. Sure, she wanted us to believe and to be moral, but I don't think I ever heard about the forgiveness of sins in a way that meant anything to me until early adulthood. While it is true that my mother and grandmother took me to the Lutheran church, where I was baptized and confirmed, I'm quite sure that I never really believed until right before my twenty-first birthday. So from my perspective, my citizenship in the kingdom of God began in the summer of 1971, when I was delivered "from the domain of darkness and transferred . . . to the kingdom of his beloved Son" (Colossians 1:13).

But from God's perspective, my citizenship in his kingdom began in time immemorial, when the Father, Son, and Spirit, covenanted to redeem me. So, at the right time, the Spirit opened my eyes to the truth about Jesus, and though I have resided in the United States for nearly seven decades, I'm also a citizen of another kingdom. In fact, my true citizenship is in the New Jerusalem, in heaven: "Our citizenship is in heaven, and from it we await a Savior, the Lord Jesus Christ, who will transform our lowly body to be like his glorious body, by the power that enables him even to subject all things to himself" (Philippians 3:20–21).

There's a certainty about our ultimate destination that is so very important for us to hang on to. In the same way that God perfectly fulfilled all the prophecies about the coming of his Son, he will fulfill all his Word concerning our participation in the New Jerusalem. Rest assured. We've been his from time before time, we're his now, and we will be his when the New City comes out of heaven and is joined to the earth.

What would our lives be like if we could see ourselves as citizens of that city right now? Yes, I understand about the *already* and the *not yet*, but I wonder how my life would change if I constantly saw myself as I will be then (and truly am now): a Spirit-born, righteous, blood-bought, beloved child, a royal priest of the King of Kings. Furthermore, how would my responses to doubts, difficulties, and disappointments differ if I remembered that his glorious kingdom is in fact, right here, right now, rather than being out there, somewhere? As a matter of fact, that's exactly what Jesus said, "The kingdom of God is at hand" (Matthew 4:17; 10:7).

Maybe it would be helpful to think of that kingdom as if it existed in a different dimension . . . a dimension that our physical sight here stops us from perceiving. Most of us have seen enough science fiction to be able to visualize what looking into a different dimension might be like. What if, remembering our Savior's ascension, it was just a mist away, or to borrow C. S. Lewis's metaphor, right through a magic wardrobe? Whether that analogy works for you or not, what would your life be like today if you could, just for one moment, break through that barrier and see what is more certain than all our certainties here?[7] How would our lives change if we knew, as we ought to, that we are already citizens of that blessed country—that the welcome mat has been put out for us? Separated for the time being? Seemingly so. But we are certainly citizens there, too. The problem is that we think heaven is so far away, so very intangible, when it really is right here with us right now.

My United States citizenship means so much to me, and I'm very thankful for it. It means that no matter where I go, I've always got help close by. I have certain rights and privileges as a citizen. I am an American. For me, that's a very comforting thought. But what if I thought about myself as a citizen of that far country? Can you imagine what that might be like for you? You're on a road right now. A road that will lead inevitably to a perfectly shaped city filled with light, where you'll be invited to see the one face you've been looking for your entire life. You'll read YHWH's name there, and you'll see your name too, and every sadness will vanish forever. Rejoice!

--------- FIXING OUR EYES ON HOME ---------

1. "That which the gospel defines as reality will come to pass for every believer. Such hope inscribed on the heart and mind by the Spirit of God has through the ages steeled the resolve of countless little people, ordinary and unremarkable men

and women (as the world counts them), to go on looking to Jesus, the Alpha and Omega, the author and finisher of our faith."[8] How have the truths presented in this chapter steeled your resolve to persevere even in the midst of great trial?

2. "The kingdom of the world has become the kingdom of our Lord and of his Christ, and he shall reign forever and ever" (Revelation 11:15). Are there situations in your life where it's hard to believe that the Lord is, in fact, reigning? How does the thought of the New Earth help you?

3. What would it mean to you to live in a city of golden light, where the Lord is ever present? How would that thought transform the way you live now?

4. You are a person with dual citizenship. What does your natural citizenship mean to you? How about your citizenship in the New Earth?

5. How does the thought of your name being inscribed in the New Jerusalem encourage you?

6. Summarize what you've learned in this chapter in four or five sentences.

7

Completely New, Yet So Familiar

In the New Jerusalem, the voice of the One seated on the throne will declare, "Behold, I am making all things new" (Revelation 21:5). "All things new." What on earth, literally, will that be like? Sure, I know what it is to have something new—a new car, a new phone—but to have everything new, and new in such a way that it never gets old? Wait. *What? All things forever new?*

Let's recap what we've learned so far: Life in this world is frequently troubled and often excruciating. Our lives rarely turn out the way we hope they will . . . and even when they do, it's not long before our pleasant reality fades into obscurity or futility. Even the snazziest new computer gets old and outdated before I have an opportunity to master everything I need to know. And then, of course, eventually everything just stops working.

Why? That old jaded preacher who said, "There is nothing new under the sun," also said, "All are from the dust, and to dust all return" (Ecclesiastes 1:9; 3:20). That includes all the words I am carefully arranging in this book. They like all else will eventually wither into insignificance. These little black lines will fade off the page, and the thought I'm laboring over now will all too soon be lost. Our lives are nothing more than "a mist that appears for a little time and then vanishes" (James 4:14). In fact, all the dreams, desires, successes, labors, and overhyped progress of all the nations are nothing more than a "drop from a bucket, and are accounted as the dust on the scales" (Isaiah 40:15). The banner hung over the whole world is "subjected to futility" (Romans 8:20). Even what we would call new is already decaying, the indestructible is destroyed, all life ends. But this world isn't all there is.

Calling Us Home

On a day that has been set by our Father,

> You hear a blast to end all blasts from a trumpet, and in the time that you look up and blink your eyes—it's over. On signal from that trumpet from heaven, the dead will be up and out of their graves, beyond the reach of death, never to die again. At the same moment and in the same way, we'll all be changed.[1]

At the physical return of the God-Man to earth, he will clothe all his children in their new resurrection bodies. The souls of those who have already died will be reunited with their new resurrection bodies; those who are still alive at his coming will be instantly transformed, "in the twinkling of an eye" (1 Corinthians 15:52).

> For the Lord himself will descend from heaven with a cry of command, with the voice of an archangel, and with the sound of the trumpet of God. And the dead in Christ will rise first. Then we who are alive, who are left, will be caught up together with them in the clouds to meet the Lord in the air, and so we will always be with the Lord.
>
> 1 Thessalonians 4:16–17

126

None of us has any idea what that will be like. As C. S. Lewis quipped, "None of us would ever imagine an orange if we'd never seen one before."[2] Who could have imagined that juiciness, that tart sweetness, those little follicles inside each segment full of such deliciousness? (Makes my mouth water just to think of it!) Who could have imagined such a thing as an orange? (Aside from the Lord, of course!)

In the same way that none of us could have imagined an orange, no one can imagine what it will be like when he causes the seed that is our present body to grow into the new body it will become. What will it be like not to suffer from the degeneration that we are subjected to every day? What will it be like to awaken every morning to a new, never-wearing-out, fully rested body that doesn't age or feel any of the effects of sin? I have no clue. As I write this, I'm coming up on my sixty-fifth birthday, and trust me, I know my body is wearing out. But my hope rests in the truth that this body will not keep wearing out forever. I will be new. Every day I will wake up in a new body that will never grow old, will never stop being new.

Creation Will Be Set Free

All of creation will be renewed: the land, the waters, the sky, the trees, the animals. The entire cosmos will be remade, completely washed by fire and finally set free from the slavery that our sin had subjected it to:

> For the creation waits with eager longing for the revealing of the sons of God. For the creation was subjected to futility . . . in hope that the creation itself will be set free from its bondage to corruption and obtain the freedom of the glory of the children of God.
>
> Romans 8:19–21

As beautiful as our world is (and it really is), it is chained to disorder, chaos, and death. Every part of it is degenerating. Wearing out. Blowing up. Falling apart, cracking, rotting, and dying. Those terrible events that we refer to as "natural disasters" really ought to be called "unnatural disasters," because the world as we know it isn't the world it was originally created to be. Cyclones, earthquakes, and tsunamis are not part of God's good creation. They are part of the groaning of a cosmos under judgment. The world has been in "bondage to corruption," to "the inevitable tendency to decay."[3] Everything we see is decomposing, turning back into dust, and all the processes of death and disaster we're all too familiar with are just signals of that slavery and creation's desire (if you will) to throw death's chains off. The creation is groaning, just like we are. It cries, "Free me from this inevitable decay, from this inescapable cycle of spring becoming winter, birth ending in death, gain resulting in loss!" And that's just what the Lord will do! Earth's shackles will be burned away in white-hot fire, and it will burst forth in strong, vibrant, glorious new life . . . life that will never wear out. And you and I will be there to rejoice in it! Life will be everywhere, unstoppable and bursting-forth-glorious life.

At this point you might be wondering how this bursting forth of life in the New Earth squares with passages like 2 Peter 3:10–13 NASB, where we are told that the "elements will be destroyed with intense heat," and "the heavens will be destroyed by burning" or Revelation 21:1 NASB, which says that the "first heaven and the first earth had passed away." Rather than viewing these cataclysmic events as a complete obliteration and annihilation of this earth, we should look at them as a reshaping or renewing of what already exists. Peter uses the same "destruction" language earlier in the chapter about the time of Noah's flood. He says, "The world that then existed was deluged with water and perished" (2 Peter 3:6). While it is true that much life on the earth perished in the flood, the entire earth did not cease to exist. Rather, it was temporarily cleansed. Because of this, it might be better to look at the "passing away" from Revelation 21 in this helpful way from Pastor John Piper: "We might say, 'The caterpillar will pass away and the butterfly emerges.' There is a real passing away and there is a real continuity, a real connection. Or we might say, 'The tadpole passes away and the frog appears.'"[4]

That the heaven and earth will be cataclysmically transformed is beyond question; this transformation does not mean annihilation but another renewal. The earth from which all living things draw their components will continue but this time without any curse; the seed that is this earth will die and life will spring forth from it.

All Creatures Great and Small

And the animals! It's not only the inanimate world that will be made new, it's also the entire animal kingdom. Because there were animals in the Garden of Eden before the world was corrupted, it's reasonable to assume that there will be animals in the New Earth, too. After all, animals are part of God's good creation. The Lord loves and pities his entire creation, even animals, as he made plain when chiding Jonah for his selfishness: "And should not I pity Nineveh, that great city, in which there are more than 120,000 persons who do not know their right hand from their left, *and also much cattle?*" (Jonah 4:11). Do you hear that? Could he destroy Nineveh for their violence and treachery? Of course he could. But he cared about the city . . . and its cows! Amazing![5]

All the beautiful animals that have spent their entire existence in futility, in killing or being killed, suffering for our sin, will finally

129

be free! On the New Earth there won't be animosity or fear be-tween them and us. We will care for them and they will serve us.

The wolf shall dwell with the lamb, and the leopard shall lie down with the young goat, and the calf and the lion and the fattened calf together; and a little child shall lead them. The cow and the bear shall graze; their young shall lie down together; and the lion shall eat straw like the ox. The nursing child shall play over the hole of the cobra, and the weaned child shall put his hand on the adder's den. They shall not hurt or destroy in all my holy mountain; for the earth shall be full of the knowledge of the Lord as the waters cover the sea.

Isaiah 11:6–9[6]

No hurting or destroying anywhere, ever! If God can trans-form my nature so that I am no longer bent in on myself, no longer a sinner, so that my body never wears out, then he can certainly change the nature (and even the physical attributes) of any animal for our joy and his glory. I know that lions don't graze right now. But that's not to say he couldn't re-create them to be just as magnificent as they presently are and yet not so bloodthirsty. Again, if he challenges us to envision a city that is 1,400 miles high, I'm guessing it's okay to suppose that children could play with cobras—then, not now!

Which brings me to the question that children always ask: Will our dogs go to heaven? I can't say definitively whether our dear dog Taz (the dog of a lifetime) will be there or not. But C. S. Lewis ventured, "As we are raised *in* Christ, so at least some animals are raised *in* us."[7] He continues, "In this way it seems to me possible that certain animals may have an immortality, not in themselves, but in the immortality of their masters."[8] In other words, the animals in which I have invested my love and care, and who have responded to that love and care by enriching my life and being a beloved part of our family, may be part of

130

the resurrection life I will know when the earth is remade to be what I've always longed for it to be: a place without aging or death. A place where I won't have to pet my dear friend Taz as the veterinarian injected her with a heart stopping drug. I don't know if she'll be there or not, but it would be really lovely to walk out onto the New Earth and see her there, wagging her little stubby tail in welcome. Lewis suggests,

> Who knows, indeed, but that a great deal even of the inanimate creation is raised *in* the redeemed souls who have, during this life, taken its beauty into themselves? That may be the way in which the 'new heaven and the new earth' are formed. Of course we can only guess and wonder.[9]

The Right Kind of New

In preaching on God's declaration that all things are made new, Manhattan pastor Tim Keller points out that there are two different Greek words that can be used for *new: kainos* and *neos*. He says that the word *neos* means "something young, something that has just been made," like "new" wine (Matthew 9:17), which hasn't been around for very long. On the other hand, the Greek word *kainos* means "new," but not in the sense of having just arrived on the scene, but rather in the sense of a quality of newness without reference to time. Keller says that in our experience, "Something has to be young in order for it to be new. But in God, all things are made new, and in fact they never stop being new. They get newer and newer."[10] I can't conceive of anything getting newer and newer. It's simply not part of the world in which we live. I've been trying to imagine what it would be like to get into my car every day and have it be new in my experience. Of course, there would be a welcome sense of familiarity but familiarity without boredom, habit without dullness. And it would go on and on without ever wearing out.

I've never experienced anything like that newness . . . and neither have you. Everything in our world is geared toward aging and obsolescence. In fact, if new babies don't grow and become older, we know there is something wrong with them. Everything in our world gets old, wears out, and dies. That's because entropy or degeneration of the world, originated in the fall. Before the fall, deterioration and death simply didn't exist. Adam and Eve could never have conceived of things wearing out, or even of boredom. They would never have said, "Familiarity breeds contempt."

But in the new world to come, God will make all things *new*, and he will never get tired of doing it. There won't be any "contempt" for things familiar. They will remain ever new. That's why he can call, "Again! Again!" over the stars and the daisies and the krill, and never get bored. He loves to say, "Mercies new every morning!" and then, "Mercies new every morning!" and then, "Mercies new every morning!" and on and on every morning forever. Everything is new to him every day because nothing has been blighted by sin. It remains eternally fresh, never tarnishing, never degenerating.

How much of the world to come is described as *kainos*? The word is used nine times in the book of Revelation alone. It is also used twice in Peter's description: "But according to his promise we are waiting for *new* heavens and a *new* earth in which righteousness dwells" (2 Peter 3:13). It remains eternally new because it is overflowing with righteousness. Remember, *kainos* doesn't refer to the length of time something has been around but rather to the quality of newness it retains. In the world as we know it, something has to be young, freshly minted or just made for it to be new. But in the world to come, everything will get "brighter and brighter, more vivid and more vivid, stronger and stronger every day, forever"[11] because sin will not tarnish it in any way.

132

All things new! Press yourself to continue to think about that for a moment. At the very least, John means that God himself will "wipe away every tear from [our] eyes" (Revelation 21:4) and that death shall be no more. Death, mourning, crying, and pain are all part of this old life, the darkness that enshrouds the former life here. Every sin we commit eventually begets tears . . . but all those tear-creating sins will be gone. Every treachery, every disappointment, breaking of promises, using and abusing, and shame will be gone. That will be a completely new day for every one of us, and that new day will *never end*!

On that day, the blessed words "The old has passed away; behold, the new has come" (2 Corinthians 5:17) will be true in every way possible. Yes, I know they are true now, as they refer to our lives in Christ, but honestly, I look around at my life and not everything seems new. I'm still living in between the *already* and the *not yet*. I am now in Christ, but there's still so much oldness, so much dying and decaying clinging to me. But that's not how it will always be. God is making everything that we've ever known—all that once carried the blight of this old sin-cursed world—into something completely new. He's making it into radiant, palpable joy.

We've never seen a world free from sin's disease. In the same way that we don't taste the pollution that is part of our air, we don't know what an environment of newness freed from sin feels like. From the very first breath we take until we whimper out our last good-bye . . . this world is, indeed, a vale of tears. It makes us old. We become jaded. But then . . . then, on that day, from the first time we fill our lungs with that pure air, we will grow stronger and stronger until we become what we were meant to be. Daughters and sons whose lives are "radiant over the goodness of the Lord . . . [our] life shall be like a watered garden, and they shall languish no more" (Jeremiah 31:12).

133

No More Tears . . . Ever

I'm not what you would call a crier. It's not that I never cry at all, it's just that I'm not like some women I know whose eyes are nearly always damp with tears. Personally, I think that's a lovely trait, but it's not the bent of my personality. Then, too, I know that I don't cry much because I really haven't had a lot of occasions to cry. I've been married for over forty years to one of the kindest people on the planet, who loves me dearly. My mother and brother, my children and their children all live nearby, and we are all in reasonably good health. I've got a great vocation. I mean, after all, who gets to sit around and think about heaven all day? Over the last few years I have shed many tears over the loss of my father; my uncle, who was a surrogate father; and both parents-in-law; over the loss of our business; and over some very sad situations in various churches and with friends, but the truth is that it takes a lot to get me crying.

My guess, though, is that when I see the beauty of that city and finally look into the eyes of the Lamb I've loved all of my adult life, I'll burst into tears of joy. Will there be tears of sadness, too? I don't know. If there are, it will only be because I'll see how much more worthy of my devotion he is . . . but then, that heartache and those tears won't be around for long because he, that is, "God himself," will "wipe away every tear" from my eyes (Revelation 21:3–4). With his hand? Really? Honestly, I'm trying now to wrap my understanding around that statement. God *himself* wiping tears of shame away from my eyes?

Perhaps it might help if we tried to envision a loving father comforting his dear child who has realized she has hurt him. Dads, what would you say? Moms, how would you console your little one? "There, there, dear one. You didn't really hurt me. My love for you is so much bigger than your lack of faith in it. Now, now. I love you. So . . . let's dry your eyes and forget

134

all about that. You are here. I am here. That's all that matters."
And then, maybe, the Lord will say, "There's a party happen-
ing out on the street right now. Let's go join in the music and
watch the dancers . . . and while we're at it, let's have a feast."
That sounds like something "new" to me. Does it to you, too?
No tears? No mourning? No death? Just joy?

Isaiah captured a sense of what that New Earth will be like,
a life where all the failures, idolatry, and unbelief of yesterday
will not be remembered or even come into our minds. Imagine
what it would be like to spend even one day completely free
from the recognition of personal sin and loss. Think of living
in a city that is *a joy*, with a people whose primary descriptor
is *gladness*. Imagine a city where you never hear the sound of
weeping or the cry of distress. If he hadn't promised it, I would
say it was impossible.

> For behold, I create new heavens and a new earth, and the former
> things shall not be remembered or come into mind.
> But be glad and rejoice forever in that which I create; for
> behold, I create Jerusalem to be a joy, and her people to be a
> gladness. I will rejoice in Jerusalem and be glad in my people;
> no more shall be heard in it the sound of weeping and the cry
> of distress.
>
> Isaiah 65:17–19

In one sense, everything will be new . . . but in another sense,
everything will remain familiar. We will know what music and
dancing is; we will recognize rivers and trees. When we see
mountains, we'll know they're for climbing. We will recognize
our friends . . . and maybe even people we've longed to meet
from the past, who will instantly be our friends when we meet
them. And when we see a lion, we'll know it for what it is.
Maybe we'll even be able to run our hands through his thick
mane, like Lucy did in Narnia, and thrill with the excitement

of it all. And maybe he'll favor us with one or two of his magnificent roars and we'll all laugh with joy.

Maybe now would be a good time to stop reading and spend some time in worship.

A Happy City

Let's look again at some descriptions of the New Earth and see what might be new and yet familiar:

> Then the angel showed me the river of the water of life, bright as crystal, flowing from the throne of God and of the Lamb through the middle of the street of the city; also, on either side of the river, the tree of life with its twelve kinds of fruit, yielding its fruit each month. The leaves of the tree were for the healing of the nations. No longer will there be anything accursed, but the throne of God and of the Lamb will be in it, and his servants will worship him. They will see his face, and his name will be on their foreheads. And night will be no more. They will need no light of lamp or sun, for the Lord God will be their light, and they will reign forever and ever.
>
> Revelation 22:1–5

Amazing, encouraging truths! Again, if the Lord hadn't said them, we would have to wonder whether or not it could possibly be so.

To begin with, John describes a river that runs through the middle of the main street in the New Jerusalem. In places where water is abundant, the thought of a river running through a city might not thrill us the way it would someone from the ancient Near East, where the land was arid and the people had to rely on rain to have water to drink and food to eat. Notice that the water is described as the "water of life," reminding us of Jesus' statement to the woman at the well. He is the One who gives sinners "living water" (John 4:10). And, "Everyone who drinks of this water will be thirsty again, but whoever drinks of the water that I will give him will never be thirsty again. The water that I will give him will become in him a spring of water welling up to eternal life" (John 4:13–14).

Later, at the end of John's vision, he writes, "The Spirit and the Bride say, 'Come.' And let the one who hears say, 'Come.' And let the one who is thirsty come; let the one who desires take the water of life without price" (Revelation 22:17).

Are you thirsty? Come and drink of the water of life. What will it cost you? Nothing. Your water bill has already been paid. The water that God freely lavishes on us in his city is both physical and spiritual. It will refresh our bodies and make us strong, but it will also quench the thirst of our souls. It has the power of life that will eternally renew us, and will ensure "the imperishability and vital freshness of the new world."[12] (See Ezekiel 47:1; Zechariah 14:8; comp. 1 Peter 1:4.)

As if that were not enough, John also says that this river is "bright as crystal, flowing from the throne of God and of the Lamb" (Revelation 22:1). His original readers would have known that rivers in their part of the world would never be described as "bright as crystal." They would be muddy and polluted, which was why the Syrian commander Naaman balked when commanded by Elisha to cleanse himself in the Jordan (2 Kings 5:10–12). No one would ever have referred to any of the rivers of Israel as bright, clear, or clean. And yet, they were told to imagine a beautiful river flowing out from the throne of God and the Lamb right down the main street of the New Jerusalem. Shining water . . . flowing out in an eternal stream to refresh and nourish every living creature in the New Earth. They would have been astounded and very, very happy. Bright, clean, fresh, life-giving water freely flowing right down the center of the city? Now, that's good news indeed.

John's vision is very similar to a vision the prophet Ezekiel had. In the Old Testament, Ezekiel spoke of a supernatural river that flowed out from God's temple that defied the laws of nature as it went. Rather than diminishing in size as it left its source, it gained depth and breadth the farther away it got. In Ezekiel's vision, the water started out as a trickle but ended up deep enough for a man to swim in. The renewal that this water brings with it will not just come to "people but [will] affect the entire natural world . . . and prefigures the living water that Christ offers through the Spirit."[13] Imagine walking through God's city with a bright river flowing through the middle of it . . . a river where everyone and everything could drink without worrying about contamination, bacteria, or drought. Where does this river of life originate? In the presence of the Lord, who is himself the "Headwaters of Eternal Joy,"[14] of course.

The Tree of Life, Plus More

John continues, "On either side of the river, the tree of life with its twelve kinds of fruit, yielding its fruit each month" (Revelation 22:2). Are you beginning to see how so much of what we can look forward to isn't utterly unique but rather a renewing and broadening of everything lost in the Garden of Eden? Following the pattern of what was once called good by God becoming even grander in the New Earth, instead of just one Tree of Life, we are invited to eat from one on each side of the river. And these trees don't have a limited season of fruitfulness. Remember how I said that everything will be remade? This is another one of those "everything remade" situations. The trees will produce twelve different kinds of fruit . . . forever. No need to worry about depleting this crop. No need to worry about famine or whether the trees will be up to the task of feeding all of God's children. Who knows how large these trees are, or the size of the fruit they bear.

Harking back to Lewis's orange analogy, we don't have any idea how nourishing that fruit will be or what it might taste like. I know that most fruit is sweet, but I'm wondering if there won't be some savory fruit there, too, perhaps fruit that will satisfy even the hungriest meat eater.[15] We can let our imagination soar. In any case, the fruit that will be there will completely nourish us and will grant us all the health and vitality that we will ever need. "The best meals you'll ever eat are all still ahead of you on the New Earth."[16]

And notice what John writes next: "The leaves of the tree were for the healing of the nations" (Revelation 22:2). Not only will the trees furnish us with abundant fruit forever, their leaves will have healing properties. "Not only the quenching of our heart's thirst but also the satisfaction of spiritual hunger, and the healing of wounds and woes proceed from the throne room of God."[17]

Think back to the story of Adam and Eve's fall. What did they do? They tried to weave leaves together to cover themselves. It's not a meaningless coincidence that leaves are spoken of again here at the beginning of the new world. The leaves they sought to cover themselves are now ours for the healing of all the nations from their sin.

The Trees of Life will be there for us to eat from freely and no longer in any probationary way. There won't be any laws forbidding any unlawful eating there like there were in Eden. In fact, there won't be any laws there at all because no one will have the desire to sin. Ever.

> Once we become what the sovereign God has made us to be in Christ and once we see him as he is, then we'll see all things— including sin—for what they are. God won't need to restrain us from sin. Sin will have absolutely no appeal. It will be, literally, unthinkable.[18]

We will eat freely and be blessed forever because our Lord, the promised Rescuer, hung on another tree and was cursed in our place. By his death there in the Old Jerusalem, suspended between heaven and earth, he joined heaven with earth and forever fulfilled every law and abolished punishment for disobedience. He has already set us free to enjoy all his bounty forever, and when we finally get there, we'll really understand what he's done for us. "No longer will there be anything accursed, but the throne of God and of the Lamb will be in it" (Revelation 22:3). When John says that nothing accursed will be there, he means that everything will be completely free from divine wrath.[19] How could there be any wrath there? All of God's wrath for all of our sin has already been poured out on the Son he loved. There won't be any laws for us to break, no occasion for sin, no desire for anything but love. Nothing but love and love and love forever and ever.

No More Night

John finishes up this section with these precious words: "And night will be no more. They will need no light of lamp or sun, for the Lord God will be their light, and they will reign for ever and ever" (Revelation 22:5).

In our world, darkness is a description of our hearts. All of that darkness that sought to overcome the light brought by the Lord (John 1:5) has now been completely banished. No more suffering in darkness. No more wicked deeds done under the cover of night. Only light and beauty forever because night and everything associated with it here "will be no more." There won't be any need. No want of anything. No starving babies, no lives of poverty. No hatred or war or unnatural disasters. Right now, everything within me is praying, "Maranatha! Come, Lord Jesus!" (See Revelation 22:20.)

140

———— FIXING OUR EYES ON HOME ————

1. Read Isaiah 42:9; 43:18–19. The Lord delights in speaking of the new things he will do. Are you anticipating them? Why? Why not?

2. He loves to give water to his people and even to his animals (Isaiah 43:18–21).

   a. Would you say that you are thirsty for the water he'll give?

   b. Can you define a spiritual thirst within you?

   c. What do you think about the fact that he even cares for wild animals, jackals, and ostriches?

   d. Why does he give us water to drink?

3. Read Isaiah 65:17–25. Respond. I know that some people may interpret these passages as applying to a millennial age, but even if you do, it's reasonable to assume that the New Earth will be at least as great as that temporary reign.

4. In talking about animals, C. S. Lewis writes, "In heaven, if you wanted a horse to ride you would walk up to the nearest herd and ask for volunteers—and the one you chose would be regarded as the lucky one."[20] Respond.

5. Summarize what you've learned in this chapter in four or five sentences.

8

Our Tears Make Us Long for Home

As I sit here trying to choose words that will speak to those who are suffering and impart hope to look past this life and into our true Home, I admit that I am not qualified to do so. I wouldn't count myself among the suffering. Yes, I've gone through some difficulties in my life, but nothing, *nothing*, like the real suffering that others have known. So, dear sufferer, please forgive my inability to deeply understand what you face every day. I don't know what it's like to wake up every day and wonder how to get food for my child who is slowly starving before my eyes. I've never had chronic, excruciating pain or had to undergo long-term medical therapies. No one in my family has committed suicide or struggles with any severe mental disorder. I don't know what it's like to have sinned in such a way that devastation has followed me for years. My family remains intact, my grandchildren are simply a phone call away, and I live in one of the most pleasant cities on the planet. My husband loves God and even as I write is away in Central America doing mission work for a week. My mother and brother live nearby, and I am able to see them often. I do not worry about being arrested for attending church or owning a Bible, and I can go to any church I choose whenever I choose. Yes, I have suffered some losses in my life, and I have sinned grievously, but these things are nothing, again, *nothing*, in comparison to what you may be facing every moment of every day. So please forgive me if my words sound shallow or if you don't see any of my blood on the page.

Even so, my heart is to encourage you. The primary reason the Spirit gave us portraits of the world to come is to comfort us in the midst of our suffering. Life in the New Earth is only good news to those for whom this old earth no longer promises satisfaction. The season of suffering I've been going through—though insignificant in comparison to what others have faced, and are facing—has made me long for Paradise and my true Home on the New Earth like never before. It is meant to do so. When I go to the Scriptures, I find comfort for those who suffer given over and over again, and the comfort that is given is filled with the Lord's sure promise of rest, vindication, relief, and joy that will be found in the age to come.

The Word of the Lord to all who trust in him is that everlasting joy is coming . . . and nothing can stop it!

> Say to those who have an anxious heart, "Be strong; fear not!
> "Behold, your God *will come* . . . and save you."
> Then the eyes of the blind shall be opened, and the ears of the deaf unstopped; then shall the lame man leap like a deer, and the tongue of the mute sing for joy. . . .
> And the ransomed of the Lord *shall return* and come to Zion with *singing*; everlasting joy shall be upon their heads; they shall obtain gladness and joy, and sorrow and sighing *shall* flee away.
>
> Isaiah 35:4–10

Our "final homecoming is through glorious abundance exploding with joy, when the curse shall be reversed."[1] The Lord, who declared that "he is God" and "we are his people" (Psalm 100:3), also declares in faithfulness his promise to come to us. Things will not always be as they are right now. He has promised to return. What a glorious picture of the life that awaits all of us. His promise to us is sure: God's salvation will include not only the promise of spiritual well-being but also physical healing and the wholeness we long for. This wholeness will be fully realized in our resurrected bodies when we finally arrive Home.

Because I feel my inadequacy so keenly right now, I've asked some of my friends to share their stories, and sought, through them, to help you see that you are not alone and that the Lord is speaking the same thing to your weeping brothers and sisters that he speaks to you. What follows are the testimonies of real believers whose hearts have been focused on Home through their trials. One of these testimonies came from a woman who wanted to remain anonymous. But wherever their stories originate, all of them know what it is to long for Home, for the New Earth, in ways that I can only faintly imagine.

The Beloved of the Lord

This world has been a sorrowful place many times in my life, and my heavenly Father has been so faithful to be here with me in the midst of my sorrows . . . even before I really knew him. However, this world has never felt like a home to me, and for many years I have looked forward to the joy of being free from this place of sorrow.

As I was a child of five when my father left our family for another woman, and because he had another family, I missed him terribly. My mother was unstable emotionally and could be very cruel. I felt lonely and unloved. As I grew up, I tried rebellion, religion, and even suicide. No matter what I tried I never felt good enough, never felt that I was loved as I longed to be.

145

Jesus reached into my life when I was twenty-one in a miraculous way (isn't it always a miracle?) and showed me that I could trust in what he had done. I realized that I couldn't ever be good enough on my own and that because he loved me, I was finally free from the debt of sin I couldn't pay! What a relief!

Still, living in a world of sin and suffering had its effects on my life. I hesitate to list the things God has called me to go through, because he has always turned what seems like tragedy into an opportunity to see his goodness. But even so, what I've gone through felt very painful to me and sometimes still does.

My unsaved husband was unkind and didn't like my being a Christian. I was eviscerated (or so it felt) when I found out he was being unfaithful to me.

I lost children to miscarriage and thought I would never be able to have a child. When I finally did give birth, I lost a baby to what the doctors called "failure to thrive."

Ten days later, I had a severe deep vein thrombosis and still have bad veins that require that I always wear compression hose. Then, I had a terrible misdiagnosed case of chicken pox when I was thirty. I was hospitalized for weeks because of it and lost a lot of my skin on bed sheets and toilets, as it turned black and peeled. My skin is still covered with a lacelike scarring today, nearly forty years later.

Then our seven-year-old son was hit by a bus and suffered a severe head injury. Even though the Lord miraculously saved his life, his injuries have required many years of special therapy. It has been so hard for me to see him suffer.

We were all in an intensely trying time, and my marriage continued to be difficult. Even though I loved my husband very much, we eventually separated and divorced.

It was during this time that a fire destroyed my house and the studio where I worked. The fire not only unsettled our living situation, but my income was disrupted and remained difficult for years. I suffered severe financial problems.

Even though I continued to long to have a relationship with my father (and his second family), I was not allowed to see him or do things with the family because his wife didn't like me. Nobody in the family really knew why, though it became more and more apparent that she resented the fact that I was a Christian.

I have continued to feel rejected by people I've loved.

And then, I lost my beloved son Richard in a car crash almost twelve years ago to the day that I write this. He was twenty-two. His death is the most enduring sorrow of my life. I long to see him again

That's what this world is, a place where we have tribulation. Though God has miraculously healed, restored, blessed, and provided for me over and over again in absolute faithfulness, and even though he has redeemed the pain many times over—so that I can say we can trust him—I do rejoice to know that in the New Heaven and New Earth there will be no more suffering for any of us. And yet, what I see of this world every day fills my heart with sorrow just knowing how hard it can be for the sick, the broken, the homeless, the unloved, and the wounded.

But God . . . doesn't leave us to this world. He has paid for the ticket home! And as Mother Teresa said in one of my favorite quotes, "In light of heaven, the worst suffering on earth will seem to be no more serious than one night in an inconvenient hotel."[2]

If I hadn't personally walked through these trials with my friend, it would be hard for me to believe that everything listed here (and more) actually happened, and that she's still praising God and looking forward to our final homecoming.

To her and to all those who have longed to be loved, who have longed to know what it is to be welcomed into a family and not rejected, the Lord says, "Once you were not a people, but now you are God's people; once you had not received mercy, but now you have received mercy" (1 Peter 2:10). The one who was "not beloved I [the Lord] will call 'beloved'" (Romans 9:25). Every daughter and son who has known the rejection of a parent choosing to leave them, every wife or husband who has been abandoned will know and savor hearing him call us his "beloved." We've all longed for Home as it was meant to be—a place where love and welcome permeate every crevice of our hearts. We won't be disappointed.

For Righteousness' Sake

I have a dear friend who has agreed to let me tell the story of her suffering, a suffering she's known for doing the good of adopting children.[3] Most of us find it easy to reconcile the suffering that we have to face when our personal sin has brought it on. For instance, if I'm in a wheelchair today because I was driving drunk and crashed my car into a tree, then in one sense, my suffering seems logical. I shouldn't have gotten behind the wheel when I was inebriated.

But what about the suffering of the righteous? What about those who suffer because they made decisions to lay down their lives in love for others? Certainly the Bible talks about the blessedness of suffering persecution for doing good, but should we call the suffering faced by my friend persecution? I think we can. Perhaps this isn't the sort of persecution that we normally think of, like what terrorists are doing to Coptic Christians in the Middle East, but I'm convinced that this kind of suffering has its origin in the depths of hell just as surely as these acts of terrorism do. Here are John Calvin's thoughts:

> Therefore, whether in declaring God's truth against Satan's falsehoods or in taking up the *protection of the good and the innocent against the wrongs of the wicked*, we must undergo

148

the offenses and hatred of the world, which may imperil either our life, our fortunes, or our honor. Let us not grieve or be troubled in thus far devoting our efforts to God, or count ourselves miserable in those matters in which he has with his own lips declared us blessed [Matthew 5:10].[4]

Certainly what my friend and her family have done can be described as the "protection of the good and the innocent against the wrongs of the wicked." You see, in living out a desire to bless and save innocents, she and her husband have adopted seven children, adding them to their own family of three. In doing so, they brought into their home two individual children, who are now well-adjusted married adults, as well as a family group that came to them through the foster care system and two other daughters, one through domestic adoption and another one through international adoption. The daily troubles they have faced as they sought to love, provide for, and protect those who had no one to protect them have been ongoing and heartrending, not to mention terribly expensive.

And this story isn't over. Two of the children have had to be sent into residential care facilities at different times because they were becoming dangers to themselves and others. One of them suffered so much trauma as a small child that he will be unable to graduate from high school or provide for himself even as an adult. Others have been so shattered by the failures of their parents to properly care for them that they now find it impossible to have trusting relationships with those who love them.

All of this suffering has been brought into a family who might have chosen to live for their own pleasure, but who instead decided to lay down their lives so that others might know the joy of living in a Christian family. Their sacrifice has been returned with blow after blow of hatred, deceit, and loss. This is what it means to take up the cross and follow Christ, to follow him

149

as he loved those who despitefully used him, to wash the feet of those who would betray him.

It is very difficult for anyone who is suffering for doing good in this way to continue to labor and to believe, which is why, at the end of Paul's letter to the Corinthians who were suffering (and would continue to do so), he writes, "Therefore, my beloved brothers, be steadfast, immovable, always abounding in the work of the Lord, knowing that in the Lord your labor is not in vain" (1 Corinthians 15:58).

I'm quite sure that there are days, even weeks, when we see our good work go up in flames, or when we are persecuted for loving, or misunderstood and punished for seeking to do the right thing, that it is next to impossible to believe that our work hasn't been in vain, because it sure looks like it has been. How many parents have spent years and years loving and training their children, only to have them throw over the faith and embrace a lifestyle that functions primarily as a slap in the face? How many missionaries or pastors have laid aside their own ambitions or careers to serve people who are not only ungrateful but downright hostile? This is the world in which we live. After all, if this is how he suffered, then we should not think we would be more privileged than our Master: "'A servant is not greater than his master.' If they persecuted me, they will also persecute you" (John 15:20).

Perhaps part of the key to making it through this kind of suffering is to actually see it as persecution for righteousness' sake. But usually that's a hard thing to do, because when we look at our own lives, we see our mixed motives and our failures, and we think that persecution for righteousness' sake is something especially holy, something different from the grind we face. I don't agree. Every time we suffer while seeking to do good—no matter how inconsequential that endeavor seems to us, no matter whether we were able to do the good we longed to do, or do it well—it is happening because we are seeking to walk in the footsteps of our Savior.

> For this is a gracious thing, when, mindful of God, one endures sorrows while suffering unjustly. . . . But if when you do good and suffer for it you endure, this is a gracious thing in the sight of God. For to this you have been called, because Christ also suffered for you, leaving you an example, so that you might follow in his steps.
>
> 1 Peter 2:19–21

Suffering for doing good is a "gracious thing in the sight of God." It is pleasing to him when we suffer in this way because it is a demonstration of his very character and the way he has ordained his person to be known in this world. Suffering like this is always a demonstration of grace, an issuing of his favor upon an ungrateful world.

And so to my friend, and to all those who are suffering in any way for seeking to love, for trying to do good, the faithful Lord reminds you that you have not been forgotten and that your prayers have not gone unheard.

"You have kept count of my tossings," David moans. This word *tossings* is what you do when you start to fall off to sleep and then awaken again.[5] It's a word that might imply wandering around looking for solace and rest. David continues, "Put my tears in your bottle. Are they not in your book?" (Psalm 56:8). Dear friend, if you are suffering because you have tried to do good, here are words for you sent from the world to come: Your prayers are heard. They are in the hands of the four elders who are before the Lamb; they are in golden bowls full of incense. He sees and hears them. They are pleasing to him.

> And when he had taken the scroll, the four living creatures and the twenty-four elders fell down before the Lamb, each holding

151

a harp, and golden bowls full of incense, which are the prayers
of the saints.

Revelation 5:8

And another angel came and stood at the altar with a golden
censer, and he was given much incense to offer with the prayers
of all the saints on the golden altar before the throne, and the
smoke of the incense, with the prayers of the saints, rose before
God from the hand of the angel.

Revelation 8:3–4

And because those prayers have arisen before God, you can
know—and I mean know with certainty—that he hears them,
that he is pleased with them, and that he will completely satisfy,
deliver, and answer them in his great kindness.

Light Shining in the Darkness

In the spring of 2014, I began to develop sensitive patches on
the skin of my eyelids, neck, face, and chest. Over a period of
weeks that turned into months, I developed painful blisters
and inflammation that basically took over my life. All the topi-
cal creams I tried to cure my problem only made my condition worse. Being out in the sun increased the pain, so I had
to be isolated in my home in the dark for nearly two months.
I wasn't allowed to be outside or even near the windows. All
the shades in my house had to be shut. I had to stop using
everything I normally used to wash my hair, my face, and my
body. At times, I used baking soda to clean myself and cold
cooked oatmeal for my skin.

There were days I didn't want to live because of the physical pain I was experiencing. But that wasn't the only pain I
felt. I faced deep loneliness and isolation. It was a dark time
physically, emotionally, and spiritually. I was cut off socially,

and for the most part I was alone in my house in the dark. I spent many sleepless nights tossing and turning and praying.

I remember one night at about one in the morning sitting on a futon bed in our extra bedroom, asking God to take the whole situation away. It was summer, and I wanted to see the ocean, to play with my grandchildren and friends, to watch the sunsets. As I was praying, I heard the words in my heart in the form of a question: "Are you willing to give up a summer for the work I am doing in your life?" Honestly, I answered, "No, I'm not willing." I didn't want to miss anything in this life, especially the summer. Right after saying the word no, I thought how shallow but honestly true that response of my heart was. I turned to God in prayer and asked him to help me value what he was doing in my soul. I said, "I surrender to you, Lord."

Throughout the dark summer months as I waited to see a specialist at a local university, I began to experience light shining in my darkness. Psalm 139:12 says, "Even the darkness is not dark to you [God]" and the "night is as bright as the day." As I was being stripped of this life, God was shining upon me with the light of his eternal message. His light felt like home to me.

I didn't belong to this world. I belonged to a world that I was called to through Christ my Savior. It would be a world where what was happening in my soul would be with me forever, a world where my soul was being transformed into the person I was meant to be. I began to experience confidence, strength, and hope even as my body was wasting away. Some part of my happiness that was dependent on this world was being stripped from me, and the treasures of my real home were being planted deep within me. There is a confidence that I now have that I know comes from the world to come, and not from this world. It is a world where the light gives us all the life we need. In my dark weeks at home I experienced this light, and it gave me the life I longed for: a life where I felt like I belonged, a life where I knew that I mattered.

This is the message that I experienced through the power of God's light. His Word is that powerful. In the darkness his light was shining through with the message of his Son, Jesus. I realized that what he thinks of me is more important than what this world offers in appreciation and recognition. I'm valued because I have been plucked out of darkness and brought into his marvelous light, and one day I will experience that light in its fullness. The light is Jesus himself, and I know he was there with me in the darkness, giving me confidence that I am his beloved and belong to him.

In God's kindness and care, I was able to correct my skin problem with the help of that specialist, and yet my real Home seems a little closer to me now than ever. As it turns out, I had an out-of-control contact dermatitis, which sounds fairly common, but was exacerbated by the fact that I was also allergic to the very remedies that my dermatologist was giving me to combat it. I was tested for over one hundred fifty allergens and was allergic to all but five ingredients normally found in skin products.

When I think about how suffering in this life helps me to look forward to the New Heaven and New Earth, the main thought that comes to mind is that suffering reminds me this is not my home. Suffering reminds me that all of life is temporal and everything I have will fade away. I know that if I do not experience the fading of my life through suffering, I will not look to my real Home. Home, the place I was meant to belong, is the place that makes perfect sense out of what I walk through now.[6]

The physical sufferings of this life never come to us without other sufferings in attendance. Donna's suffering isolated her from the very people who were given by the Lord to comfort and encourage her. A great part of her suffering was the very isolation her condition necessitated.

And so to Donna, and to all who are isolated in their pain, the Lord speaks:

> Fear not, for I have redeemed you;
> I have called you by name, you are mine.
> When you pass through the waters, I will be with you;
> and through the rivers, they shall not overwhelm you;
> when you walk through fire you shall not be burned,
> and the flame shall not consume you.
> For I am the Lord your God,
> the Holy One of Israel, your Savior.
>
> Isaiah 43:1-3

Because you are the Lord's, because he knows you and has called you by name, you will not suffer any loss that will ultimately burn, overwhelm, or consume you. He makes this promise to us because he is the Lord and the Holy One who is also our Savior.

Anyone who has known chronic pain or sickness also knows that after a while, and usually too soon, friends and family become weary with the battle. They want you to be better, but your pain feels like it's more than they can bear. And they still have their own lives to attend to. The pressure to care and keep caring seems unendurable to them at times. I watched both of my in-laws degenerate in slow and painful ways until the Lord finally took them a few years ago. I am trying to be attentive to my own mother, who is ninety-two at the time of this writing, and needs my care more and more frequently. Job's so-called friends wearied with his suffering and demanded that he repent. The blind man in John 9 and the lame beggar in Acts 3 were sent out to beg for a living. If people hadn't given them alms, they would have starved. Our suffering seems unending both to us and to those who are caring for us. But the truth is that there will be an end to all the suffering, crying, and pain that we know here. He has promised.

As I mentioned before, the man who acted as my father, my uncle Mitch, died just a few days before the end of a difficult year. Although his death was expected, it occurred more swiftly than I had anticipated. These are some of the words that I delivered at his memorial service:

> Mitchell was a significant source of strength, encouragement, stability, generosity, and love in my life. Uncle Mishy—as I always called him—did for me what he was so good at doing for so many others: He stepped into my need and did his best to love me and be there for my brother and me, not only as we were growing up, but even into our adult years. I knew that whenever I would contact him, he would always say, "There's my beautiful niece, Elyse. How are you, darling?" With him, I knew I was loved. The Lord used him powerfully in my life as a source of blessing.
>
> I have precious memories of spending weeks during my childhood summers with him and his family as we played in the pool together at the house in Whittier. He loved his children Si and Gayle deeply and was a devoted father to them, and uncle to me. I have particularly fond memories of him making breakfast for us, and of his gentleness and patience with a houseful of overly rambunctious and loud kids, even though he was enduring a significant suffering of his own. He never let on, at least not to me. His heart was open and welcoming, and he went out of his way to say kind things not only to me but also about others to me. He was a faithful, diligent man. I mean, who has the same phone number at his business for fifty years? Mitchell did.
>
> At his marriage to Susan, I saw a man who had finally found joy. He and Susan were a beautiful and seemingly inseparable match. I recall a conversation I had with Susan one evening when she and I were working a show in San Diego together because Mitchell had been unwell. She was deeply troubled

about how she would go on if she ever lost him. We talked about faith and the probabilities of an afterlife with the Lord, and she was encouraged. Neither one of us had any idea at that time that she would precede him in death. It's been less than two years since Susan left us, and every time we saw Mitchell in the interim, he would bemoan his loss to us. "I miss my sweet girl"; "She went too soon"; and "She was so beautiful . . . she never had anything bad to say about anyone" were words I heard from him on more than one occasion. It is fitting, then, that he would leave us and go to her on her birthday.

In closing, I'd like to share with you about the last time I saw my uncle Mishy. My husband, Phil, along with my brother, Richard, and our son Joel, visited him in his room in the hospital. He greeted me as he always did, with "There's my beautiful girl." At that visit we read Psalm 23 to him and told him that we believed that the Lord was his Shepherd and was awaiting his arrival. He said, and I quote, "I buy that."

Uncle Mishy enriched all of our lives, and for that we are eternally grateful, but, as this day has made so sadly obvious, this world is not our home, this is not the house we were made to live in eternally. By faith, I personally look forward to the day when I will see both him and Susan again, and we will all recognize the blessedness and veracity of these oh, so familiar words from King David:

Psalm 23

The Lord is my shepherd; I shall not want.
He makes me lie down in green pastures.
He leads me beside still waters.
He restores my soul.
He leads me in paths of righteousness for his
    name's sake.
Even though I walk through the valley of the
    shadow of death,

I will fear no evil, for you are with me,
Your rod and your staff, they comfort me.
You prepare a table before me in the presence of
    my enemies;
You anoint my head with oil; my cup overflows.
Surely goodness and mercy shall follow me all the
    days of my life,
And I shall dwell in the house of the Lord forever.
    Amen.

I continue to mourn the loss of my uncle. I miss him deeply, but I know that we will dwell in the house of the Lord together forever.

I'm now going to let my dear friend Nancy Guthrie, who has suffered the loss of two children, close our time together. The hope that each one of us has—the confidence that everyone who suffers can claim—is that our suffering is not in vain and that a day is coming, and sooner than we think, when all that is presently darkness will be light, all that is lost will be found, and all those who are wandering will finally be welcomed Home. Don't despair, dear friend. He knows. He sees. He loves. There is something more.

Word of Faith From Nancy Guthrie

A while ago David [Nancy's husband] and I did an interview for a radio program about our experience of loving and losing our daughter, Hope, and son Gabe. As we came to the end of the program, the interviewer seemed to be setting us up for a sentimental closing in which we would talk about our anticipation of seeing Hope and Gabe again when we enter into the presence of God when we die. And certainly we look forward to that day. In fact, sometimes it becomes so real that my heart skips a beat.

But as good as it will be to see my Savior and my children on the day I go to be "at home with the Lord," my fondest hopes will not yet be fulfilled. My hopes are set firmly on a greater day. The hope the Bible tells us to set our hearts on is resurrection.

In 1 Thessalonians 4, Paul draws a distinction between those who grieve with no hope and those who grieve with hope. We want to be people who grieve with hope! So what is the nature or substance of the hope held out to us in this passage? Paul did not command us to comfort one another with the truth that the spirits of Christians who have died are in heaven, although that is very true and precious. Rather, he commanded us to comfort one another with the truth of the resurrection to come.

The substance of our hope is not in a bodiless-spirit existence in the presence of God. The substance of our hope is in our spirits being reunited with our resurrected bodies, fit for eternal enjoyment on a renewed earth (see Romans 8:18–25; Revelation 21–22). I'll be there, with David and Matt and Hope and Gabe. And there, at the center, seated on the throne, will be the source and substance of our hope. Together, we'll hear a loud voice from the throne saying, "Look, God's home is now among his people! He will live with them, and they will be his people. God himself will be with them. He will wipe every tear from their eyes, and there will be no more death or sorrow or crying or pain. All these things are gone forever" (see Revelation 21:3–4).[7]

FIXING OUR EYES ON HOME

1. There are no sufferings that can be compared to the sufferings of Christ. Read Isaiah 52:13–15. Respond.

2. John Calvin wrote, "If, while conscious of our innocence, we are deprived of our substance by the wickedness of man, we are, no doubt, humanly speaking, reduced to

poverty; but in truth our riches in heaven are increased: if driven from our homes, we have a more welcome reception into the family of God; if vexed and despised, we are more firmly rooted in Christ; if stigmatized by disgrace and ignominy, we have a higher place in the kingdom of God; and if we are slain, entrance is thereby given us to eternal life."[8] Respond.

3. Martin Luther wrote, "There is no other way—if we desire to possess Christ, to live and to rule with him in eternity, then suffering must first be endured."[9]

4. Hymn writer William Cowper wrote the great hymn "God Moves in a Mysterious Way":

> Ye fearful saints, fresh courage take,
> The clouds ye so much dread
> Are big with mercy, and shall break
> In blessings on your head. . . .
> Blind unbelief is sure to err,
> And scan His work in vain:
> God is His own interpreter,
> And He will make it plain.[10]

Perhaps now would be a good time to sing this hymn. (If you don't know it, you can access it at http://cyberhymnal .org/htm/g/m/gmovesmw.htm.)

5. Summarize what you have learned in this chapter in four or five sentences.

9

The End of Our Bucket List

Every one of us is longing. We're thirsty. There is a desire residing within each of us that drives us all of our lives. It is simply impossible to ignore. We are yearning for something deeper, something that won't fade like everything we've encountered on this earth. We all have an "inbuilt longing for what is permanent."[1] We long for happiness. I'm not talking about the happiness we feel when we get the birthday present we've been hoping for. Or even when we finally meet the *right* person to marry, find a job to invest our lives in, or are in a position to afford the home of our dreams. I'm talking about the happiness that comes from life in the presence of God, where there is nothing but satisfaction, wholeness, love, and holiness. I'm talking about a place of "refreshment and an eternal home."[2]

This endless longing and seeking and laboring in vain to find these things aren't new to the twenty-first century. It all began on the day the cherubim was stationed at the gate of the

Garden of Eden to keep us out, and has continued unabated ever since.

Yes, everything you're experiencing now, even those things you're sure will satisfy, are nothing more than fickle shadows sure to disappoint. Most Christians know that what we long for won't be found here. Like Abraham, we recognize that we're "looking forward to the city that has foundations, whose designer and builder is God" (Hebrews 11:10). Even though we've been taught this, we still spend our lives searching for something more. When we hear that happiness and permanence are being found in *something else,* we chase after it—deceived, again and again. We have a terrible time learning that nothing here will satisfy us, that everything here is no more sturdy than a shadow. This is how Digory from THE CHRONICLES OF NARNIA describes our seemingly solid, yet completely vaporous world:

> [The Narnia Lucy knew] was only a shadow or a copy of the real Narnia which has always been here and always will be here: just as our own world, England and all, is *only a shadow or copy of something in Aslan's real world.* You need not mourn over Narnia, Lucy. All of the old Narnia that mattered, all the dear creatures, have been drawn into the real Narnia through the Door. And of course it is different; as different as a real thing is from a shadow or as waking life is from a dream.[3]

In one sense, we're living in a dream world that will only take on true solidness, authentic life, when he shakes us awake in the resurrection. The world as we know it now is simply a faint snapshot of the resurrected world to come. In light of that, we would be wise not to spend our lives taking selfies, trying to prove that we're really living life to its fullest, really going for the gusto, while we fall backward off cliffs into that bottomless bucket list.

The Bucket List

I had never heard of a bucket list, until the movie with that title, starring Morgan Freeman and Jack Nicholson (which, I admit, I have not seen), came out in 2007. Since then, though, I've heard a lot about bucket lists. In short, a bucket list is a list of things you want to accomplish before you die. You might make a list of countries you'd like to visit, people you want to meet, or experiences you'd like to have, like hang gliding, scuba diving, or writing a book. In fact, there are even websites that tell you how to construct your own unique bucket list. And if that's not enough, you can read a book about it or even take a course on it—maybe that course is something to go on the list: *On my bucket list, is a class about how to construct a bucket list.*

There's so much wrong with this impulse—it's so futile and shortsighted—that I won't spend time critiquing it, but needless to say, the idea of crafting a bucket list has resonated deeply within our culture, a culture bent as it is on pleasure-seeking and self-justification.

The bucket list resonates with us because we are seeking to justify ourselves by our experiences. We might call it "Justification by Facebook." In other words, many of us find passing satisfaction and pride in the knowledge that we're able to share (or brag) about the great food we've just eaten, or the wonderful arrangement of our Christmas decorations, or better yet, our smiling family as we pose beside the Grand Canyon or an ancient fountain in Rome.

An entire industry has sprung up around our drive to share about how much we're enjoying life. Whoever invented the selfie stick really understood this impulse. And in case riding a twenty-five-foot wave isn't enough of a thrill, the GoPro is a necessity. *Look at me!* the post proclaims. *See, I really am happy, well-heeled, in control, fun, strong, brave . . . wonderful. Don't you wish you were me?* Justification by social media is one of the primary reasons that Facebook exists. And the other one is our intrinsic desire to envy. We've lost sight of our true Home, and are trying to find satisfaction and justification where it will never be found.

The bucket list resonates with us because we are all seeking our own happiness. We want to survey our lives and assure ourselves that we really did live a life worth living, after all, as if scuba diving would ever satisfy that criteria. The bucket list phenomenon is simply the fruit of a culture that has lost its sense of transcendence, the childlike ability to believe in life after life, in an eternal existence, a forever relationship. Even Christians who know better still live as though this world were all there was. So on and on we chug, making the entertainment, travel, and exercise industry rich.

We think we know what we want, but when we get it, it never really satisfies, does it? That's because it's not strong enough to bear the weight of our desires. The newness and happiness of a spouse or child or church or job or degree all too soon disintegrates and wears thin, old, and boring. (That's not to say that we can't or shouldn't seek to renew our relationships, it's just that we weren't meant to be satisfied by anything this world has to offer.) Here's French philosopher Blaise Pascal:

> All men seek happiness. This is without exception. Whatever different means they employ, they all tend to this end. . . .
>
> What is it then that this desire and this inability proclaim to us, but that there was once in man a true happiness of which there now remain to him only the mark and empty trace, which *he in vain tries to fill from all his surroundings, seeking from things absent the help he does not obtain in things present*? But these are all inadequate, because the infinite abyss can only be filled by an infinite and immutable object, that is to say, *only by God Himself.*[4]

Why this universal craving? Because we've got an "infinite abyss" within each of us, and will only find true happiness when we stand face-to-face with the One for whom we were created, the One whose face we've searched for day after day throughout our entire lives. As Saint Augustine wrote, "Thou madest us for Thyself, and our heart is restless, until it repose in Thee."[5] Restless hearts . . . yes, that's an apt description of our experience here, isn't it? Into my restless heart I try to cram everything on my bucket list, but no matter how many experiences I check off, my heart just won't rest because I was created to thirst for something more, for Someone more.

Imagine a man who is starving,

> and to satisfy his craving stomach he should gape and hold open his mouth to take in the wind, and then should think that the reason why he is not satisfied is because he has not got enough of the wind; no, the reason is because the thing is not suitable to a craving stomach. Yet there is really the same madness in the world: the wind which a man takes in by gaping will as soon satisfy a craving stomach ready to starve, as all the comforts in the world can satisfy a soul who knows what true happiness means.[6]

We are longing for the living water that will flow out from under the eternal throne of the Father into the river in the New Jerusalem, where we will drink and drink and drink of a liquid so refreshing the only way to describe it is "living." We are thirsty, in need of him. We need to spend an eternity letting him satisfy our thirst.

Contemplating the truth about our Home helps free us from the futility of the bucket list, while it whets our thirst for the real thing—for the eternal drink that only the truly thirsty can enjoy. What is the Spirit's response to our thirst? Does he chide us? No. He bids us *come,* and *drink.* What is the church's message to a parched world, a world trying to quench its thirst by gulping down another cup of mud? "All who will, come and drink!"[7]

165

Completely Satisfied

What is it that we're thirsting for? Is it just a space of safety, or are we actually longing for relationship, for a person, for him? In the upper room, the Lord had given his friends the bad news: He was going away. They were heartbroken and afraid and felt like he was deserting them. But then he also gave them the good news: that they would learn to rely on him more and more as the years of his absence grew: "I will come again and will take you to myself, that where I am you may be also" (John 14:3).

What is the joy of heaven? Listen, we could have all the beauties of a New Heaven and New Earth, with creation remade and resurrected bodies, but none of that would be satisfying without *him*. What is the joy of heaven? Seeing God the Father, Son, and Spirit: "No longer will there be anything accursed, but the throne of God and of the Lamb will be in it, and his servants will worship him. They will see his face, and his name will be on their foreheads" (Revelation 22:3–4).

Think of it, we will see the Lamb, his very face. Why is Jesus called the "Lamb" here? Because he's the One who was slain, "who takes away the sin of the world!" (John 1:29). We will see him forever as the One who took away all our sin, who cleared the path to this love feast, who bought us and brought us to himself for our eternal joy. We will never forget that; it will be the focus of our song and work forever.

Have you ever noticed how hungry our eyes are? Always looking, searching for something more and never satisfied: "The eye is not satisfied with seeing, nor the ear filled with hearing" (Ecclesiastes 1:8). The Lord has made our eyes and ears in that way. He's made us to want to see him, to behold him, and heaven will be heaven simply because *we will see him*! Nothing will get in the way of our vision of him; he won't let that happen.

The Good Shepherd

"For the Lamb in the midst of the throne will be their shepherd, and he will guide them to springs of living water" (Revelation 7:17). Remember who he is: He's the Good Shepherd whose eye is always on his sheep . . . and not just sheep in general, but each one of us individually. He will watch over you always and will guide you forever as the strong, courageous, and loving Shepherd he is. "I am the good shepherd. The good shepherd lays down his life for the sheep" (John 10:11 NIV). This is who he is and what he has done. When he calls himself "good," he doesn't just mean that he's morally good, which of course he is. He means that he's the strongest, most loving shepherd in the field. He's using a word that has been used to mean courageous or excellent. He's saying that he's our Heroic Shepherd.[8] Jesus, the one our eyes will see, is the hero whose shadow we've seen hundreds of times in good books or movies. He's Aragorn, who is willing to fight to the death to save the world of man from the evil Sauron in Tolkien's *The Lord of the Rings*. He's Aslan, who went to the stone table to ransom Edmund from the White Witch in C. S. Lewis's *The Lion, the Witch, and the Wardrobe*. He's every hero who ever faced down death to rescue his beloved. He's our Good Shepherd: "He will tend his flock like a shepherd; he will gather the lambs in his arms; he will carry them in his bosom, and gently lead those that are with young" (Isaiah 40:11).

What precious words Isaiah uses to describe our Shepherd. He's not like some parents who drag their unruly kids along, nor is he a shepherd who beats his sheep to force them to get going. No. He's the one who picks us up and carries us. He gently leads those of us who can't quite keep up. This is the One we've been dying (literally) to see—a strong, courageous, gentle shepherd. This is the face that will so enrapture us, it will instantaneously transform us: "We know that when Christ appears, we shall be like him, for we shall see him as he is" (1 John 3:2 NIV).

This is the face that David, the courageous shepherd, loved and longed to see. "The Lord is my shepherd; I shall not want," he said (Psalm 23:1). David knew that because it was the Lord who was responsible to guard, guide, and lead him, he would never have any true needs. We're very accustomed to reading that psalm and believing, by faith, that that is what the Lord is doing for us now. But I want you now to reread it and think about it in light of the New Jerusalem. Although it is certainly true now, the truth of it now is only a shadow of the truth of it in the age to come:

> The Lord is my shepherd; I shall not want [there, in
> the age to come]
> He makes me lie down in green pastures [in the New
> Jerusalem]
> He leads me beside still waters [of the River of the
> Water of Life]
> He restores my soul [feeding me from the Tree of Life]
> He leads me in paths of righteousness
> for his name's sake [so that I will worship him
> forever].
>
> Psalm 23:1–3

Think about this: looking into that throne room where the Ancient of Days is sitting, and seeing a Lamb who is also your valiant Shepherd. What are his promises to you? Your entire existence from that moment on and forever will be completely free from any want. You'll never again say, "I wish I had . . ." You will be completely satisfied in him. *Completely.* He will say to you, "Here, dear one, lie down in these rich pastures and rest with me for a time. Let me get you a drink that will quench your thirst and restore you to the *you* I always meant for you to be. Here are paths for you to walk in, and they will lead you into more and more righteousness. Yes, I know you love me. Your joy in my name is all the world to me."

Meeting Him Face-to-Face

In Exodus 33, Moses asked that he might have the privilege of seeing God's glory. The Lord granted his request partially but also said,

> "You cannot see my face, for man shall not see me and live." And the Lord said, "Behold, there is a place by me where you shall stand on the rock, and while my glory passes by I will put you in a cleft of the rock, and I will cover you with my hand until I have passed by. Then I will take away my hand, and you shall see my back, but my face shall not be seen."
>
> vv. 20–23

The Lord loved Moses and communed with him as with a dear friend. But not even Moses was able to stand face-to-face with God in his glory. To do so would mean instantaneous annihilation, even for Moses. No one could see God's face and live. *But you will.* Here's the promise: "[His servants] will see his face" (Revelation 22:4). That means you. And me. And everyone who has been loved by him and longed to see him (1 John 3:2), everyone who has ever whimpered out a song of thanksgiving or love for their Shepherd. We will do what no one in the history of the world has ever done: stand before the Lord in our physical bodies (though resurrected to be strong enough to face that light) and see his face (Revelation 22:4). That sight will permanently eclipse every item on your bucket list. Not even our tears of joy will obscure that sight, for God will wipe away every tear from our eyes (Revelation 7:17).

You are welcomed. You are beloved. You are on the inside. You now have eyes that will eventually see everything you have ever longed to see. Like Job, in your flesh you *will* see God: "And after my skin has been thus destroyed, yet in my flesh I shall see God, whom I shall see for myself, and my eyes shall behold, and not another. My heart faints within me!" (Job 19:26–27).

169

Is your heart fainting for joy within you? Me too. This might be a good time to stop reading and thank God for his promise to you.

The Best Promise in the Whole Bible

There are thousands of beautiful promises in the Bible, but the best one of all is this: "And you shall be my people, and I will be your God" (Jeremiah 30:22). How is it that we are not only pardoned and adopted now, but we will be forever? How is it that the One who sees us as we really are, before whom nothing is hidden, can say, "You are mine now and I will be yours forever"?

His declaration over you is this right now: "I will show my love to the one I called 'Not my loved one.' I will say to those called 'Not my people,' 'You are my people'; and they will say, 'You are my God.'" (Hosea 2:23 NIV). And this will be his declaration over you forever. You are his. He is yours. Forever. His promise is, "I will make my dwelling among them and walk among them, and I will be their God, and they shall be my people" (2 Corinthians 6:16).

His name is on our foreheads; we have already been sealed as his "protected property"[9] throughout all of our turmoil and trials. This is his *No Trespassing* sign posted in the sight of any enemy who might try to get in the way of our meeting with him. I suppose when the Lord posts a *No Trespassing* sign anywhere, it gets obeyed.

We are his people. He is our God.

May we strive to live in the light of that declaration every time our longings for something more whine at us or demand attention or whenever we look at the lives of others in envy. We are his. We belong to him and he belongs to us. We don't need to worry that we'll never have lived a life we can take pride in.

170

We no longer need to fight for our rights or despair because nothing ever seems to turn out the way we hope it will. We are his. He is ours. Forever. And on that day, when we finally awaken from the sleep of this earth we'll jump around and sing and hug everyone we see. And then we'll fall down and worship him for thousands of years, and it will seem like nothing in our eyes.

Only for the Thirsty

What prerequisite, what credentials will you need to present to attain that thirst-satisfying drink? What sort of ID is required? None. Just your thirst. "Only those aware of their deep thirst, which God alone can quench by grace, will taste the water of life."[10] Are you thirsty? Then come and drink. Are you hungry? Come and dine. You'll never be hungry again. You'll never again wish that you could have or experience something that would make you think you're really a person of worth. You'll never wonder why so-and-so gets to do such-and-such while you just watch life pass you by. Everything that would make heaven *heaven* will be there, and all for you to freely take. Come and dine and drink and dance and gaze upon him and hear him say to you, "You are mine. I am yours. Forever." Deeply satisfying words.

─────── FIXING OUR EYES ON HOME ───────

1. "For as the new heavens and the new earth that I make shall remain before me, says the Lord, so shall your offspring and your name remain" (Isaiah 66:22). Respond.
2. The psalmist wrote that as the thirsty deer, "My soul thirsts for God, for the living God. When shall I come and appear before God?" (Psalm 42:2).

a. What are you thirsty for? Sometimes you can figure this out by asking questions of yourself such as, "What am I afraid of?" "What would make my life worth living?" "What makes me really happy or sad or depressed?"

b. Do you long to come and appear before God? Why or why not? Would you say that you feel confident in his presence?

3. Read Jeremiah 30:21–22 and respond.

4. Jeremiah 31:33–34 is reiterated in Hebrews 8:10–12. What are the promises given to us in these passages? Why is it encouraging that we will all "know the Lord," even the least among us? How does this relate to the New Earth, where we will live in his presence eternally?

5. Have you ever been envious when you hear of others' vacations or experiences? How does the promise of Home help you to fight against those feelings?

6. Summarize what you've learned in this chapter in four or five sentences.

10

Gazing Through the Thin Places

The church on earth is the doorstep of the church in heaven. No, it isn't heaven on earth . . . it is still located here on this dark planet, with its roots in dirty soil, yet it is the shining portal through which we catch glimmers of golden light, hear whispers of the angelic choir's refrains, and smell the aroma of baking bread. It is here that we feel the water of life on our skin and taste the bread and wine sent to sustain us from the table at the Lamb's wedding feast. And it is here that we listen to the King who is sitting on his throne, speaking words of welcome and comfort to us: "I am yours. You are mine. Forever." Here he declares his kingdom rule and marshals his forces out to do the work in this world that will ultimately unite our work here with our work there. His kingdom will come; all his desires will be done, on earth as they are in heaven. In the meantime, it is through the church that we are reminded that he provides all our needs, pardons all our sins, and protects all of us all our days.

Most of us don't think about church in this way. We don't see it as the doorstep of heaven. Many Christians think that church is sort of a social club: a place where you go to visit with your friends and hear an uplifting message. Some view it as a service organization, a place where community organizers get us fired up to do good in our neighborhoods. Others think of it as their weekly duty: They put in their time on Sunday so that God is obligated to give them the wage of a pleasant life during the rest of the week. And still others use it as penance. They know they're in debt to a holy God, so they go to church to make up for all the bad stuff they've done through the week. It's their time of self-atonement. And far too many parents look at it as a way to keep their children off drugs and out of gangs—in kind of the same way they expect youth sports to accomplish that. How would our relationship to church change if we viewed it as the foyer of heaven?

Most churches have a foyer or a lobby. It's the place where people catch up with one another and gather information about what will be happening in the sanctuary. Everyone knows that what happens in the foyer is different from what happens in the sanctuary. The foyer isn't serious . . . it isn't holy; it's just a lobby. But it is also the door to the holy. And we all know it. When we walk through those doors—whether we have a free-flowing worship service or a very liturgical one—the moment we leave the foyer and step into the sanctuary proper, our attitude changes, or at least it should. We calm down a bit. We start thinking of what will come. We begin to focus on realities unseen. We know we're stepping into another realm, the foyer of heaven.

The Thin Places

You may not be familiar with it, but the idea of "thin places" is well known in Celtic spirituality. Thin places "are locales where the distance between heaven and earth collapses and we're able to catch glimpses of the divine, or the transcendent."[1] The Celts believed that heaven and earth were only three feet apart, "but in thin places that distance is even shorter."[2]

Without making too much of what is not a strictly biblical construct, I think it's allowable for us to use our imaginations and stretch the borders of the ways we normally think about the relationship between the church and the world to come.

The church, when it's functioning as it should be, should almost enable us to experience the world to come; it should make the division between here and there nearly transparent. That's not to say that every moment of every time we gather together as a church is to be a rapturous experience of the New Earth; rather, that the church should be a place where we get glimpses, whiffs, whispers of it from time to time.

In saying this about the church, I'm not saying that the church building *itself* is a portal, although there are some places where, when you walk in, you find yourself more disconnected from what we might call the "thick places" outside. The mall is certainly a thick place, isn't it? On the other hand, there is a church property in San Diego that I have visited on several occasions simply because it feels different. I know that sounds weird, and yet I can't deny the experience. Theologian N. T. Wright recognizes that there are "such things as places sanctified by long usage for prayer and worship, places where, often without being able to explain it, people of all sorts find that prayer is more natural, that God can be known and felt more readily."[3] I'm willing to admit that maybe the place feels "thin" to me because of my expectations when I go there. And yet . . .

Of course, I don't mean to imply that there are some places where God is and other places where he is not, since he is so obviously everywhere, as David confessed:

Where shall I go from your Spirit?
Or where shall I flee from your presence?

If I ascend to heaven, you are there!
If I make my bed in Sheol, you are there!
Psalm 139:7–8

Still, I have gathered in prayer with a group of believers who have come in faith with the specific intent of being with the Lord, of remembering that we are his and he is ours, of experiencing now in part what we will know in full on the New Earth. There have been times when I have experienced a holy presence that enveloped everyone in the room, and everyone knew that something had happened. The Lord calls us to worship him together as his body, the church, and to expect him to be there, sometimes more palpably than others. The church, being his body and the place where he has promised to dwell with us, would by its very nature be a place where he would be nearest to us . . . if we can use that sort of spatial language.

The Definitive "Thin Place"

Of course, Jesus himself is the primary example of a "thin place." It was through him, through the joining of his person with our earthy flesh and blood that he literally brought heaven down to dwell on the earth. Certainly his miraculous transfiguration, where he was suffused with the white light of heaven and spoke with men who already inhabited Paradise (Moses and Elijah), was a thin place (Matthew 17). We have to assume that he could have bridged this gap at any time, stepping into the world to come as it pleased him and as he did at his ascension.

It is also through him that the invisible God is seen on earth. "No one has ever seen God," John said, but "the only God, who is at the Father's side, he has made him known" (John 1:18). Or as Eugene Peterson writes, Jesus "has made [God] plain as day."[4] Jesus said that anyone who had seen him had seen the Father (John 14:9) and that "no one comes to the Father except *through*" him (John 14:6). He is the kingdom already arrived on earth (Luke 17:21), a foretaste of what life and relationship will be like when we cross over. We will find our way to God's throne in the New Jerusalem because his flesh and the curtain in the Old Jerusalem were torn open, thereby ending the separation between holy God and sinful man. And it was through him that heaven and earth were finally reconciled: "For in him all the fullness of God was pleased to dwell, and through him to reconcile *to himself all things, whether on earth or in heaven, making peace by the blood of his cross*" (Colossians 1:19–20).

Where once there was enmity between earth and heaven that kept us apart, now, by the blood of his cross, we are reconciled. In a word, things between God and man have been made right. The door to Home has been opened. He himself is the key, the lock, the threshold, and the door itself. He has made us one with heaven. The church on earth and the church in heaven are one in him and will be completely one for us all to see on that day.

But it's important to note that his work is for the church, of which he is the head and we are the body. God has put "all things under his feet and gave him as head over all things to the church, which is his body" (Ephesians 1:22–23). If Jesus is the ultimate connection, the fundamental thin place between heaven and earth, between head and body, it is certain that he stands in the church and for the church, connecting us to realities beyond these.

When Jesus ascended into heaven, he sent his Spirit upon his people, the people who would ultimately be known as the church.

> From Pentecost onward, *the church was to be the thin place of the world*. . . . To put it differently, in the time after the ascension of Jesus and the descent of the Holy Spirit, God has chosen to make himself known most of all through the church . . . in a very real sense, the church is to be the world's preeminent thin place.[5]

Jesus has promised to be with his people, the church, of which he is the "firstborn," in very specific ways. He has promised to be with us when we gather (Matthew 18:20), to be with us in mission (Matthew 28:20), and to be with us when we worship (Hebrews 2:12). Any way that he is with us by his Spirit, and especially with us where we gather together collectively in his name, certainly has to be a thin place, a place where this world and the world to come are as near to unity as is possible here.

So, if the church is in fact a thin place, a portal, the foyer of heaven, then it makes sense that we welcome babies and bury our dead there. It is also right that it should be the place where all Christian marriages are performed, since our marriages are merely shadows of the marriage to come. Everything that has been traditionally part of the function of the church tells of its proximity to heaven. If the church is the thin place near to heaven through the work of Jesus its Lord, then, of course, every significant event in our lives should be celebrated there. And the dead who have gone before us to Paradise should be remembered there, which of course is why graveyards are often properly placed near churches.

The Sacraments

But there are other significant events in the church that speak loudly of the world to come. They are the preaching of the Word of Christ and the sacraments, those ancient rites without which the church becomes nothing more than an impotent civic organization. The sacraments are the very heartbeat of the church and are "one of the points where heaven and earth overlap and interlock."[6] The French reformer John Calvin wrote, "In this sense the preaching of the gospel is called the kingdom of heaven, and the sacraments may be called the gate of heaven, because they admit us into the presence of God."[7]

178

There has been much discussion in the church about whether the bread and wine in the Lord's Supper are actually his body and blood or whether they are simply meant to represent or remind us of it. Even if one holds to the remembrance view, I don't think it is beyond the bounds to say that they might be thought of as a meal sent to us through Christ, the One whose body was broken and whose blood was spilled, from the table where we will celebrate our marriage and his sacrifice for us at Home. In our eating and drinking we are participating in "the blood of Christ" and "the body of Christ" as Paul wrote (1 Corinthians 10:16), and in doing so, "we anticipate the heavenly marriage-feast: *the symbols of creation, bread and wine, are shot through with heaven, with God's dimension, with the life and love of the Lamb.*"[8]

It's more than just a meal to remember. Perhaps we should think of it as food infused with heaven's life, sent to nourish us from the world to come, food that we will enjoy again in the New Earth. The Communion service surely should be thought of as a thin place. Aren't we nearer Home there than we are anywhere else?

The other sacrament that we celebrate is baptism, and again, there has been much argument and disagreement in the church about the proper mode and meaning of baptism. Whatever we think about baptizing infants or whether baptism demands immersion, we can say that this strange rite, even because of its innate strangeness, speaks to us of a world different from this one. That baptism is a thin place is made plain first of all by the fact that at Jesus' baptism, "the heavens were opened" (Luke 3:21; see also Acts 8:39). Of course, that's not to say that every time someone is baptized the heavens open in that same way, but we do have to say that this sacrament, like the Lord's Supper, is one of those places where heaven is especially near. Could we say that the water might be thought of as a foretaste of the water of life? Is it merely coincidental that water is in both places?

We are to take hope in the sacraments and not view them as "ho-hum." They bring us nearer to our heavenly home, though perhaps only for a moment. They speak to us of invisible heavenly realities, making them visible to our eyes, accessible to our senses. Here we see and hear, taste, smell, and touch. Here we are commanded to do what we are otherwise commanded not to do: use earthly substances to remind us of heavenly realities. We use something common here on earth to connect us with the uncommon, to remind us of what—or rather who—awaits us in heaven as we look forward to our eternal home.

As I have struggled through this year of loss, the sacraments, especially the Lord's Supper, have been the food that has strengthened my soul. In the same way that a soldier needs rations on the battlefield, or better yet, chocolates sent from home, I have desperately needed food sent from my eternal Home to refresh, revive, and strengthen me.

The Word of Christ

In the sacraments, the Word is present, speaking to us and drawing us toward the world that is to come. So also, in the preached Word, he is present, planting, and growing our faith. (See Romans 10:17.) Thundering out from the throne in the New Jerusalem we will hear these words:

> "Behold, the dwelling place of God is with man. He will dwell with them, and they will be his people, and God himself will be with them as their God. He will wipe away every tear from their eyes, and death shall be no more, neither shall there be mourning, nor crying, nor pain anymore, for the former things have passed away."

And he who was seated on the throne said, "Behold, I am making all things new." Also he said, "Write this down, for these words are trustworthy and true." And he said to me, "It is done! I am the Alpha and the Omega, the beginning and the end. To the thirsty I will give from the spring of the water of life without payment. The one who conquers will have this heritage, and I will be his God and he will be my son."

Revelation 21:3–7

These are the words we will hear there, and they should be the words we hear every Sunday. The church's Lord is speaking through the thin place into the hearts of his people. He's assuring us that a new reality is coming, a reality where he declares that he is with us and we are with him, where all the former things are passed away and he has made all things new. Are you thirsty? Come and drink from the "spring of the water of life without payment." This is the good news. The Alpha and Omega's work is, as he said, finished (John 19:30)! Oh, how we need to hear this voice from heaven every week. "In the sermon it is Christ who wants to visit us and wants to be himself our heavenly joy."[9] Jesus visits us through the good Word preached to us. His home is open to all who are thirsty, to all who are willing to come. But to those who refuse his gracious invitation, there awaits an eternity as terrible as heaven will be blessed.

In the sermon we also hear the call to welcome and love our neighbor, a call to plant his kingdom here on earth even while we await it from heaven. (More on this in chapter 11.)

Prayer

One of the primary signs that the church is heaven's foyer is that it's a place where we pray. It's the place where his ear and our hearts are attuned to each other. His people are gathered.

He is there listening. For some of us it may be the only time we are quiet and speak to him all week. It is right that we are led in prayer here, for Jesus himself said that his house would be a place of prayer.

Thieves who plundered the worshipers had overrun the temple in Jerusalem. Jesus, the One who knew what the temple was to have prefigured, was outraged. "Is it not written," he asked, "'My house shall be called a house of prayer for all the nations?' But you have made it a den of robbers" (Mark 11:17). "A house of prayer for all the nations"—that's a thin place for sure—a place where all sorts of people can gather together in prayer to him, and a place where he has promised to listen. Since prayer is simply conversing with God, we will pray in the New Earth. Not, of course, as confession of sin or prayer to be relieved from some difficulty, but certainly in thanksgiving and perhaps also as we go forth to reign with Christ and ask for wisdom in how to do so.

Perhaps there will be days when we are considering the best choice, the one that will most glorify our Father, between exploring underwater caves, visiting the Horsehead Nebula, or taking a class where Paul will be sharing his testimony, and we can pray knowing that he will speak to us and guide us into the right pursuit. Of course, since we'll have all eternity to do whatever our hearts may desire, we won't worry there at all about whether or not we're going to lose a special opportunity. Still, I do think we will pray both in Paradise and on the New Earth as well, and we will certainly spend time speaking with the Lord and trying to learn words that properly express our love for him.

Singing

One of my favorite thin places is when we gather to praise the Lord through song. Like everything else of deep import, we all have our opinions about what form of worship is most God-glorifying. Personally, I'm not terribly concerned about the tempo or even the instruments used. I am, however, very concerned that we sing the same sorts of things here that we will sing in the world to come. I'm fairly certain that we won't be singing about ourselves or about our determination to do more and try harder. Worship there will be all about the Father and his Son, just as worship here should be.

Because Revelation is a thin-places book, a place where the curtain that separates heaven and earth is nearly transparent, we would expect to find a lot of singing there. And, of course, we do. What do we hear them singing?

Praise to the Lord God Almighty:

> Holy, holy, holy, is the Lord God Almighty,
> who was and is and is to come!
> Revelation 4:8

> Great and amazing are your deeds, O Lord God the
>   Almighty!
> Just and true are your ways, O King of the nations!
> Who will not fear, O Lord, and glorify your name?
> For you alone are holy.
> All nations will come and worship you,
> for your righteous acts have been revealed.
> Revelation 15:3–4

> Hallelujah!
> For the Lord our God
> the Almighty reigns.
> Let us rejoice and exult
> and give him the glory,
> for the marriage of the Lamb has come,
> and his Bride has made herself ready;

it was granted her to clothe herself
with fine linen, bright and pure.

Revelation 19:6–8

Praise to Our Creator:

Worthy are you, our Lord and God,
to receive glory and honor and power,
for you created all things,
and by your will they existed and were created.

Revelation 4:11

Worship of the Lamb:

Worthy are you to take the scroll
and to open its seals,
for you were slain, and by your blood you ransomed
people for God
from every tribe and language and people and nation,
and you have made them a kingdom and priests to our
God,
and they shall reign on the earth.

Revelation 5:9–10

Worthy is the Lamb who was slain,
to receive power and wealth and wisdom and might
and honor and glory and blessing! . . .
To him who sits on the throne and to the Lamb
be blessing and honor and glory and might forever and
ever! . . .
Amen!

Revelation 5:12–14

Salvation belongs to our God who sits on the throne, and to
the Lamb! . . . Amen! Blessing and glory and wisdom and
thanksgiving and honor and power and might be to our God
forever and ever! Amen.

Revelation 7:10, 12

Who Is Serving Whom?

I think that for most of my life as a Christian, I've always thought about church as one of the primary places where I go to serve God. I think about the things that I do there—volunteering in ministries, giving my offerings, praying, and singing—as ways to serve God. Church has been for me mostly about my working for God.

But . . . if church really is a thin place, then perhaps I need to reorient myself to think about it in a different way. Home is the place where our Father and Husband have done all the hard work. Therefore, perhaps we should think about church as being the place where he serves us. He's given himself for us, has brought us to himself and overcome by his work *all* our enemies and *every* impediment to our being there with him. So our gathering together in church ought to primarily be the place where we remember what he's done and let him speak to us about his grace and forgiveness again.

Most Protestants are uncomfortable with the thought of absolution. They're not used to hearing anyone stand in the place of God and say, "You are forgiven." But isn't that really the message that the Lord speaks to his bride? Shouldn't we hear that comforting message every week, while we eat food from the coming feast and watch as others are bathed in the water from the River of Life?

As I've confessed throughout this book, this has been a very difficult year for me, especially in church. If I had thought that the main reason I needed to go to church was so that I could "do my duty," I wonder if I would have quit. But because I knew that I needed nourishment from him, that I needed to hear that I was forgiven and hear the Word of Christ spoken into my heart, I kept attending. As a matter of fact, I've been attending two churches for months now. . . . Just because I'm that needy.

Do we serve in church? Yes, of course. But our service is primarily for our neighbor because our neighbor needs our good

185

works. God doesn't. So, yes, I do serve in church, but that's not the reason I go. I have to go because I need the One who washes feet, the One who was crushed and deserted for my unbelief, the One who was raised victoriously and who reigns sovereignly to speak to me. And I need him to feed me bread and wine from his table. Otherwise, I'll simply die spiritually.

I know that sometimes it's hard to make it to church every week and that all sorts of events and obligations demand our allegiance on that day, especially since the youth sports movement has claimed Sunday as its own. But there is something "thin place" about Sunday . . . the day of the new beginning, begun at the first Easter. We would do well to remember that in the ancient Near East it was just as difficult for believers to worship on that day, probably even more so, since for them, Sunday functioned like our Mondays do.[10] Days of the week matter, and the eighth day, the day of the resurrection, is a day sent to us as a gift for our nourishment, encouragement, and edification.

Dietrich Bonhoeffer, German pastor and martyr to the Nazi regime, once preached:

> He is close to us in his church, in his Word, in his sacrament, in love among the brethren. Here he comforts us who are abandoned; here he soothes our homesickness ever anew; here he takes us who are estranged from God, who are in barren, empty places, who don't know the way, who are alone, and makes us joyful in his Christly presence. Joy in the sermon, joy in the sacraments, joy in brothers and sisters—that is the joy of the believing church in its unseen, heavenly Lord.[11]

I think there are places where the experience of the world to come is more common, more natural, nearer. If you will give me the benefit of the doubt that there is such a thing as a "thin place," then I think it's obvious that church is the primary one. Of course, there are people who will push back and say that they experience God in nature . . . and I do, too. And that's not without biblical support (Psalm 19:1). But I don't think that's the main place where the Lord has promised to speak to us. The psalmist knew that the heavens declare God's handiwork, but declaring God's handiwork by looking at the stars and by receiving bread from the Lord's Table are worlds apart. Yes, I can see his power as I gaze down into the Grand Canyon, but nothing—*and I mean nothing!*—is more amazing than watching water speak of a soul's cleansing, partaking of bread and wine from a brother's hand, or hearing a word of forgiveness from God's mouth through his servant.

Don't you think it's interesting that there are specific places where we speak to, sing about, and hear from unseen realities, as though it were the most normal thing in the world? I mean, every day most of us eat bread and wash ourselves with water as though they were the most common and natural events in life. But then we get to Sunday, and all of a sudden, presto! They change. They have power. They mean something.

And then, in the power of God's Spirit, each one of us becomes a portable thin place; a portal, a conduit of heaven to our neighbor. "God's purpose, it seems, was for all the world to be a thin place, a place where human beings experienced intimate and immediate fellowship with him."[12] We'll think more about this in the next chapter, but for now, ask the Lord to open your eyes to the purpose and power of the church.

FIXING OUR EYES ON HOME

1. C. S. Lewis wrote about the thin places in an interesting way. He said, "The blackout [between earth and heaven] is not quite complete. There are chinks. At times the daily scene looks big with its secret."[13] What do you suppose

Lewis meant by "chinks"? Does the daily scene look big with its secret? Are you beginning to see the realities hidden by the blackout curtain? Respond.

2. Have you ever heard of the concept of thin places? Have you thought about it? If so, how?

3. Have you ever thought about church as being a place where though we are presently still moored to this reality, we can see glimpses of the one to come? Do you think church functions as a foyer for heaven? Why or why not?

4. What importance do you assign to the sacraments? Have you ever considered them as part of your true Home? Why or why not?

5. What importance do you assign to the preached Word? Do you ever think about it as the Word of the King from his throne? Why or why not?

6. Summarize what you've learned in this chapter in four or five sentences.

11

Hurrying His Return

In light of the fact that our lives are spent, at least in part, in significant suffering, and because it seems as though the work we try to accomplish for the Lord is so difficult, and at times even futile, it is very tempting to simply give up and say, "Let us eat, drink and be merry, for tomorrow we die." (See 1 Corinthians 15:32.) I think this hopelessness and apathy is what the Lord meant when he cautioned, "Because lawlessness will be increased, the love of many will grow cold" (Matthew 24:12). When churches implode, when our children thumb their noses at our faith, when dear friends misunderstand, deceive, or desert, when the pain just never seems to end, it's doubly hard to keep the fire of faith and love burning. The bent of our hearts is to simply quit. It's hard to continue working when it seems as though there is a tsunami of evil breaking over our heads, when it seems like everyone we know is resigning themselves to "going with the flow," even though the flow appears to be headed off a cliff. Every time I hear that a friend has left the faith or stopped attending church, it becomes more and more challenging for me to persevere. Sometimes I have wondered whether it's worth it or not.

And then, if we add into this harmful brew our typical assumptions about heaven, especially the belief that the world is wildly careering toward an end where everything will be destroyed and all our work will be burned up, it's easy to throw in the towel and say, "What's the point?" I mean, if everything is destined for destruction, including even the good that we do, then why bother? Why not just enjoy ourselves as best we can, try to live peaceable, quiet lives, and then hold on till the end? If the work we do in faith now will ultimately be obliterated, if it won't somehow live on after us and get transferred into eternity, then let's just forget about suffering for the cause and enjoy ourselves today.

Paul's Ultimate Hope

Paul had heard these same questions from the church at Corinth, but also surely from his own heart as he faced suffering and setbacks. "What do I gain if, humanly speaking, I fought with beasts at Ephesus? If the dead are not raised, 'Let us eat and drink, for tomorrow we die'" (1 Corinthians 15:32). Rather than trying to cheer himself up with be-happy affirmations, Paul squarely faced his approaching death and longed for his ultimate resurrection.

> For we do not want you to be unaware, brothers, of the affliction we experienced in Asia. For we were so utterly burdened beyond our strength that we despaired of life itself. Indeed, we felt that we had received the sentence of death. *But that was to make us rely not on ourselves but on God who raises the dead.*
>
> 2 Corinthians 1:8–9

Paul's answer to the trouble and suffering he faced, to the continual war with his brothers and seeming loss of ground in

190

so many areas, to the "sentence of death" he felt within himself, was his hope in the resurrection of the dead. He wasn't working to prolong his life here on earth. He knew death was coming, but he also knew that death wouldn't mean his ultimate demise. He was counting on the fact that this life wasn't all there was, that his mortality would eventually be overcome in immortality, that the work he was doing here, though filled with sorrow and setbacks, was not in vain. So he spoke not only to the Corinthians but also to us, "Therefore, my beloved brothers [and sisters], be steadfast, immovable, always abounding in the work of the Lord, knowing that in the Lord your labor is not in vain" (1 Corinthians 15:58).

Why would Paul speak of the resurrection when considering the futility of this life? What does the resurrection have to do with our life here? Why be immovable and steadfast? Additionally, how could he say that his work was "not in vain"? Didn't he know that the end of all things meant the end of his work also? Wouldn't that end make his labors the very definition of futility? Paul knew that though the world would be destroyed and days were coming when even fellow believers would vilify him, he should continue to labor on until he finally faced martyrdom in Rome. Why? Because of the resurrection of the dead.

Silencing Death's Lies

Paul's answer to futility and impending death is that we have a hope that reaches past this life of loss and into a reality of gain to come. This isn't all there is. Death won't have the final word. And so we are able to live our lives today in freedom from the grave's lie of failure and loss. Because of the resurrection we are no longer afraid to die. So "Christians overwhelm every barrier: not fearing death, they fear nothing at all."[1] After all, if we have already lost our life to gain Christ's (Matthew 10:39), what do

191

we have left to lose? And if he has done the same, given his life in order to capture ours, and if he promises us that we will live with him forever, wild self-sacrifice is our only logical option. Christians are the only people who believe that good exists beyond the loss of good—and even life—that we experience here.

Those Coptic Christians who were martyred by Islamic terrorists in 2015 had already given their lives over to the Savior. They knew that they would have whole bodies again . . . stronger and more alive than they had ever been before. They knew that their number would be added to those martyred saints in Paradise who are given white robes to wear and told to "rest a little longer" (Revelation 6:10–11). Terrorists won't have the final say, no matter how much blood they demand.

The resurrection of Jesus is the proof that our final resurrection is sure:

> For if we have been united with him in a death like his, we shall certainly be united with him in a resurrection like his. . . . Now if we have died with Christ, we believe that we will also live with him. . . . Death no longer has dominion over [us].
>
> Romans 6:5, 8–9

The resurrection furnishes us with hope to endure everything the world and the enemy throws at us. So it follows that the more we let the truth of the resurrection and our true Home slip from our daily thought, the more difficult it will be to hold on to hope and its outcome, perseverance: "Not only that, but we rejoice in our sufferings, knowing that suffering produces endurance, and endurance produces character, and character produces hope, and hope does not put us to shame" (Romans 5:3–5).

Spending time as we have, considering our life to come, will build a heart-transforming hope that will spur us on to love and good works, even when we fail, even when we are unappreciated or persecuted. Will we have to face great peril or staggering loss?

Perhaps. But grace awaits. Home beckons. The resurrection is sure. Death will die. Love will win.

Who shall separate us from the love of Christ? Shall tribulation, or distress, or persecution, or famine, or nakedness, or danger, or sword? As it is written,

> "For your sake we are being killed all the day long;
> we are regarded as sheep to be slaughtered."

No, in all these things we are more than conquerors through him who loved us. For I am sure that neither death nor life, nor angels nor rulers, nor things present nor things to come, nor powers, nor height nor depth, nor anything else in all creation, will be able to separate us from the love of God in Christ Jesus our Lord.

Romans 8:35–39

Imagine the joy of the Coptic martyrs when they awakened in the company of the saints who welcomed them to their new Home, a true Paradise of rest and joy, and the final vindication of a life that appeared wasted, though was anything but. They may have looked like fools who fought bravely and lost shamefully. But, as Paul reassures us, *here* is not all there is. The terrorist sword may have severed their heads from their bodies, but nothing could ever sever their souls from "the love of God in Christ Jesus our Lord."

Eternal Rewards

Our resurrection is not the only incentive we have to live zealously, though. We have been given the motivation of eternal rewards. While it is true that we are counted righteous and enter into heaven only by faith in the work of Jesus Christ, we are also promised rewards for our work. Our work, whether outwardly successful or not, whether appearing to be something great or not, when offered to him will earn rewards for us. Even the ordinary vocation of our lives lived in faith and charity, offered in weakness, is pleasing to him and will reap blessings for us. In the midst of all of our suffering, we can say, *I know that he sees what I'm trying to do here and that he will graciously accept my offering as a sacrifice well pleasing to him.* The sermon written to the suffering church of the Hebrews said, "Do not neglect to do good and to share what you have, for such sacrifices are pleasing to God" (Hebrews 13:16).

As someone who firmly believes that we can't earn any merit from God, I admit that the thought of earning a reward for my work creates some tension within me. I'm not saying (and neither would Paul, I'm quite sure) that we can earn salvation by our acts of love for our neighbor. But I am saying (with Paul) that the reward we earn as Christians is given to us as a gift by his grace, "knowing that whatever good anyone does, this he will receive back from the Lord" (Ephesians 6:8). Through our actions in this life, we are "storing up treasure for [ourselves] as a good foundation for the future" (1 Timothy 6:19).

"For we must all appear before the judgment seat of Christ, so that each one may receive what is due for what he has done in the body, whether good or evil" (2 Corinthians 5:10). Christians will not stand before God's bar of judgment as criminals, for we have been declared not guilty and are no longer condemned (Romans 8:1). But we will stand before Christ's judgment seat, where, as his beloved bride, we will receive rewards for the work we have done out of love for his grace to us. "Behold, I am coming quickly," the Lord has lovingly promised, "and My reward *is* with Me, to render to every man according to what he has done" (Revelation 22:12 NASB). Jesus' words at the end of John's Revelation should not cause fear for any believer but should rather spur us on to faithful labor for him.

Perhaps one way to think about our heavenly rewards is to change up the paradigm a bit. Rather than thinking about rewards like a grade on a report card, we should think about them in the context of relationship. We know that there is such a thing as a *rewarding* relationship with a friend or spouse. If I seek to be a good wife out of love and genuine desire to bless Phil, I will certainly reap the reward of that work. In doing so, I am not merely trying to amass Brownie points or earn a good Christmas present. I'm not thinking about what I'll get from him at all. But one of the by-products of my faithful love for him will most likely be the blessing and reward of a long and stable marriage. We will both enjoy the reward of a deep and enjoyable friendship. It's obvious that love for others is its own reward, isn't it? Perhaps the rewards that the Lord has for us are like this. They are the reward of relationship and joy in serving our Beloved.

Even so, in saying that there will be rewards in heaven, after everything I've already written about the joys of Home, you might be feeling a bit confused, so let me state this unequivocally: We will *all* be completely, utterly, fully, and unendingly happy and satisfied there no matter what. Period. As theologian J.I. Packer writes, "In heaven there will be no unfulfilled desires."[2]

But having said that, I won't negate the clear teaching of Scripture that rewards are accrued to his children who act in faith and out of love for him.[3] Here is Dr. Packer again:

> There will be different degrees of blessedness and reward in heaven. All will be *blessed up to the limit of what they can receive*, but capacities will vary just as they do in this world. As for rewards . . . two points must be grasped. The first is that when God rewards our works he is crowning his own gifts, for it was *only by grace that those works were done*. The second is that the essence of the reward in each case will be more of what the Christian desires most, namely, *a deepening of his or*

her love-relationship with the Savior, which is the reality to which all the biblical imagery of honorific crowns and robes and feasts is pointing.[4]

You might be wondering, "If heaven is heaven, what difference will rewards make?" After all, if we get God and glory and all things blessed already, why on earth would we want rewards? I think that at the very least we can respond by saying that the Lord has offered them to us as an incentive to live lives of love, and we should want them, even if we can't imagine what would be better than what he has already promised.

Interestingly, John Calvin even proposed that it was by our good works that we "are prepared for receiving the crown of immortality."[5] Perhaps the labors we do here, the striving and failing, the daily pressing out of our love into the lives of our neighbors, the dying to ourselves and our desires, the coming to him in repentance and hearing the word of forgiveness, are the very things that are preparing us to receive the inheritance and crown of immortality he has prepared for us. For he has promised to give us,

> A crown of rejoicing . . . for bringing people to Christ (1 Thessalonians 2:19); a crown of righteousness, for loving His appearing (2 Timothy 4:8); a crown of life, for enduring testing with love for the Lord (James 1:12), and a crown of glory to elders who are faithful to their responsibilities in the church (1 Peter 5:4).[6]

Let us then think of our rewards as bridal tiaras placed upon our heads to wear on our wedding day. As we bow before him, our Savior, who purchased them and us and who made this marriage possible, will gently lay these golden wreaths on our heads. We are his bride and he will clothe and beautify us for our mutual joy. And on that day although we will be radiant, he will be the One everyone will be looking at.

John writes about that day:

Let us rejoice and exult and give him the glory, for the marriage of the Lamb has come, and his Bride has made herself ready; it was granted her to clothe herself with fine linen, bright and pure"—for the fine linen is the righteous deeds of the saints.

Revelation 19:7 8

We will be dressed in some indescribable manner with luminous cloth that will have been woven out of the deeds we have done in faith and our love for Jesus. Our clothing will be fine, bright, and pure only because it has been washed in the blood of the Lamb (Revelation 7:14), for our good deeds are certainly stained with sin and are nothing more than filthy rags (Isaiah 64:6 NIV). How could sinners be clothed in such a way? Only by the grace of God as he works in us "both to will and to work for his good pleasure" (Philippians 2:13). It is his work in us that causes us to want to work and then eventuates in love for our neighbor, in righteous deeds. And the fine linen that we'll be wearing is not made only from our own good works, *but from everyone else's as well, all of our deeds of love clothing one another in shared beauty.*

C. S. Lewis proposes that clothes in heaven "are not a disguise." They are not a way to hide ourselves, as they are here, but rather who we are in our spirits is seen in our beautiful attire. Our "spiritual body lives along each thread and turns them into living organs."[7] Who we are inwardly by his grace—who we have been made to be—will be seen outwardly. And then he will present us to himself, a bride beautified for her husband, in splendor, without spot or wrinkle or any such thing, that she might be holy and without blemish (Ephesians 5:27). Oh . . . and unlike the clothes most of us got married in, these clothes will be oh so comfortable . . . so comfortable, in fact, that we will forget we're even wearing them, except when we happen to glance down at ourselves for a moment . . . which, of course, will eventuate in more and more songs of worship to the One who caused us to be clothed so beautifully.

197

Beautifying Our New Home

As we strive to fight apathy and discouragement, perhaps we should consider that at its foundation, much of what we believe about the work we do here may simply be wrongheaded. As we've already seen, the Lord has promised that we will continue to live here on this earth, in strong, resurrected bodies. And not only that, we are also taught that the work we do here will receive a reward and that our heavenly clothing is made up of the good we have sought by faith to do. We have more than ample incentive to live lives of loving service to our neighbors in that truth alone. But that isn't the only incentive there is.

In the same way that our homes here reflect and express our faith, our work, our loves, and even our personalities, our Home there will do the same. Heaven itself will be beautified by the work we do here. Rather than thinking that all the work we have accomplished here will be for nothing on the last day when the earth as we know it is cleansed by fire, we should understand that the good we do will live on after us, and even be resurrected with us into the New Earth. We are not . . .

> . . . oiling the wheels of a machine that's about to fall over a cliff. You are not restoring a great painting that's shortly going to be thrown on the fire. You are not planting roses in a garden that's about to be dug up for a building site. You are—strange though it may seem, almost as hard to believe as the resurrection itself—accomplishing something which will become, in due course, part of God's new world. Every act of love, gratitude and kindness; every work of art or music inspired by the love of God and delight in the beauty of his creation; every minute spent teaching a severely handicapped child to read or to walk; every act of care and nurture, of comfort and support, for one's fellow human beings, and for that matter one's fellow non-human creatures; and of course every prayer, all Spirit-led teaching, every deed which spreads the gospel, builds up the

church, embraces and embodies holiness rather than corruption, and makes the name of Jesus honoured in the world—all of this will find its way, through the resurrecting power of God, into the new creation which God will one day make. . . . It will last all the way into God's new world. In fact, it will be enhanced there.[8]

You see, the truth is that nothing we do here is in vain. If it were all to vanish away, to be burned or dissolved or annihilated, there would be no point to our work. It would mean that Satan and his scheme to destroy all of God's good creation would have won and the church would have lost. Sure, we might be taken out of this world into a new "heavenly" one, where we would receive rewards, but if he gets to claim this world as his domain to such an extent that God is forced to simply walk away from it and all the work we've done here, then Satan will have won. He will have stolen and so defaced God's good creation that it would no longer be salvageable. And we know that could never happen.

We are working on something that, though we may not see its completion in our lifetime, is being constructed nevertheless. God's kingdom *will* come to this earth. His kingdom is a world without end. "I cannot believe," Charles Spurgeon preached, "in that world being annihilated upon which Jesus was born and lived and died. Surely an earth with a Calvary upon it must last on. Will not the blood of Jesus immortalize it?"[9] This earth and all the good works the church has ever done here—in faith, in weakness, flawed, or glorious—and certainly the work of the Savior whose blood sanctified its ground . . . all of it will live on and beautify our Home to come . . . forever. Those beautiful walls in the New Jerusalem will have names engraved on them . . . perhaps we will be able to look at them and see a vision of the work that made it as glorious as it is. And the thanks we will give to the saint who accomplished the work will be his reward.

Daniel, the Old Testament saint, foresaw a kingdom that would last forever . . . a kingdom that would "never be destroyed," nor "left to another people. . . . It shall stand forever" (Daniel 2:44). He prophesied that to Jesus, the Son of Man, would be given "dominion and glory and a kingdom, that all peoples, nations, and languages should serve him; [for] his dominion is an everlasting dominion, which shall not pass away, and his kingdom one that shall not be destroyed" (Daniel 7:14).

The apostle Paul also foresaw that after the resurrection of the dead, when we will finally be Home with him, the end will come and the kingdom will be delivered to God the Father, who will destroy "every rule and every authority and power" (1 Corinthians 15:24). John proudly declares, "The kingdom of the world has become the kingdom of our Lord and of his Christ, and he shall reign forever and ever" (Revelation 11:15).

When Jesus told Pilate that his "kingdom is not of this world" (John 18:36), he didn't mean the physical earth as he created it, but rather the "world system" or "standards"[10] that are in a constant state of rebellion against him. The Lord rather claimed this earth as his own by placing his stake in it on Calvary. He will overcome all the world's resistance and idolatry: "But the saints of the Most High shall receive the kingdom and possess the kingdom forever, forever and ever" (Daniel 7:18). Jesus and his bride will reign forever and ever together here.

We May Not See the Finished Product . . . Yet

N. T. Wright uses the image of a "stonemason working on part of a great cathedral" to illustrate the belief that the work we do here will not be annihilated when this world's systems are, when the earth itself is cleansed and renewed. It stretches our imagination to consider that the work we're doing now will somehow be of value there. That's why his stonemason image is so helpful. Even though detailed plans have already been drawn up by the architect, and even though all the materials necessary to complete the project have been delivered, it may take years for the cathedral to finally be completed. If he happens to die before he can see how his work will fit into the structure, a specific stonemason may never see how what he has done added to and fit into the edifice when it was completed. In the same way, we Christian stonemasons are not the ones who will bring to completion all the work God has tasked us to do in the world. We are simply one of many builders, and whether we see the completion of our work right now or not, we can be assured that the building he is constructing will stand, and stand forever.

The work we do here matters. Those things we labor at, whether it is merely the changing of a diaper or a tire, the cleaning of a house or a computer, the love of walking with an old friend, or being willing to try to love an enemy, it all matters and it will all . . . in some way . . . be transferred into those beautiful stones that will decorate the walls of the great city. Even kings will bring their glory into it (Revelation 21:24), which may refer to the best that mankind has developed throughout history. Our "contribution to the new Jerusalem should not be downplayed."[11]

Think about it. . . . Won't it be wonderful to talk with Michelangelo and find out what was in his heart as he painted the Sistine Chapel . . . to actually look at, into, and behind his work up close? Might it actually come to life? Or to visit with believing scientists like Galileo or Kepler or philosophers like Pascal or Kant or Kierkegaard . . . and be able to ask them questions and have enough time to really understand what they're talking about? Wouldn't it be wonderful to take a writing class from Tolstoy or Dostoevsky and to sit with Victor Hugo and ask him what made him portray Jean Valjean the way he did? I can hardly wait.

Hurrying His Coming

Further, in his second letter, Peter wrote that it was *because* the world was about to change and a new kingdom was about to be inaugurated that we ought to "live lives of holiness and godliness" (2 Peter 3:11), refusing to give in to apathy and unbelief. In this passage, he says that we are waiting for a coming day, when the "heavens will be set on fire and dissolved, and the heavenly bodies will melt as they burn!" (v. 12). But then he says the most astonishing thing: He writes that we are not only "waiting for" that coming day, but are also "hastening" it by living godly lives:

> Since all these things are thus to be dissolved, what sort of people ought you to be in lives of holiness and godliness, waiting for and *hastening the coming of the day of God,* because of which the heavens will be set on fire and dissolved, and the heavenly bodies will melt as they burn! But according to his promise we are waiting for new heavens and a new earth in which righteousness dwells. Therefore, beloved, since you are waiting for these, be diligent to be found by him without spot or blemish, and at peace.
>
> vv. 11–14

That's an astonishing thought, isn't it? Peter is clearly teaching that we "can advance or hasten the arrival of God's day by living godly lives."[12] Our lives and prayers do matter in the cosmic scheme of things. Otherwise, why are we taught to pray, "Your kingdom come" (Matthew 6:10)? If God is sovereign, and he is, and if the day of Christ's return is fixed eternally, and it is, then why are we told to pray for its arrival or that our godliness can somehow speed his coming? *Simply because God is both sovereign and a God who answers our prayers and responds to our acts of faith.*

We all certainly believe Jesus' words that the mission of the church is to spread the gospel "throughout the whole world as

202

a testimony to all nations, and then the end will come" (Matthew 24:14). So it shouldn't be that much of a stretch for us to believe that somehow, and in some way unfathomable to us, God is using our work, our words, our lives, our prayers, to bring about the events that he has foreordained must happen before the Lord's return. Peter referenced this same idea in the sermon that he preached after the healing of the lame man in Acts 3. There he talked about Jesus, the one whose return we are awaiting, as being held in heaven until certain things . . . things done by human beings . . . are accomplished. He said:

> Repent therefore, and turn back, that your sins may be blotted out, that times of refreshing may come from the presence of the Lord, and that he may send the Christ appointed for you, Jesus, *whom heaven must receive until the time for restoring all the things* about which God spoke by the mouth of his holy prophets long ago.
>
> Acts 3:19–21

The Lord Jesus is being held in heaven until the restoration of all the things God has promised. We don't know exactly what he is waiting for. Perhaps it is the salvation of another soul, the building of another brother's faith, love poured out on the poor, or one more song sung in grateful response through tears. Perhaps it's just one more diaper changed in love, one more sermon faithfully preached, one more prayer, one more martyr, or one more instance of refusing the temptation that we so easily succumb to. We do know, though, that he "is not slow to fulfill his promise as some count slowness, but is patient toward you, not wishing that any should perish, but that all should reach repentance. But the day of the Lord will come . . ." (2 Peter 3:9–10).

The day of the Lord will come. For those of us who long for that day, the thought of its arrival should draw us forward into the life of joy and blessedness we long for while we remain here. There are rewards to come—it is right for us to consider them. Perhaps the good work you do today will function as part of the robe of righteousness I will wear. The city is being constructed right now. Perhaps picking up your children out of love when your back already hurts and they don't want your love will be a glowing stone in the New Jerusalem. Perhaps the prayer you weakly murmur tonight as you long for sleep and find it once again eluding you, the "Lord, I love you. Please be near me now" will so enhance your relationship with him that it will feel like a reward, though just being near him is reward enough. "I heard your prayer, daughter. I was there all the time."

The work you are doing now, "your work of faith and labor of love and steadfastness of hope in our Lord Jesus Christ" (1 Thessalonians 1:3) will be part of his kingdom of faith, love, and hope that will last forever, and forever and ever. Your labor is not in vain. My work is not for nothing. Our love will never be overcome. We will see the fruit of it once again . . . in the world to come.

─────── FIXING OUR EYES ON HOME ───────

1. Athanasius's most important proof of the resurrection of Christ from the dead was this: "Look how these people live in this world . . . imparting strength to meet death."[13] Respond.

2. John Calvin wrote, "First, let it be a fixed principle in our hearts, that the kingdom of heaven is not the hire of servants, but the inheritance of sons"[14] (see Ephesians 1:18), and yet he also said, "It is not strange that [his children] are said to be crowned according to their works."[15] We aren't told to *work for* our reward in heaven, but we are

at the same time told that *there will be* rewards in heaven. Respond.

3. Our enemy would like us to believe that there is no reason for us to continue to work for the Lord now. He tells us that our work is in vain and that nothing we're doing is making any lasting difference. How do the resurrection and the promise of future rewards silence these lies?

4. Martin Luther wrote that if we did not have the consolation of rewards in heaven, "we could not stand the misery, persecution, and trouble we get in exchange for doing so much good, nor . . . be rewarded with nothing but ingratitude and abuse. Finally we would have to stop working and suffering, though it is our obvious duty to do so."[16] Respond.

5. J.R.R. Tolkien wrote, "There is a place called heaven, where the good here unfinished is completed, and the stories unwritten and the hopes unfulfilled are continued. We may laugh together yet."[17] Respond.

6. Summarize what you've learned in this chapter in four or five sentences.

12

The Forever Hello

We have all said good-bye. Perhaps we've said it to friends who are moving out of state, to children who have been accepted to colleges too far away, to aged loved ones whose dear hearts finally gave out, like my uncle's did. Or we've said good bye to churches that we were devoted to after realizing that in spite of all our love and all our work, we still couldn't keep them afloat. Maybe we've said it to relationships that were once dear, because too much water had passed under the bridge to go back and try again. We've said it to our expectations and dreams, to the good we've tried but failed to accomplish, to our hopes of lives filled with love and a home warmed by hearts committed to one another and to faithfulness. I've said it to my plans to love and love and never stop loving. We've all said too many good-byes.

I'm longing for the day of eternal hellos. I'm aching for the day when I'll hear the endless "Welcome Home" and for the joy of awakening day after day after day with no possibility of good-byes, no "I'm sorry . . . I meant to be kinder," and no shame or covering up or duplicity. I need to live in the land where I will no longer hear, "You should have tried harder" from others, and especially from myself.

I'm sick to death of all this failure and loss and tearing apart, of shattered dreams and sin upon sin upon sin. David described life here as existence in a "besieged city" (Psalm 31:21), and I know what he meant. What is life like in a besieged city? Constant warfare, fear, and want, a bleak future, daily tears. Existence in a dungeon.

One part of this psalm particularly describes my personal besieged city experience:

> Be gracious to me, O Lord, for I am in distress;
> my eye is wasted from grief;
> my soul and my body also.
> For my life is spent with sorrow,
> and my years with sighing;
> my strength fails because of *my iniquity*,
> and my bones waste away.
>
> Psalm 31:9–10

I'm sick to death of living here with my own sin, of the way I've wanted to make a home, to put people at ease, to spread love to everyone I meet only to find myself falling into selfishness again and again. I'm tired of sinning against the people I love the most. And I'm tired of living in this broken-down body, with its weaknesses and aches and demands and failings.

Mean Girls

I recall a time when I was in seventh grade (a terrible time for everyone, even the popular—which I certainly wasn't!), when the school newspaper asked if anyone had ever seen me without a run in my stockings (in the days when girls wore nylon stockings to school and didn't purposely run them). I remember the day I read that sentence, written by some mean girl somewhere, like it was yesterday. It hurt deeply. I knew I was the object of scorn. I was known for having runs in my stockings and pretty much wearing the same wrong thing day after day to school. I responded in rebellion and soon left that school. I confess to being hurt by the shaming remarks of mean girls.

But I also confess that there have been times when I played the role of the mean girl. There have been times when I meant to be kind and what I said came out all wrong. There were other times when I meant to offend and I did. I've spent many hours wondering if I said the wrong thing again. Did I make the wrong choice when I meant to make the right one? Did I betray a friend's confidence or speak words off-handedly that went like arrows into a loved one's heart? Am I really that proud, that selfish, and that faithless? I'm sorry if this is too gritty, too raw, too real, but this is life in a besieged city. I've been the object of scorn, and truthfully, I've dished out my share of it, too.

This is a hard world. This is the place in which we live. The real heartbreaker to me, though, is that I'm a mean girl, too, and I can't seem to get past it. On many days I feel like I've been consigned to the middle seat on a nonstop flight to failure. I have wanted to love people, but I keep acting like a mean girl.

Yes, the Lord has been so very kind to me. David writes:

> Oh, how abundant is your goodness,
> which you have stored up for those who fear you
> and worked for those who take refuge in you,
> in the sight of the children of mankind!
> Psalm 31:19

Don't misunderstand. He has generously gifted me with family and friends, and ministry and immense open doors . . . and one of the kindest husbands in the world. I'm not saying that there is nothing good in my existence here. I'm not saying that at all. I am saying that this isn't Home, and I'm really longing to lie down in green pastures beside still waters in Paradise. I long for fellowship in the New Jerusalem and to hear him say, "I am yours. You are mine. Forever. Welcome Home." It's very true that even now I'm able to say, "Blessed be the Lord, for he has wondrously shown his steadfast love to me when I was in a besieged city" (Psalm 31:21). But . . . I'd still like to be freed from that besieged city. Wouldn't you?

So, for today, I say that I'm done with pretending that life here is a place where, as if we were in the Magic Kingdom, dreams really can come true. I've finished with the pretending that begins by believing I could have a great life right now if I could just discover the secret liniment to rub into my soul that would make all my sin-triggered tears disappear. I've bought that snake oil way too many times. This isn't Home. Nothing can make it Home. It remains a besieged city. Could it be worse? Of course. I could be in this place without any hope of deliverance, without the light of his grace, without faith, without the knowledge of his wonderful steadfast love, without the promise of Home. I could be there, but I'm not. Through the Spirit, David has encouraged me, "Be strong, and let your heart take courage, all you who wait for the Lord!" (Psalm 31:24). *"O Lord,"* we pray, *"grant us courage and strength."*

The People of Faith

I know this seems pretty bleak, but I also know this is the way that the ancient people of faith viewed their lives in this world. It isn't a mark of faithlessness to describe this life as it really is or to refuse to imagine that we can turn our exile into Home. Faith isn't faith when I obtain what I'm longing for; it is rather being convinced of things I can't see now (Hebrews 11:1).

210

The lives of the people of faith have always been like this . . . even from the very beginning. Eve's second-born son, Abel, lived a life of faith, was declared righteous, and yet was murdered by his brother. Noah acted in faith and watched while the entire world was remade into a sludge-covered graveyard. His very righteousness and faith condemned the world and everything he had ever known. Abraham wandered for decades seeking an elusive inheritance, living in tents with his sons who were also heirs of the promise of blessing. He never lived in the Home he longed for. How many times did he regret listening to Sarah's advice regarding Hagar? How many arguments did he endure or even instigate? How much did he cringe over his spineless desertion of his wife before pagan kings? How many times did he long for the blessed life God had promised him?

Abraham knew this wasn't Home. He certainly knew that the desert land he sojourned in here was not Home, for he was "looking forward to the city that has foundations, whose designer and builder is God" (Hebrews 11:10). Sarah gave birth to a son in her old age, but he didn't bring her the ultimate happiness she longed for—even though she named him "laughter." Neither of them actually witnessed their descendants numbering more than the "grains of sand by the seashore" (Hebrews 11:12). They saw wandering, conflict, trouble, and ultimate death.

> These all died in faith, *not having received the things promised*, but having seen them and greeted them from afar, and having acknowledged that they were strangers and exiles on the earth. For people who speak thus make it clear that *they are seeking a homeland.*
>
> Hebrews 11:13–14

God's people of faith weren't jolly and they certainly weren't comfortable here. They hunted for a homeland their entire lives.

That's not to say they didn't experience the true happiness that is born out of relationship with the Lord. But they weren't giddy with happiness, and they didn't have perfectly tidy lives. They knew their own sin and the sins of others against them. They desired "a better country, that is, a heavenly one" for God has "prepared for them a city" (Hebrews 11:16). They longed for a Home where righteousness lived. Death was part of their everyday life. The city they longed for wasn't here. They knew it. They wanted a better one. That is, heaven.

The continuing look at the people of faith, in Hebrews 11, describes them as being tested, as struggling to believe the resurrection in the face of ultimate sacrifice, as blessing future generations in death, as choosing mistreatment rather than pleasure, as leaving earthly home and comfort because by faith they saw "him who is invisible" (v. 27). The ancient people of faith attempted the impossible, watched their homes being destroyed,

> . . . conquered kingdoms, enforced justice, obtained promises, stopped the mouths of lions, quenched the power of fire, escaped the edge of the sword, were made strong out of weakness . . . were tortured . . . suffered mocking and flogging, and even chains and imprisonment. They were stoned, they were sawn in two, they were killed with the sword. They went about . . . destitute, afflicted, mistreated . . . wandering about in deserts and mountains, and in dens and caves of the earth. . . . *All these, though commended through their faith, did not receive what was promised.*
>
> vv. 33–39

Faith doesn't mean that we pretend that life here is all that we hoped it would be or that every promise given to us is fulfilled in the here and now. The saints in Hebrews 11 saw only "preliminary glimpses of what was promised."[1] They were living in the hope of a better, a greater future. Like them, we are on a pilgrimage, heading toward a heavenly Jerusalem, "the city of the living God" (Hebrews 12:22). We are members of the church "of the firstborn who are enrolled in heaven" (v. 23). We are just like them. We are anticipating a future home . . . a Home that really is Home where all the old, tired, hurtful things are erased, and all the world is as it should have been all along, dressed in God's glory and our true joy.

> Each one of these people of faith died not yet having in hand what was promised, but still believing. How did they do it? They saw it way off in the distance, waved their greeting, and accepted the fact that they were *transients in this world*. People who live this way make it plain that they are looking for their true home. If they were homesick for the old country, they could have gone back any time they wanted. But they were after a far better country than that—*heaven* country. You can see why God is so proud of them, and has a City waiting for them.[2]

Let Your Heart Take Courage

From beginning to end, from the Old Testament to the New, the besieged people of faith are told to take courage, to be strong, to conquer. They are not told that every wish-prayer will be answered or that their lives here will ever rise much above life as it would be in a besieged city. But they are told how to conquer and they are given glorious promises about what life will be like in their new Home. This is where they find their ultimate victory: through conquering their enemy "by the blood of the Lamb and by the word of their testimony," and not loving their lives here, even until the day of their death (Revelation 12:11).

We are told to keep believing, to keep hold of our testimony. This isn't the testimony of how great our life has become or how we have been ever so victorious over all our troubles. This testimony isn't about us at all. Rather, our testimony is the witness of the bloodied Lamb, the One who took upon himself all our sins and sorrows, lived the life of perfect obedience we have longed for, and took all the shaming and attack that we each deserved. He died in the besieged city alone, and his body was laid in a cold stone tomb alone. He said good-bye to his mother, Mary, as he hung dying on the cross . . . and even more shockingly, he said good-bye to his Father, who turned his back on him in wrath over our sin. But then the power of God broke into this besieged city and raised the New Man from the dead. From there he would open the door to our real Home. For him, there would be no more good-byes, only the promise of endless delight and fellowship with the Father and the Bride he loves.

The Rewards of Our Testimony

And so, even in the midst of all our sorrows—those we've brought upon ourselves, and others that have come to us as by-products of life in this sin-cursed world—we hold on to our testimony. We hold on to our testimony of a redeemed life and our bloodied Warrior Prince who has rescued us.

Our words of faith conquer Satan and assure us that we will be able to eat from the "tree of life, which grows in the paradise of God" (Revelation 2:7). We know that we will not be hurt by the second death (v. 11), the hellish good-bye that those who have refused grace will murmur forever. Our hungering souls will be fed hidden manna, and we will be given a white stone with a new name on it (v. 17). We don't know what that name is . . . but we will instantly recognize it when we read it and know that we were intimately known by our true name all along. Surprisingly, we'll be given authority to rule over nations in his name. We will spend eternity ruling as his vice-regents over this ever-expanding universe (vv. 26–27). I don't know what that means, but it sounds amazing, doesn't it?

We will receive the Morning Star, as the Lord Jesus describes himself (v. 28) as our constant friend, companion, protector, and husband. He is the eternal sunrise that will never end. Our faith and testimony in his work on our behalf will grant us the blessing of throwing off our soiled robes and being clothed in white garments that will never be stained with our sin—ever again. Because we will be completely remade into perfection, there will be no need to fear that our names will be blotted out of the Book of Life. In fact, our names will be confessed by our Savior before his Father and his angels! (Revelation 3:5). Oh! Amazing grace!

Instead of being formless wraiths, we will be pillars, part of the structure in the temple of God. We will be forever marked by him with his name and with the name of his city (v. 12). Without losing our individuality, our identity will be completely intertwined with his. We will sit with Jesus on his throne (v. 21) and stand next to a "sea of glass mingled with fire" where we will play music and sing the song of Moses and the song of the Lamb (Revelation 15:2). He will be our God. We will be his children (Revelation 21:7). Forever. No more mean girls. No more bullies. No more sin or suffering or good-byes. No more besieged cities. Ever.

We are an embattled people. Every day we live is warfare on some level. But the promise God has given us that this isn't all there is, that the Lamb will ultimately triumph over all our sins and suffering, is more certain than anything our eyes can see today. Three persons have guaranteed the reliability of his promises: "God, the divine author (Revelation 22:6); Jesus, the divine revealer (v. 16); and John, the faithful recorder (v. 8)."[3] These are sure promises that we can hang on to not only in the storm but also in the boring, mundane, soul-deadening onslaught of our day-to-day battle against sin and unbelief. Three witnesses have promised that our Home awaits us. We can be sure enough of

215

it to lay down our lives . . . even unto death, for we know that death itself will only function as a doorway to Paradise and to our ultimate Home.

The Fourth Man in the Furnace

At my mother-in-law's memorial service, I asked if I could bring a message to the congregation. I entitled the message, "Come With Me, I Know the Way," and I'm quite sure that many in the audience thought the title referred to her. While it was true that she had led many to faith, I wasn't going to talk about her, because though she was very wonderful, she, like the rest of us, was a sinner. I could tell because I could see her remains lying cold and stiff in a coffin near me. She needed Someone to come to her and show her the way. She needed Someone who had been through death and had come out victorious on the other side. She needed Someone who knew the way to Paradise. Just like the rest of us, she needed Jesus in her death.

The family was with her during her final breaths, but we weren't what she needed. At the very moment when her heart stopped, when death was stepping in to seize her, her Savior grasped her hand and said, "You're coming with me, my dear daughter. I've got you. I know the way." And at that moment she knew rest and joy and freedom from fear and pain that had eluded her for years.

You've probably heard the story of the three Hebrew exiles that were thrown into the fiery furnace at King Nebuchadnez-zar's command. They had refused to worship the king's idol in exchange for their release, so he had condemned them to an excruciating death: being burned alive in a fire so hot that those who even got near it were killed. Into the pit they went, but when the king looked in he exclaimed, "I see four men unbound, walking in the midst of the fire, and they are not hurt; and the appearance of the fourth is like a son of the gods" (Daniel 3:25). The Lord Jesus, in his preincarnate state, not only entered into the suffering of his three faithful servants, he also entered into their deaths . . . and that, my sisters and brothers, is the best news you'll ever hear.[4]

On the day when you say your final good-bye, when whatever family you might have around you is crying, when you're no longer able to keep your eyes open or your lungs expanding and contracting, you won't say good-bye to him. You'll be saying hello . . . and when he takes your hand and leads you into Paradise, you'll immediately know who he is and what he's doing for you.

The story of the fiery furnace doesn't end with the glory of his presence in our death. It also speaks to us that the suffering and fiery wrath that are our just deserts for the mean, bullying, anxious, faithless, selfish, and guilty lives we've lived won't even touch us. The Lord Jesus received all the wrath due us, which is what the word *propitiation* means. It means he's the one who bore God's righteous anger, a wrath heated up four times hotter than any furnace by his anger against sin. "In this is love, not that we have loved God but that he loved us and sent his Son to be the propitiation for our sins" (1 John 4:10). Our Savior loved us so he willingly cast himself into the fiery furnace of God's wrath so that we wouldn't suffer under it. Ever. And what's the outcome for us? Just like the furnace had no power over the three faithful Hebrew men, God's wrath will have no power over us at all.

> And the satraps, the prefects, the governors, and the king's counselors gathered together and saw that the fire had not had any power over the bodies of those men. The hair of their heads was not singed, their cloaks were not harmed, and no smell of fire had come upon them.
>
> Daniel 3:27

"There is therefore now *no* condemnation for those who are in Christ Jesus" (Romans 8:1). None. Ever. We'll walk right into Paradise with our Savior with no smell of fire on us at all. And we'll never say good-bye to love or life again. I'm longing for that day . . . aren't you? Home. Finally. Hello!

Black Lines on a White Page

We've come a long way together, haven't we? It is my sincere desire that these black lines, these letters and squiggles have created in you a deeper understanding and desire for your ultimate Home. I trust that you've learned what it is you're really longing for and have determined, by God's grace, to live whatever life you still have ahead of you in loyal faith and allegiance to your true citizenship. You and I aren't going to find the life we're looking for here . . . but that doesn't mean it is completely lost to us. It is coming, that's for sure.

The difficulty that I have faced in trying to use words to describe our ultimate Home is that no matter how I strive, I know I haven't been able to even come close. I'm trying to describe and even make you long for something neither one of us has ever experienced. Remembering the analogy we used before, how could I possibly tell you about something as simple as an orange if you had never tasted one? How could I tell a color-blind person about the sea in the Virgin Islands . . . or try to describe what it will be like when we have more than just the three types of color receptors our eyes presently have . . . or that we'll have unlimited strength and a new body that is perhaps as changed as an acorn is when it grows into a seventy-five-foot oak? Everything will be changed. And we'll love all the changes more than we can ever imagine.

C. S. Lewis tried to get at the disconnect I have been faced with in his address "The Weight of Glory." In it he created a fable about a pregnant woman who is thrown into a dark dungeon that has only straw on the floor and a little window high up in the wall . . . too high to see anything but the sky. While in the dungeon she gives birth to a son. But this poor woman is also an artist, and using pencils and a drawing pad, she seeks to portray for her son the world he has never seen. She draws rivers and fields, mountains and cities. She sketches out what waves on a beach look like. He loves her and believes her, but then the day comes when she realizes that he believes that her pencil drawings are exact representations of what the real world looks like. He thinks that everything there is outlined in pencil. He doesn't understand the nuances of light or color or texture, or the fact that shapes are not actually outlined but "define their own shapes" with . . .

> . . . a delicacy and multiplicity which no drawing could ever achieve. The child will get the idea that the real world is somehow less visible than his mother's pictures. In reality it lacks lines because it is *incomparably more visible*. . . . So with us. "We know not what we shall be"; but we may be sure we shall be more, not less, than we were on earth.[5]

All that we have been through in these pages filled with black lines, all the drawing, erasing, and redrawing I've done for you are at best pencil sketches by a woman in a dungeon, trying to sketch a world I've never seen, seeking to employ words I'm not skilled enough to arrange, trying to create for you something more than a child's stick-figure drawing. In fact, that's all any of us can do from here. For all of us still live in the land of penciled lines on flat paper. Have I succeeded in whetting your appetite at all? I hope so, but I also know that if I have it is simply because the Holy Spirit wants to impart truth to us all. On the other hand, let us not forget the thought we opened this book with—about Jesus laughing with me about my drawings. "Well, Lord," I'll say, "You know I tried."

What is coming toward us is far more solid, far more beautiful, far more sensory and magnificent and alive than anything we can even imagine. We are presently, as Lewis says, "too flimsy, too transitory"[6] to even begin to get a grip on what's to come.

So Let Us Live on in Faith

We don't know what tomorrow, or even the next moment, holds. Perhaps some lonely piece of cholesterol that has been floating around in my bloodstream looking for a home will find a comfy place to plant itself in a coronary artery and within moments I'll be gone. Perhaps I won't even have a chance to say good-bye to those darlings I love or to tell them how I meant to be kinder. None of us knows what lies ahead.

And so, we must live our lives now in faithfulness, recognizing the realities of this difficult, dark place, and yet rejoicing in the truth that this isn't all we've been granted. Let us hold on to our testimony about the blood of the conquering Lamb, even when it seems as though there isn't another believer within a hundred miles. Let us continue to love our neighbors and long for their welcome into Home with us. And let us keep ever before us the truth that we have an inheritance awaiting us that will be far more glorious than we have words to describe.

> The Spirit and the Bride say, "Come." And let the one who hears say, "Come." And let the one who is thirsty come; let the one who desires take the water of life without price. . . .
> He who testifies to these things says, "Surely I am coming soon." Amen. Come, Lord Jesus!
> The grace of the Lord Jesus be with all. Amen.
>
> Revelation 22:17, 20–21

FIXING OUR EYES ON HOPE

1. Pastor Tim Keller said, "Jesus Christ is the only God who goes objectively into that ultimate furnace. No other god and no other religion talks about a god that suffers."[7] Respond.

2. Christian martyr Dietrich Bonhoeffer encourages us to pray,

> *King of the church, Master of joy beyond compare, give us great longing and desire, a mighty homesickness for you—and then come and comfort us with your ascension; make us certain of your promise, that one day the curtain that separates us from you will fall. We cannot see you, but we love you; we do not have you before our eyes, but we believe in you.*[8]

Once you have prayed through that prayer, contemplate what he meant. The next time you attend church, why not ask the Spirit to enable you to be joyful and to see through the "thin places" into the heavenly realities beyond.

3. When we get to heaven, it is a "hand like ours that will open heaven's gates" and a "face like ours which will greet us in love." We will "see with our own eyes that Jesus ever remains incarnate."[9] No more good-byes. Only life with the physical God-Man forever. Respond.

4. Summarize what you've learned in this chapter in four or five sentences.

5. Summarize what you've learned in this book.

Appendix

Coming to Saving Faith

Welcome. I'm glad you're here, because I have some really amazing news for you. This news is actually so amazing, so *good* that the people who lived when it was first being talked about called it the *good* news or *gospel*. You've probably heard that term *gospel* before and might have wondered about it. When Christians are using it, it really does mean "good news," and in particular, good news of a certain sort.

So . . . what's the good news and what does it have to do with "saving faith"? First of all, it is news. Think of a news story you read on your computer or hear on the nightly news. News is generally thought of as a story about actual events. But unlike the daily news feed on our phones, the gospel is about events that happened thousands of years ago in the Middle East.

This story starts out with a husband and his wife, in fact, the first people who ever lived. The Lord, their loving Father, placed them in a very beautiful garden; he had given them life and everything they needed to be completely happy. But one day Satan, a creature that hated both them and their Father, tricked them into disobeying their Father. This disobedience brought sadness and death to them and to all of us, as the Lord said it would.

In disobeying the Lord, they transformed from people who were capable of sinning into people who sinned because it was their nature. They began to die. Their bodies began to degenerate and, saddest of all, their relationship with the Lord and with each other began to die also. The Lord exiled the man and woman from their beautiful garden home, but before they left, he gave them a promise: Someday a Son will be born who will crush this Enemy and make everything right again. Yes, they had to leave their home, but their Father promised them that someday they would be able to return.

Thousands of years passed, and after God had accomplished many things through his people Israel, the world was finally ready to receive the One he had promised.

About two thousand years ago, a young virgin girl from Israel was visited by God. She was told that she would be the one who would bear the longed-for Messiah, the Promised One. Her name was Mary. By a miraculous act of God through the Holy Spirit, she became pregnant with the Son, the second person of the Trinity. The Messiah's birth had to happen like this because, though a human being was necessary to complete God's work, only God could actually accomplish it. The Promised One had to be both man and God at the same time. The Father needed to send someone to his people who would obey all his commands and never sin, but yet be willing and able to bear the punishment of death for our disobedience. The girl's child was named *Jesus,* which means "God saves!" and he was the Christ, or the Messiah, the Promised One. He was the One for whom the Jewish people had been longing for thousands of years. Jesus was Mary's son, but he was also God's Son.

Jesus grew up in an ordinary Jewish home, but in one way he was very different from everyone else. He never sinned. Another way to say that is to say that he perfectly loved his Father with his whole heart, soul, mind, and strength, and he always loved his neighbor the same way he loved himself.

You would think that a person who was so loving would be really popular, wouldn't you? And while there was a time when he really did have a lot of friends, there were also other people who were jealous of him and of the fact that he was getting more popular than they were. They also hated him because he called them out about their sin and hypocrisy. So they decided to shut him up and, of course, the best way to do that permanently was to kill him.

One day, they talked their corrupt rulers into conspiring with them, and eventually they killed him. That happened on a day we now strangely call Good Friday. Jesus, the man who always loved everyone, was laughed at while he was being executed on a cross. He died in exile, even from his Father. He was standing in the place of every person who had ever sinned; he was being punished and exiled for them. And he was imputing or transferring to them his record of never sinning, of always loving his Father and his neighbor.

While all of this might seem like really bad news, the truth is that everything was going according to God's plan. Remember how he gave his promise to send someone who would defeat Satan, the one who had tricked the first man and woman? This was how he accomplished that. In that ancient prophecy, God said that the Rescuer would crush the Enemy, but he also said that the Enemy would strike the Rescuer.

After Jesus died, some of his followers took his lifeless body down from the cross and carried it to a cave in a garden. The jealous religious leaders were afraid that people might steal his body and say that he hadn't died after all, so they had soldiers roll a large stone in front of the cave where his body had been laid. Then a group of them were stationed by the cave as guards to make sure there wasn't any trickery going on.

But . . . God had a different plan. On the third morning, Jesus' Father declared that his Son had completed everything he had sent him to do, and so he raised his body from the dead. We celebrate that day on Easter. Easter proves that Jesus was who he said he was and that he accomplished everything his Father had sent him to do. It proves that he is God.

After his resurrection, Jesus was seen by hundreds of people, many of whom died because they wouldn't change their story and say that he was still dead. They were completely convinced, and because of that they were willing to suffer in terrible ways.

You might be wondering how this story is good news and what it has to do with you. I understand. Here's why it is good news: The truth is that you and I, all people in fact, are sinners. We all fail to love God and our neighbor. Sometimes we fail to love in little ways, like being angry at someone because our coffee isn't exactly the way we like it. Other times we fail to love in really big ways, like lying or stealing or even committing adultery. No matter how we fail, we all fail to love *all the time*. And none of us puts God first in our lives like we should. In fact, we don't even live up to our own standards most of the time. Because we are sinners, we have the sentence of death hanging over us. God promised that all who sin will die (Romans 6:23).

The good news is that all the punishment you and I deserve for all the sin we have committed was poured out on Jesus. That's why he died. That means the punishment of death for disobedience no longer applies to those who believe in Jesus' sacrifice for them. But that's not all the good news there is. The next part of the good news is that the whole record of all the love that Jesus showed to his Father and to all people is ours. We are forgiven for all our sins *and* we have Jesus' perfect record besides! Amazing, yes? That's what the Bible means when it says we are justified. Justification means two things. First of all, it means that as far as God is concerned, when he looks at us it is just as if we had never sinned. Second, it also means that when he looks at us it is just as if we had always obeyed. Because of the work of Jesus, those who believe on him are both completely forgiven and made completely righteous.

But there is more good news still. We are not only forgiven and counted obedient, God also welcomes us back into his Home in heaven, which is what this book is about. You remember that the first couple was exiled out of their beautiful garden because they disobeyed God. Well, the great news is that Jesus has reopened the gates to that garden for us and is welcoming us back Home.

You might be wondering what you have to do to get rid of that death sentence, get a perfect record, and procure an invitation into God's house. The really, really great news is this: *All you have to do is believe.* Really. Just believe. Believe that the story I've just told you is true and then put your trust in Jesus, his life, death, and resurrection and all that I've just said will be true for you. It's called "saving faith," which simply means this: You believe you have sinned and need a Savior, and you believe that Jesus is the Savior you need. And you are saved. Period.

Now, of course, if you believe this is true, you'll want to be around other people who believe this, too, and you'll want to learn more about it. You need to find a Bible-believing church and become a part of it. That's why I have gone to church almost every Sunday for forty-five years since I first believed. No church is perfect. It's a place that is full of people just like you and me, sinners who need a Savior. But church is the place God has promised to meet us. Look for a church near you that has a statement of faith that you can read and see if it declares the same story I just told you. (Mormons and Jehovah's Witnesses are not Christians.)

The next thing you should do is get a Bible, or go online and find one that is available to read for free. I really like the translation called the English Standard Version, but there are other good ones, as well. You might want to start reading in the New Testament, which is the part of the Bible that starts with the stories about Jesus and the books called the Gospels. And, of course, you'll want to start praying—talking to your Father God, and to Jesus, your Brother. They will love to hear from you, and will answer your prayers in the way that is best for you.

Does this sound too good to be true? I know. It really is amazing. That's why they call it the good news! But if you sense God is calling you to come to him, just put your faith and trust in him and in his Word. Believe in him, that he is loving and good and wise, and has great things in store for you.

If you have come to faith through reading this book, I'd really like to know. You can contact me through the publisher or my website, www.elysefitzpatrick.com. Thanks!

Now it's time for you to turn back to the front of this book and start reading about the place you and I are headed.

Notes

Chapter 1: On Loss and Homesickness and Baking Bread

1. From now on, whenever I refer to our ultimate Home in heaven, I'll be capitalizing the word. When the word is not capitalized, I'm referring to our temporal home here.

2. *Homesickness*, Wikipedia, https://en.wikipedia.org/wiki/Homesickness.

3. Susan J. Matt, *Homesickness: An American History* (New York: Oxford University Press, 2011), 26.

4. Philip Graham Ryken, *Jeremiah and Lamentations: From Sorrow to Hope*, Preaching the Word (Wheaton, IL: Crossway, 2001), 51. The Walker Percy quote is from *First Things* (May 1993), 48.

5. R. Laird Harris, Gleason L. Archer Jr., and Bruce K. Waltke, *Theological Wordbook of the Old Testament*, Walter C. Kaiser, ed., (Chicago: Moody, 1999), 412. "(tôšāb). Sojourner. Occurring fourteen times, seven times in Leviticus 25, this noun refers to the temporary, landless wage earner. The term is used with gēr (permanent resident, alien) to describe Abraham in Canaan (Genesis 23:4), and the Israelites in God's eyes (Leviticus 25:23, 35; Psalm 39:12; 1 Chronicles 29.15)."

6. Johannes P. Louw and Eugene Albert Nida, *Greek-English Lexicon of the New Testament: Based on Semantic Domains* (New York: United Bible Societies, 1996), 351: "συνέχομαι ἐκ: (an idiom, literally 'to be held together from') to be in a mental state between two alternatives—'to be pulled in two directions, to be betwixt and between, to have conflicting thoughts.' συνέχομαι δὲ ἐκ τῶν δύο 'I have conflicting thoughts' or 'I am in the middle between two sets of thoughts' Philippians 1:23. In a number of languages the rendering of this statement in Philippians 1:23 must be expressed idiomatically, for example, 'my mind is pulling me in two directions' or 'my thoughts are going in two different directions' or 'my heart is speaking two different words to me.'"

7. Philip Yancey, *Disappointment with God* (Grand Rapids, MI: Zondervan, 1988), 246; quoted in Randy Alcorn, *Eternal Perspectives: A Collection of Quotations on Heaven, The New Earth, and Life After Death* (Carol Stream, IL: Tyndale, 2012), 291.

Chapter 2: Let Not Your Hearts Be Troubled

1. A. J. Conyers, *Eclipse of Heaven: The Loss of Transcendence and Its Effect on Modern Life* (South Bend, IN: St. Augustine's Press, 1992), 42.

2. Johannes P. Louw and Eugene Albert Nida, *Greek-English Lexicon of the New Testament: Based on Semantic Domains*, "ταράσσω[b]: (a figurative extension of meaning of ταράσσω[a] 'to stir up,' 16.3) to cause acute emotional distress or turbulence—'to cause great mental distress.'"

3. C. S. Lewis, *Mere Christianity* (New York: HarperOne, 2001), 137.

4. "A term introduced into Greek by Xenophon to indicate the game parks and pleasure gardens of Persian kings and nobles. By the third century BC, it came to mean any park or garden. The three occurrences of *pardēs* in the Old Testament are all late and all have a literal, secular meaning (Nehemiah 2:8; RSV 'forest'; Ecclesiastes 2:5; RSV 'parks'; Song of Solomon 4:13; RSV 'orchard'). The LXX uses *parádeisos* to translate Heb. *gan, gannâ* 'garden,' including references to the garden of Genesis 2–3, as does Philo." *Eerdmans Bible Dictionary*, reference to "Paradise."

5. "Gagarin Never Said He Did Not See God in Space—His Friend, an Air Force Colonel," Interfax, April 12, 2006, www.interfax-religion.com/?act=news &div=1287.

6. Of course, that's not to say that there is any part of the entire created universe where his Spirit doesn't dwell. Just that what we would call his throne room, the place where he can be seen, isn't in outer space or "up there" somewhere. Maybe he dwells in the "dark matter," the part of the cosmos that the astronomers and physicists know exists but can't understand.

7. See http://www.epm.org/resouces/2010/Jan/5/do-people-now-heaven-pray -those-earth/. For more information, see Randy Alcorn, *Heaven* (Carol Stream, IL: Tyndale House, 2004).

8. Maybe this is a little outside of your eschatology. Just go with it for right now. Wherever you want to put this day is fine with me as long as you realize that a day is coming when he will re-body us and renew the earth to be our eternal home.

9. C. S. Lewis, *The Weight of Glory: And Other Addresses* (New York: HarperOne, 2001), 41.

10. Ibid., 42.

11. Blaise Pascal, *Pensees* (New York: Penguin Classics, 1995), 45.

Chapter 3: Surprises in the Garden of New Life

1. N. T. Wright, *Surprised by Hope: Rethinking Heaven, the Resurrection, and the Mission of the Church* (New York: HarperOne, 2008), 12.

2. Alcorn, *Heaven,* 117.

3. The mist also might have resembled the cloud that covered the mountain when Moses met with God (Exodus 24:15).

4. Alcorn, *Heaven,* 59.

5. The big-deal theological word for *essence* is *ontology,* which just means "the nature of being." The point is that our ontology won't change; we'll still be us.

6. Elyse Fitzpatrick, *Found in Him: The Joy of the Incarnation and Our Union with Christ* (Wheaton, IL: Crossway), 2013. My guess is that for most of

evangelical Christianity, teaching and celebrating the ascension has been lost, because we no longer preach according to the church calendar, so we never get an Ascension Sunday message, thereby missing these glorious truths.

7. "Rock of Ages," Augustus M. Toplady, 1776. Public domain. While it is true that at death we will be instantly transferred to what is known as the "intermediate state" (more about that in the next chapter), ultimately, we won't be headed to worlds "unknown," but rather to this known world, cleansed and redeemed as it will be. Anyone who has heard me speak on the gospel knows that I love this hymn and quote it frequently. It's just that this last verse gets us a little off track.

8. For example, see 1 John 2:16; Romans 13:14; Ephesians 2:3; 2 Peter 2:18.

9. *ESV Study Bible*, note on Romans 7:5, (Wheaton, IL: Crossway, 2008).

10. C. S. Lewis, *A Year with C. S. Lewis: Daily Readings from His Classic Works*, 1st ed., Patricia S. Klein, ed. (New York: HarperOne, 2003), 172.

11. "In the new creation, the ancient human mandate to look after the garden is dramatically reaffirmed, as John hints in the resurrection story, where Mary supposes Jesus is the gardener." Wright, *Surprised by Hope*, 210.

12. Lewis, *Mere Christianity*, 200.

13. Martin Luther, *Luther's Works, Vol. 22: Sermons on the Gospel of St. John: Chapters 1–4*, Jaroslav Jan Pelikan, ed., Hilton C. Oswald, and Helmut T. Lehmann (St. Louis, MO: Concordia Publishing House, 1999), 269.

14. Gerrit Scott Dawson, *Jesus Ascended: The Meaning of Christ's Continuing Incarnation* (Phillipsburg, NJ: P & R Publishing, 2004), 182.

Chapter 4: A Glimpse of Our Garden Home

1. Lewis, *Mere Christianity*, 136–137.

2. J. Richard Middleton, *A New Heaven and a New Earth: Reclaiming Biblical Eschatology* (Grand Rapids, MI: Baker Academic, 2014), 71.

3. Wright, *Surprised by Hope*, 212.

4. C. S. Lewis, *The Collected Letters of C. S. Lewis*, Vol. 3, Walter Hooper, ed. (New York: HarperCollins e-books; HarperSanFrancisco, 2004–2007), 778.

5. Albert M. Wolters, *Creation Regained: Biblical Basics for a Reformational Worldview* (Grand Rapids, MI: Eerdmans, 1985), 49.

6. *ESV Study Bible*, note on Genesis 1:28.

7. Ibid.

8. I was first introduced to this concept by G. K. Chesterton, *Orthodoxy* (Ortho Publishing, 2014), 58, through my friend Rondi Lauterbach.

9. I know that Revelation 21:1 says that "the sea was no more," but most theologians take this to mean that "the source of earthly rebellion, chaos, and danger—the sea from which the beast emerged . . . will no longer threaten creation's perfection" rather than there will no longer be any oceans. *ESV Study Bible*, note on Revelation 21.

10. The concept and the quotes taken from Chad Louis Bird, *The Missing Verse in the Creation Account*, blog post at www.chadbird.com, August 28, 2015. Used by permission.

11. Lewis, *Mere Christianity*, 137.

Chapter 5: Seeing the City Abraham Saw

1. "In the Garden," Charles Austin Miles, 1912. Public domain.
2. The apostle Paul also visited what he called the "third heaven," but he wasn't allowed to share what he saw and heard there with us (2 Corinthians 12:2–4).
3. Online Etymology Dictionary, "City," www.etymonline.com/index.php ?term=city.
4. "List of Cities Proper by Population," Wikipedia, https://en.wikipedia.org /wiki/List_of_cities_proper_by_population.
5. Timothy J. Keller, *The Timothy Keller Sermon Archive* (New York City: Redeemer Presbyterian Church, 2013).
6. Eugene H. Peterson, *The Message: The Bible in Contemporary Language* (Colorado Springs: NavPress, 2005), Revelation 21:9–21.
7. Keller, *The Timothy Keller Sermon Archive.*
8. *ESV Study Bible,* note on Matthew 24:29.
9. Keller, *The Timothy Keller Sermon Archive.*
10. C. H. Spurgeon, *The Metropolitan Tabernacle Pulpit Sermons,* Vol. 39 (London: Passmore & Alabaster, 1893), 43–44.
11. Alcorn, *Heaven,* 253.
12. Bruce Milne, *The Message of Heaven and Hell* (Downers Grove, IL: InterVarsity, 2002), 321.
13. Alcorn, *Heaven,* 251.
14. Dennis E. Johnson, *Triumph of the Lamb: A Commentary on Revelation* (Phillipsburg, NJ: P & R Publishing, 2001), 335.

Chapter 6: His Kingdom Has Come

1. I hope that you are a member of a local church, because that membership speaks of this heavenly church where you've been enrolled.
2. N. T. Wright, *New Heavens, New Earth: The Biblical Picture of Christian Hope* (Cambridge, UK: Grove Books, 1999), 7; Quoted in J. Richard Middleton, *A New Heaven and a New Earth: Reclaiming Biblical Eschatology,* 220.
3. More about this in chapter 10.
4. "Holy, Holy, Holy," lyrics by Reginald Heber, 1826. Public domain.
5. J. Ryan Lister, *The Presence of God: Its Place in the Storyline of Scripture and the Story of Our Lives* (Wheaton, IL: Crossway, 2015), 67.
6. Johnson, *Triumph of the Lamb: A Commentary on Revelation,* 307.
7. Elisha prayed that his servant's eyes would be opened so that he could see unseen realities all around him. "So the Lord opened the eyes of the young man, and he saw, and behold, the mountain was full of horses and chariots of fire all around Elisha" (2 Kings 6:17).
8. Graeme Goldsworthy, *The Goldsworthy Trilogy* (Waynesboro, GA: Paternoster, 2000), 316.

Chapter 7: Completely New, Yet So Familiar

1. Peterson, *The Message: The Bible in Contemporary Language,* 1 Corinthians 15:52.

2. Lewis, *The Collected Letters of C. S. Lewis*, Vol. 3, 778.

3. Louw and Nida, *Greek-English Lexicon of the New Testament: Based on Semantic Domains*, 276.

4. John Piper, *Sermons from John Piper (1990–1999)* (Minneapolis, MN: Desiring God, 2007).

5. Even on a day as important as his triumphal entry into Jerusalem, Jesus was unwilling to separate the mother donkey from her foal on which he rode, not wanting them to be apart, and knowing that her foal would be calmer with her by his side (Matthew 21:2).

6. I am aware that this passage can be interpreted in one of several ways. The ravenous beasts may be referring to a messianic age, "when the predatory nations will no longer hurt or destroy God's people. . . . Other interpreters, however, understand this as a reference to a future time when God will bring about a transformation of the earth, extending even to the animal kingdom, when the curse of Genesis 3:17–18 will be removed . . . that is, a future time when the present working order of the natural world will be changed, removing the carnivorous nature of the wolf, leopard, lion, and bear. Some interpreters think this will occur in a future millennial period, while others think it will occur in the new heavens and new earth." (*ESV Study Bible*, note on Isaiah 11). Even if this passage is referring to a millennial period, I don't think it is too much of a stretch to say that the good that may be there during that time will not be lessened in the renewed earth at the end of time.

7. Lewis, *The Collected Letters of C. S. Lewis*, Vol. 3, 1383.

8. Ibid., 458.

9. Ibid., 1383–1384.

10. Keller, *The Timothy Keller Sermon Archive*.

11. Ibid.

12. John Peter Lange et al., *A Commentary on the Holy Scriptures: Revelation* (Bellingham, WA: Logos Bible Software, 2008), 388.

13. *ESV Study Bible*, note on Ezekiel 47.

14. Randy Alcorn, "Cumulative Daily Decisions, Courage in a Cause, and a Life of Endurance" in Justin Taylor, *Stand: A Call for the Endurance of the Saints*, John Piper, contrib. (Wheaton, IL: Crossway, 2008), 91.

15. I am convinced that since there won't be any suffering or death on the New Earth, we won't slaughter animals there. I'm as much of a carnivore as anyone, so I'm looking forward to fruit that will taste savory. The avocado and the tomato are both fruits that are not sweet, so this isn't even that much of a stretch here. Why couldn't some of the fruit that will grow on trees there satisfy our longing for steak (if we still have that longing)?

16. Alcorn, *Heaven*, 309.

17. Johnson, *Triumph of the Lamb: A Commentary on Revelation*, 320.

18. Alcorn, *Heaven*, 313.

19. *Accursed* is used of "something delivered up to divine wrath, dedicated to destruction, and brought under a curse," Gerhard Kittel, Geoffrey W. Bromiley, and Gerhard Friedrich, eds., *Theological Dictionary of the New Testament* (Grand Rapids, MI: Eerdmans, 1964), 354.

20. Lewis, *The Collected Letters of C. S. Lewis*, Vol. 2, 460.

Chapter 8: Our Tears Make Us Long for Home

1. *ESV Study Bible,* note on Isaiah 35.
2. From Julie Pascoe. Used by permission.
3. Anonymous.
4. John Calvin, *Institutes of the Christian Religion,* Vol. 1, John T. McNeill, ed., Ford Lewis Battles, trans., The Library of Christian Classics (Louisville, KY: Westminster John Knox Press, 2011), 707.
5. Louw and Nida, *Greek-English Lexicon of the New Testament: Based on Semantic Domains:* "*nûd* basically denotes a going back and forth. It is applied to a physical movement or an attitude. Cf. Arabaic *nāda,* 'move to and fro' (as the head of one falling asleep).' "
6. Donna Turner. Used by permission.
7. Nancy Guthrie. Used by permission.
8. John Calvin, *Institutes of the Christian Religion.*
9. Martin Luther, *Luther's Works, Vol. 43: Devotional Writings II,* Jaroslav Jan Pelikan, Hilton C. Oswald, and Helmut T. Lehmann, eds. (Philadelphia: Fortress Press, 1999), 177.
10. John Piper, *The Hidden Smile of God: The Fruit of Affliction in the Lives of John Bunyan, William Cowper, and David Brainerd* (Wheaton, IL: Crossway, 2001), 167–168.

Chapter 9: The End of Our Bucket List

1. Derek Kidner, *The Message of Ecclesiastes* (Westmont, IL: IVP Academic, 1984), 23.
2. Johnson, *Triumph of the Lamb: A Commentary on Revelation,* 306.
3. C. S. Lewis, *A Year with Aslan: Daily Reflections from The Chronicles of Narnia,* Julia L. Roller, ed. (New York: HarperOne, 2010), 464.
4. Blaise Pascal, *Thoughts, Letters, and Minor Works* (1910, 2007), 138–139.
5. Saint Augustine, Bishop of Hippo, *The Confessions of St. Augustine,* E. B. Pusey, trans. (Oak Harbor, WA: Logos Research Systems, Inc., 1996).
6. Jeremiah Burroughs, *The Rare Jewel of Christian Contentment* (Carlisle, PA: Banner of Truth Trust, 1648/1995), 91.
7. Peterson, *The Message: The Bible in Contemporary Language,* Revelation 22:17.
8. Louw and Nida, *Greek-English Lexicon of the New Testament: Based on Semantic Domains:* "In origin, καλός is to be grouped with the Sanskrit *kalja* 'sound,' 'powerful,' 'vigorous,' 'excellent.' A linguistic relation has been indicated to the Old German *hoele,* which means a 'hero' or 'strong man.' "
9. *ESV Study Bible,* note for Revelation 22:4.
10. Johnson, *Triumph of the Lamb,* 306–307.

Chapter 10: Gazing Through the Thin Places

1. Eric Weiner, "Where Heaven and Earth Come Closer," *New York Times,* March 9, 2012, www.nytimes.com/2012/03/11/travel/thin-places-where-we-are-jolted-out-of-old-ways-of-seeing-the-world.html?_r=0.
2. Ibid.

3. Wright, *Surprised by Hope*, 272.

4. Peterson, *The Message: The Bible in Contemporary Language*, John 1:18.

5. Mark D. Roberts, "Thin Places: A Biblical Investigation," Patheos, www
.patheos.com/blogs/markdroberts/series/thin-places.

6. N. T. Wright, *Simply Christian* (London: Society for Promoting Christian
Knowledge, 2006), 155.

7. John Calvin and John King, *Commentary on the First Book of Moses Called
Genesis*, Vol. 2 (Bellingham, WA: Logos Bible Software, 2010), 118.

8. N. T. Wright, *Following Jesus: Biblical Reflections on Discipleship* (London:
Society for Promoting Christian Knowledge, 1994), 49.

9. Ibid.

10. Wright, *Surprised by Hope*, 274.

11. Dietrich Bonhoeffer, *Berlin: 1932–1933*, Vol. 12, Carsten Nicolaisen, Ernst-
Albert Scharffenorth, and Larry L. Rasmussen, eds., Isabel Best, David Higgins,
and Douglas W. Stott, trans., DIETRICH BONHOEFFER WORKS (Minneapolis: For
tress Press, 2009), 469.

12. Mark D. Roberts, "Thin Places: A Biblical Investigation."

13. C. S. Lewis, *The Problem of Pain* (New York: HarperOne, 2001), 153.

Chapter 11: Hurrying His Return

1. A. J. Conyers, *Eclipse of Heaven: The Loss of Transcendence and Its Effect
on Modern Life*, 42.

2. J.I. Packer, *Concise Theology: A Guide to Historic Christian Beliefs* (Wheaton, IL: Tyndale, 1993), 266.

3. Matthew 16:27; 2 Corinthians 5:10; Romans 2:6; John 5:29; Matthew 25:34;
Proverbs 12:14; 13:13; Matthew 5:12; Luke 6:23; 1 Corinthians 3:8.

4. Packer, *Concise Theology*, 266.

5. Calvin, *Institutes of the Christian Religion*.

6. Charles Caldwell Ryrie, *A Survey of Bible Doctrine* (Chicago: Moody Press,
1972).

7. C. S. Lewis, *The Great Divorce: A Dream* (New York: HarperOne, 2001), 118.

8. N. T. Wright, *Surprised by Hope*, 219–220.

9. Charles H. Spurgeon, *Spurgeon's Sermons*, electronic ed., Vol. 19 (Albany,
OR: Ages Software, 1998).

10. Louw and Nida, *Greek-English Lexicon of the New Testament: Based
on Semantic Domains*, 507: "41.38 κόσμος^c, ου *m*; αἰών^c, ῶνος *m*: the system of
practices and standards associated with secular society (that is, without reference to
any demands or requirements of God)—'world system, world's standards, world.'"

11. Middleton, *A New Heaven and a New Earth: Reclaiming Biblical Eschatology*, 173.

12. Thomas R. Schreiner, *1, 2 Peter, Jude*, Vol. 37, *The New American Commentary* (Nashville: Broadman & Holman Publishers, 2003), 390.

13. Conyers, *Eclipse of Heaven*, 45.

14. Calvin, *Institutes of the Christian Religion*.

15. Ibid.

16. Martin Luther, *Luther's Works, Vol. 21: The Sermon on the Mount and the Magnificat.*

17. J.R.R. Tolkien, Christopher Tolkien, Humphrey Carpenter, *The Letters of J.R.R. Tolkien* (Boston, MA: Mariner Books, 2000), 55.

Chapter 12: The Forever Hello

1. *ESV Study Bible,* note on Hebrews 11:39–40.

2. Peterson, *The Message: The Bible in Contemporary Language,* Hebrews 11:13–16.

3. Johnson, *The Triumph of the Lamb: A Commentary on Revelation,* 305.

4. I first heard this perspective from Pastor Ted Hamilton, in a sermon he preached at New Life, PCA in Escondido, Califormia, on November 22, 2015.

5. C. S. Lewis, *The Weight of Glory: And Other Addresses,* 109–111.

6. Ibid., 111.

7. Keller, *The Timothy Keller Sermon Archive.*

8. Bonhoeffer, *Berlin: 1932–1933,* 470.

9. Dawson, *Jesus Ascended,* 154.

Elyse Fitzpatrick is a nationally sought-after speaker and author, speaking at such events as The Gospel Coalition and Nancy De-Moss Wolgemuth's Revive Conference. Along with her husband, Phil, Elyse is a member of Valley Center Community Church, a reformed congregation in the community of Valley Center. VCCC is a member of FIRE, the Fellowship of Independent Reformed Evangelicals.

She holds a certificate in Biblical Counseling from Christian Counseling & Educational Foundation (San Diego) and an MA in Biblical Counseling from Trinity Theological Seminary. She has authored twenty books (and one booklet) on daily living and the Christian life.

Elyse and her daughter Jessica have written two books together, *Give Them Grace* and *Answering Your Kids' Toughest Questions*. Elyse has been married for over forty years and has three adult children and six grandchildren. Learn more at www.elysefitzpatrick.com.

More Insight From Elyse And Her Daughter, Jessica!

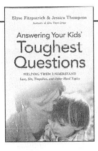

MATES DON'T GROW ON TREES

How to Meet the Man or Woman for You

BY

TODD LANDEN, Ph.D.

Dancing Hearts & Company, Greenwich, CT

MATES DON'T GROW ON TREES

HOW TO MEET THE MAN OR WOMAN FOR YOU

BY TODD LANDEN, PH.D.

Published by:

Dancing Hearts & Company
310 Greenwich Avenue
Post Office Box 466
Greenwich, CT 06836-0466

See last page for order information.

Publisher's Cataloging in Publication Data

Landen, Todd
Mates Don't Grow on Trees: How to Meet the Man or Woman for You/
by Todd Landen-First Edition
1. Dating Social Customs, I. Title
2. Courtship
3. Single People
4. Success

ISBN: 0-9644671-9-4   14.95   Softcover

Illustrations by Cecilia Soprano

TABLE OF CONTENTS

Author's Preface

Where, with Whom, and Which Love Song?

Single people often have a problem when wishing to meet that special other, that singular person with whom they can have a loving relationship. What does she say if she happens to meet such a person? How does he put forth whatever it is he says, and more importantly, where, when and how does he or she meet this person to begin with? Meeting, dating, the early stages of a relationship, or all three combined can make us feel like we are trying to follow some complex road map. A three dimensional map complete with inherent obstacles and detours which often frustrate or delay our getting to where we wish to go.

In time, the odds are that a person will meet someone else with whom he or she can have a serious, lasting relationship. The question is how long does a person stay alone if he or she is not happy being single? How long must a person wait? Most of us don't want just any relationship. At some point in our lives we begin to look for the real Mr./Ms. Right, whoever that may be, for marriage, living-together, or some other mutually accepted situation. And then how do we know if we have found the real Mr./Ms. Right?

While many individuals fall into a lasting relationship effortlessly, others need time, self-improvement, expanded social/cultural perspectives, specific techniques, and a hearty dose of common sense. There are, after all, very few courses on the subject of meeting people and developing a romantic relationship. Admittedly, there will always be gender, cultural, and personality differences but, for the most part, human nature (e.g., emotions, egos, expectations, and fears of rejection), is basically the same for everyone, everywhere.

The road we must navigate will often be a curving path and it, undoubtedly, will have its share of frustration, loneliness and indecision. Yet, if well-traveled, this road will also have its share of some of the most uplifting and rewarding times of our lives. To wish the reader "good luck" on this journey is not enough. To *create luck* through knowledge and skill is the aim of this writing.

Here then, is a manual: humorous, because human nature is humorous and, at times, autobiographical because it makes the book's message personal and heartfelt. My goal is not to summarize or psychoanalyze, but to lead the reader through practical, everyday, common-sense decisions, actions and perspectives designed to greatly *increase the odds* of meeting his or her mate. Our Mr./Ms. Right is out there somewhere, especially if we work to find this person and, even more so, if we work on improving and preparing ourselves in the process.

Listening to your car radio, you'll hear love songs and sing along.
Reach this destination and you'll be singing hundreds of them,
like billowing flocks of birds — only you won't need
a radio or other people's songs.

T.L.

On Your Mark,
Get Set...

I

CREATE YOUR OWN LUCK

1.

PROLOGUE: THE CASE OF MISTAKEN IDENTITY

YOU MAY OR MAY NOT BE THE JAMES BOND KIND-OF-GUY or the Wonder Woman kind-of-gal, but... you're walking down the street and *Va-Voom!* You are definitely in love. Maybe this street is your office hallway or it happens while at a friend of the family's picnic in suburbia. Wherever, whenever, *you* are moved. Moved to take action on your own behalf? A smile at least, to communicate the promise of your great love? Maybe

Walking down Main Street, it is evening and getting darker by the moment. You happen to be the author of this book, and you spot two women walking together, one of whom dazzles you to pieces with her delicacy and poise; at least, that's what you register from this angle. She is potentially *Ms. Right.* I kid you not. Yes, I admit, this response has occurred before. Maybe I have some distant kinship with that furry little Arfer, one of Pavlov's dogs, who salivated whenever a certain dinner bell rang. But I'm also the Bond kind-of-guy: cool, collected, and willing to take a chance on love.

The sidewalks are full of people returning home from work, so I am able to walk just to the side of these two women, unnoticed — me, a smitten passerby in the ever-dimming light. *Wait!* I can hear them speaking a foreign language. "German?," I ask myself, knowing enough of this language, at least, to be amusing if I could only start a conversation. No, it's more like Swedish, I think, but like nothing I've ever heard. I fall back, somewhat stymied; still haven't seen her face very clearly.

They move on into a boutique for women. Shucks. Perhaps it's better if I wait outside. No one will notice me, my hair askew in the cold, snow-filled breeze. I'm waiting ... but I'm getting tired of waiting. Think I'll go in for a browse...maybe start a conversation about the benefits of rayon or... *suddenly,* they turn to leave. It's too late. My foot's already in the door! Now if I ask what language they are speaking, it will look like a come-on: too obvious I've been checking them out.

I've got one second to adjust to the store's bright light and finally get a look at this charming potential mate when I hear my name, "Todd! Hi! How've you been?" *Todd?! Hi? Who knows me here?!* In a split second I put it all together with my first face-to-face glance. *Auschildur,* that new editor from Iceland. I just sent her a manuscript of mine last week. Shoot, this darn lack of street light. I mean, sure, she's terrific, but she's *married* already!

"Hello. What a surprise," I muster. "What are you doing in this neighborhood?," half-trying to sense if she's aware of the instantaneous flush of blood through my veins. I mean, what if I had approached these two women speaking German or with some opening line like, "Are you two from Sweden?," and I didn't even recognize my new editor. How potentially embarrassing!

Walking the few blocks home, the night now a pitch, coal black, I'm feeling more like the bungling Inspector Clouseau* than anyone resembling that slick Bond-kind-of-guy. Hey, I was making the best of an opportunity and I'm not going to blame myself for that. What if I hadn't already known Auschildur? That might have been *Her* and I might have had a chance. I mean, people speaking Icelandic on a New York City street can be very friendly. They're travelers, tourists maybe, expatriates looking for meaning and love in the New World.

Humiliated? Perhaps for a while. But I've made up my mind to meet a woman for that *long-lasting* relationship. I'm looking for the girlfriend who turns into the fiancee who becomes my wife. I am distinctly tired of the singles' life — of one night stands or two month affairs that fizzle-out in question marks or sighs of relief. Ultimately, I know I *will* meet my mate. Here, somewhere, but in this life, soon.

---

* Inspector Clouseau: a fictional detective depicted in films: neither sauve nor brilliant but a bungler *par excellence:* best known for his comic charm.

We begin our quest imperfectly. No superheroes here — just you and me, riding the ups and downs of this roller coaster until it stops and we're all there.

SERIOUSLY NOW

How can you encourage opportunity to knock when good luck seems to be missing in your life? Maybe you don't have the extraordinary good looks of, say, a Marilyn Monroe or the irresistible allure of a James Dean. Perhaps you are one of the many single people who need to work at learning techniques and actually *developing a strategy* to meet your mate. You don't want to wait around until your Prince Charming, or Cinderella, accidentally drops by, do you?

Let's start by thinking about this problem using a scientific analogy. Way back in physics class we learned, while discussing molecular behavior in a hypothetical vacuum, that objects in motion stay in motion and that stationary objects remain stationary. Well, objects in motion often collide with other objects and, *hey*, if these objects are people, then people in motion collide (bump into, interact) with other people too!

---

*Stay "in motion," while keeping this motto in mind:
Motion ... Creates Opportunity ... Creates Luck.*

MEETING ACCIDENTALLY...WELL, SORT OF

Seems simplistic to make such a technical analogy when discussing the problem of meeting new and interesting people? Opportunities to meet people often happen when you help *create the environment* for them to occur. Often these meetings are not completely accidental, as illustrated in my own example above; albeit this led to greeting someone who was romantically *unavailable*, and whom I already knew. (Heck, I'm only human too.)

Other opportunities arise unexpectedly, without being planned or consciously worked on, and these are indeed *accidental* — like picking up the proverbial handkerchief which someone drops, and finding yourself gliding into a conversation with a grateful and attractive person. Regardless of the purity of origin, you can encourage a *chance meeting* to develop into a relationship that lasts, using the right charm and skill, and *that* is creating your own luck.

To begin with, you will need to be somewhere you *might* meet someone, either through chance or by his, her, or your *intentionally planning it*. You've heard it before: go places, do things, and the odds increase that, in time, you will meet people and eventually your mate, either accidentally, or by consciously encouraging Lady Luck to look in your direction. Even placing an ad in the personals column, like dropping a fishing line in the right pond, places you *indirectly* in a position to meet someone *by chance*.

Don't worry yet about the how, what, and where of it all. We will examine many different specific actions you can take to help create the right circumstance for meeting men and women throughout this book. One thing for sure: being motionless is the last situation you'll want to find yourself in. Opportunities rarely happen staying home curled up on the couch, watching television or reading a good book. Prince Charming does not come knocking door-to-door ... most of the time, that is.

Creating the Right Circumstance

Step #1: Situate yourself where the odds increase that you will meet someone accidentally, like at a party or in an everyday setting like your local laundromat or library.

Result #1: *It will be a spontaneous meeting, even though you were hoping to meet someone and you helped it along just by being there.*

Step #2: Help create the right set of circumstances by starting a conversation yourself. Or, invite a conversation by making yourself available: smiling, making eye contact, or physically *positioning* yourself near the person so the odds increase that he or she will initiate a conversation.

Result #2: *It will seem like a spontaneous meeting, yet you actually helped it along, even considerably, by taking specific action(s).*

Necessity is the Mother of Invention

One of the best motivators for solving the age-old problem of mating is *need*, instinctual or otherwise. When the bachelor's, or bachelorette's life-style has run its course, you may start having thoughts like, "It's time to settle down," "I've got to start thinking about having a family," or "Gad Zooks!, I can't stand being alone; I really want to be involved in a serious relationship."

Once we identify the *need* to find Mr./Ms. Right to live with, marry, or for some other mutually accepted situation, we must make the *decision* to find this person with whom we long to spend a large part of our life. Some people feel the need but make this decision gradually; others are clear in their goals from the outset. Need is not hard for most individuals to establish. Yes, we all want good companionship, great times, social and sexual fulfillment, but *marriage? Commitment!?*

Unfortunately, this first step is difficult for many people to take. However, it's easy to understand that being indecisive weakens our motivation to take action and make the necessary changes in our lives. When we are truly ready to proceed, we will need to be open and self-directed. With both *need* and a clear *goal* firm in your mind, you won't waiver or shy from the path as the early stages of a relationship develop to the point where you can identify Mr./Ms. Right.

Getting Started

Most of us start our search with positive feelings about ourselves and other people. We begin with the knowledge that we have something good to offer, good qualities which seem only natural to share with another person.

In the earliest stages of attempting to meet Mr./Ms. Right, we will each have our own style and feel more comfortable in different situations or places. Some of us may opt for a relaxed scenario, like getting to know that pleasant librarian while asking about a certain periodical at the local library. Others will feel freer dancing their way over to that decked-out person at the disco and yelping out an invitation to dance like some ancient mating call.

To each his or her own. Perhaps we are not about to identify with some fictional TV character or some mythical super-person like a Captain Marvel or a Wonder Woman. We think of ourselves as the mere *Homo Sapien* type, the more lovable bungler, just the average singer-along of popular love songs. All the better to come down to Earth, out from the clouds, and interact, directed and decisively with other people.

To feel strongly about this need is a good start. To make the clear decision to find your mate: this alone is your best compass for the road ahead.

OTHER PEOPLE

Other people are what it's all about. If you like people, you'll have better chances of them liking you. If you like people and can develop the skills of being personable and diplomatic, you will increase your odds of getting along with other people. It is surprising how simply this principle complements the first motto stated earlier. If you stay *in motion* and at the same time are a friendly conversationalist, the odds of meeting someone new *increase dramatically*. After all, one person can lead to another person and before you know it, a mutual friend may even become that special person you've been looking for.

With more than four billion people in the world, there must be *millions* of individuals with whom you could, in theory, have a friendship. There are surely *thousands* of individuals with whom you could have a romantic relationship, that is, if the right circumstances evolved. Of course, the best news is that you don't need thousands, you are simply looking for *one* person. With the help of this book, you will discover that he or she probably exists somewhere *nearby* — where you live, work, or travel. I'm not just being glib. Get ready!

THE TREND IS UP, AND EVERYWHERE

A financial-wizard friend of mine named Brook often talked about the stock market in catchy phrases. I was amused by his lingo and often took his advice. More often, however, he asked for *my advice* on his love life, which was in constant flux just like the stock market. When Brook advised me as to when to trade a financial security, he reasoned "the trend is your friend." If the stock market was in a major bull market and moving higher, or a bear market and moving lower, he suggested moving in the same direction; avoid standing in front of the stock market coming on like a moving train. The large trend identifies the "path of least resistance," and going with the trend is an easier path than going against it. Logical?

Well, easier said than done, because the financial markets are huge and, as you probably know, unpredictable. But Brook's Wall Street jargon is also of interest to those of us in another market: the *Mr./Ms. Right market!* After all, the world of Other People is huge and unpredictable. Its overall trend is also constantly *in motion*. It may not go up or down, but it is a trend I recommend moving with; to move with the flow of its vast energy by *interacting with other people*. Do not choose to stand aside while this promising flow of other people moves on.

The problem for most individuals, however, is that the process of seeking their mate and interacting with other people is not so simple. Again, it's easier said than done. Most of us share common difficulties in dealing with others. Other people aren't perfect, that's for sure. Often they can be quirky, oversensitive, difficult, or defensive. It's reasonable, however, that the sooner you begin to *accept* their differences and try to enjoy people (even with all the various personality quirks and faults you may encounter), *the sooner you will move more easily among them.*

It doesn't take a financial wizard to recognize the fact that money doesn't grow on trees, it has to be *earned.* We all have our immediate likes and dislikes but unfortunately, we are not *super*-perceptive like Captain Marvel or Wonder Woman. We often make mistakes when registering first impressions, good or bad, about other people. We frequently miss subtle invitations for conversation when a potential mate is nearby because we are momentarily self-conscious or preoccupied — daydreaming about that hoped-for raise at work or mentally listing what we need at the supermarket.

Don't stand aside when that friendly trend of Other People begins to move. At least go along for the ride because you'll never know who else might be on board. Meeting someone new may mean acting against your natural inclinations, like accepting an invitation to a party when it makes you nervous to socialize and meet new people. If shyness isn't a character trait of yours, what might some of your social or personal imperfections be? It isn't always *someone else's* fault if we don't take advantage of the many romantic opportunities which pass us by.

---

*Consider the "path of least resistance" to be the trend of
Other People moving around you. Move with them,
not against them and, certainly, not alone.*

YOUR LUCKY CHARM

"On your Mark...Get Set...," the title of this section, implies two
things: first, you must be prepared *to begin* and, second, you must be
willing *to proceed* on this journey. You will undoubtedly experience
repeated starts and stops. That is the nature of the game. Each
attempt at meeting someone, every date or romantic endeavor will
not lead to a success story. You may not always win, but you can
be prepared and ready at the starting line.

An old proverb states: "A little person can fight a big person if
they are in the right and keep on coming strong." That may be too
idealistic. To shout good luck to the "little person," while giving a
push in the right direction is not going to help. The soothsayers should
have added, "especially if he or she has a black belt in karate!" *We
want to be optimistic but we also need to be pragmatic.*

While ours is a peaceful endeavor — to meet, love, and live with
a mate — it doesn't always come easily. Numerous factors will undoubtedly thwart your efforts, like the twists and turns of an obstacle
course which Fate has mischievously designed.

A rabbit's foot or an Irish Leprechaun are not the good-luck
charms you will need. The numerous techniques, strategies and good
social habits which are profiled in these pages are the mettle which
will coax Lady Luck in your direction. Let perseverance be your virtue.

Becoming involved in a positive romantic relationship may take
self-improvement, experimentation, dedication, time and effort. But
like any other worthwhile endeavor, what else is new?

---

*Develop the best attitudes, social behavior, and
physical presentation possible to increase your odds for success.
Don't be discouraged if this takes some practice.*

WHAT'S YOUR ALTERNATIVE?

2.

LONELINESS CAN BE AWFUL. YOU ARE GOING TO EXPERI-
ence it sometimes whether you like it or not. However, aloneness
doesn't have to mean being lonely. Each of us has our own tolerance
for being alone, and some loneliness is a normal part of life. But
alone for how long?

Those happy holidays, Saturday nights and formal social functions (like other people's weddings and sit-down dinners) can be sad
or depressing without a loving partner at your side. Family expectations, societal pressures, not to mention the tick-tock of the proverbial biological clock, can make loneliness even more painful. The
very urge for a shared life is an *animalistic* need, and while most
humans are thought to be loftier creatures than most, few of us can
escape this instinctual pull. The need to mate and, for many, the
need to have children can be *very* real.

PLAYING THE ODDS

How many times have you passed someone on the street or seen
someone at a social event and felt *potential* for love? How many times
did you miss getting to know that nearby stranger when he or she
was just a few feet from you, without even an innocent attempt at
meeting them? The answer is probably *hundreds* of times, more than
you're even aware of or care to remember.

Wouldn't it be nice to give yourself and that *potential mate* a
chance? Even if you try and meet just one of the next twenty interesting, attractive people that come your way, it would probably be an
improvement. Each encounter doesn't have to result in a spirited
conversation or a promising first date; count it as practice and stay in

motion. After all, when you're out fishing you may have to throw some of the little fish back in the water and, at other times, you'll spend hours in your boat without even getting a nibble.

Loneliness is an unacceptable alternative and can actually interfere with our maintaining a friendly, positive frame of mind. It's a Mating Catch-22: you are less likely to meet someone new if you are lonely and feeling blue.

THE VAPOR FACTOR

Kirsty, a thirty-two year old advertising executive, told me a story partly out of frustration that she was single and did not know what to do about it, and partly because she knew I was compiling anecdotes for this book. She had just moved to a suburban town in California, an hour's drive outside of Los Angeles, and had finally settled into her new job in an up-and-coming advertising firm.

After a few weeks, she adjusted to her new life-style and settled into her five-room apartment with its pretty views and blue-tiled Jacuzzi. It sounds great, but her social life was limited; her new colleagues were older and seemed too busy to include her in their social affairs. Kirsty hadn't been romantically involved with a man for almost a year, and she missed having someone to share her good fortune with.

The Tease of Temptation

One Saturday morning, she decided to go to the post office at the college campus, a few minutes away, rather than drive the extra mile into town. She parked her car and walked though the student-center towards the post office, pausing at a large community bulletin board. Looking over the multicolored posters and signs, she overheard a conversation between two men in their late thirties who were standing in front of the faculty mail boxes.

One of the men was nicely dressed in a purple checked shirt and gray pleated trousers, and Kirsty found him quite handsome. She liked the way he talked and smiled, and admired his thick brown hair. He sounded like someone she could be friends with, and Kirsty couldn't help noticing the absence of a wedding band. The two men also noticed Kirsty and half-turned in a friendly greeting, momentarily stopping their conversation.

Kirsty said hello, but felt somewhat out of place as the two men returned to their conversation. She glanced over two or three more posters, and continued on to the post office to mail her letters. Feeling slightly embarrassed about walking past the two men a second time, Kirsty returned to the parking lot using the side door.

Kicking Yourself in the Pants-Syndrome

Starting her car, Kirsty belittled her social awkwardness thinking, "Why did I have to go out the side door?" However, just as she turned the ignition, she saw the man she liked step through the front door of the student center and walk towards his car in the parking lot. Her pulse quickened as they both, coincidentally, drove away from the campus towards the local highway.

Kirsty stopped at the traffic light in the right lane, to turn towards home as she'd planned, when the man pulled up alongside her in the left lane, apparently heading in the other direction towards town. Waiting for the light to change, they turned towards one another. He smiled and waved in recognition, and Kirsty returned the gesture. It was a warm day, and both car windows were down. It was one of those nice, friendly moments with a person you might have found interesting and had something truly in common with. It felt good and was filled with promise, fresh, like a budding flower.

Yet, Kirsty felt nothing but disappointment when the light changed and the brown-haired man drove on to town, and she dutifully turned towards home, alone. She fantasized about the loving relationship he and she might have had, and wondered if she would ever see him again. She was frustrated because, as a woman, *she* wanted to be approached first, to be asked for a date. She didn't want to have to approach *him*.

Recognize this picture? What's wrong with it? What's right? Events like this happen every day in the life of most single people. Kirsty reasoned, in retrospect, that he probably already had a girlfriend, and that he might not have been *available* or *interested* in her anyway. Certainly she didn't know a lot about him other than his appearance, the color of his car, the sound of his voice, his height and approximate age. Would she see him again? Maybe...possibly, but probably not and who knows in what context?

What Should Kirsty Have Done?

Was there anything Kirsty could have done? Chase and tackle him? *No-oo!* On the other hand, she could have leaned through her window at the traffic light and asked him an innocent question like, "Hi, I'm fairly new in town. Do you know where there's a good bakery nearby?," *even if* the question was fabricated for the occasion. (It's not like there was any traffic or cars waiting in line behind them.)

Kirsty did shy away from walking past the two men a second time at the student-center which was, admittedly, counterproductive. If she had paused a second time at the bulletin board or asked an innocent question like, "Are you familiar with the gym here? Is it possible to get a community membership?," maybe the two men would have warmed-up to a three-way conversation.

Was Kirsty's behavior surprising? Not really. People often lack the necessary experience or social charm to accomplish something quite simple, like making small talk with a potential mate when a promising opportunity presents itself.

Was Fate simply tempting her? The promise of the moment and the possibility for love can be exhilarating but *if never tested* in the earliest stages, even with a small conversational exchange, those moments of promise disappear. *Poof!* Like water dissolving into the invisible rays of the sun, a fleeting opportunity will turn into the thin air of memory. It's not as depressing as it sounds; just an example of what we shall know as the *Vapor Factor.*

Make a commitment to reduce the ever-growing number of opportunities lost to the Vapor Factor. Remember: fantasies won't make good company, at least ... not to live with.

THE REALITY TEST

Heck, I'm not saying that every time you spot an attractive, potential mate that an opportunity exists! You will experience the loss of so many opportunities to meet new, interesting and attractive people that it's best to get used to it. You just cannot meet every person that strikes your fancy. Many situations are *next to impossible* to navigate, and others *are impossible:* not even worth your consideration.

Of course, the more skills you possess in moving freely among people, the more adept you will be in evaluating those *seemingly* impossible situations. First, you will need to determine which candidates and situations pass the *Reality Test*.

Reality Test:
Given your perception of the person and the particular set of
circumstances, is there a realistic way
you might meet this person, and do you think:
1) he or she might be interested in you?
2) he or she is available?

YOU PAYS YOUR MONEY
AND YOU TAKES YOUR CHANCES

While Brook, my financial wizard friend never made me rich, he did lace our conversations with witty sayings. A principle he often referred to was the ratio of "risk versus reward." When describing his stock picks, he'd say that the stocks of established companies tend to move higher and more predictably over time, but slowly. They also involved less risk. Stocks of the smaller, lesser known companies could move higher quickly, but involved more risk. That is, sometimes these smaller companies failed miserably and their stock prices dropped precipitously!

What does that have to do with people and a new relationship you ask? I'm certainly not going to equate the decision of which stock you're going to buy with the decision of which person you're going to try to meet. But you can analyze situations in terms of *risk and reward,* assessing the amount of risk in terms of the effort, time and resources involved in taking certain action(s).

If you spot someone you are attracted to on a ski lift, as they ride up the mountain while you are skiing down the crowded slope, trying to meet that person may not be worth your effort. Ski outfits and goggles are very concealing, so what would you base your first impression on anyway, nice fabric? On the other hand, as you take off your goggles at the bottom of the slope and head over to the concession stand, it might be a perfect time to say something to that attractive brunette: "The snow's great today, isn't it?" You are in a snowy environment together and you have something immediately pleasant in common: outstanding ski conditions!

Some effort will be necessary but, in the next twenty opportunities which come your way, there will be a chance to meet someone new and interesting. We will examine scores of examples which are suitable for both men and women, ranging from the most passive behavior to somewhat aggressive behavior.

It may involve a small risk of rejection. It may prove successful or it may turn out to be a waste of your time and energy. Some strategies will be more suited for females than males and vice-versa. Don't be concerned. *All sorts of opportunities exist* in your daily life without having to be too aggressive or having to chase after people as if they were moving targets ... unless you want to.

Determine which situations present a realistic opportunity to meet someone. Ask yourself, "What are my risks and what is the likelihood of some success?"

THE POLLYANNA/FATALIST SYNDROME

Waiting for Mr./Ms. Right to appear, while patiently enduring the passage of time, could take forever. That is not an acceptable alternative. Yet, perhaps you simply want to be yourself. If Mr./Ms. Right does not come along on his or her own, you'll accept that fate as destiny. Perhaps you believe that good things happen if they are supposed to happen, that you don't create your own luck and circumstance. You do not want to analyze information, real or imagined, for any so-called *mate-search planning.* Nor do you want to involve yourself in personal salesmanship or spend time and money dressing to please some unknown suitor.

Do these rationalizations sound like your own? If so, you are not alone in the world: many other people feel the same way. *I just wish you could meet them.* But, consider the following irony: what if one fine day, Mr./Ms. Right walks up to you and through his or her social skills and perceptions, the two of you meet, fall in love, get married and live happily ever after?

What if this same Love of Your Life has read this book and,

through its pages, gets up the nerve and develops the necessary skills to make his or her way into your life? Will you really wait until this special someone *makes the choice for you?* Sure, you might like this person, but you might have liked a dozen other people, maybe months or years before, had you acted in a more resourceful and sophisticated manner.

Personally, I have always preferred nudging Fate along. Make the decision to act on your own behalf and you already take the responsibility for *some* control over your destiny. With a little effort, you can increase the *number* and *quality* of opportunities in your daily life to meet people and develop relationships. Ask yourself, "What's the alternative?"

Don't leave it up to Fate. Fate may leave you out of the picture because Fate is very busy taking care of lots of other people.

The Most Talked About Thing

3.

HAVE YOU EVER NOTICED HOW YOUR FRIENDS WANT TO know about the romantic relationships in your life; that relationships are high on the list of questions people ask you? This questioning can be a little disconcerting if you are single. Aren't you enough on your own? Sure, your career is interesting, your work, money, and the future is important but, "How's John?," "What's going on with Susan?" These questions promptly arise, or the conversation switches to your friend's own romantic concerns: "What do you think about my going out with that woman I met last night?"

The promise and intrigue of love can turn a dry conversation into something involving and exciting. The passion with which we vicariously share the irrational energy of love would make an alien believe love was some ubiquitous drug on which humans thrive. This human fascination is not lost on advertisers. Television and print ads flood our senses with unspoken promises of sex and relationships. "Use this mouthwash...this cologne...wear this brand of clothes," and you can be attractive, find yourself in love, or be lovable just like the high-paid models you see; their beauty romanticized by the latest fashion and photographic techniques.

We are constantly made aware of men and women pairing-off or getting married, and we realize once again that, worldwide, the family structure is here to stay. Go back in time to Antiquity: Helen of Troy, Antony and Cleopatra — through history, romantic relationships could be *the most thought about and talked about thing.*

If a romantic relationship is the most talked about thing or even a close second, then you can talk about it too. You can think about it and act on it when the opportunity arises. It's human nature and why should you be any different? But, you'd be surprised how many people feel ashamed and embarrassed by his or her predicament of being single. Ironically, these very feelings and hesitations often hinder the needed flexibility to act when he or she *really needs to.*

Make the goal of finding a mate a priority in your life.
Don't belittle it, hide it or deny it but, rather, feel good about it.

HEALTHY, WEALTHY, AND WISE

Have I convinced you yet? The bank considers you favorably for being married when you apply for a mortgage because your credit rating generally improves. The I.R.S. gives you special status, and so do insurance companies. It's a well-known fact that doctors believe, and it has been statistically proven, that marriage contributes to longevity, physical well-being and emotional stability. But, of course, the best reason for finding your mate lies in the daily satisfaction of good companionship and the positive qualities of love and a partnership based on commitment.

I grew up in a neighborhood where lots of older couples lived and one such couple were the Marvins up the street. They were a friendly couple, but one day, sadly, Mrs. Marvin died. Our neighbors said Mr. Marvin was only sixty at the time, but he soon became crabby, unkempt and chronically unhappy. Children no longer played in his front yard and he let the weeds grow tall. He didn't seem to care about anything and grew older quickly, hunched over and grayer. He died four years later. Everyone said that having lost his mate, he mourned her and passed away from loneliness.

I'm not suggesting that his mate was replaceable; mourning a lost mate can take time, often years. But a person has to wonder: if Mr. Marvin had met another companion, perhaps after a few years, would he have continued to live a happy life? We'll never know, but we often hear of a person dying relatively soon after a lifelong mate has passed away. This may be part of human nature, and depending on age and other variables, this phenomenon may not change.

On the other hand, many fine and wonderful people are not inventive, emotionally resilient, or willing to change their habits and improve the quality and tenor of their lives either — not necessarily Mr. Marvin, but possibly someone like *you.*

Another neighbor on the same street was Miss Conway. She was eighty years old and never married. People that knew her well said she had lived alone for many years and spent most of her time in her garden, planting and harvesting the vegetables she grew. We all liked and respected Miss Conway, but she was not much fun. Not for us kids, and apparently she did not spend a lot of time socializing with her other neighbors either. She liked to be alone in her great big garden.

I can't say how satisfied she was with her life, if she was lonely, discontent, or if she would have done anything differently if she could have started over. But, with the *right* mate by her side, not just *anyone*, it's easy to picture a more prolific garden, with summer barbecues and children in the underbrush playing hide and seek. A year is a long time to be alone with your garden. But years gone by represent lost time and opportunities never to be recovered.

"Hold it, Todd! Anyone can go out and get just any ol' mate. There are plenty of bad marriages and lots of divorces in the world." That's correct, and you don't want that. You are special, and we all know that good mates don't grow on trees. Also, given people's emotional complexity, committed relationships are not for everyone. Sure, there are always exceptions to the rule, but why should you be one of them? Why, when the rewards of a long-term relationship are so certain, the social need so great and part of our human experience?

A good relationship is a gold mine for almost anyone, anywhere, anytime. It needs no special justification, explication, or rhyme. It does need your high priority, your concentration and your time.

ALL ON BOARD

What are the odds of your being successful in finding a mate? I can't give you a precise statistic but who needs it? I suppose that popular statistics support your being between the ages of twenty through fifty rather than fifty through eighty, but if the statistics are against you, will you give up here and now? Or, will you take control of the situation, make some changes in your life and help tip the odds in your favor?

Single people are *everywhere, in every country, county, city, and town.* Every day newcomers get on board: thousands of young people mature and join the ranks, relationships dissolve, couples divorce, a mate passes away, and single men and women decide for themselves that now is the time to settle down. All of these people sail forth in the same big boat as you. No need to feel that there is something wrong with you if you are single, even if the process of finding your mate takes time. Even if it takes *a lot* of time.

Remember, you are not alone when you are single.
Surprisingly, you've got plenty of company.

WHO IS MR./MS. RIGHT?

4.

I DON'T KNOW WHO HE OR SHE IS IN PARTICULAR, BUT I DO know that there are many Mr./Ms. Rights out there in the world for you. Maybe hundreds, maybe thousands of people with the looks, professional circumstances, and positive personality traits which would be more than compatible with your own. Some of these people are waiting impatiently to be discovered by you and others are even looking for you, at least, *in theory*. Of course, these people are not destined to meet you in particular; they are potential Mr./Ms. Rights for many people like you.

Wait a minute! I thought that Mr./Ms. Right was that one special person *just for me*. That is a nice, idealistic thought, but if that were so, if there were really some magic person out there with a label on them just for you, our task would be like looking for a needle in a haystack. There are more than four billion people in the world!

So, who is Mr./Ms. Right? He or she is the person you can love and have a relationship with for a lengthy period of time, hopefully, for the rest of your life even though there will be adjustments and problems to work out. When a problem in your relationship does come up, you don't have to run for the Exit to find the real Mr./Ms. Right because you are *already* committed to him or her as a person, friend, and mate.

Mr./Ms. Right can be one of many people if you will accept a person's imperfections. This is especially true when you are truly ready and willing to meet Mr./Ms. Right.

THE GREAT LIST

Do you have a list of characteristics that belong to your Prince Charming, or a perfect glass slipper that fits your Cinderella? People often make a mental shopping list but, unless you have a lot of time, you can't afford to wait for some idealized Mr./Ms. Right to stand up and identify themselves. Chasing after dreams and abstractions can be futile and, unfortunately, the tick of your biological clock does not wait for anyone. I'm not suggesting you marry any person to get it over and peg the name "Mr./Ms. Right" on a someone who does not deserve it. I just want to point out the folly of having a Great Big Long List for your prospective mate to fulfill.

My good friend Franz had an attitude problem about finding his Ms. Right. Why, even Cinderella couldn't fit the shoe Franz picked out for her. He had a list which seemed to grow longer as he grew older. His Ms. Right had to be beautiful, younger than he by so many years, have a good job and be handy around the house. She also had to be faithful but not mind if he had a mistress. She couldn't be taller than he, could not gain weight, but she had to bear him as many as six children. I felt sorry for him because no human being I ever knew could meet all of his standards. What was especially odd was that he seemed quite serious about his requirements.

Was Franz really ready to meet his mate? I don't blame him for being choosy, just for being so shortsighted about that list of his. Franz was from lumberjack country, the north woods of New Hampshire, but he could not see the forest from the trees. He was stuck counting birch and maple; the rest of us were off getting married.

Franz might be misguided, but he has a lot of company. Too many people have very long lists, and that overlong list is like the Great Wall of China: built to keep others out. As time goes on, the wise single whittles down the list and, at the same time, gets closer to really wanting to meet Mr./Ms. Right. (Franz, however, was an *unwise* forty.)

Some people feel that no one they meet is quite good enough.
Paradoxically, the people he or she considers worthy
are often not that interested.

LET ONE SLIP BY?

I have known people to be involved with many people, one after the other, and then finally to settle down. Strangely enough, he or she passed by one or two relationships which seemed appropriate and, in their own words, someone who *could have been* Mr./Ms. Right. These people were hoping for a mate but, at the same time, were not really ready — not ready to work things out, adjust to a person that had a history, needs, complications, or who was imperfect. In their fantasy, Mr./Ms. Right had no imperfections. Since they did not see a need to compromise, their quest continued.

Regardless of who we pass by in our search for a mate, the decision to give up one person is often made in the hope that someone better exists. Yes, we might have stayed with "Alan" or "June," but the psychic chemistry was wrong. He or she was a Pisces, did not speak French, and/or was impossible to live with for many other reasons. Maybe we saw the truth, the insurmountable differences, and made the intelligent decision. Most people settle with someone for good reasons and, likewise, decline others for good cause. But not everyone makes such intelligent decisions. How about you?

If you have let a potential mate slip by, learn from your mistakes without regretting the past. Set yourself up for the discovery and the arrival of the *real* Mr./Ms. Right. That person will be as imperfect and as present as you are; no ghosts from the past, no fancy images off in the future.

It is the decision and need to find Mr./Ms. Right that will propel you on this journey, not clear logic nor the fulfillment of all of your wishes and dreams.

KNOW YOURSELF:
YOUR NEEDS IN A MATE

5.

HEY, DON'T THROW AWAY THAT LIST YET. JUST WHITTLE IT down! After all, you probably know what attracts you and, sometimes, you might even know for what reasons. True, there may be many potential Mr./Ms. Rights out there, but you might be attracted to personal or physical characteristics in a certain *type* of person. If you are repeatedly drawn to particular qualities in people, be aware of them because some qualities may be essential ingredients for a *lasting* attraction and relationship.

If you are repeatedly attracted to redheads, for example, is it important to know why? Not necessarily, because, in fact, you may never know. Some seemingly superficial needs and desires, as well as those we consider to be fundamental, *are not rational*. Hopefully, your concerns are less superficial than just liking the color of someone's hair. But your preferences, while perhaps illogical, may have a life of their own.

The Great List is negotiable. Your needs may revolve around personality or physical preferences, or they may involve issues of finances or time. If you have an unending attraction for redheads who are very good looking, highly intellectual, thirty years old, independently wealthy, and fascinated with your stamp-collecting hobby, well, you may be asking too much. Whittle it down: someone who is an attractive redhead and shares your active interest in stamp collecting may be fine.

Unfortunately, with some personalities, a particular attraction may also be responsible for repeated failure. You may feel like a lonely hamster going round and round on a wheel in his cage. Any variety of neurotic or self-critical tendencies can interfere with a lasting and rewarding personal relationship. There are many people who exhibit

destructive social patterns or who exercise poor judgment in select-
ing a partner. In such cases, professional pyschotherapy may be the
only true way to change deeply rooted problems and emotional habits.

---

*Recognize your needs, separating fundamental from the more
superficial. Be true to these needs...if they seem positive.*

GOOD LOOKS, AND BRAINS TOO

I once knew a man who was extremely charming and appealing
to numerous and varied women. After many years of being the Don
Juan, he told me that he was aiming to marry. He was aware of his
problem with fidelity, and believed that the woman with whom he
could be monogamous had to be exceptionally beautiful *to begin with.*
Of course, she had to be both intelligent and amiable because socializing and networking were important aspects of his livelihood.

Many people may clamor, "Hey, that's on my list too! My mate
has to be exceptionally good looking." Maybe extraordinary appear-
ances are fundamentally important and maybe they're not. Ultimately,
a person might wind up with someone who looks okay, but also
excels in making him or her feel loved and needed. Perhaps this
person shares a mutual obsession with the game of golf, involved
conversations about politics or relishes shared challenges in business. These may become the more important qualities which a person attributes to his or her mate.

However, the man I'm talking about, my friend the Don Juan,
had a problem with monogamy. After years of experience, he was
aware of his compulsions and excesses. So, to begin with, he felt he
needed to be with a very beautiful woman. Of course, he and she
would have to be compatible on many different levels. And, to his
credit, he spent the next three years in psychotherapy coming
to grips with his personality and fears of making a commitment
to one woman.

Given that his forte was charm, in excess, Ms. Right was not far
away and, yes, she was exceptionally beautiful. I happily attended
their wedding and the two of them now get along fabulously. In his
own words, they are "happily monogamous." If he had ventured into
a serious relationship with a woman he did not consider exception-

ally beautiful, it is doubtful that he would have succeeded *despite the efforts* of even the best psychoanalyst in the world.

Some needs may dominate your choice and behavior. Question each of your idiosyncratic needs as being "friend" or "foe."

No Time to Find

Jana was a lawyer at a large firm in a medium-sized city. She felt she might best relate to a person who shared her fascination with logic. Her mate did not have to be exceptionally good looking but since she worked long hours, she needed a man who understood her *workaholic* schedule. Jana did not have extraordinary needs as a person; she just wanted companionship. She had limited experience with men, yet she was attractive and not picky.

Luckily for her, the law firm where she worked employed a significant number of men, also lawyers: several of whom were single. Maybe this small pool of fish was limited, but when would she have the time to look elsewhere? Even if she met the perfect man on a weekend in the Bahamas, she would barely have time to get to know him. She was dedicated to her job, expected to work long hours and her schedule was *not* negotiable.

When she first met Tom, Jana was not swept away with passion, nor was she wooed with romantic dinners on the town. However, she was very close to him. Very close because he worked at the same firm. At the time Tom and Jana began seeing each other, they shared an assignment: a corporate restructuring for which the contractual language was extremely demanding. They spent long, late hours together without ever having the time, or need, to go out on a date and see a movie.

Jana may not have been the most socially engaging person from some perspectives, and my friend the Don Juan might have had some deep-rooted problems, but no one said they were perfect. Both were aware of a specific need which related to their livelihood and personality; a need that if not met, would probably have led to an unsuccessful relationship. Clearly, this was not their only need, just at the central nervous system of their needs.

Be flexible, so you don't paint yourself into a corner but, certainly, not all points on the List are negotiable.

THE FIRST IMPRESSION FACTOR

6.

HOW MANY TIMES HAVE YOU SEEN SOMEONE FOR THE FIRST time and said "Wow, He or she looks great!" First impressions are fallible but, nevertheless, they can be a valuable tool when seeking your mate. If you can improve on accuracy while interpreting first impressions, you may discover a hidden source of information which will save time, energy, and ultimately could lead to your mate.

Beware, however, because while our perceptions may be working overtime, the First Impression Factor (with its inherent fallibility) can be an early stumbling block, foiling us here and fooling us there. Frequently our first impressions are based on something superficial or the belief we can see through a person's appearance to the inner workings of their soul. While observing a person at a party, you might notice, "I like the way he moves his hands when he speaks," or, "She's very open and warm, and I like the way she dresses." On the contrary, you might have negative impressions and find he or she inappropriately dressed or too crude in speech and behavior.

But as imperfect as your methods for gathering first impressions may be, you'll have to judge a book by its cover, at least *partially*, especially when it is a person and not a book. When it comes to meeting our mate, we *must* make such judgements because our time and emotional energy is at stake. We cannot give everyone a chance to prove him or herself and to correct those first negative impressions. If you have loads of time, you may opt to give someone a second or third chance, but it could take years of wining and dining to weed out all of the inappropriate people you could encounter.

There are many fish in the sea,
but only some you'll really want to swim with.

Sherlock Holmes to the Rescue

In analyzing our first impressions, we occasionally share characteristics with the great fictional detectives of the past: Bond, Holmes, maybe even the bungling Clouseau. We may prefer not to act in such a *calculating* manner, but if we do not scrutinize information and determine the risk/reward ratio of a given romantic encounter, we may wander aimlessly, exerting time and effort ineffectively.

The image of Sherlock Holmes and his large magnifying glass is somewhat comical, but it is also to the point. Focus your lens while giving room for human imperfection — that only seems fair. Gather both visual and behavioral information; watch the tell-tale signs fill in and form a larger first impression. Is someone conventional or unconventional? Are they witty or dull? Are they friendly, sophisticated, a nervous Nelly, simple, sexy, loud, modest, or conceited? Is his style and manner attractive? Which characteristics matter to you?

Surface details can reflect inner qualities. Did your magnifying glass observe the religious symbol on his or her necklace? Is that something you have in common? Do you care? Are his facial expressions inappropriate for the occasion, or is he just nervous? Is anyone hiding behind that makeup? Does she have a sexy, svelte figure under those baggy clothes? Does she use too much hair spray, dress tastefully, is the voice mellow or shrill and do you mind one way or the other?

Each observation you regard as significant will add a weight,
light or heavy, and tips the scale of the First Impression Factor.

Flip Through a Few Pages

Since we interpret a great deal of information *subjectively,* the deductive reasoning of a Sherlock Holmes may not be the only assistance you'll need. Imagine that our perceptions are viewed on some magical Screen of Interpretation, that our task is to decipher incom-

ing information — whether an extraneous detail or a fundamental clue to a person's character. Superheroes and fictional sleuths may have that kind of special vision but we humans, well, we'll just have to try.

While our first impressions may guide us, our Screens of Interpretation may go haywire, over-analyzing here or under-doing it there. Each of us can lose sight of important personality traits when presented with such a collection of visual, audio, and other sensory features, *good or bad*. But, it's a shame to turn away someone prematurely just because he or she hasn't quite got the good looks or dress-code of the day. Nor do we want to be intimidated, needlessly, by someone who is attractive beyond our expectations.

Are you overly critical? Is your Screen of Interpretation on full blast? You might notice a chipped tooth in an otherwise attractive smile, or an unflattering hairstyle that makes you pause. Maybe so, but if other signals flash green for, "Yes," at least flip through the pages: take another look, and say hello! And if your Screen flashes green in bright neon and hopes sparkle through your brain like fireworks on the Fourth of July ask yourself, *"How often does this happen?"* Having a conversation allows a person's character to shine through or cloud-over your first visual impressions at a *very low risk* of involvement for you.

Is your Screen of Interpretation switched on too low? Do you gravitate to anyone who wants to talk with you and err on the side of acceptance? You purr like a cat; "I love the expensive clothes he is wearing," but when he opens his mouth you experience his crude grammar and bad breath which was not exactly what you had in mind. Do you end up talking with him for hours even though you know he is not the man for you? In this case, "flipping through the pages" may mean just that: close the cover before you're stuck reading the book!

Refine your observation skills while gauging your criticism of others.
Use a process of elimination early on, but remember:
words often say more than a thousand pictures.

SMOKE SCREENS OFTEN DECEIVE

Getting the best of the First Impression Factor is not always easy. People often aren't willing to wear their bad qualities scrawled in red on their T-shirt, and most of us don't sport the kind of egos which brag about our better qualities for all to see. Some people are adept at clouding-over first impressions he or she gives with a *smoke-like shield*.

It may take time for you to see through this tactic (often a well-practiced system of defense) and to re-evaluate your feelings. A person who is potentially unpleasant may also send the subliminal message, "I'm compatible. I am a nice person." In contrast, a genuinely nice and sensitive individual might be scared of personal interaction or be intimidated, sending his or her own message, "Don't come near me, I bite."

Interpreting the First Impression Factor is an art, not a science. Someone who seems obnoxious or awkward may simply lack social sophistication. Maybe he or she is just hard to get to know. While meeting new people and looking for our mate, we must stress our commitment to the process. We cannot be dissuaded by the defensive behavior of other people. Getting to know someone may take time. It may take *numerous situations and conversations* to uncover those personality traits you will either like or dislike.

---

*Pay close attention to the telltale signs of a person's character
so as to take fewer detours on your journey.
Also, you won't want to miss that turn in the road
when you've finally reached your destination!*

GETTING BEYOND SHYNESS

7.

IN THE EARLY STAGES OF GETTING TO KNOW SOMEONE, ANY hesitation in using our communication skills may interfere with our getting closer to another individual. Not all of us share characteristics of shyness, per se; many people have strong nerves and self-confidence. Even so, most of us hesitate, from time to time, to speak, flirt, make ourselves socially available, or ask someone to accompany us to the town fair or local zoo. Repeatedly triggering these moments of hesitation is a *fear of rejection* of one sort or another.

While shyness is often the culprit, a lack of conversation skills often keeps us from successfully navigating the early stages of getting to know someone, even *after* getting over the butterflies-in-your-stomach symptoms of shyness. Before we look at specific conversation techniques, which quicken the pace in meeting and dating prospective Mr./Ms. Rights, let's identify common patterns associated with shyness which we'd like to control and weed-out from our behavior.

The better we manage our fear of rejection, and the better our ability to converse with others, the more people we'll find ourselves talking with — just what you need!

THE TRAP OF SHYNESS

The trap of shyness is that thousands of opportunities to meet people are wasted; they are lost in a never-ending black hole which is colored by the fear of rejection. *I wish I could say this more strongly.*

The shy person is afraid of being treated coldly when his or her intentions are put forth warmly. At conflict with himself, the shy person debates what he can, should, do or say. The shy person believes that his statements and actions must be correct in both form and content or he will look foolish and be vulnerable. Unfortunately, shyness sets a cycle in motion in which a person repeatedly loses confidence to act when he or she really wants and needs to.

The Trap of Shyness keeps us in a state of in-between-ness where, afraid of rejection, we stay quiet and inactive.

HE MIGHT LIKE ME AUTOMATICALLY

A shy person wants to be liked and respected by other people. She reasons that if she does not offend others, she will be liked for her politeness and presence, *if not* her personality. The problem with this rationale is that most people prefer friendliness and social interaction to the asocial behavior of keeping quiet and restrained. How can we respond to, or get to know someone who keeps safely to themselves?

Remember "Show and Tell," the game in elementary school where a child gave a short report in front of the class on a subject of his or her interest? Not only did this entertain and educate ones peers, but it gave children the chance to speak out in turn and to get to know one another. Today, a shy adult, without the benefit of a teacher's supervision and encouragement, debates the wisdom of this undertaking: exposing his or her thoughts and personality to the whims of other people.

Still, the shy person often suffers a mild, underlying pain of regret, wishing they too could play the social games other people play — laughter, storytelling, flirting, handshakes, smiling, small talk — even though at times such social behavior may seem superficial, hypocritical, or just plain silly. The shy person hopes that other people will be entertained without *their* assistance and hopes he or she will be liked and noticed, *automatically.*

A shy person is safe, but they are not necessarily liked. In fact, people prefer it if you aren't shy. That makes socializing easier for them too.

NOTHING VENTURED, NOTHING GAINED

Shyness is a product of conditioning, and like Pavlov's dogs who learned to salivate at the clang of a dinner bell, we humans can be *de-conditioned*, at least to some extent. I was once *very* shy, introverted, and alienated from the world of Other People. I was young at the time but needless to say, I lost many opportunities for friendship and romantic relationships over the years. Yet, in my mid-twenties, I made a conscious decision to try and dig myself out of that black hole. I'm pleased to say that I have succeeded to the point where friends today are shocked in disbelief to hear that I was once a very shy person.

However, it took years of experience and practice and still, at times, I have to fight the tendency to clam-up in order to protect myself in social settings. Since *many* people are shy and socially awkward, do shy people protect themselves from other shy people too? It seems a shame. A turtle protects itself with a big heavy shell, but a turtle doesn't get a lot accomplished in this world.

Have you ever noticed that some elderly people can be refreshing in their lack of shyness? They won't hesitate to say the most direct, childlike things. It's as if they don't care how they appear to others; they've seen it all, done it all, and they've wised-up to the fact that very little really matters when it comes to conversation and protecting some self-made image. As you gain perspective about people, this important realization hits you: *there is no productive reason to be shy.*

Certainly, nothing is gained in the social arena of looking for your mate by being shy. The fact is that most people respect, and are attracted to, those who go out on a limb, show themselves and take a risk. You can help yourself and other shy people at the same time, by coming out of that black hole which is so destructive. Rise to the occasion. You are needed to help. Be brave: take a small calculated risk. *Talk.* No James Bond here, no Wonder Woman — just you and me — more like the charming Inspector Clouseau: bungling at times, but *talking.*

Shyness does not pay. No one reads your mind, treats you special or gives you credit. But...you do miss out on a lot of good times.

YOU, THE CONVERSATIONALIST

8.

IN SCHOOLS ALL OVER THE COUNTRY, THERE SHOULD BE A required course: "The Art of Conversation." In social life, love life, the business world or in friendship, the skilled conversationalist is always better off while moving freely through the world of people. With an added sense of humor, a conversationalist can do wonders in paving the way towards meeting people in all walks of life.

If you are not skilled in wit and repartee, don't worry about it. Be aware, however, that hiding in your shell is not the way to stimulate conversation. You don't need a Blue Ribbon in the Art of Conversation in order to practice. Anyone can practice the skills of navigating the unexpected dips, curves and uplifts that take place in almost every conversation. While some of you may not need a refresher course in the basics, it's surprising how often even the most experienced conversationalist will need to avail himself of these common principles.

Ten Basic Rules of the Road

Rule #1: A Two Way Street: Find a subject in common, or one which interests your conversation partner and develop it...gladly.

Tip: Don't worry about composing perfect questions, answers or opinions. Your conversation partner will be interested in the topic as a whole.

Rule#2: Don't Stop Now: The greater part of a conversation is the activity itself: talking and listening. The actual topics discussed are less important than maintaining a comfortable flow of conversation.

Tip: Concentrate on the bigger issue of enjoying the conversation and getting to know one another.

Rule #3: Look Ahead: Introduce new subjects and keep the flow of conversation fresh by asking questions and making observations.

Tip: Any detail can serve as a pivot and turn into a new topic of conversation: "You mentioned the Bahamas a moment ago. I was there two years ago...."

Rule #4: Do Not Pass: Always keep your conversation partner in mind when introducing or developing topics of conversation; observe and respect his or her responses.

Tip: Do not pursue a topic with someone if he or she seems to resist it by being uncomfortable or defensive. Also, don't be too quick to hotly discuss an issue; argumentation is not your goal.

Rule # 5: Use Your Directionals: If the pace of conversation slackens, take it upon yourself to vitalize the conversation by changing the subject.

Tip: Your goal is a free-flow of thoughts and good feelings, where each person feels free to express his or her thoughts without fear of rejection.

Rule #6: Drive Courteously: Confirm his or her statements, whenever possible, with positive, affirmative responses which help create a relaxed atmosphere: "Yes, I agree," or, "I know what you mean."

Tip: Smooth over your own mistakes and the mistakes of others: be generous and don't dwell on, or point out, mistakes. Encourage your conversation partner with smiles and laughter when appropriate.

Rule #7: Yield: Avoid being monotonous and do your share of listening. Too much cynicism, egotistic bragging or nervous domination of the conversation can be alienating.

Tip: "Enough about me, what do you think about me?," gets boring fast. Give room for the other person to share the spotlight.

Rule #8: Deer Crossing: Don't freeze in your tracks if someone brings up a fact or subject you are not well-versed in.

Tip: Be honest and ask about the subject up-front so that the conversation includes you. You will feel better being honest, and the other person will be happy when he or she is the expert on the subject.

Rule #9: *Beep Your Horn:* If you are listening to a compulsive talker or a nervous chatter-box, you can usually interrupt and get a word in edgewise without insulting them.

Tip: Do not wait for a long pause because a short one will do. A compulsive talker will probably not stop talking on their own and, most likely, will be used to being interrupted.

Rule #10: *U-Turns Are Permitted:* If you are bored with your conversation partner, politely move on when the opportunity presents itself.

Tip: Be polite and smile but don't worry about the precise timing or particular comment which allows you to move on. Think of the time-consuming consequences of continuing the conversation.

There are, after all, many pitfalls along the way which might interfere with your developing a conversation with a prospective mate to the point of getting a date. Even as you converse, you will need to check and make sure your conversation partner is still interested and willing to continue. Is she shifting about or looking over your shoulder whenever she gets a chance? Or is eye contact, a smiling face and participation in the conversation moving in sync at a smooth pace?

Being easy-going and accommodating is a good rule of thumb. It's only a conversation; try and get beyond stiff formalities and enjoy the other person's company.

DETAILS AND THE USE OF PIVOTS

A small detail within a conversation can easily develop into a larger conversation piece. Which detail you choose to develop is not important because any detail will easily relate to a variety of topics. I like to think of a detail in a conversation which develops into a related topic as a *pivot,* a turn in the road which keeps the conversation fresh and interesting.

In the world of physics, or mechanics for that matter, a pivot is, technically, a fixed pin on which something else turns. By coaxing a conversation to turn, using an opinion, place, person, article of clothing, hobby, work-related issue, etc., you can *shift* the topic of conversation, logically and smoothly, to new areas of exploration.

You have just been introduced to a man named Alvin at the reception after a church service and he offers, "I live in Ellensville." If you simply nod or acknowledge the comment with a static, "Oh really?," the conversation may come to a stop, since Alvin may assume you were not impressed and are not really interested in pursuing a conversation with him. That may, or may not, be the case.

You don't need immense knowledge of a great variety of subjects; you just need to use a few simple techniques for *extending and expanding* conversations. If you are interested in talking with Alvin, confirm his statement with a smile and take it upon yourself to develop a detail related to the place he lives in like, "Oh yes, I know that place. Sometimes I go to church service at that big, old church in the center of town," or, "Oh really, how do you like that new restaurant which recently opened in Ellensville?" Maybe you have tried the fare at this new restaurant and can continue the conversation by talking about its great menu and reasonable prices.

Stream-of-consciousness and a creative imagination will be your best resources; common sense will be your best guide. Once the discussion of the new restaurant in Ellensville has taken its course, freely bring up the subject of other restaurants: cuisine, prices, or even other townships. "There is a restaurant on the island of St. Maarten that has the exact same big yellow bananas on its wallpaper as the restaurant in Ellensville. Have you ever been down to the Caribbean?" From Ellensville to the Caribbean all from one afore-mentioned detail? While that may seem a far-fetched connection, your conversation partner will probably be only too pleased to follow your lead.

---

*Evaluate each conversation individually. Sometimes you may
need to work hard at stimulating a conversation and,
at other times, you can just listen.*

THE HERO OR HEROINE IN YOU

Occasionally you may feel a given conversation is drifting unproductively but that, with some direction, it could be invigorated. A James Bond or Wonder Woman could help here, but how about you? A polite person faces a predicament, wondering, "Should I steer this conversation in a more satisfactory direction by gently changing the subject, or is it proper etiquette to pretend this endless debate on corn-oil margarine and a comparison of different brand-names is fascinating?"

For example, imagine that you are with a group of five people and that two of the people have branched off into a loud but private discussion about how to cook escargots. Interesting topic for some, but the rest of the group suppresses a collective yawn while listening politely. You, the Conversationalist, can salvage the situation by skillfully energizing group dynamics. After all, there are five of you, not just two.

"Escargots?," you gracefully inject at a pause. "Have you guys ever gone clamming (addressing the entire group)? We should all go sometime. I hear there's a good beach over in Charleston." It's true; you have interrupted a private conversation, and that may not have been polite. But with the group dynamic floundering, you were actually more courteous to the group as a whole.

It's more constructive to take the helm and direct a ship out of troubled waters, than to politely go down with it.

I'M NOT SHY, BUT I'M TOO POLITE

Politeness is a very important and charming attribute indeed but, on occasion, the *overly-polite* person may lose control of a variety of situations and regret it. There are numerous individuals who will take advantage of your good manners. You may wind up spending the duration of a cocktail party listening to someone ramble on about a subject you have no interest in: like a drawn-out history of the Swiss watch industry and the development of the Cukoo Clock. You may find yourself backed up against a wall, your wine glass hopelessly in need of a refill. Think of the many other promising conversations you could be having; at the very least, think about that refill!

Being overly polite often hinders your finding a mate, because you end up on some detour just when you spot someone you'd really like to talk to across the room. Being a good conversationalist means being able to navigate the many obstacles which inevitably come up in a conversation and, to some extent, to make your own decisions about *what* you'd like to talk about and with *whom* you'd like to speak.

Don't leave it up to others to be responsible, polite, or have social sophistication. Very few people actually take a course on the subject.

THE SILENCE RULE

One of the simplest rules, because there can be very little social interaction without it, is the Silence Rule. Silence is golden and very peaceful in the right context, but within a conversation, it's not usually very helpful. The rule goes something like this: *"Other than the practice of meditation or watching butterflies in the park, who needs it?"*

An overdose of silence in a social setting can create unnecessary awkwardness. For instance, how many silent moments have you sat through at mealtime, listening to the nerve-wracking clink of silverware on dinner plates interspersed with someone clearing his or her throat? How many painful seconds have you spent hoping for someone to break the ice and come up with something to say?

A natural pace of conversation, needless to say, will contain silences and pauses. A good conversation will have a natural rhythm. You will need to sense when to give or take, listen with interest, speak faster, change the subject, dramatize, show the tender side of your personality, flirt, joke, ask questions or reveal personal information about yourself. In other words, the actual silence you will be comfortable with is relative to the *particular circumstances and personalities* involved.

Some people react quickly, while others are just as clever but take more time. I once had an attorney from Texas who was as slow as molasses when he spoke, "Todd, (pause) I believe this situation needs (pause) well...perhaps...uh...to be reconsidered," pausing and drawling, charmingly, but for what seemed like forever before he made his point. He was very smart, however, and ultimately worth the high fees I paid him. Luckily, his fees weren't based on an hourly rate! Be sensitive to the *style* and *manner* of your conversation partner; adjust your expectations and gauge your implementation of the Silence Rule accordingly.

Avoid too much silence. Do not nervously ramble on either.
Just do your share to keep the conversation
flowing at a natural pace.

PRACTICE MAKES YOU
FRIENDLIER ANYWAY

WE WILL LOOK INTO THE PSYCHOLOGY OF REJECTION AND how to deal with it later. In the meantime, if you experience similar hesitations, simply open your mouth and say (almost any tone of voice will do), "Hello," "Good morning," "You make my day," "Top of the morning," "Hi (quiet)," "Hi (normal)," or "Hi (loud)." Get into this friendly habit, even when it doesn't serve any particular romantic purpose, like greeting your colleagues at work or neighbors on the street. If you can greet a person in a friendly and casual manner when you *partially* care about them, think how you will greet someone whom you *really* care about.

Stay in practice. Condition yourself to be friendly and greet people at the drop of a hat, both for the pleasure of it and so you won't miss that person who really matters.

FATHER KNOWS BEST

In the apartment building where I used to live, there was a charming man who was in his mid-sixties. He would hold the elevator door for other people before he got in or out. He would smell pleasantly of cologne, dress in a handsome suit, and say hello to everyone with a smile. Maybe he was going to retire soon and was happy about that. It doesn't matter. You did not need to engage him in a long conversation to vote him the friendliest, sweetest, and most considerate man in the building. He had that presence about him, and he *contrasted* the good number of unfriendly people in the building.

He wasn't just being friendly to attract one of the many eligible, older ladies in the building. He was genuinely friendly, contagiously so, and he attracted lots of smiles and greetings in response. Now, if I had these feelings about this fellow, think how many other people in the building felt this way. How about his colleagues at work, his friends and relatives? I mean, word gets around. Even if other people didn't introduce him to their favorite single lady friend, he would do well enough by himself if, and when, he wanted.

Even people who keep to themselves greet someone they know to be friendly. Friendliness that goes around definitely comes around.

Small Talk is Risk Free

If you have not picked up this point already, you've probably sensed it wasn't long in coming. One of the best devices for meeting a mate is often right in front of our noses: *small talk*. Some people think small talk is beneath them, too silly or frivolous to take seriously, but once you get the hang of it, you will undoubtedly agree with me. Perhaps what you say won't sound original; it may seem slightly worn or predictable. That's not the point. As long as what you say functions to start or continue a conversation at a particular point in time, what does it matter?

One perennial topic for small talk is the weather. How hot, cold, or will it be rainy or sunny? We all have subjects in common, like the weather, which are *safe* to talk about with strangers or acquaintances because these topics are *not personal*. That is the beauty of small talk. A person will recognize the tone and language of small talk and be *less* defensive about talking with a stranger. Furthermore, if you enter into a conversation using an *impersonal* topic, you can usually lead into a more personal discussion, thus using small talk as a conversational pivot: "Golly, it's cold (impersonal). Well... at least you got the chance to wear that terrific hat (personal)!"

Small Talk #1: On a summer day at the mall, you volunteer to a friendly shopper, "I came down for the air-conditioning and to buy a newspaper, but they've sold out already (smiling as you say this)! By referring to yourself first, you deflect the attention away from the other person and make it easier for him or her to respond. You add after a moment's pause, "Did you hear about the hurricane in North Carolina last night?"

Let's analyze this opening line. Using small talk, you have inadvertently volunteered a great deal of information about yourself:

1. You are a friendly sort of person; the kind who will speak to a stranger.

2. You read the daily newspaper and are interested in current events.

3. You care about the heat, and value comfort.

4. Life's curve balls amuse you, such as the paper being sold out. (It does not make you throw an angry fit, for example.)

5. Other body language or first impressions you manage to convey, relaxed posture, your good looks, character, choice of clothes, etc.

Clearly, many different levels of communication will overlap and the list above could go on and on. If he or she responds favorably to your opening line, you can *pivot* immediately: "It's really *so* hot! Have you been to the beach yet this summer?" While this example serves as an introduction to later chapters on Opening Lines, I would like to backtrack and continue with another illustration of the *no risk venture of small talk....*

Small Talk #2: Imagine that you are walking down a city street and, for a few moments, you are walking directly next to a person you would like to meet. You are both passing in front of a French restaurant and there are unusually huge, round planters filled with red gardenias. It is simply a detail in the total scheme of things, but it is a welcomed sight both from a stray hummingbird's point of view, and also to a couple of people walking home from work. "Wow, I've never seen such huge flower pots," you remark. *Risk free.*

Risk free because, in fact, they are inappropriately sized planters (the restaurant owner's faux pas is your entree), and you are half-talking to yourself anyway. You offer the phrase *coincidentally* in the other person's direction with a friendly tone of delight. You are being indirect so to appear casual and give the impression that it is the planters which have given rise to your observation, *not* your romantic inclinations towards him or her. Given that most people are brought up to be polite, often overly polite, he or she will probably be friendly and respond in one way or other to this *something-in-common-bond* you have creatively identified.

Of course, it is possible that a person may not be inclined to have a conversation with a stranger and will ignore you. The man or woman may become defensive and feel that, indeed, you are coming-on to them. But the beauty of small talk is that even if you speak to someone directly, with a smile and flirtatious sparkle in your eye, you are just being friendly and making *small talk*.

Skeleton key:

Almost everyone accepts (and expects) small talk with a stranger — especially, when presented in a casual, easy-going manner.

Thanks to an Actor's Self-Confidence

What? You say you lack the self-confidence to initiate greetings or make conversation? To say, "practice makes perfect," helps promote your general attitude but isn't enough to open a conversation with a stranger? Yet, you are aware that by being restrained and introverted, you limit yourself socially and thereby, *romantically.*

Sometimes it's difficult to stop thinking about our problems or inhibitions, and to move more freely among those people we would like to associate with. While there are numerous techniques, here are two which have been instrumental to many people in need of a jump-start from time to time.

Jump Start #1: Imagine an actor professing great love with a red rose clutched to his chest as he speaks words of passion. (Deep inside, however, he worries that the audience can hear his stomach growl: "Darn that pizza I ate for lunch," he laments.)

Just for a moment, try being that actor but recite a different line like, "Hello, my name is Bob. I see you drive a Volvo. I've had one for six years — great car, isn't it?" No need to change professions or become a movie star — just make a cameo appearance from time to time.

Jump Start #2: Invoke the image of a person you know who is naturally friendly and personable. Surely, the roster of your past acquaintances contains one person whose friendly, outward nature you admire.

Imitate his or her character just for a few moments, using their social charm as a good example. Think how he or she would react in such a social situation when you need an opening line or a response.

Does it seem too drastic to *jump-start* your personality into action when it hesitates in neutral? Try it. *Fake* the confidence and muster up the nerve to speak when you need to. No one can read your mind, and if you are nervous about starting a conversation, you are probably the only one who knows it. Very few people are perceptive enough to notice your nervousness. It's more likely, however, that other people *will be impressed* by your actions and the confidence you display.

After all, actors take-on the character of another person, temporarily, and the successful ones get paid generously for it as well!

THANK YOUR NATURAL HIGHS FOR BONUS DAYS

Depending on the frequency of *natural highs* in your life, you will sometimes get a "freebie." That is, there will be days when you naturally possess the confidence to meet people and socialize in situations you would otherwise find inhibiting. These boosts of confidence are not borne out of desperation, or of newly-found communicative skills, but out of being in such a *good mood* that you find yourself more friendly and open than in the other three hundred-plus days of the year.

My cousin Sarah met her mate, quite accidentally, on one of her *bonus days.* Sarah was not the most outgoing of people, and she often displayed the bad habit of discouraging men who made passes at her, regardless of her interest. One fine day, her boss surprised her by announcing in front of her peers that she was being promoted. Not only did this solve her immediate financial problems, it did wonders to raise her self-esteem and good will towards others. In her own words, she walked out of the office that day "smiling from head to toe." Normally, Sarah would go home after work, cook for herself, watch television, and retire early. This particular evening she decided to celebrate, even if by herself.

She drove to one of the popular restaurants in town and sat down at the bar, not wanting to sit at a table alone. Unaware that she had *positioned* herself precisely in the right place at the right time, a conversation ensued with a man sitting next to her. He was not in a good mood, in part, because his arm was in a cast from a recent ski accident. Sarah had noticed him when she sat down and had an inkling to start a conversation with him. But, miracles don't happen, and my cousin Sarah did not do the obvious: ask him what had happened to his arm. However, she was open to talking with someone new and it was her good mood that made the difference.

His name was Michael, and he opened the conversation by reacting to her friendly glow: "You look like *you've* had a good day," he smiled dryly. Observations, which are *obliquely* complimentary are perfect conversation openers as we will examine soon. Sarah, meanwhile, was off to the races. She was so pleased with her promotion at work that she forgot her usual behavior towards strange men was to spurn them. It had been so long since she had allowed herself the luxury of meeting a man, and she decided that she liked Michael right away.

Michael and Sarah talked at length about her promotion and then he told her about his unfortunate ski vacation. You could call it good timing, winning a bonus-day lotto, or being in the right place at the right time. The two of them started dating and the rest is history, because Sarah and Michael have been together ever since.

Bonus days are not the only times, but they are prime times for practice. The next time you are in an exuberant mood, for whatever reason, recognize its potential. It does not have to be some great change in your career like Sarah's. It can be anything that brings out the brighter, more sociable side of you. There is no greater substitute for acting confidently and being friendly. If you are serious about finding your mate, don't waste this potential sitting around watching TV or talking to an old friend on the phone. Do ask your friend to come along. Place yourself in a social setting, the best available, and let your good mood work for you effortlessly.

Conversation is both a means and an end. With it as a skill,
you can be generous. Without it, you are dependent
on the generosity and skills of others.

A Scout is Ready, Willing, and Able

10

Maybe you were never a Boy or Girl Scout, but... you are doing a bit of your own scouting now. You see possibilities in every situation, no matter how simple or complex. You are open to surprises and chance meetings. While others expect to meet their mate in conventional settings or situations, you are *creative* and *flexible*. While you are only looking for one merit badge, one for love in the shape of a wedding band, you repeat this motto: *Anywhere, Anyplace, Anytime.*

When Opportunity Knocks

Now, you must be prepared because, when the time comes, no one holds up a sign saying, "This Way to the Yellow Brick Road." The Scout must smell opportunity by the tell-tale signs which are always present, like the soft pull of some seductive cologne or perfume. With this second sense, alert and focused, a scout makes decisions in a disciplined manner. When opportunity comes knocking, you will need to open the door (try not to shut it on the very person you've been waiting for).

My friend Justin was a scout, but not necessarily a good one. One Saturday, Justin called to say he was coming to a party I was giving, but that there had been a change of plans. He could only stay for an hour or so because he wanted to go to another reception given at the same time. Just the day before, I had told him about a woman named Lena whom I had invited; actually, I gave her rave reviews and he seemed excited about meeting her. I also let Lena know there would be a single man at the party whom I thought she would like. In response, Lena planned on coming alone.

I asked Justin if he might meet a woman at the reception to which he was intent on going. He said, "No," it wasn't that kind of event, just a gathering of good friends whom he already knew, but "some were from out of town." He said it was rare they all got together and he didn't want to miss it; they were old college friends.

Given that Justin was lonely and wanted to meet his Ms. Right, at least so he said, his decision to miss the party seemed self-defeating. I understood his conflict but did he want to socialize with old friends, or be at a party with several new women to meet including one in particular who came highly recommended by a friend? Wouldn't it be possible to see some of these old college friends later that evening or perhaps the next day? Of course, there was no guarantee Justin and Lena would hit it off, and it did sound like he would definitely have a good time with his college buddies, but what was his priority?

Good Scouts have positive and flexible attitudes. When a Scout senses opportunity, he does not place obstacles in the way. Rather, he removes obstacles whenever possible.

Flexibility Can Win the Day

As I thought, Justin was charmed by Lena and I could tell that she was warming up to him as well. He spoke to me, aside, saying that he felt pressured to be at his friend's reception on time. Justin went so far as to ask Lena if she wished to accompany him to the reception he was going to, but Lena politely declined. After all, she had only talked with Justin for twenty minutes, had just recently arrived at my party, and there were many other interesting people to meet in the room. He and she agreed to get together another time soon, and so they exchanged phone numbers. Under normal circumstances, this might have led to a budding, romantic relationship.

The night was young, however, and Lena met another man whom I did not know, but who had been invited through a mutual friend. The two of them spent a lot of time talking and dancing together. As the party wound down, around 2 A.M., he offered to give her a ride home and the two left together. Lena called me the next day to thank me for the party, to say what a great time she'd had, and to comment on how many interesting single men I knew.

When Justin got around to calling her, several days later, his opportunity had been lost. Lena told Justin that she had liked meeting him, but that she had recently started seeing someone. Lena didn't like to date more than one person at a time.

A good scout knows that a window of opportunity sometimes closes quickly. If Justin wanted a merit badge, he should have revised his plans on the spot.

Getting Your Priorities Straight

Now, we can't assume that Justin would have been the man Lena would meet and start to date that evening, but the odds were favorable in my estimation. As far as Justin was concerned, it was just a case of lousy timing and bad luck. However, it might easily have been a case of *perfect timing* and *good luck* had Justin been flexible and given his love life the priority it deserved. He was *ready* and *willing*, but Justin lacked the *ability* to be flexible. He was rigid in his decision to leave the party, especially given that he liked Lena, and this ultimately cost him an opportunity to date a potential Ms. Right.

Convenient opportunities to meet a potential mate don't float by all that often. Swim with the current or you may find yourself treading water.

THIS COULD HAPPEN TO YOU

Ready: You may enroll in an adult education class hoping to meet Mr./Ms.Right, but you actually meet him in the bookstore while looking for the textbook. You may have great expectations in going to a friend's dance party, but happen to meet your future spouse while walking home after the party. You may meet someone unpredictably, *because you are ready.*

Willing: "Anytime" means it could happen when you least expect it: at the stationery store while buying an envelope before rushing to the post office; at the coffee shop, first thing in the morning while your eyes are still adjusting to the light; on a biking trip, even though you are perspiring and not dressed your best. You may be caught off guard, but *you are willing.*

Able: You are dancing at some hot new club when the music stops, and the potential mate you have been watching gives you a look that makes you melt. For any variety of reasons, you can't muster the friendly opening line needed to introduce yourself, or you are too shy and hold back the necessary smile and eye contact that would have gotten things going. You may be ready and willing but, *if you are not able,* the opportunity might be lost anyway.

It takes more than repeating the motto:
"Anywhere, Anyplace, Anytime." You must live and
breathe it by being Ready, Willing, and Able.

ALWAYS KEEP THESE
RULES IN MIND

11

1. *Make the decision to meet a person whom you will call your mate. Remember, don't leave it up to Fate because Fate is busy taking care of lots of other people.*

2. *Make the goal of meeting this person a serious priority. You don't need to justify your efforts. It's the number-one topic on the minds of most other single people. Why not yours?*

3. *Discipline yourself to go places and do things outside of your normal habitat. Increase activity which will bring about opportunities for chance-meetings, group activity, or formal introductions.*

4. *Shorten the list of your requirements for Mr./Ms. Right. Since you haven't met him or her yet, how do you know so much about them?*

5. *Accept imperfections in a prospective mate as long as the basic personal and physical chemistry seems right. Don't compromise too much or the relationship may not last.*

6. *Give the person a chance to shine through negative first impressions which are often fallible. On the other hand, don't waste your time either.*

7. *Recognize shyness as being a counter-productive trait. What are some of your fears and bad habits which lock you into non-productive patterns of aloneness? Concentrate on improving and adjusting your behavior accordingly.*

8. *Increase your efforts at being friendly. Don't wait for the other person to greet you or start a conversation. Condition yourself to take action when an opportunity to meet someone arises; it may only require a subtle or non-aggressive action.*

9. *Practice conversation as an art in itself. You never know when conversation may help create a social situation where you meet a prospective mate. After all, what if he or she is shy, less socially sophisticated than you, and could use your help?*

10. *Monitor and improve your attitudes towards openness and friendliness. Are you self-disciplined and flexible in your search? Are you really Ready, Willing, and Able, "Anywhere, Anytime, Anyplace?"*

Take Your Positions...Go!
II

THE ART OF "POSITIONING."

12

You DON'T HAVE TO BE THE MOST CHARMING, ATTRACTIVE, or persuasive person, but you must first *position* yourself in the physical proximity of the person whom you would like to meet, naturally. And, of course to be successful, any Positioning Technique must lead to a second goal: a conversation.

For the moment, let's look at several examples of what is usually the first action taken when meeting someone new: *Positioning*. There are three basic levels of Positioning: *passive, active, and aggressive*. Each will have its own set of variables determining the level of complexity and type of Positioning it takes to meet a person.

One could invest as much as a quarter-hour trying to unobtrusively include yourself in a group conversation at an office cocktail party (with that cute new executive you've been eyeing), or just a few seconds by accidentally bumping into him in the local hardware store one Saturday morning. It often will depend on where you are, the specific individual(s)involved, and any obstacles in your way.

For example, if you have accepted an invitation to a social event and you walk into a room full of available single people, well, that wouldn't involve much effort at all. You have not met anyone yet, but you have *passively positioned* yourself just by being there. Perhaps an interesting man or woman will help you out and start talking to you!

Creating coincidental meetings out of thin air is, definitely, an art worth cultivating. Unless you are a rock star or some other kind of Very Beautiful Person, you may have to *make an effort* to get within the proximity of a person you would like to meet. That is, you may have to go to him or her. If you are swimming laps at the town pool, you may need to swim an extra length and get out on the same side

as that handsome lifeguard. You could then casually position yourself by walking slowly past, and starting a friendly conversation by
asking about the temperature of the water.

Positioning can be thought of as priming the canvas
on which you are going to paint.
When the conversation begins, the painting starts.

PEOPLE USUALLY SAY "YES"

More often than not, an opportunity to meet someone can exist
... yet, you might not recognize it. Unless your mate comes wrapped
in a red ribbon with a note saying, "Here, Jill. This is the man you
will marry," Positioning Techniques can be very useful. They can also
be *very creatively* employed.

Did you happen to take an introductory ballroom dance-class
when you were in junior high? Crossing the floor to ask someone to
dance was a tense moment. Will he or she say yes or no? And yet,
getting a partner to dance usually just meant *asking* because it was
rare that someone would refuse. It was, after all, just a dance.

Now that we are older, the principles are basically the same. It's
still inevitably awkward to cross the floor and introduce yourself to
someone. Why, it's a tricky dance in itself and the culprit is (always
has been) that dastardly *fear of rejection.* Today, we find ourselves
tapping the shoulder of someone by the punch bowl at a party, and
getting out the conversational equivalent of, "Awhhhhh... Hiiiiii...
(can we test the waters of a potential relationship?)." The good news
is that people usually say "yes"... at least to a conversation.

This two-part action will become a practiced reflex in time.
First, get physically close to the person (positioned) and,
second, have a conversation.

AVOIDING THE HEAD-ON COLLISION

When you were twelve years old and in that same dance class mentioned above, you tried hard to be charming when approaching that special dance partner. You took care in combing your hair or choosing the color of your dress.

Today, male or female, you still want to approach a potential partner in a charming manner and you want to *avoid being obvious* about your romantic intentions. After all, this time around you may want a relationship, not just a dance. You may want to eat, live, and sleep with this person — you don't want this prospective mate to get defensive or form a negative impression about you before he or she even gets a chance to know you!

I used to know a man named Adam who behaved in a way which I'm sure you are familiar with. He was less than sophisticated in making his initial approach to women. In fact, he came-on to women as if he were the Great Drooler. Not much "dancing" to it all. He just wanted to get down to the nitty gritty. Very few women trusted his overtures, however, or found him to be an appealing prospect. His "Your place or mine?" routine is probably best remembered during the 1960s in the era of hippies and "free love."

Today, many people will become defensive if he or she feels you have an ulterior motive (sexual, romantic, etc.). Even people who are attracted to you prefer not to be taken for granted. So, rather than colliding head-on with the psychological defenses of a potential mate, approach the person obliquely; don't display your trump card before the game begins.

I'll always remember the advice my gymnastics instructor in college gave me just before I began work at the parallel bars. He'd say, "Todd, the 'amateur' is always in a hurry, but the 'professional' (and he'd stress that word with the greatest respect) has *aaaa-llll* (and he'd stretch that word until I'd relax and give full concentration to what I was doing) the time in the world." Of course, in the process of finding your mate, you are not concerned with professionalism — just try not to bungle it, *amateurishly.*

Remember, you first want to elicit a friendly response.
Secondly, you would like to avoid being rejected.

THE OBLIQUE APPROACH

The Oblique Approach is probably one of the most important principles I can recommend as it embraces the all-important virtues of patience and diplomacy. It respects the other person's space and personality. It masks your more obvious romantic intentions, and enables you to meet people whom you might otherwise not. It allows people to save face and participate in the dating game with less fear of rejection.

The Oblique Approach is a method which can be transferred to many different diplomatic activities. You can apply it to any form of salesmanship, negotiation, group dynamics or relationships of any type. It is simple and yet so difficult to implement with consistency, sincerity and charm.

In the early stages of meeting people, an Oblique Approach can be most useful in disguising your eagerness, nervousness, or romantic intentions (or lust). Calculating and circumspect, an oblique approach allows the prospective mate to accept and like you when he or she had no previous intention of entering into a friendship with you.

The Oblique Approach minimizes risk of rejection and can be described like this: *approach a person in a gradual, step by step, mutually agreed-upon manner. Consider, diplomatically, how your words and actions will effect the other person, rather than impulsively acting out your own immediate wants and desires.*

Make a potential mate feel that your action(s) is spontaneous, even if premeditated. Win the trust of the other person first, before acting-out your own whims.

MAKE IT HIS IDEA: PASSIVE POSITIONING

No technique could be more oblique than *Passive Positioning*. In such instances, one person is relying on the interest of a second person to begin a conversation. Passive Positioning requires placing yourself next to someone, e.g., sitting next to a person on a bus or standing next to them at a party where, *hopefully,* one of you will initiate a conversation. Passive Positioning takes skill, nerve, timing, and insight. Yet, it is the least demanding of Positioning Techniques to employ when meeting a prospective mate; it is also the most widely implemented.

In ballroom dancing, where a polite, old-fashioned etiquette still exists, one of the easiest dances is the Two Step, or "front-step, back-step." There is little chance of falling down on the dance floor or making a fool out of yourself with such simplicity, no matter who takes the lead.

Two Easy Exercises

1. **Can I Help You?** More than once I have positioned myself, simply and passively, in the proximity of a woman I was interested in meeting by walking nonchalantly in her direction. I may have originally planned a different route, but think how pleasantly surprised I was to hear her unfamiliar voice asking me for directions, "Excuse me, but do you know where the movie theater is?"

2. **Merely A Coincidence.** Your name is Melissa. You notice a man in the town library whom you recognize from your place of employment, but he is someone you've never actually met. You don't have the nerve to go over to him and introduce yourself directly, even on this Sunday afternoon when you both have some free time. Yet, if you browse through the stacks (close to where he is reading) and wait for the right moment to make eye contact and smile, a conversation might begin.

Sit, stand, or walk next to someone. Create the impression that your presence does not harbor an ulterior motive. Hopefully he or she will say something to you ... but you can't always count on it.

STOPPING IN YOUR TRACKS

You've joined an organization or signed up for an activity in your community. Perhaps you are taking Ballroom Dancing at the Y just to brush up on your "Whose leading here?" and "That's my foot" vocabulary. One evening, you're hurrying to class a few minutes late and you recognize that attractive, personable fellow from class in line at the drinking fountain.

Yes, you've paid your tuition to learn how to dance and, yes, you are nervous about being late, but you also joined class in hopes of meeting a man who fits *his* description exactly. After all, your career is not riding on this particular diploma, but your love life might be. Why not turn on a dime? Stand in line for a drink of water. What better place is there for you to be?

Quick-Step and Turn:
Condition yourself to react constructively even when a situation takes you by surprise. Timing can be crucial and you may have to be the first to act. Hopefully, one of you will say something.

MAKING AN EFFORT: ACTIVE POSITIONING

Getting to talk to a new, interesting, and attractive person often demands an effort and some risk of appearing obvious. The particular technique employed can't always be termed "passive" or "aggressive" because, at times, you must rate the effort somewhere *in-between* those extreme levels. *Active Positioning* will lie somewhere in the middle on a scale of one to ten.

For example, noticing a man across the room at a cocktail party hasn't always meant meeting him in the past. Perhaps you were discouraged when you watched him talking with someone else. You didn't act quickly enough to position yourself nearby and so, when he was free and ready to mingle, you lost your chance to another.

The next time a similar situation arises, try moving over to whatever, or whomever, is located conveniently next to this man, perhaps it's the punch bowl. Your risk so far is that you may drink more than you bargained for, and that no one will call you a Scout or give you a merit badge for *just standing there.* So, when you notice a pause in the conversation, say something pleasant about the color of the punch or the tie he is wearing. You may feel awkward waiting your turn, and you may nervously blurt out your sentence while accidentally making a slurping sound in your glass as you speak, but no one said it's always comfortable or easy.

It may take some effort and often there are obstacles along the way.
But you can't always leave it up to him or her to approach you first.

ASSUMPTION OF SOME RISK:
AGGRESSIVE POSITIONING

When Positioning runs the risk of being obvious and/or takes quick thinking or quick talking, we refer to it as *Aggressive Positioning*. Oh, it's not as bad as it sounds. An analogy might be that when picking a peach off a tree, you may have to reach higher up on the tree to find one ready to eat. You may need to stand on a stool to reach it and you may even fall off. No big deal; just brush off the dirt and try again. *In such cases, you will undoubtedly need to work harder to keep your approach oblique.*

Aggressive Positioning, Level One:
TWO PEOPLE THINKING IN A BAR

He: I'm drinking at the bar and she is with a group of people at a table across the room. She seems to like me because I keep making eye contact and she doesn't turn away.

She: Every time I turn around he's looking this way and he's really cute. I wish I could talk with him but I'm with these people and we're all sitting at a table.

He: She's getting up, probably to use the ladies room. When she walks by, I'll try to say something with a smile like, 'Hi, I see you are with a rowdy bunch of people tonight.' After all, I can't expect her to walk across the floor and whisper sweet nothings in my ear. (*He's also thinking, 'Don't lose an opportunity which may be fleeting. Sometimes it is now or never.'*)

She: If I go the ladies room, maybe we'll have a conversation on the way back. At least I'm Positioning myself, even if *passively,* and I can smile at him as I go by.

Hopefully, he will get the idea and say something to me at which point I will be encouraging. *(She's also thinking, 'Don't expect him to go to extraordinary lengths to meet you. Encourage him by making yourself available.')*

Remember, the other person will only do so much before losing the opportunity to the Vapor Factor.

INVENTIVE TECHNIQUES FOR THE SOPHISTICATED AND DARING

The term *Aggressive Positioning* implies that more skill and effort will be necessary in order to succeed in meeting a person. The skilled conversationalist can maneuver through a variety of potentially awkward conversations and yet, each conversation can be socially acceptable and entertaining. Likewise, a person who is skilled in Positioning Techniques can create opportunities to meet men or women seemingly out of *thin air.*

Aggressive Positioning, Level 2:
THE CAPPUCINO AFFAIR

Picture yourself, a gentleman, in a restaurant with two male friends having a cappuccino on a Saturday afternoon. You've noticed a woman sitting by herself whom you would love to meet. For most people this situation might seem impossible. You are in a public place, sitting a few tables away from this person, and you lack the necessary flexibility given your commitment to socialize with your pals. Also, let's not forget, you know very little about her. She may be waiting for her boyfriend to show up!

While there are several obstacles in the way, anyone with some basic conversation skills could easily make an attempt to meet this individual while maintaining an Oblique Approach. This particular set of circumstances may be complicated by the presence of your two friends who may, or may not, be sympathetic to your cause. Start by appealing to your friends' understanding, "As she leaves, I'm going to walk out the door with her and try to start a conversation. If I succeed I may be back in several minutes, after I've gotten her number or some other way of getting in touch with her. Otherwise, I'll see you in a *few seconds*."

"Sure," they joke and give you a hard time, but your friends are likely to be envious of your daring and skill. "Ssshhh," you reason, "Don't give it away; you'll break the spontaneity." *Option:* avoid consulting with your friends and find an excuse for your absence; you are going to buy a paper or a pack of cigarettes and will be back in five minutes.

As your prospective mate starts to leave, you pay your share of the bill. You appear as genuine as possible, perhaps taking a mint near the door. Looking straight ahead, as if you have somewhere important to go, you (the friendly sleuth), casually walk out the door. As you pass her, you turn slightly and nod towards the restaurant with a smile, "That's a *great* place, isn't it? I go there a lot to have a coffee and read the paper." This, admittedly, is an example of a *hunter's* mentality and is for more confident and somewhat aggressive personalities. The principles behind these actions, however, are for everyone: flexibility, inventiveness, and the willingness to take *some* risk.

---

*Creating a cover is a sleight of hand trick, and is another use of
the Oblique Approach. Like the magician, you do one thing to mask
another. Like a good dancer, you make it all look easy.*

The Quandary of the Empty Seat

Like the Scout who is ever industrious, you can learn to view a large variety of obstacles as surmountable. Passive, Active, and Aggressive are fine terms, but numerous *variables will exist in each and every situation*. Versatility is required; some problems involve simple solutions and others, complex solutions.

To illustrate how circumstances and specific obstacles can change, consider the Quandary of the Empty Seat. Not a Chinese puzzle or riddle, the Quandary of the Empty Seat is a model problem which illustrates correct thought process and discipline with regards to Positioning. I'm sure you've had the experience of stepping onto a commuter train (bus, airplane, etc.) and noticing the perfect travel companion sitting alone and adjacent to an empty seat. The quandary which you may find yourself in is whether or not you will attempt to meet this person by taking limited, but definite action, or none at all. Whatever, you will certainly choose to sit — that much we know.

PASSIVE POSITIONING, SIMPLE EFFORT

Since each situation will bring about its own challenges, we need to be prepared to deal with any obstacle *as long as we perceive it to be surmountable*. Imagine that you get on the train and you are lucky: the train is crowded with only a few empty seats. If you casually sit down next to this man or woman and take out the latest mystery novel, he or she won't think it aggressive or strange.

Note: With little risk, you are passively positioned and your effort was simple. A more complex action would be needed if, to get to the seat, you waited for twenty seconds for a man in front of you to take off his coat and place it on the seat rack above. You may become impatient and give-in by sitting in a closer seat (but too far from your hoped-for companion). Obstacles in this case would include both your own impatience and lack of commitment to the process.

Don't be discouraged when an obstacle delays your approach. Learn to expect and solve problems patiently, or you will run the risk of appearing too obvious.

ACTIVE POSITIONING, MODERATE EFFORT

What if the train is half empty and there are fifteen empty seats? You may have feelings of conflict, because you don't want to appear too eager by sitting next to him. However, the important fact to keep in mind is that he or she *cannot read your mind*, and everyone knows you must sit somewhere.

It would be easy enough to camouflage your interest by looking distracted and placing your coat on the rack above. When you sit down, avoid looking directly at him by glancing through your magazine instead. The person you are hoping to meet has probably not counted the number of empty seats. You can be assured that he won't turn around and do so when you sit down. At some point, you can casually ask for the time ("How soon before this train departs?"), and hopefully a conversation will result.

If you do not know a person, you'll want to come across in a friendly and casual manner. Later on, you can be yourself — once you can count him or her as a friend.

AGGRESSIVE POSITIONING, COMPLEX EFFORT

What if only a few people are on the train and there are thirty empty seats? If you sit several seats behind or in front of a prospective mate, you will probably miss any chance you may have had to meet this person. You feel conflicted because you don't want to invade his or her space or appear too obvious. Probably it is smarter not to jump into the seat directly beside this person because he or she may not want you there.

You could simply say, "Hi. May I join you?," and while that is occasionally appropriate, it could make the person feel pressured. A prospective mate may be polite and tolerate the invasion of privacy, or it could put him or her ill-at-ease for the rest of the journey. Of course, on the other hand, if you were to sit several seats away, you could only cast wistful glances from over the empty seats.

Compromise. Sit down adjacent to the person, directly across the aisle if possible. While placing your jacket on the coat rack, or while standing in the aisle as you take off your jacket, look around and say in his or her direction, "I've never seen the train so empty at this time of day." Or, you could smile as you take your seat while holding your newspaper (as if you are intending to read), "Are we early (looking at all the empty seats)? I forgot my watch this morning." Remember, a stranger does not know you. You may be one of those friendly people who like to make small talk. Maybe you are, or maybe you aren't, but you have succeeded in transforming a commuter train into a friendly conversation piece.

Until You Meet Your Mate, Remember This:
If you meet someone, enter into a relationship, date, and later marry, what difference does it make what type of effort it took on your part to meet them?

Finding Something in Common

= 13

When you fish in a pond you can try for hours without getting any nibbles. So what else is new? With the know-how of when, how, and where to fish, you will increase your odds of making a catch. Now that you have studied some basic principles of Positioning, you need to be prepared for one of two things:

1. You will be the first person to talk.
2. You will need to respond if the other person talks first.

Both situations may require quick reflexes.

You May Need a Hook

In journalism, a hook is a term used for a catchy theme, or a particular angle of presenting a story, so it carries extra appeal. If you are the proud owner of a new fishing bait and tackle store in a town on the coast of Maine, you may want to submit a press release to the local newspaper to announce your grand opening. You want to make the story attractive to the editors, and readers alike, and you discover a "hook" in the upcoming fiftieth anniversary of the Maine Lobster Fishermen Association's Lobster Dinner.

It so happens that your opening week coincides with this event, precisely when the fishermen are holding their conference on new lobster traps and changing trends in sales. What a coincidence: the

anniversary dinner and conference occurring during the opening week
of your store. Not only will the newspaper print your article, but the
local readers and participants of the conference will be very interested in viewing your new lobster traps!

Now, back to the reality of meeting a new date. The more *appropriate* and *catchy* your opening line, the more assured you will be of
a positive response and conversation to follow. While we don't want
to sell bait, per se, we are interested in presenting the most amiable,
charming and interesting sides of our personality.

If your opening line is light and bright,
it may encourage a positive response.
With an appreciative laugh or smile, you'll stand a
better chance of starting a conversation.

A LINE YOU CAN BOTH SHARE

Wherever you are, people share *common denominators:* a something-in-common bond which can serve as an *entree* to a conversation because it relates directly to the person you are talking with. We
introduced this concept earlier as part of a discussion on small talk.
Whether or not it is small talk or a profound comment is immaterial;
the two of you have it in common.

If you are on a business trip in Paris, speaking English would
clearly be something you have in common (in Oklahoma, *poof!*, this
bond would be taken for granted). "Are you an American too?," you
ask a man, huffing and puffing, while making your way up the Eiffel
Tower, having heard him speak to the tour guide.

The Something in Common Bond:
Almost any person will respond to a friendly opening line which
identifies something you both have in common.

FISHERMEN USE LURES THAT SHINE

Simple Openings

You are leaving your favorite shopping mall, walking through a busy parking lot, and you pass by a man approaching his car. You would love to say something, so you focus on his yellow convertible Ferrari, "Oh, I hear those are fantastic cars. It must be a lot of fun to drive," you offer. If he responds positively, you can ask about the mileage per gallon and eventually shift gears to find out how far of a commute you both have.

Complex Openings

At the checkout counter in the local liquor store, you are in line and notice a woman in front of you carrying a small computer bag over her shoulder. It so happens that you are taking your portable computer on a flight to Los Angeles for an editing job this week. You need a similar bag yourself, maybe slightly bigger, but nevertheless you *zero-in* on this common bond.

"Excuse me, where did you get that computer bag? I have to take my computer on a flight to Los Angeles next week, and I'm looking for one just like that." Good! Not only are you relating to something she probably likes and has spent money on, but you are including details of your life which might invite questioning. What kind of computer do you have and why are you going to L.A.? What line of work are you in that you need to bring a computer?

A complex opening line which includes personal information about yourself may stir a person's curiosity. It may also allow the other person to feel more comfortable and lower his or her defenses.

THOSE UNUSUAL OCCURRENCES

An unusual situation does not have to be that special to qualify for use in an opening line — just something you both have in common.

Example A: You are walking down the main thoroughfare in your hometown, and a video store is having a grand opening with those red, white, and blue banners on their windows to grab your attention. You stop in front of the display window right next to a gentleman you would love to meet. "It's nice to see we are finally getting a video store in this town," you remark.

Example B: You are sitting with a friend at a luncheonette, next to a table with a woman you would like to meet. You determine that she may be approachable, but you can't figure out how to open a conversation. At that moment something unusual happens: the lights unexpectedly dim as if there's a power shortage or the manager accidentally switched-off the wrong light.

You joke, "I thought it was too bright in here anyway," or "It's getting spooky." If she responds to your humor with a smile, you may have received an invitation to continue talking. If she doesn't seem encouraging, oh well, you can always recheck the menu.

"Looks like a storm is coming our way!" With dark rain clouds approaching, it's a good time to cast out your line — a good time to fish too.

DIDN'T I SEE YOU DOWNSTREAM?

Once upon a time I had hoped to meet a woman who lived in my neighborhood in Manhattan. I liked her because of her intelligent looking face, her great shock of red hair, and the fact that I overheard her talking to her grandfather one day and liked the way she sounded.

On Wednesdays, my schedule included an aerobics class at a gym which was twenty minutes walking-distance across town. Unexpectedly, who stepped out of the door to my gym but the charming redhead who lived in my neighborhood! She didn't seem to notice me, but looked straight ahead and started walking towards *our* part of town.

In one quick sensation of buzzing synapses, I decided to forget about working-out that day. Perhaps I may have caught up to her a bit too obviously, but when I began to pass her (as if I were in a hurry to get home), I feigned surprise as if I were just recognizing her. "Hmm, Ahhh ... I've seen you around my neighborhood at ... what's-the-name of that store?" (I *really* couldn't remember.) She smiled, agreed that she recognized me, and named a few stores to help me out. We definitely had our neighborhood in common, so it was easy for her to accept my starting a conversation.

Well, by the time we reached our neighborhood, it became clear that my new redheaded friend was married. Nevertheless we became neighbors and friends and, later, when my wife and I gave parties, she and her husband would come over to socialize with our other friends and we all had a good time. Each endeavor does not have to turn into a romantic affair. It's always nice to know more people in town

---

Your approach doesn't have to be perfect. Sometimes being awkward is charming because it shows vulnerability which, in turn, makes the other person feel at ease.

OUT OF THE DINGHY, INTO THE CANOE

Entering and exiting almost any place or location often creates a *window of opportunity*. It's easy to comment on the specific environment which you both are about to experience, or already have experienced.

Example 1: Leaving the shopping mall, you walk by a woman who returned your smile while looking over the apples and pears in the supermarket. You call out an amused, "Did you see the long lines to get into that new movie?" The two of you have just passed the theater and are heading towards your cars. You add, "I hear that movie is really good."

Example 2: Let's imagine that Thursday evening happens to be your bowling night. You notice a man or woman approaching the entrance of the bowling alley. As the two of you reach the entrance to the alley you complain lightheartedly, "It was hard to find parking tonight." Or, if the two of you are leaving, coincidentally, you offer modestly, "I didn't bowl that well tonight — How did you do?"

In entering or exiting a place, you can look forwards or backwards.
To some degree, you have experiences from the immediate past
or expectations for the immediate future in common.

Always Nicer to Fish with a Friend

Remember, the easiest solution to your mating problem is when you get that call, "Mary! Have I got the fellow for you. This is the guy you are going to marry!" Usually, however, those calls seem far and few between. Quite often, when you do get an introduction, one or both people feel a mild disappointment like they've just lost the lotto. Even so, this type of blind date or introduction is the easiest, safest and often the most successful method to meet your mate. *There is probably no better source for entering into a romantic relationship than meeting people through people you already know.*

Even from the standpoint of making conversation alone, it's a highly compelling something-in-common bond. People that are recommended by mutual friends are already screened. Having a mutual friend creates an immediate bond based on positive (hopefully) associations . If you are at Marissa's wedding party or some other kind of social function, what easier opening line could there be than, "How do you know Marissa?"

Encourage friends to introduce you to their friends. When they have
someone appropriate in mind, do not hesitate or put-off the event.
Recognize the opportunity and say, "Sure! Anytime."

Business May Create the Ideal Fish Pond

Philip and Cynthia were introduced by a mutual friend, but the introduction wasn't quite enough to get things going, at least, not right away. The friend they had in common was named Gloria, and one Sunday afternoon Gloria took Philip to the restaurant where Cynthia was co-owner. Ostensibly, they went to have pastries and catch-up on what each other had been doing; *also*, Gloria thought her friends would like to meet one another.

Everything went as planned, and Philip definitely liked Cynthia. Unfortunately, Cynthia didn't take instantly to him. After all, men came into the restaurant every day, and making small talk with customers was simply part of her job. In the next couple of weeks, Philip stopped by the restaurant to say hello, but found Cynthia continued to respond to him in that same polite, but uninterested way.

He had all but given up when he needed a caterer for his architectural firm's annual party. Of course! He would ask Cynthia about her restaurant's specialties and checkout her rates. Philip wasn't expecting anything romantic to come out of this, how could he? — just a price list, some friendly talk about business and the possibility of getting to know her better.

In the meantime, Gloria had a phone conversation with Cynthia which included talk about Philip. Actually, Cynthia had started getting used to seeing Philip come into the restaurant, and Gloria's positive comments made her feel less resistant towards him.

It was Philip's inquiry about catering, however, that became the catalyst their friendship needed. It wasn't just that she wanted his business, but talking about a project he and she had in common made it easier for her to take him seriously. She invited Philip into the kitchen to explain what her restaurant would prepare, and she couldn't help admiring the warm quality of his dark brown eyes and smile. She was beginning to like him.

Philip was no different from previous days when he'd stop by to say hello. It just took some time, Gloria's recommendation, his repeated visits and, eventually, having more in common.

Don't press your luck by being overly present or familiar.
Do help the friendship along by being personable and available.

Other Opening Lines and Responses

$$14$$

IF YOU CAN'T FIND SOMETHING DIRECTLY IN COMMON, SOME-
thing indirect will do. To review, if a person is available to have a
relationship and is at all interested in you, almost any comment will
do to break the ice. In order to improve your odds of success, and to
avoid detrimental comments like, "You look like a man I'd want to
marry only you have too many pimples," or "My, but you have terrific breasts," let's examine several types of opening lines and *responses*.

Cast Your Line Observantly

"Is this Forsythe Street?" you ask, walking in the same direction
as a potential mate. When she turns and answers "Yes, it is," you add,
"I've never seen so many daffodils this soon in the season. Maybe
Forsythe Street is an early bloomer," you suggest in good humor.
Well, there you are: observant about nature and a sense of humor
to boot. Of course, if daffodils are in bloom, they will be blooming
all over the place not *just* on Forsythe Street! The soundness of
your logic is not always important but, rather, the spirit in which
you present it *is*.

---

*An observation about the surrounding environment is always
acceptable. How late is the train or how hot is this sun?
An added sense of humor helps create a quick, personal
exchange without any strings attached.*

THE T-SHIRT PRINCIPLE

T-shirts are fashionable from time to time and they often sport witty phrases, pictures, or names of places. People pay to purchase these *publicly displayed* statements, often customized with pop-culture comments like, "I Love Daytona Beach." It may be a phrase he or she thought was amusing, or it may simply be the first piece of clothing that popped out of their bureau drawer. It's not hard to think of any variety of lines to offer in response like, "I've never been to Florida, but I hear Daytona has a great beach!"

If the message is offensive, try not to judge the person simply by his or her T-Shirt. Consider it a conversation piece, par excellence. What better opening line than focusing on his or her own tacitly offered invitation? Not everyone likes to wear T-shirts, but the same principle can be applied elsewhere. If someone is engaged in an activity that invites comment like polishing the car in the driveway, or picking a bouquet of wildflowers in the grassy lot across the way, *any relevant comment will do.*

You don't necessarily have something in common, but you are acknowledging an activity or statement which, to some degree, a person makes public.

NOW THAT'S A FISH-FIN I LIKE

I recently observed a young man on a New York City bus, sitting next to a beautiful young woman he seemed interested in meeting. She was wearing elegantly carved leather boots, perhaps from Spain or Italy. "Wow, where did you get those boots? They're really great," came out of his mouth almost automatically. The woman appeared to be a model or an actress, and I admired how he deflected his compliment to her boots, not to her face or anatomy, *and* that he seemed genuine.

Sure, he could have said "I really like your eyes," but it would have been too soon and too public for such familiarity. Of course, there is always a chance that a forward approach will produce positive results. But, probably he would only have succeeded in making her feel self-conscious or defensive, rather than want to participate in a conversation with a stranger on a city bus. After all, what did he know about this woman that he could assume she would play by his rules?

*"I really like that tie," for example, acknowledges the probability
that the person wearing the tie also likes it. Few people will reject
this indirect form of flattery if presented obliquely, genuinely,
and without excessive enthusiasm.*

A WHITE LIE MAY BE HELPFUL

There are times when we may need to manipulate the other
person's perception of the truth because it is the most productive
thing to do. No one likes to lie outright, nor am I recommending it.
However, a white lie can be very productive from time to time.

Remember how I met my redheaded woman friend while walking home from my gym? Thinking back on that example, I *was* feeling a bit self-conscious about my Stop Everything and Turn Approach.
As I passed her in the street, I admit to having *feigned* surprise in
order to create an air of spontaneity and make it appear I had been
walking in her direction *anyway*. That functioned, deceptively, as a
kind of white lie.

In retrospect, I suppose I could have blurted out the whole truth
and nothing but the truth like, "Hi, I've seen you around my neighborhood. Perhaps you observed me walking towards the gym, but I
was so moved by your persona and charm that I decided to forget
about working-out today, and I paced myself or, you may have noticed, *loped,* in order to catch up to you."

However, I did not speak the whole truth and I would not
always advise it. Revealing the inner workings of each and every
thought can be counterproductive, not to mention *naive*. Most people
do not want to feel they are being chased after, *especially* based
on their looks or sexual attributes. The guilty conscious you'll have
for telling a white lie, once in a while, is probably minor when compared to the opportunity of meeting a lifelong companion you,
otherwise, might lose.

*An occasional white lie may help facilitate an opening line.
Later, you can be your true-blue self, once you can
count him or her as a friend.*

FLAVOR YOUR BAIT WITH OPTIMISM

One basic common denominator among people is an attraction to positive, easygoing attitudes about life. Easygoing people encourage other people to let their guards down and relax. Make a person feel good about talking with you, and they may find you charming and personable. A man or woman conversing with an easygoing person will experience less fear of rejection on the one hand, and less fear of getting involved in an uncomfortable conversation on the other. Life is hard enough. While there are individuals who have depressed personalities, few people actually want to be with a stick-in-the-mud.

1. An Easy-Going Action, and the Double Opener:

You are in line at the Post Office waiting to weigh a small package, and you are searching for something to say to the woman in line behind you. You study the postal stamps you happen to have in your hands, the ones with pictures of birds twittering and fragrant flowers. You imagine a smell which you can't help confuse with the scent of her designer perfume. Since one never knows who the stamp collector might be, you half-turn and smile, "I wonder what kind of bird this is (looking at the stamp)...do you know (looking up at her)?"

Maybe she smiles, and glances at the stamps with eyelashes you secretly admire. "I don't know," she answers with a voice you want to spend your whole life listening to. Perhaps she's shy, and you've caught her off guard by testing her recall on the wingspan of sparrows.

Free her from the demands of ornithology and continue with a *Double Opener:* "It's amazing how many different stamps the Post Office keeps coming out with." You smile and appear understanding even to small things like stamps and, especially, the tentative way she responded to your question the first time. If she is interested and available, she will adjust to the idea that you are easy to talk to. But, it may take a Double Opener before she begins to respond.

2. Upbeat and Positive...but Loud:

Now, there are times for subtleties and there are times for quick action. The Attention-Getter Opening may be what you need for starters. This approach need not be subtle because its function is to get the other person's attention. You can't always have the luxury of perfect Positioning, smooth timing, and a charming presentation.

The man or woman you want to meet might be walking in the opposite direction from you. Or, he or she will be among a crowd of people at a party with music screeching and lights flashing.

Solution: Use any opening line, tap him or her on the shoulder at a party, or greet this person in the hall with a self-confident, "Hi, I've seen you here before. Do you work here?" It may be aggressive and involve some risk of rejection, but if you are friendly and keep smiling, it may be the solution to an otherwise impossible problem.

Coax a person to respond to your opening line by making it easy. Good feelings and positive attitudes are like magnets which can pull people towards you.

YOUR TURN TO RESPOND

A fish will normally tug on the line if he is hungry. But, if the fish does not tug, the fisherman has no other way of gauging its interest. Likewise, if a man or woman starts a conversation with you, *you may have to adjust* to the fact on short notice, often *unexpectedly.* If a woman says something to a man, for example, she may simply be making innocent conversation or she may be interested in getting to know him. He won't know until he interacts with her.

Imagine that sitting beside you at the counter of your local luncheonette is an attractive coffee drinker who asks you to watch her belongings while she makes a phone call. True, she may mean just that. You muse, "That wasn't a come-on, was it? She just wants me to watch her things. Right?"

But, remember, everyone is capable of using the Oblique Approach. Even if looking after her things *was* the extent of her request, she found you to be a trustworthy kind of, may I say, Scout? Since *she* broke the ice, you are free (expected) to respond. When she returns you lose no time and joke lightly, "No one tried to take anything," or "I noticed you are reading a book I'm interested in. Is it good?"

---

*Do not be surprised if someone approaches you
with an opening line. It doesn't cost anything, it's friendly,
and he or she is the one who took the risk.*

CROSSING LINES AND THE QUICK RESPONSE RULE

The Quick Response Rule states: *Almost any response is better than none.* This rule recognizes that when a man or woman has spoken to you first, it is at his or her risk of rejection. A quick response from you makes the same man or woman feel it was worth the risk. Respond if you are interested, even if your line is not perfect. Combine verbal response with encouraging body language (smiles, eye contact, or nodding your head affirmatively).

Moreover, if you want to respond in an encouraging manner, there is no better way to tie the knot than by *crossing lines*. If you glance away sheepishly while silently cussing the fact you can't think of anything else to say, he or she may lose confidence, and *you may lose them.*

Crossing Lines, in Three Parts

1. *Person One's Opening Line:* "Do you know what time it is?"

2. *Person Two's Quick Response:* "Yes. It's five o'clock."

3. *Person Two's Second Line Which Crosses:* "I'm looking forward to daylight savings time this weekend. I can use the extra hour."

---

*Supply a quick response and "cross" their line with your own
contribution to the conversation. You may need to
encourage the other person to keep talking.*

INTRODUCTIONS, AND THE FEAR OF LOOKING FOOLISH

15

A FORMAL INTRODUCTION IS THE MORE DIRECT APPROACH to meeting someone, with all its trimmings of handshakes, smiles, and saying "Hello, my name is Jane." As a technique for starting a conversation with a stranger, an introduction differs somewhat from the two-part action (Positioning and an opening line) which we have been discussing.

Anytime people gather to socialize, or in everyday business, introductions are not only socially appropriate, they are to be *expected*. Better yet, in some situations, like a party, introductions are not only expected, they are *hoped for!* When people gather for one purpose or other, like bowling or a wedding reception, it may be more efficient to approach the person directly and formally introduce yourself. No need to go through an elaborate Positioning Technique and cast your flirtatious fishing net in his or her direction with an opening line.

Decide which is more appropriate: a formal introduction or a combination of Positioning Technique with an opening line.

BUSINESS PEOPLE HAVE EXPERIENCE

Business people, at least in the corporate world and particularly in sales, understand the value of making introductions. People tend to do business with people they like, know, and trust. Salespeople have a lot of practice and training in warming up to other people whose trust they would like to gain.

Business people dress the part and groom their hair; they have learned it is productive and profitable to be charming. Salespeople, and politicians for that matter, address other people by their first names as if addressing an old friend, even if they are talking with someone for the very first time.

You are not making business contacts, necessarily. You are making personal contacts. The motivation is different, the expectations are different, and therein lies the fear of rejection.

SCARY REJECTIONS DON'T HAPPEN HERE

A remarkable characteristic of almost every introduction is a built-in *positive momentum*. People are conditioned from childhood to respond positively to almost each and every introduction made to them. "Jill, I want you to meet Wilson." ("Okay," thinks Jill, "No problem.") Even if Jill and Wilson never say another word to each other, they smile and look as pleased as punch as if they were being introduced to a new best friend.

If introductions can be considered second-nature, then people shouldn't have a problem meeting other people at social gatherings through introductions. Right? If that is true, why do so many people keep to themselves in social settings and choose not to walk over to a potential Mr./Ms. Right and introduce themselves? Why do people hesitate to go to a party or social functions alone, preferring to go with a friend for moral support? I mean, everyone is supposed to be there to talk with other people and have a good time anyway!

Introductions are easy and involve very limited risk of rejection. They don't cost money and are second nature to most people — but you'd never know it.

THE TIME-LAG PRINCIPLE

It's easy when someone takes it upon themselves to introduce you to a third person. The problem begins when you have to make your own introduction. Potentially, you are exposing yourself to one form or another of *rejection*. The mere hint of rejection, a social snub or a cold shoulder can hurt a person's feelings.

Imagine that you are at a party and have observed a person whom you would like to meet. You can think of something to say, but the butterflies in your stomach make you queasy. You are waiting for that precious moment when the timing is perfect, your eyes meet, the music is low, and when her breath (like honeysuckle) is so close you could swoon. Then reality hits you like some nagging frustration; that perfect moment *rarely arrives* without some effort on your part.

Once a decision is made to introduce yourself, either with an opening line or a formal introduction, the Time-Lag Principle comes into play: *There is a greater or lesser distance in time between the decision to act and the acting.* Simply put: "Don't put off tomorrow, what you can do today."

Ten Reasons To Shorten the Time Lag

1. You could waste a lot of time trying to overcome stage fright while waiting for that perfect moment.

2. Having butterflies in your stomach is no worse than the pain of an insignificant rejection or lack of success in meeting someone.

3. While being subtle with timing may produce a more spontaneous meeting, the end result will be about the same anyway.

4. You are only trying to meet someone — you aren't asking them over to dinner...not yet.

5. You will feel better if you try; you are being sociable and staying *in practice.*

6. If you discover there is no possibility for romance, you will be freer, once again, to meet other people.

7. A small calculated risk is part of the process to which you are committed. "Hi, I'm Jennifer," or "My name is Robbie," is *not* too simple an opening line for starters.

8. Any risk of rejection is low, given the built-in positive momentum of introductions.

9. If you are waiting for a third person to introduce you, you cannot count on other people to help. Other people are often self-involved, busy, or may even have forgotten someone's name.

10. Making your own introduction is more polite than smiling awkwardly and shifting aimlessly about. Be helpful. Remember, he or she may be shy, inexperienced or socially awkward.

Waiting for that perfect wave is an obsession with many surfers. In the meantime, they continue to surf. When he or she occasionally wipes-out, well, that's just part of surfing.

LEGITIMATE STALL TACTICS

Sometimes you need a little more time, it's true. *Legitimate Stall Tactics* can do wonders when you need to set up a seemingly spontaneous meeting, or if you are not one hundred percent sure about the first impressions you've gathered about a person. Certainly the great detectives, like Bond or Holmes, were aware of Stall Tactics, pulling up newspapers in front of their newly-donned sunglasses while waiting for clues, an important observation or a revealing action.

Maybe you work in an office and you'd like to get to know a co-worker from another firm down the hall. You choose to *stall* before attempting to meet him. You know he is at the office five days a week, and that a good opportunity will present itself, either on the elevator or in the corner luncheonette during your coffee break. Also, you are a little timid, in part, because you have this all-encompassing *crush* on him.

Instead of being aggressive and risk coming-on to someone you will have to see every day at work regardless of the outcome, you hold back. If you err, you want to err on the side of caution. You'd prefer to overhear him talking with his co-workers in the hall once more, and observe his personality traits and habits from a distance. When the time seems right, you will position yourself and one of you will start talking.

*Don't confuse the benefits of Legitimate Stall Tactics with
the procrastination of the Time-Lag Principle. Stalling can be
positive as long as you act, sooner, than later.*

ALONE AT A SOCIAL EVENT?

A special situation and *opportunity* exists when you are interested
in meeting a prospective mate and he or she happens to be alone at a
social event. It's not so special if you're the one alone because it can
be a lonely experience. Most likely, the man or woman who is alone
is hoping to bump into an acquaintance or to meet someone new. A
person that goes alone to a social event and is not busy socializing is
probably thinking something like, "How long should I stay here? I'll
give it another half hour."

He or she may feel self-conscious about being alone when most
other people are supposedly having fun socializing in groups of two
or more. Unless you think he is waiting around for his date to show
up, don't wait for an invitation but mosey-on-over and introduce
yourself: "Hi, my name is Susan." If it doesn't seem too forward you
might add, "There seems to be mostly couples here tonight." That
type of statement implies that you also came alone and are happy to
talk with another individual who seems unattached.

*You can count on the fact that most people have social needs,
especially in group situations, and that he or she will prefer
good company to being alone.*

THE PARTY PHENOMENON

16

I COULD GO ON AND ON ABOUT THE OPPORTUNITIES PARTIES present. I love them and you should too since they are the perfect environment for meeting new, interesting, and available people. The Party Phenomenon will exist anytime people gather as a group to engage in a fun activity be it a game of badminton, a clambake, or a formal reception for the new congressional candidate in town.

At a party, people are taking a break from the day-to-day routine of work, errands and chores. Problems are temporarily put aside in order to socialize. What better time to meet someone when he or she is open to meeting strangers to talk, relax and have a good time.

The Party Phenomenon is a state of mind, when introductions flow freely and meeting people is both expected and easier.

WHERE PEOPLE GATHER

People gather at parties to have a good time, talk, and *meet people*. Many people may not be comfortable at parties — they may be shy or defensive. The best is yet to come, however. A single person may not be planning to meet someone to date, but you can *bet* that it has entered his or her mind. The *plus* at a party is that everyone who is single *expects* to meet someone new. The *big plus* is that most everyone who is single is *hoping* to meet someone new!

In fact, a single person who goes to a party and doesn't talk with *anyone* thinks, "Heck. This is a lousy party." He or she feels badly and muses, "Maybe I'm not a party-animal. Maybe I'm not socially attractive," or, "Gee. What a waste of time this is." From a perspective of Positioning, a party is a *goldmine*. I mean, there you are in a room full of people. You spot a man or woman who you'd like to meet and who seems to be by themselves...need I say more?

WHAT MAKES A PARTY?

A party is not only a planned and festive occasion for drinking and dancing. It can be a church function, an art gallery opening, a small cocktail or dinner party, or a reception of any kind. A party-like atmosphere can be present in an infinite variety of gatherings, especially events with *group participation* like organized games —volleyball, hiking, softball, bingo — where people lose their inhibitions and are there to share good times.

We can find the Party Phenomenon in group travel, club meetings of all sorts, or even somewhere seemingly mundane like shared activities of the cleanup crew after the town's annual picnic. If you travel on a weekend (when more single people are off work), we can include special locations like a particularly sunny beach (where single people are known to gather), or a popular winter ski lodge where having shared the exhilaration of the slope, singles are thrilled to meet someone romantic in front of a warm fire.

A Word on Singles' Bars: Some bars might occasionally have a party atmosphere, but people usually gather in such places for a wide variety of reasons and often intend to socialize with the friend(s) they came with. Only in some singles bars (where the clientele are familiar with each other), or in the most festive establishments (where people are clearly interested in meeting others), will a party atmosphere be in play.

Use your imagination and be flexible in seeking a party environment.
You name it but, when looking for your mate, don't miss it.

MINGLING: WORKING A CROWD

Now that you have found the party, how do you go about meeting all of the various and interesting single people? In fact, how do you determine who is single *and* available and who is not? Word of mouth? Trial and error? The First Impression Factor? The answer is all of the above through the good-humored process of *mingling*.

Have you ever been square dancing: that ol' time, country fiddling kind of dancing? Just for fun, let's think of mingling as analogous to some of the movements and calls of the square dance. Most of these dances are not only gracious and civil with respect to your dance partner, but also allow you to dance with many different people either in a group or individually. Why, it's just like mingling!

Bow to Your Partner

1. The square dance caller yells out, "Bow to your partner (at the beginning and ending of the dance)." *In a party situation, you'll make your initial contact with a potential partner and, later, make your bows good-bye.*

2. The caller yells out, "Doe See Doe (arms folded, each dancer takes a turn circling around their partner)." *In a party situation, each person exchanges a few words about himself or herself in an initial exchange.*

3. "Grand round," the caller yells (right hand grabs your neighbor's as you dance past him; then your left hand grabs his neighbor's as you dance past her and so on around the circle). *In a party situation, you'll mingle with one person before going to the next.*

4. Finally, "Promenade your partner around the town (arm around your partner, escorting her around the circle)!" *In a party situation, you'll hopefully find someone you will talk to in depth.*

In the process of mingling, every person you greet does not have to be a potential mate, a business contact, or the Albert Einstein you've always wanted to meet. Once you've become adept at making introductions to people you want to meet, it's not hard to be generous and introduce yourself to people you aren't so sure you *need* to meet (Remember, what goes around, comes around).

Since many people feel awkward about introducing themselves, *you* could do it for them. It's socially correct for you to help keep the flow of conversation circulating in the room and to improve group dynamics. It doesn't take a lot of effort to turn around and say, "Hey, Peter. Have you met Jonathan? He's also into computers in a big way." Exchange phone numbers with those people you'd like to see again regardless if they are a potential date. Say, "Hey, I might have a party of my own soon and I'll give you a call."

Everyone respects and appreciates a person who is socially generous and makes introductions easier. Improve your skills at making introductions, and when that special person comes marching into your life, guess who's going to meet them?

THOSE COMIC STRIP CHARACTERS

There is always the risk you will not care for the person you've met during the process of mingling. You may even get caught in a conversation with someone you had hoped to avoid like the Laser-Beam-Nasal-Voiced-Woman, her voice piercing your psyche in rapid pulsations, or the Onion-Breathed-Dandruff-Man. Horrors! It sounds unkind, but it may be true.

Your departure from the company of these comic strip type characters need not be graceful or perfectly timed to a natural pause in the conversation. However, you, the Friendly Mingler, bow with a smile and say, "Excuse me. I see someone I need to speak with," or "I think I'll go get another drink. See you in a bit."

Always respectful and polite, you, especially you, must excuse yourself in order to continue your quest.

THE ONE-LINER: EASY COME, EASY GO

Mingling requires an easy-come, easy-go attitude. Getting bogged-down in a lengthy conversation can be unproductive. Imagine that you were the President of the United States. You couldn't get involved in a long discussion with every person you knew or met, and yet you certainly couldn't afford to hole-up in the Oval Office and not say anything to anyone either.

Politicians, and other busy and successful people, develop the skill of using the *one-liner* because they are aware of the need to appear friendly and appeal to the likes of others. While the one-liner may seem superficial at times, and overused by some, it can be a graceful conversation technique if used in moderation.

If you are strategically moseying across the room to position yourself next to that attractive man in the blue tie at the office holiday party, you won't want to have a lengthy chat with every person who says hello on the way. Yet, you can't sneer or snub all of the well-intending people that come your way either. You can be polite and greet each person by mentioning something *in passing,* "How do you like the new paint job in the hall?," or "I love that necklace you are wearing," or "Too bad the Patriots lost last night," or "I really liked the presentation you gave yesterday."

A one-liner does not have to be the most appropriate or sophisticated comment. When combined with body language, such as a smile, an appropriately friendly touch on the shoulder or handshake, the one-liner will be understood as, "He can't stop and talk right now, but I know he or she likes me just the same."

Ending an ongoing conversation with a one-liner is also extremely useful. When you want to end a conversation, a one-liner (with a perky, upbeat inflection) can lead gracefully to a peak at the close. You'll want to communicate how you've enjoyed talking with this person but that you need to move on.

The content of your one-liner will most often fit naturally within the context of your conversation. If you were listening to a woman speak about the benefits of air-conditioning in large office buildings, you might close with, "Well, I'm certainly glad Bill and Lisa have *their* air-conditioner on (as you smile and make your way through the crowd).

People understand that you cannot have a lengthy conversation with everyone. One-liners add an element of cheerfulness both to greetings and summing-up at the end of a conversation.

May I?: The Art of Blending

Mingling also involves blending-in and blending-out of various conversations. One person leads to the next and, hopefully, you will find someone you are interested in seeing again. In ballroom dancing, an old-fashioned etiquette allowed a man to tap a gal's dance partner on the shoulder saying, "May I cut-in?"

The dance floor may not be as gentile today, but you don't need to be shy about working your way into an ongoing conversation at a party. Unless you detect a very serious atmosphere, or hot and heavy flirtation, blending into a conversation at a party is *expected*.

Since you don't want to confuse blending-in with *butting-in,* you will need to develop the special technique of blending. There are always opening lines which, with good timing and charm, facilitate your blending into any ongoing conversation. As always, think before you leap in order to increase your odds of success.

Blending-in Strategy

1. Listen to the conversation from nearby and determine the pace and subject matter of the conversation. Time your entrance (placed best at a pause) so it doesn't appear like you are butting-in.

2. If you have overheard a proper noun or an activity which you may have in common, use it as a pivot, "Did I hear you mention water-skiing (speaking to them both)? I was in Honolulu last weekend — the water was terrific."

The Party Phenomenon permits and welcomes friendly, whimsical behavior which might otherwise be interpreted as erratic or pushy.

NOT EVERYONE TAKES THE COURSE

In the social arena, the principles of charm and diplomacy are our guiding lights. After all, we are not playing football, aggressively thrashing and kicking about. However, not everyone practices good manners or is all that familiar with the principles of charm and diplomacy. You may need to guard against the occasional rudeness and clumsiness of others (sometimes intentional). You may also need to guard against your own sensitivity and self-destructive reactions to other people's rudeness. If you take a social slight or small rejection too seriously, you may find yourself limping off the playing field and not participating just when the real Mr./Ms. Right comes along.

Two Defensive Plays

1. A person may interrupt a conversation you are engaged in. He or she may cut-in and place their back between you and your conversation partner. Whatever the imposition: loudness, standing in front of you, or any other obnoxious behavior, *reposition yourself* and join the conversation again.

2. A person to whom you are talking may not be that interested in you (Whaaa...unbelievable?). The person may communicate it by not smiling, staring elsewhere, using a monotonous tone of voice, or by not asking any questions. Take the hint: *excuse yourself,* and continue to mingle until you find a more willing conversation partner. As in the example above, your defensive action is to regroup and try again.

Be resilient, and don't be surprised by someone's occasional lack of good manners. Navigate the sea of social awkwardness and don't allow someone else the pleasure of sinking your ship.

DECOYS CAN BE HELPFUL

We are not hunting for ducks, but concepts like the Oblique Approach lead us, indirectly, to the discussion of the *decoy*. A decoy is a third person who distracts the unsuspecting potential Mr./Ms.Right from the fact that you are attempting to meet him or her. Just having another person at your side in a social environment can give you a sense of confidence and security while you are waiting for a prospect to come along.

Inactive and Active Decoy: An Inactive Decoy may or may not be aware of his or her function, while an

Active Decoy may even lend a helping hand such as scouting-out the situation with your goals in mind. Like the straight-man in a comedy routine, a decoy functions to support the main player, *you*.

Cooperative Decoy: A generous friend is usually pleased to lend a helping hand. Picture a man named John who goes with a friend named Marleen to an art gallery opening (town bazaar or barbecue). Marleen independently starts a conversation with a woman (whom John has indicated an interest in meeting). He then casually joins their small talk (without risk of rejection), "Hey, do you have a new friend, Marleen? Hi, I'm John." If Marleen is really trying to help, she might excuse herself to phone her boyfriend (making it clear that John and she are just friends). John's initial approach is less of a come-on given Marleen's presence.

Uncooperative Decoys: Hopefully, if you go with a friend to a party or a social event, you can talk with him or her and still have the freedom to branch-off on your own. Occasionally, you may make the mistake of inviting a friend who feels jealous about your attempts to meet someone new. If you feel that you are obligated to this friend, because he or she feels insulted or left out, you have selected an Uncooperative Decoy and this results in a lack of flexibility and independence.

There are many variations and applications of Decoy Techniques, and most depend on the personalities involved.

AVOID THESE FIVE COMMON MISTAKES

Missed opportunities at social functions extend your waiting time for the relationship you seek. If you are focused on your goal of meeting your mate, don't let an opportunity go to waste *especially* when the Party Phenomenon tilts the odds in your favor. Unless you are privy to a steady stream of social activities, you cannot afford to make too many of the mistakes listed below. How often do you get the chance to meet someone wonderful and exciting in an environment where single people both *expect* and *hope* to meet someone with whom to have a romantic relationship?

1. **Do not get lazy:** Avoid using a friend's presence as an excuse not to meet new people. Do not spend a lot of time with a friend(s) you already know when you can socialize with him or her another time.

2. **Do not forget your purpose:** Once you have met someone attractive and interesting, use the small amount of time you have at a party to become familiar with him or her and to establish an immediate rapport (assuming he or she is interested).

3. **Do not walk away from a good thing:** How many times have you been at a party, met someone you liked, played it too cool, and lost the opportunity to get to know a prospective mate. Perhaps you excused yourself, mingled, and walked over to the bar for a drink. When you returned a few minutes later, you found this Apple of Your Eye engaged in conversation and hitting-it-off with someone new. Next time, forget about mingling and say, "Would you like to get another drink together?"

4. **Do Not Forget the Follow-Through:** You must get whatever information you need in order to see him or her again: a phone number, address, place of work, name of a mutual friend or, at least, give him or her the information needed to contact you. You may be having a great time at a party and talking with the potential mate of your life. You may have established the kind of rapport love songs are made of, but if you don't have the means for Follow-Through, you'll miss the boat. When you are saying good bye, *Follow-Through information is the only thing that really matters.*

5. **Do not shy away from the challenge:** If you worry, "Oh. I can't go to the party because You-Know-Who will be there," you deny yourself a chance to meet someone new. If you have so many opportunities to meet men and women, it might be okay to miss a social event or two. But why should your ex-spouse, lover, or business associate, have all the fun and meet new people? Weather the awkwardness. Smile, if possible, wave from across the room, and then move on with your love life.

---

*Try to avoid these and similar mistakes
because the Vapor Factor is cruel.*

KEEPING PERSPECTIVE:
A SENSE OF HUMOR

17

NOW, YOU DO NOT HAVE TO TELL GREAT JOKES OR BE THE life of the party, but a general resiliency and sense of humor are invaluable attributes. Unless you are the type of person for whom meeting prospective mates comes easy, you will occasionally find yourself in some rather humorous, partly ridiculous and sometimes humiliating situations. Having the ability to keep a broad perspective, and to appreciate the various trials and tribulations which come our way, makes the dating process more tolerable, if not more fun.

THE LESSON OF COMIC OPERAS

Surely, you are familiar with some of the great operas which have been composed. In comic operas, mostly Classical Italian operas composed in the 18th and 19th centuries, audiences are amused by one mishap after the other, usually centered around love and relationships, greed and infidelity. There may be political infighting, deceit and misdirected passions, yet, the characters keep singing, gloriously, from beginning to end. While these often silly plots are filled with clumsy fiascoes, they most often conclude with a happy ending.

Unsuccessful attempts at meeting your mate should not deter you from your pursuit of happiness and a committed relationship. You may face slight humiliation on occasion or small loss of dignity, but that is part and parcel of the process. As with other disciplines in this world, finding a mate may involve one percent inspiration, the easy part, and ninety-nine percent perspiration, the difficult part. Learn to brush-off disappointments by keeping a broad perspective; file away your unsuccessful attempts at romance under the label "A Means to an End."

The Case of The Chinese Ice Cream Bar

When the occasional false start occurs and one thing or other frustrates a successful relationship, we must guard against disappointment, frustration and tears. If the Vapor Factor is detrimental, our own lack of persistence is somewhat *fatal*. Again, if we are reaching up high to harvest ripe fruit, the lofty nature of our quest is such that we sometimes fall off our ladder. Not all false starts are so painful, but others might be considered a waste of time and energy, it's true.

The author of this book, Yours Truly, has had more than his share of James Bond-like stories and, certainly, many ridiculous episodes worthy of the bungling Inspector Clouseau. One episode that posed a few interesting challenges, like a small comic operetta in itself, was my getting to know Tracy.

Walking home alone after a dinner date with my great aunt in Greenwich Village, I was watching the autumn leaves fall amidst the evening traffic on Bleecker Street. That is, those few leaves one can spot in New York City after eating a four course meal of Japanese food and downing several ceramic bottles of almost purely alcoholic *saki*.

Suddenly, out the door of a Chinese restaurant emerged a beautiful young woman. I could hardly conceal my conviction that this was surely Ms. Right as I *skidded* to a halt. Casually stepping over to the curb to stall for a moment, like maybe I want to look over my shoulder to see if my aunt was following me (she's always saying I should settle down with a woman like this.... "No, seems okay....coast clear"). With a single person's enthusiasm and hope, I perceive the warm glance of my future bride on the nape of my neck. Whirling around to emote my feelings about her, I...

Whooa! ...Where is she?! I've lost her in this crowd. *Over there!* But who's the older couple hovering a few paces behind like they're trailing her. The Bond in me emerges: suspicious, like I'm watching some evil ready to descend on my damsel in distress. Then, floating through city lights and traffic noise, the older couple coos her name with the softness of butterfly wings, *"Traaaa—ccccy."* I am contemplating this breeze, still warm with the sweet smell of summer and this strange mix of Chinese and Japanese food. Wait a sec...*her parents?!*

Holy cow! In some momentary fantasy, I almost had the old man in an arm lock. A lot of good that would have done me! This *saki* has definitely gone to my head. Maybe so. But when a single person is desperate for love (or so it seems), reality blurs *with enthusiasm and hope*. Now, reality hits me like the loss of a five dollar Lotto ticket: Eeegads! If I want to meet this woman, I'm going to have to meet her parents too — that won't be easy!

Tracy and her parents descend into a basement-level ice cream parlor (Sure, I'd love to join them, but I'd blow my cover...not just yet). No sooner do I regain my composure when the trio appears back on the street, this time with large cones. I stroll a few paces behind them, inconspicuously, though I'm starting to develop a taxing itch in my left lower leg; can't help my arm extending down towards the ground like some escaped ape from the zoo.

Straightening, I casually saunter past...maybe I can get a better sense of her personality if I can hear their voices. *Hmm*...English accents — all three. *Hmmmm*. I remember being in London, but that was fifteen years ago. What could I possibly talk about even if I could start a conversation? Westminister Abbey? Big Ben?

I slow down as I approach the intersection; my mind drifting on the scattering of pigeons and yellow taxis in the intersection. Oh, well...I might as well call it quits and go home to bed.

Psshsam! Pooosh! Wiiisssooah! — The moment we single people dream of magically eclipsed all doubt! "Excuse me," Tracy's voice wafted pure and seductive. "Do you know where the Sixth Avenue subway is?" (This is what I mean! You are Passively Positioned, minding your own business, and the man or woman of your choice comes up to *you* and starts talking.) "Yeah, sure... it's up this way," I manage to creak out, casually joining the group as if I were also heading in that direction. After all, no one really had any idea which direction I was *supposed* to be walking in at this point, myself included.

"I heard your accents," warming up to the parents, deliberately not coming-on to their glorious daughter. I mentioned my trip to England and expressed my hope to return one day. We had some kind of instantaneous synergy, her parents and I. "Are you tourists?," I asked. "Yes, we are visiting our daughter, Tracy, for a few days."

I glanced over at their daughter, smiling, as if this were my first serious contemplation of her existence (Oh yes, the young woman who asked for directions). "She works in an art gallery in the city," they continued. "Oh, really? Which gallery?," I politely asked, looking over to Tracy (my heart pounding with the promise of Follow-Through information). "The Premier Gallery, uptown," she chimed, her words pealing in my ears like wedding bells.

I sighed with relief because I knew that without this information, any Follow-Through would have been almost impossible. I mean, what was I going to do? Ask Tracy to go out with me in front of her parents after two minutes of conversation? So, with this information, and a few more jolly phrases, I took my leave at the next intersection. I figured that even these nice people probably wouldn't be inviting me, a perfect stranger, to have a *second* ice cream cone with them. I waved with a smile, "It was nice meeting you. Have a good time in New York, and maybe I'll see you around, Tracy."

A few days later, I stopped in at the gallery where Tracy had said she worked; I asked if she'd like to go out for a drink that evening. Well, you might imagine a hot and heavy relationship would be developing in just a matter of days, if not hours. However, it doesn't always work that way. Tracy turned out to be, for better or worse, one more romantic wrong turn, or dead end, in the long road-map of finding my mate. Not that it was a painful experience or a regrettable waste of time, it just fizzled out.

After two or three dates for dinner and drinks, I arrived at the realization that Tracy was inappropriate for me, even though she was *just* right for some other lucky guy. (I never really asked her what she thought of me.) You see, I learned that Tracy was only nineteen years old, fifteen years younger than myself and, unfortunately, *she acted it.*

Our perceptions may become exaggerated by our enthusiasm and desire for a loved one. Keep focused on your goal of finding Mr./Ms. Right, and ride the waves of challenges, obstacles, and occasional wrong turns.

THE DUTCH SWEATER CAPER

Background

Any discussion about keeping perspective and maintaining a sense of humor, has to touch on my short friendship with Jill. A year before I met her, I had been in Holland for a few weeks on business. I bought a wonderful sweater in Amsterdam: in fact, it was my favorite sweater.

The night I met Jill, in New York City, I went to a birthday party for a friend of mine. Ten of us had reserved a back room in a restaurant for a private party. Of course, I went to the restaurant to celebrate my friend's birthday, but you can't blame me if I was keeping my eye out for someone to have my own private parties with...

More than Just a Greeting

First Attempt: Our waitress had a pleasant sense of humor and I found her attractive to the point of wanting to find out what, if anything, we had in common. While she hadn't offered any encouragement, I decided to excuse myself from the bustle of the birthday table and take a stroll around the restaurant. I knew that our waitress would be busy, so I positioned myself by leaning against the long mahogany bar and calmly observed the room's busy proceedings.

Soon enough, she came over to call-out the drink orders to the bartender. Our eyes met and we smiled at one another. I gestured towards one of the tables and chuckled, "That's a boisterous crowd." (I was sharing something we had in common: the *noise*.) She nodded in agreement, laughed, and added cheerfully over her shoulder on her way to another table, "They're drinking up a storm." So far, so good, I thought.

Getting to Know You

Second Attempt: A week later, I returned to the restaurant with a friend of mine to have dinner. He agreed to come along for moral support and to play the part of a Cooperative Decoy. Unfortunately, a different woman waited on our table, but I spotted my waitress friend across the room. We acknowledged each other with a smile, and I waved casually as if to say, "Hey, what a coincidence. You're working tonight?" Since my friend and I were eating dinner, why would she think twice about my being there?

Third Attempt: In a few days, so not to come on too strong, I returned late one evening hoping she might get off work around midnight. I seated myself at the end of the bar and tried to appear natural. Frankly, it was unpleasant to go out of my way to the restaurant, sit at a bar and order several drinks which I did not really feel like having. I mean, I am a patient kind-of-guy, but add the waiting around for the few moments she had free to exchange small talk like, "So, which days do you work?," or "Which nights are busiest?," and a single person can get pretty frustrated by the whole process.

Nevertheless, she was very friendly although I observed she was very friendly to almost anyone who spoke to her. During our conversation, which was squeezed-in over the course of the next hour or so, she told me that her name was Jill and surprised me when she revealed how late she worked that night: 4 A.M.! Call me an old fogy, but after a few more exchanges of flirtatious small talk, I said good night and went home to bed.

Things Were Looking My Way

Fourth and Final Attempt: One week later, about 2 A.M. on a Wednesday night, a time when I knew she was working, I ambled in. I was fairly confident of my mission. I carried a copy of Thursday morning's *New York Times*, a *prop*, so as not to appear too obvious sitting down smack in the middle of her waiting-section. After all, my nocturnal habits, however newly acquired, did not seem strange to her. She worked till 4 A.M. And many people read the next day's morning paper at 2 A.M., not *most* people, but many.

We greeted each other like two good friends before she bolted into a distant corner with a pitcher of beer. I was wearing my favorite sweater, the one purchased in Amsterdam, and I have to admit I was looking rather spiffy and feeling quite debonair. I mean, here I was successfully pulling off more brilliant small talk with Jill like, "I love all the candles in this dark room — makes it look like some religious order." She thought about it and chuckled, "Yeah. It does."

Picture this restaurant: a large space with stone walls, old-fashioned woodwork and very tall ceilings. On each table was a candle giving the room a dark, cavernous atmosphere. There I was, strictly in my Bond mode, although stretching out my newspaper somewhat self-consciously across the table so to look occupied. My thoughts rested happily on the fact that this romantic endeavor was going along just as I had planned. Tonight, I would try to have a lengthy conversation with Jill and see if she might like to get together on her day off.

Then Something Happens

Just as I was peering through the morning's news, I glanced around because I smelled something funny like some synthetic plastic, polyester or nylon. Holy smokes. *My sweater!* My cuff was in the flame, snapping and crackling like a bowl of Rice Crispies. *Damn!* Half-frantic to see if anyone was noticing, especially my waitress, and half mad to save my sweater, I smacked it with my newspaper, dashing out the flames, the small cusps of smoke smelling like some noxious petroleum product. Desperately clinging to my Bond image but with the ever gnawing sensation of feeling distinctly like the bungling Clouseau, I lurched into a reading pose like a puppet being jerked around in a French matinee.

Nothing had happened, I pretended, though a flood of hot blood rushed through my veins and I stared blankly at the blurred print with a retention level not unlike someone's pet dog named Goof. I certainly did not want Jill to detect my clumsiness and sully my up-till-then near perfect image. What on Earth would Bond do? Ridiculous mishap! Worse than that, I couldn't swear she hadn't seen the flames or that someone hadn't told her about it.

All too quickly the moments passed and she came walking by my table, beaming at me with those clear blue eyes. I distrusted her smile, like maybe she smelled the nylon or noticed the deep creases in my newspaper smudging the now indecipherable headlines. Maybe she could read my mind and thought it funny that I lacked the retention capability of a four-year old staring absently into the morning paper. I mean, who reads by candlelight anyway for Pete's sake?

Bond Turns in His Badge

That night I gave up on my waitress-love named Jill, not because of the burned sweater, but because I had determined that my attempts at getting to know her were not passing the *Reality Test*. I determined that it would take a major effort on my part to gain her true affections, *if at all*. I felt like I was chasing after a rainbow, grabbing for colors which evaporated whenever I came near. She just wasn't responding. Sure, she was personable, but only in the polite and naturally friendly manner which I judged to be her style. Of course, maybe I was wrong...

What's Missing in This Picture?

But... weeks later, I was sitting at an outdoor cafe with the same male friend whom I had dined with that night at the restaurant, and Jill passed by. I called out to her and she stopped and turned. It took her a couple of seconds to remember who I was. She smiled momentarily, as if she were both in a great hurry and not all that glad to see me. She said, "Oh. Hi," with this beautiful, but blank look on her face, and then happily went on her way — never returning the interest in me that I had shown towards her.

Depressing? Oh well, that's life. Look at the brighter side. At least I have the sweater story to tell.

THE MORAL OF THESE STORIES

In the two illustrations above, the ultimate lack of success in achieving a romantic relationship is not important. It is the process and determination that is laudable. I eventually did find my Ms. Right, and whether or not I was able to emulate the great Bond or the famous bungling Inspector is inconsequential.

When searching for our mates, we don't need to justify our endeavors. Often we make an effort towards finding love and many times a romantic connection is simply not in the cards. Everyone goes through trials and tribulations; it's human.

Remember the funny twists and squalls, the human folly of the characters in comic opera. Keep singing, laugh a little, and know that there will be a happy ending, eventually.

Exposure: You Can't Win If You Don't Play

=== **18**

It's a little like playing the Lotto. You've got to take chances and you've got to play or you probably won't win. However, take heart. The dating game is much better than playing the lotto because the odds are higher that you will win. Eventually you will win because there are so many other people playing, and guess what many of them are trying to win? *A relationship with someone like you.*

Where Fish Swim

The odds of meeting your mate will increase when you situate yourself around people with whom you have something in common. Naturally, you want to be in those places where the odds support your meeting someone compatible with yourself. If you do not like sports, you probably will not meet your mate at the baseball stadium. You may imagine throngs of single people calling from the bleachers, but finding your mate there may be like looking for a needle in a haystack. If, on the other hand, you discover an environment where you feel comfortable (a library, a favorite pond) but the number of available single people are limited, you may also be looking in the wrong place.

I once had a friend named Alan, an investment banker, who was a closet-pianist. He loved classical music as well as dance and the theater. As a bachelor, he discovered that the women he was most attracted to, at least physically, frequented modern dance and ballet concerts.

Well, that's not all that strange when you think about it. His theory was that the audiences for these events were partially composed of female dancers, and that dancers placed a premium on staying in shape and looking good which appealed to him. He also determined that after years of dating, he wanted to marry a woman who was artistic because of his love of culture and music.

To Alan, intermission was a land of opportunity where he would attempt to meet any attractive woman who seemed to be at the concert alone. Over time, his strategy paid off. Call him determined or even obsessive, he concentrated on going to dance-related func- tions *even on occasions when he would have preferred a symphony concert or the theater.*

When he finally met Melanie, a dancer, it was during intermis- sion at one of those dance concerts. He had a lot to talk about with her. His experience in the audience all those past months had pre- pared him, and he and Melanie jumped right into a conversation about their favorite choreographers and dance companies. While he was only an amateur, Melanie felt comfortable speaking with him about her profession, and that smoothed the way for the pair to get very personal. Melanie and he were married within the year. Alan said *only then* did he subscribe to those concerts he actually pre- ferred: season tickets at the local Philharmonic Orchestra.

You may have to fish in waters you are unfamiliar with, but where you determine the best fish swim. Unless you are a gambler, invest your money where the smallest risk pays the highest return. Since the reward you seek is finding your mate, invest your time and emo- tions while being with those people in those places where the odds are greatest for success.

Don't search for a guppy in the ocean but, rather,
a goldfish in a clear pond.

USING YOUR EXPERTISE

There may be a meeting place right outside your back door but perhaps you've never really thought of it that way. If you are an art historian, what better place to *position* yourself than in an art gallery or at a special lecture (tour, visiting show) at a museum?

If you are a computer programmer, what better place to meet someone than at a computer software convention displaying new products and services? You certainly will never need to explain your presence. You will have something in common with whomever you meet, and you will feel comfortable while being there.

Salmon swim upstream to lay their eggs and that takes a lot of effort. Go with the current because it's easier and it will increase the odds of meeting your mate.

THINKING BIG

Give thought to Positioning yourself *globally*, just as you give thought to Positioning yourself *locally*. Can you imagine a door-to-door salesman staying at home, hoping to make a sale but refusing to touch the phone? Or, how about a salesman trying to sell tractors door-to door in a non agricultural location like New York City.

Making the initial contact with another person is a bit like making a sale. You may have a great product, but you won't have success unless you make the effort *and* approach the right market.

An example of someone not thinking in these terms is exhibited by my friend Brenda in her job search. Brenda and I were classmates in college. After completing her dissertation, it was immediately published and her ideas were acclaimed as innovative in the field of Business Management. She was offered a teaching position at two colleges, one in Philadelphia and the other in a small college town in Montana which is known, in part, for being the least populated state in the country.

Brenda chose to move to Montana. While the teaching position in Montana paid the highest, Brenda, thirty-three years old, found herself in a town where it seemed everyone was married. The town and surrounding areas were very beautiful but also very rural. Being a farmer's wife did not really suit her temperament, and Brenda was unhappy with her prospects of finding a mate.

Brenda probably made the wrong choice as far as her social life was concerned. The second job offer had been at a perfectly respectable university in Philadelphia, a major metropolitan city with a large population of single people. However, she felt the business school in Montana had better facilities, colleagues, and professional contacts.

Perhaps that was true, but these faculty members were married,

the town was provincial, and after many years of graduate school and getting her Ph.D., Brenda had hoped to concentrate on her romantic life and, eventually, start a family. Brenda will hopefully succeed in these goals, regardless, but it will probably take longer to accomplish. When I last spoke with her, she was applying for a position in another location.

What about your place of work, the town, neighborhood, or even the building you live and work in? Increasing your odds for success in meeting Mr./Ms Right means being available to the vast pool of available single people who are appropriate in age, occupation and, most importantly, *state of mind* (likes and dislikes). Where are they? Anywhere near you?

Give serious thought to your social and living environment.
Are you swimming with the current or paddling upstream?

CREATING EXPOSURE

Where is Mr./Ms. Right and what might Mr./Ms. Right's interests, schedule or habits be? Since you just don't know which potential Mr./Ms. Right you will eventually meet, you need to be open to new experiences and make yourself available to new people. List those places which are accessible to you and where single people might meet. Focus your energies on being in those places when at all practical.

Common sense indicates a concentration of activities on weekends, certain holidays, and weekdays after work when exposure to single people will be maximum. As always, a Scout is flexible. If you are used to an early-to-bed, early-to-rise schedule, recognize that it will be more difficult to meet a prospective mate on that schedule. Consider adjusting your life-style and being socially available at optimum times, at least, until you find Mr./Ms. Right.

If you are a free-lance architect, for example, you may not enjoy taking a Saturday morning walk to the local church fair when you normally would be at home working at your drafting table. But, if you are serious about meeting your mate, you will need to involve yourself in various activities which *stretch* the regularity of your schedule and interests. Join as many and diversified group activities as practical: classes, church groups, outdoor or indoor sports (bowling leagues, volleyball teams), nature clubs, travel clubs, etc.

Search through newspapers, magazines, and bulletin boards for local events like auctions, promotional sales, concerts, garage sales, block parties or bingo. It's logical that if you've noticed a special event, and are at all interested in it, others like you will be as well. Having a membership in a cultural or educational organization will often place your name on mailing lists; you will likely receive invitations to private fund-raisers or preview events.

What about events in neighboring localities? Why remain at home alone when you can drive to the next town's annual pet show! There is virtually no end of suggestions but, as always, the limitations lie in our lack of imagination, time, energy, money, and, most importantly, *our skills at employing strategies for meeting people.*

Talk to travel agents about group trips or vacations for single people. If you have funds for travel, a vacation club that single people frequent may be an excellent addition to your itinerary. Wherever you travel, choose a destination where at least your trip will be fun and productive even if you don't happen to meet someone. But if you like to ski, be sure to choose a lively weekend ski lodge over an invitation to ski at your relative's isolated hilltop.

Certain activities and places will attract certain types of people. Be selective, and then make yourself available.

MAYBE A SHORT TRIP WILL DO

If you have a choice when making your travel plans, then a shorter distance is more practical from a mating point of view. Long-distance relationships can be problematic. If you are traveling in Alaska, what good will it be to meet someone to date in Anchorage if you live in Philadelphia?

Janet, who was a colleague of mine in graduate school, and I got together for lunch one day after not having seen each other for several years. After we had a chance to catch up on each other's lives, she felt comfortable enough to tell me about her recent relationship with Charles.

Janet was a clothes buyer for a major department store in Chicago, and traveling far and wide was part of her job. On a trip to Paris, Janet took an afternoon off and decided to go on a museum tour. She met a man, an American named Charles, who started their conversation asking her to repeat what the tour guide said about one of the sculptures. After the tour, he and she talked, had dinner, and walked through the streets of Paris.

The next day they met for breakfast, rented a car and drove through the beautiful countryside in southern France. Janet felt that she had finally met a man with whom she could fall in love. He and she had a wonderfully romantic affair in Europe which lasted for two weeks.

On returning to the States, there was one major obstacle in continuing the relationship. He lived in California and she lived in Florida, both sunshine states but very far apart. After a few months of regular letters, long-distance calls, and romantic trysts in various cities, Charles began to seriously date another woman in California. Janet and he both had good jobs, and the idea of one of them relocating was too large a problem and financial risk for both individuals to overcome. After all, Charles and Janet had only short periods of time together to test their relationship.

Long-distance relationships do work out from time-to-time but, logically and logistically, the odds of long-term success decreases as the distance in miles increases.

Whether you travel alone or with a group, there are many opportunities to meet people outside of your normal habitat. The closer you travel to home, however, the more the odds increase you will meet someone who lives nearby.

NEED MORE LUCK? TRY THIS

Everyone knows that practice makes perfect. But what if you get all dressed up and have no place to go? You recite opening lines in front of the mirror. You say you are doing your best, but that you cannot manage to go out on a date. Friends around you seem to be married or already involved in relationships. No one is introducing you to his or her friends, and you aren't interested in those men or women you have met. When all is said and done, you could use some help.

Dating Services

Dating services may charge you top-dollar to do what you could do on your own. However, if you need increased exposure, a local dating service will offer just that. You will peruse through a combination of photos, prerecorded phone messages, videotaped interviews, curriculum vitae, and every other available method to get you interested in dating one of the service's clients. Likewise, *you* will become part of a dating service's electronic and voice files for their other clients to consider.

This may save you the time and exasperation of the Needle in the Haystack Syndrome. We all have heard how our great grandparents had marriages prearranged by their families. *So, why not an institutional dating service for modern day matchmaking?* For many people who decline to use these services, high cost is the culprit. Others find it embarrassing.

Are you embarrassed to admit you need help with your love life? Don't deny your needs if all else seems to fail. While often expensive, a good dating service can be a step in the right direction. A dating service may work for you and, if so, it could save you months, even years of looking around on your own. You might be guaranteed a number of dates and that alone can be a big improvement!

One day, dating services will be even more popular. With a greater pool of participating clients, more competition among the services, cheaper fees and new technologically advanced services, *success stories will abound* — that's a prediction. At the present time, such a businesslike, mechanical system of match-making will often pair couples who seem more compatible on paper, a computer screen, or a statistical, first impression basis than in reality.

Most individuals are complex and choosing a mate is a very personal undertaking. In fact, attraction is hard to categorize, and even if you match one hundred-and-one likes and dislikes, a basic dynamic will often be missing, be it psychological or physical.

A dating service might be helpful as part of your overall strategy. But, if you are at all particular or unconventional, you may need to do the searching and choosing on your own.

REALLY, HOW COULD I SEND AWAY FOR THAT?

Years ago I purchased a booklet from a mail order advertisement I found in the back pages of some magazine I noticed lying around my dentist's office. The ad sounded good: "Ten Ways to Pick Up Women," or something frothy like that. I decided to send in my money and start collecting the dividends the ad promised. In a few weeks, long after I had forgotten about my purchase and was, coincidentally, due back at my dentist's, *it* arrived.

I tore open the package, impatient to learn these new and deep secrets about love and seduction. A harsh reality hastened my disappointment. The same promising picture of ten beautiful women was on the cover, but inside on page one were five examples of *personal ads,* the likes of which I was advised to place in local newspapers and magazines. On page two were five examples of the kinds of ads I was advised to read and answer in local newspapers and magazines. In one swirling instant I knew that I could count and that five and five made ten. *I'd been gypped!*

The disreputable organization that sold me this product backed it up with their guarantee: if I was not satisfied, my money would be returned to me *after* one year. I tucked the booklet into the bottom of my sock drawer and swore I'd send it back when the time came. (Unfortunately, I lost it by the time month twelve rolled around.)

Most people at that time knew about personal ads, and I had already decided that they were not for me. Why? It seemed impersonal, as if I could be reduced to three or four lines in a newspaper along with dozens of others. I reasoned that at least a traditional blind date, arranged by a mutual friend, and accompanied by a reference from someone both people knew, would be better.

True enough. But if you don't have the luxury of having promising blind dates arranged for you, what then? Consider placing or answering personal ads in any variety of newspapers, magazines, and/ or a growing number of computer online services. Now, you may say, "Todd, you ol' skunk. You're trying to nab us with the same line those sleaze bags did when you were twenty years old?!"

Since that time, not only have I known numerous couples who have met successfully through personal ads, but an entire culture has grown up around them. In this day and age, twenty years later, personal ads have achieved a respectability and are subscribed to by many intelligent, sensitive, and prosperous individuals.

Consider the Basic Pros...

1. You can receive, or answer, mail at an anonymous mailbox or voice-mail code where the ad is placed.

2. It's up to you to decide if you want to meet the person based on his or her ad, correspondence, e-mail, photographs or phone message.

3. You decide if you'd like to pursue a meeting with the person. Further correspondence or a phone conversation can bring you closer to making that decision with little effort or risk.

4. All of the above can be designed to respect your privacy and anonymity in the event you find the person inappropriate.

And Cons...

1. It's difficult to judge a person by how he or she looks in a photo, talks on the phone, or writes a few phrases. It's when you are meeting someone in person that one utilizes the First Impression Factor most efficiently.

2. You may go out on numerous dates with people you would never have dated if you had only met, or seen them, in person.

Four Tips on Getting Personal

1. Take your time scouting-out the personal ads and gathering information about a prospective date. You want to avoid going out on too many pointless or inappropriate dates.

2. A woman, especially, might want to keep her full name, address, and phone number private, at least, until she decides that she wants to go out on a *second* date.

3. When you decide to meet someone in person, arrange a first, short meeting at a neutral time and location, such as a local diner on your coffee or lunch break

(not a candlelit dinner, for example). That way, if you have doubts about the appropriateness of his or her romantic prospects, the meeting can be short and simple.

4. You can always end the acquaintance after the first meeting: "Let me call *you*. I'm very busy this month, but I have your number. Thank you (polite, but firm)."

ALWAYS GET THE AD RIGHT

Think of the Personal Ads as one more "place" to meet someone. It may seem contrived and unnatural. *So?* All you really care about is finding your mate. How you first meet a person is less important than the fact you have come to know them.

Start by browsing and getting to know today's jargon and style. You will need to be flexible in judging and reacting to an ad. Keep in mind that it costs money to list an ad and that most people are not professional copywriters. The fact that each word costs money makes lengthy ads prohibitive, and also results in a myriad of abbreviations and clichés. Be aware that, very often, a professional in the classified department will help write an ad if requested.

This has resulted in a slick, impersonal, braggartly style of ad which is very difficult to see through. For example, a modest person, who might make a wonderful spouse, might not feel comfortable touting her good looks or better qualities. A conceited person might exaggerate his or her better qualities deceptively.

Writing an ad that communicates something truly personal, and not just witticisms and physical dimensions, is not easy. *You may need to play the odds and respond to a large selection of other people's ads, or consider numerous responses to your own ad.* Once you receive correspondence, a photo, and view or listen to messages and other information, start to narrow down your selection.

Expect a small percentage of return (of appropriate dates) when using personal ads. Try to guard against the occasional odd-balls you may come across.

DON'T GET TOO PERSONAL, YET

The specific composition of your ad may result in an overwhelming response or just a few responses, depending on your sense of marketing. My friend Stephen had a problem in composing his personal ads. He wasted a lot of money on ineffective ads because he liked to design them to his own eccentric tastes and immature attitudes towards relationships. For example, he ran this silly and insensitive ad for a couple of weeks:

> Good looking man, 35, waits for woman to share seas of sensuous fantasy. Music is better with the lights low. No freeloaders, must be college educated, and no children. Send Photo.

I mean, really?! Even if a woman did not want children and happened to be college educated with a well-paying job, why would she want to respond to this ad, unless she was either a masochist or just playing the odds and giving him the benefit of the doubt? Not only is this ad *not* addressed to Stephen's market, i.e., *most* women, but it is not very nice. Also, sex is usually a benefit of having a romantic relationship and is something to bring up *after* you have physically met the person, and even then under the right circumstances.

The misleading and ironic thing about it all is that Stephen is actually a fascinating and entertaining man, though not especially sensible. He eventually met a woman who also recognized his better qualities and he and she married shortly thereafter. Two years later, she gave birth to a very beautiful child. *Needless to say, he did not meet her through the ad above!*

Expect a lot of false alarms and false advertising, i.e., "very attractive" might be an extremely subjective description a person uses to appraise themselves. Nevertheless, pay attention to general characteristics which are important to you: appropriate age, general description of a person's looks, height, occupation, and certain hobbies which you might like to share like gourmet cooking or bridge.

Don't be too picky in the initial stage unless you are aware of a quality which has fundamental importance to you. People *can* change. If you read an ad which requires a love of water-skiing, perhaps you would be willing to learn how to water-ski, *especially* if you were involved in a relationship which you thoroughly enjoyed.

The following, taken from a popular newspaper, are examples of ads which are generally inviting, indicate serious intent, sincerity and an interest in a long-term relationship. Certain specifications and characteristics will attract different people, of course, and these examples are not meant for everyone.

> Warm, mature man, 38, seeks serious relationship with sensitive and attractive female, age 30-40. College educated, well-read, financially stable, would appreciate the same. Please include Photo.

> or

> Attractive, amiable female, 32, looking for a marrying kind of guy. Love cultural activities and outdoor sports. Friendly and talkative, but serious about work and love. Please send letter and photo.

My friend Andy placed an ad in a newspaper for two weeks which I found snobby. I felt that it would discourage a lot of his readers and I predicted that he would receive very little response. The ad went something like this:

> Literary Minded, WASP 39, writer-teacher, Harvard educated, Menssana Incorpore Sano, looking for attractive, well read 25-33, sense of humor, good taste and traditional values. Send photo with letter or call.

> (Note: according to Andy, "Menssana Incorpore Sano" means, in Latin, "Of sound body and mind." — *Geeesssh! I didn't know that.*)

When he reported little luck, I rewrote the ad for him to tone down his narrowly defined interests. The result was a more friendly ad which was much better received:

> Handsome, WM, 39, writer/teacher looking for attractive female, 28-38, for serious relationship, warmth, and children. Well read, with a sense of humor and appreciate the same. Call, send photo with letter and I will respond likewise.

EXPOSURE: YOU CAN'T WIN IF YOU DON'T PLAY
121

*Ads should be written for the reader, not the writer. Think of all
the nice and interesting people who will not respond
if certain specifications rule him or her out.*

*　　　　　*　　　　　*

A woman friend named Louise, whose wedding I recently attended, was quite unhappy as a single person. She had been dating without success, and so I recommended that she give the Personals a try. She was too shy to place an ad in a local magazine because she felt embarrassed about it. She declined my advice and choose to do nothing.

The next time I spoke with her, she had not been on a date for several weeks. I volunteered to place an ad in the most popular Personals column in her area. Louise agreed, and she received twenty responses in the first week.

During the days she was going through the responses to her ad, she met the man whom she was destined to marry within the next eight months. Meeting Randall had nothing to do with the personal ad I had placed because she met him through a mutual friend at a dinner party. Nevertheless, here is the ad I placed which might help out one of *your* friends, that is, with some variations, of course.

> My good friend is a very attractive woman, single, intelligent, blonde, 40, looking for a relationship with the marrying-kind of guy. She is highly literate, sincere and warm. Since I am married, it's too late for me, but send photo and letter to her at Box 549.

*Men tend to place and answer more personal ads than women.
Ladies, when you place a personal ad, be prepared for
a large number of responses!*

Always Keep These Rules in Mind

19

1. *Approach obliquely rather than with a head-on approach. Unless you are greeted with flirtation, mask your true intentions because you don't want a prospective mate to get defensive upon meeting you.*

2. *While Positioning is a technique in itself, it is incomplete without an attempt at a conversation (if only it were that easy!).*

3. *In your opening line, try to begin with a topic you both have in common. Be flexible; the topic need not be profound, interesting or perfectly presented.*

4. *In appropriate social settings, introduce yourself as a matter of habit. What goes around comes around. Also, you'll want to stay in practice.*

5. *Be sure to respond to another person's opening line and be encouraging. "Cross" their line with a line of your own. This helps establish continuity, and lets the other person know of your willingness to converse.*

6. *Follow-Through is one of the most important early dating techniques. You may have met the most wonderful person in your life, but without having a way to talk with him or her again, you might as well say good-bye forever.*

7. *Recognize that a party atmosphere is a prime environment in which to meet your mate. Seek those group activities where the*

Party Phenomenon is present and will naturally increase your odds of success.

8. *Keep a long-term perspective and a sense of humor. When an attempt to meet your mate ends inconsequentially, remember that life is not unlike a comic opera. Learn from your mistakes and have faith that you will eventually meet someone with whom you will have a serious relationship.*

9. *Create exposure for yourself by being imaginative and flexible. Think globally as well as locally. Choose activities which are fun and productive since they represent an investment of your resources and time.*

10. *Personal ads and dating services, while imperfect, can be positive avenues to explore on the road map to finding your mate.*

GETTING THE FIRST DATE

III

Now You Are Talking

20

THE PREVIOUS CHAPTERS DISCUSS *WHERE* AND *WHAT* TO say as you meet or introduce yourself to a potential mate. The following pages discuss *how* and *when* to develop early conversations after meeting a man or woman in order to *arrange a date*.

As we have defined it, Follow-Through is the *means* by which you get in touch with a person after your first meeting. If you had to ask for Follow-Through, you took a *measured* risk of rejection whether large or small. If you did not have to ask, and the information was forthcoming, how fortunate! While we have discussed the concept and practice of Follow-Through, a broader examination is now called for. From the beginning of this book, the classic event we wish to avoid goes something like this:

> *Girl meets Boy. Boy likes Girl.*
>
> *Girl likes Boy, but....*
>
> *one or the other feels awkward.*
>
> *Neither takes a measured risk.*
>
> *Boy goes his way. Girl goes hers.*
>
> *Neither gets what they want.*

There are many situations, early on, when opportunities to get to know a person better are lost because of a lack of technique. In this section, we will try to improve your *reactions* and keep you directed towards your goals during those important first seconds and minutes early in an conversation.

During your first conversation with a potential mate,
estimate the amount of time with which you'll have to talk.
Guide the conversation towards your goal of practical
Follow-Through, be it information or an actual date.

CLASSIC CASE OF...OOPS!

I recently observed a smart young man start a conversation with a wonderful young woman. Both were in their early twenties and it all happened so fast in a public place, well...you can't really blame either for their failure to achieve Follow-Through. Actually, I mentioned their exchange previously, in connection with his opening line about her great leather boots.

He blurted out, "Wow. Where did you get those boots? They're great." I happened to be sitting across the aisle on a city bus, and observed what might have been a perfect meeting situation. She responded in an open, friendly manner. Of course, in a public place, somewhat put-on-the spot, you might expect a polite person to respond in a friendly manner. Nevertheless, their conversation continued and became quite spirited. Her participation was genuine; she wasn't just being polite to a stranger's advance in a public place.

After ten minutes of terrific progress on the young man's part (I was admiring his conversation technique), the young woman said, "Oh, I get off here." He said, "Really. Nice talking to you." "Yeah," she warmly agreed, "It was great," and hopped off the bus. *Wow!* These two people really seemed to have a lot in common.

Well, I looked over and couldn't help but feel sorry for that young man I had been cheering along. He had that self-satisfied look like, "Pat me on the back. I started a conversation with an attractive woman in a public place," but at the same time, he looked a little disappointed. It is that mixed feeling you'd like to avoid, when after a lot of hard work you receive polite applause but no cigar, so to speak. That's all he got from it: a feeling that he was a successful, attractive social being, but that he remained alone, single, and still looking for a girlfriend (or so I projected).

Okay. But what could he have done? She didn't exactly volunteer, "Hey, this is fun. I have to get off at the next stop, but let's get together sometime! Here's my number." Frankly, it is probably uncommon that she would be so forthcoming. But neither of them directed the conversation towards a subject which might have gracefully led to their getting together again like, "What part of town do you live in?," or "Yeah, I like to go to the Rock-A-Bye Club on the weekend. Do you?" Instead, he and she talked about each other's travels in Europe, the leather boots that he wanted to buy in Italy but didn't, because he ran out of money taking trains through northern Italy, Spain, etc.

It was like driving a car to a destination where you've never been, but not spending a lot of time looking at the map or reading the road-signs. No direction. No goal anywhere in sight... just driving.

I have to hand it to him: he managed a successful opening line in a difficult public setting, elicited good reactions from a wonderful young woman who returned his inquisitive conversation with flirtatious and encouraging body language. Unfortunately, there are *rarely* second chances when meeting new and interesting people, particularly in a public space. Most often, there *are* obstacles such as time constraints, too many other people around, shyness, inexperience, or the other person is not yet sure if he or she is truly interested.

---

*Try any variation of, "It's been nice talking with you! Is there
a way I could reach you somehow?," or hinting, "I get over to the
neighborhood where you work quite a bit. Maybe I'll run into
you sometime (and wait to hear his or her response)."
"Can I give you my card?"*

IN MOTION: THOSE PRECIOUS FIRST MOMENTS

As we illustrated when presenting Positioning Techniques, the person you wish to meet may be someone you are either walking with or sitting next to. There may be a reasonable amount of time for you to talk and get to know one another but, at other times, you'll need to make a good impression *quickly*.

In situations where you have less control, and a smaller *window of opportunity,* one obstacle or another will inevitably get in the way. It could be as simple as the other person's busy schedule, or a rainstorm which sends him or her scurrying for cover. How will *you* react if and when an obstacle presents itself? If an obstacle proves to be tricky and you can't surmount the problem it poses...*poof, like vapor!*

Often the obstacle may be a lack of communication. You might meet someone walking out of a park (you both converge from separate pathways and walk towards the exit to the street). If you both smile, say hello, and exchange flirtatious small talk, that's a good start. But leaving the park he may say, "This is my car," take out his keys and drive away.

He may do so *not* because he wasn't interested or available, but because he was shy, inexperienced, and did not know how to stall for time or walk with you for a few blocks before turning around and saying, "Actually, my car's back this way, but I'll give you a call next week so we can have lunch (after you suggested he contact you at work since you both are employed in the same neighborhood)."

Or, if you perceived he was slowing down as he approached his car, you could also have slowed down and continued a spirited conversation while standing in front of his car. Naturally, there would be fewer obstacles walking the *other* direction, *into* the park, where potentially you'd have more time together.

Whether you have all the time in the world or just a few minutes, you need to establish a friendly, free-flowing momentum where one topic of conversation leads to the next.

Something Like A Business Card

Sabre, a psychologist friend of mine, summed it up quite well when she recalled her experience riding a Washington, D.C. subway.

> Sitting next to her in the subway car, she noticed a charming man. He was intelligent looking and resembled one of her favorite movie stars, Robert Redford. First, she asked about the book he was reading because it was a psychology book, a field she had a lot of experience with. They talked at some length as the train started and stopped under the streets. Sabre knew that she would have to get off at the next

station — she had an appointment and needed to be on time.

Sabre mentioned that her stop was coming up, to which the man responded that he would like to see her again. She asked if he had a business card, but he did not. The train pulled up to the station and the doors opened. He asked if she had a card, but she did not. If you know how crowded Washington, D.C. subway cars are during rush hour, you know one needs to make a quick decision: get on or off. They both smiled in sympathy and laughed at the absurdity of the moment. Shaking her head, she got out of the subway car — I guess you could say they were both *unprepared*. Chalk one up for not having a business card.

Questions: Why didn't he or she quickly adjust to the particular obstacle of the moment? If he had fewer time constraints, couldn't he have gotten off the train even though it was not his stop? He could have always made the excuse, "Oh, I'm not in a hurry. I'll catch the next train. Let me write down your number." A bit forward perhaps, but *she* had asked if he had another solution: a business card.

Could Sabre have thought quickly, "I can ride to the next stop and walk back, or even get a cab — I'll probably still be on time." Would that have been too much to ask of the sophisticated lady she is, since she sensed he and she were both interested in seeing one another again? She could have voiced the excuse, "Oh, I can get out at the next stop. I have an appointment walking-distance between the two stops (regardless if true or not). We can exchange numbers if one of us has a pencil or pen."

However, neither person could take advantage of the positive momentum that had been established. Both were swayed by an obstacle of logical circumstance: the train pulling up to Sabre's stop. Who knows if he and she would be together today if Fate had been persuaded to hold off a bit and look in their direction.

Many people say, after I recommend keeping a business card handy, "Yeah, you know...I really ought to have a business card." *But they rarely get one.* True, it will always look genuine if you have to stumble, "Ahhh-hh...Do you have a pen or pencil?," or if you borrow one for the occasion from a passerby. But what if there isn't anyone else around? Do you make a big, long scene trying to find one, and will the opportunity still be there if you do?

Sometimes people agree to give out their phone number but aren't sure it's the right decision. It can be awkward to ask for the other person's number, but you can always offer your business card without the hassle of searching for that misplaced pen or pencil and scribbling illegibly on scrap paper. A card adds an element of respectablility, displays your place in society, and lends the feeling, "Hey. This new person I just met *is for real.*"

Alternative to the Business Card Rule:
Always carry a pen or pencil.

THE MOMENTUM RULE: OPEN OR CLOSED RESPONSES

The Momentum Rule: Sustain conversation, maintain positive body language, and be attentive to the other person. Momentum is like riding a wave when you are surfing. If you get off the wave, it may be difficult to reestablish momentum, at least, on that particular wave. Do not allow the pace of conversation to falter (even if you find yourself sounding stupid or nervous) or one of you may become defensive and distant.

Is it manipulative to think this way? Calculating? *Absolutely.* Social manipulation, in one way or another, is part and parcel of the dating process. It may even remain so, in many respects, until a couple agrees to commit to one another by living together, pledging monogamy or getting married.

Zen, as an ultimate and pure way of life, is not always present in the dating process. You don't have to socially manipulate another person, but be prepared to be manipulated in one way or other.

TRAFFIC SIGNALS: GREEN, YELLOW & RED

Open Response: When a person is open to talking and responds in a friendly manner with corresponding body language, proceed with confidence. Open responses are common among friendly people and, yes, they are the best kind of response.

Semi-Open Response: When the other person is slightly uncomfortable speaking with a stranger, but gives mixed messages (some of which are positive), proceed with consideration. He or she may gradually be won-over by your charm.

Closed Response: When a person is not interested in talking with you, communicated by lack of participation in the conversation and defensive body language, spare yourself. If some persistence yields no change in behavior, do not waste your time or be a nuisance.

Observe another person's signals and give out your own.
Try to make your own signals easy to read.

SIXTEEN TIPS FOR SUSTAINING MOMENTUM

Do Not Come-on Too Strong: Do not try too hard, unless you sense the person is trying to charm you as well. If you are too obvious, he or she may think it inappropriate and get defensive.

Be Flexible and Upbeat: Be flexible on the topic of conversation and be patient if the other person happens to say something you feel is factually incorrect. Some opinions are best left alone. Perhaps the comment was rhetoric, banter, or perhaps he or she is nervous and trying to impress you.

Honest Abe and the Girl Next Door: It's okay to be awkward and unpolished, but smile and be friendly. Appear immediately trustworthy (that's you), like the next door neighbor he or she grew up with. Make it clear that the

conversation is special: "I don't often get to meet someone new and interesting. This is really fun." If the other
person senses you are genuine, he or she will probably
be more forthcoming.

Stress Positives. Avoid Negatives: Encourage participation in the conversation by using affirmative body
language. Use eye contact and smiles to communicate
encouragement. If your eyebrows rise as your head
bobs, communicating, "Yes," it's clear you are attempting to be compatible and make him or her feel comfortable. Avoid intense political or religious discussions
which some people feel passionately about or quickly
become polemic over.

Avoid Sarcasm and Be Clear: Sarcasm, or dry humor,
can backfire early in a conversation because people may
not be sure how to interpret it. Rather than ask, "Why
are you all dressed up tonight?" (perhaps misread as,
'You think I am dressed inappropriately?'), say, "You look
really great tonight!" (There is no question that you appreciate him or her.)

Alternate "You," then "Me:" Volunteer personal things
about yourself and learn by asking about the other person. Get personal quickly, beginning with yourself, so
he or she doesn't get defensive.

No Interviews At This Time: Asking for a person's name,
rank, and serial number at the outset may put them off.
You may be in earnest, but if you come-on like you are
holding an interview, you may appear dry, cold, mechanical, or all of the above.

When the Person is Shy: If you sense he or she is shy,
you need to be patient and not take her shyness personally as a rejection. Hopefully, his or her smiles and ac-
companying body language will encourage you to keep
the conversation going.

If You Make a Faux Pas: Rebound, with a humorous
rejoinder. If a potential mate asks you, "Where are you
going?," and you reply (honestly), "To a shrink appoint-

ment!," he or she might wonder, "Gee. What am I getting involved with here? A nut?" *Rebound:* Add (lightly),
"Not that there is anything *wrong* with me (smiling)!" A
congenial tone of voice can do wonders to keep a problematic comment light and fun. If you say something
confusing like, "I guess your hair looks good that way,"
she may wonder, "Whaaaa-aat is this guy saying?"
Rebound: "That sounded funny! I meant to say that you
have such pretty hair — I'd like to see it down on your
shoulders rather than up in hiding."

Rapt Attention: In early conversations, listen to the other
person attentively. Good listening, accompanied by positive body language, confirms your interest in getting to
know the other person. Accepting the other person right
away, her personal history and point of view, can be flirtatious and seductive.

Subtlety and Charm: That's your middle name alrighty.
"Your place or mine?," is an approach which works only
with a very small percentage of the population. While
acceptable behavior in the '60s and '70s, people are presently more cautious about getting involved with others
sexually and, therefore, romantically. If he or she seems
to be attracted to you, guide the conversation towards
setting up a date by hinting at activities you like, or by
offering some other form of Follow-Through.

Playing It Cool: Don't express your infatuation right off
the bat, if you happen to be infatuated. It may scare-off
the other person if you treat them as a sex-object or an
idol. Control your desire or you may appear insincere,
sex-driven, or desperate.

Subtle Flirtation: Flirtation should communicate a) an
appreciation of the other person's sexuality and b) your
own availability. Flirtation is usually best when not too
obvious, at least, in the earliest stages of conversation.
Of course, getting a date or Follow-Through will be that
much easier if you sense the other person is flirting with
you. Naturally, a potential mate is not always guided by

physical attraction. He or she will often want to see you again simply because you seem to be a nice person.

Make the Other Person Feel At Ease: If you start a conversation with a man, or he takes the risk and starts a conversation with you, make him feel at ease. Recognize the awkwardness of two people attempting to have an initial conversation: relax your defenses to make him feel more at ease.

Grab For Any Straw: In early conversations, it is your *style, appearance, tone of voice, and positive body language* which makes the best impression. What you say, the content of your words, is often less important. If available and interested, he or she will respond positively to almost anything you say, however nervous or awkward you seem in the beginning.

Your Best Behavior: This is not the time to let it all hang out, so to speak. Your private habit of pulling out strands of your hair and playing with them between your fingers is not okay here. Before this new friend can accept the more seamy side of your human nature, let's impress him or her with your best manners and behavior.

The Momentum Rule is a must if you are going to develop a first meeting to the point of getting a date. The opening line can be good and the response may be encouraging but, if momentum is not sustained, the fish slips off the line anyway.

WHICH WAY ARE YOU GOING?

Lost Momentum

Here was James, a man about thirty-three, a literary scholar working weekends at a word processing job at a law firm. He was riding on a New York City subway and noticed a woman he thought he would like to get to know. The two made eye contact, which he claims was mutual and rich in innuendo (men often do make those claims). Coincidentally, he and she both got off at the same stop.

As James and the woman left the train, James tried to appear spontaneous while walking through the subway doors right next to her. He asked, smiling, through the side of his mouth, "Are you a painter? (James had noticed that she carried a painting kit.) She said, seeming quite relaxed and looking him in the eyes, "Yes. Are you?" James reached into the deep pockets of his past, "A little in high school, but not really." (I knew him in high school and I remember his class artwork: he was *really* reaching.) They walked up the stairs to the street and, to avoid silence, he continued, "Do you live around here?" The woman did not seem at all bothered, but was interested to talk with him. She answered, "No, I'm just visiting a friend." (James started to wonder, "male or female?")

The pair soon reached the top of the stairs. He paused (not knowing the direction she would walk in and unprepared for the confusion of the moment). She kept walking (what else was she supposed to do?) since she didn't know James and had only said a few words to him walking out of a busy subway. He was faced with the awkward choice of *calling* out, "Bye...Nice meeting you," or catching up to her (she was a few paces ahead by that time). He watched hopelessly and did nothing. After all, she was a stranger and they had shared very little together. She, sensing after a second or two that James was going a different direction, called over her shoulder, "Bye."

Now, she probably did not have any regrets. She was an attractive woman in her mid-twenties and, besides, maybe it *was* her boyfriend whom she was visiting. But, James was depressed about it and couldn't stop thinking about her for days. "I mean, Todd. This woman was really great and you should have seen the eye contact we had. I mean, I think we really had something in common." Possibly. But with no way of finding out, he would have to get over it. It was just one more devious event in the long, rich life of the Vapor Factor.

No one is saying that it is easy. Some situations are actually *next to impossible*. What could James have done, realistically? He was quite skilled just to start the conversation and get to the top of the stairs, wasn't he? True, he could have called after her and walked alongside her for a block or two. But he was considerate of the fact that maybe she was not interested in having him do so.

Next time something like that happens to you, keep the following tips in mind before it becomes too late to act:

Four Tips for Conversations in Motion:

1. It Just So Happens: Make an excuse for continuing in the same direction (as if it was the way you were heading anyway). "Oh. Are you walking this way too? I'm going to a friend's house (white lie). He lives up this way (so the person won't think you are just tagging along, like a little brother or sister, being a pain in the neck).

2. Which Direction? Antennas Alert: Let him or her *lead* but avoid giving the impression you are following. Keep an eye and ear pealed for change of direction. Don't stop or turn in such a way that it will be hard to shift once you notice his or her direction is changing. Keep the reason for your continued presence both believable and mutually acceptable.

3. Try to Lengthen the Short Time You Have Together: *a)* Let's say you are walking together out of the grocery store and the conversation between you is spirited. Stall by saying something like, "Oh, this is heavy (the package you are carrying). I've got to readjust something here (not really). Have you ever bought one of these (holding up an exotic tropical fruit)?" If he or she does not stop, either the person is not interested in continuing the conversation, or he or she is too shy to take you up on the offer to linger.

b) In a similar scenario, ask, "Which way are you going?," adding (after he or she indicates direction), "Oh. I'll walk up that way for a moment and I'll take a right at the end of the block (making it clear you are not tagging along forever)." In this case, you are making it obvious that you enjoy talking with him or her and that you would like to accompany the person, just to make conversation.

Positive Momentum

Jean was self-conscious at the Express checkout counter while paying for her groceries, because the man behind her asked how she liked the particular brand of cereal she was buying. "It's good," she said, faking some excitement about it. Actually, she had noticed this man in the aisle and now liked what she saw and heard. After she paid, she spent a few moments reading the headlines displayed in the newspaper rack near the exit. Consciously or unconsciously, this was her Stall Tactic.

The man only had a few items to pay for and, soon, was walking right behind her saying, "Whenever I shop at Grand Shopper, the florescent lights make me dizzy," trying to make light of a day-to-day shopping experience. Jean, nodded in agreement, now less self-conscious since no one else was around. "I know. The owners should really get some new lighting in there. But this sun isn't a lot better (squinting at the hot noon sun and *crossing lines* so to encourage him)."

The man continued, now walking next to her in the parking lot. "Actually (gathering momentum), I usually buy things up at Ed's Market. It's closer to where I live." Jean noted, "where I live" does not sound like, "where I live with my girlfriend." It also implies that he is a local citizen and is, perhaps, capable of having a relationship with another local resident. (He is not visiting his great aunt, for instance.) Jean looks at him as he speaks, giving him an Open Response, "Oh, do you live near Ed's? I have a girlfriend who lives on Oakdale Drive (once again crossing lines)." So far, so good. This conversation is gathering momentum. Both participants are open and interested in meeting someone new who seems to be available.

An early conversation may not always be the most sincere or deep-felt communication, but it can leave one feeling like the chance-meeting was a friendly one. No one's feelings are hurt if the person has other things to do and can't talk. It's understandable and is usually glossed-over in a friendly way.

CAMOUFLAGE TECHNIQUE, BODY LANGUAGE, AND THE USE OF PROPS

We are not in a jungle, nor are we hunting ducks at a pond, but avoiding being obvious sometimes requires covering-up your intentions. *Camouflage Technique* is an extension of the all important Oblique Approach. While we have touched on related principles, the added use of body language and props increases the effectiveness of the Oblique Approach.

Camouflage Technique

Often, when positioning yourself, you may need to appear to be doing something other than trying to meet a person. To be effective, you may need to appear genuine, casual, and give the impression you are ready to take their company or leave it.

Very rarely will he or she fall directly into your lap and give you sweet kisses. More often, the other person will be slightly defensive, and unsure of whether or not he or she might really enjoy your company. Inventive ways of concealing or covering up your ulterior motives are a central part of *Camouflage Technique*.

When meeting a stranger, discipline yourself to use body language, tone of voice, and props to express a *casual*, non-aggressive posture. If you are mutually attracted and flirtation is present, then sure, you can forget about Camouflage Techniques. But, in early conversations the fact that you are not coming-on aggressively will lessen any pressure he or she might feel. It may buy the time you need to charm the person and gain their interest.

> **Example One:** You are walking in one direction, but the person you would like to meet is walking the other way. You do not know where you are and, luckily, need directions. "Excuse me, Do you know where the Post Office is?," you question, in order to casually start a conversation and camouflage your intent.
>
> You point towards the street where he indicates the Post Office is located (looking in that direction to show a genuine interest). You've given the impression that you are ready to walk away towards your destination. You then glance back and relax your arm which falls to your side (communicating, "Well, I guess we could talk. I'm not in *that* much of a hurry"). "Have you ever been to this Post Office? I was told the lines are really long at lunchtime (looking at your watch)."
>
> A variation of this technique might include walking slightly beyond where someone is sitting or standing, before turning around and asking for directions (as if you are *really* intent on going somewhere and only stopped for directions).

Example Two: You are in a museum. You notice a potential mate looking at paintings, and you have positioned yourself in front of the same painting and offer a comment or two. *Create the illusion* that small talk is all you have in mind. You give the impression that you are just making one last comment about the great purples and yellows and that you are, slowly, on your way. Your body language shifts slightly, like you are heading over to the next Picasso (as if it doesn't matter if the two of you continue talking or not). If his or her response is Open, smile and gesture (including them) towards the next painting, "Have you already seen this one?"

If, on the other hand, their response is Semi-Open, the two of you can drift apart. You can always bump into him or her in the next room a few minutes later, though it may seem like starting over again (requiring Positioning and an opening line). If that is the case, your new opening line should continue the tone and substance of your first conversation. If it appears you are simply trying to meet a prospect for a romantic or sexual encounter, you may be setting yourself up for a Closed Reaction.

FIND SOME THING(S) TO HELP

Props: If you have started a conversation in your local dry cleaners, for example, bring up a topic which is not direct or personal: "I left a coat in storage two years ago, and I'm just picking it up now! Did you know you can put clothes in storage here?" You are engaging the other person in small talk and allowing him or her to become used to you.

If she becomes busy talking to the owner about the red wine stain on her blouse, *stall*. Look through your shirts and count them again; reconsider the amount of starch you'll need. By using *props* at hand, you remind your conversation partner of the legitimacy of your being there, and you don't lose patience or walk away without giving the conversation another chance.

Other examples of Camouflage Technique might include kneeling next to your bicycle on the sidewalk, fidgeting with the speedometer as if you are fixing it (maybe you really are), sitting at a table in a coffee shop glancing at the local paper (which you have little

interest in reading), or pretending that you really want to drink that extra glass of wine while you stall for time at the bar talking with a Decoy. All of the above might create a credible picture of *purpose and independence* to the eyes and ears of an unsuspecting potential mate.

Keep a face-saving statement in mind in case the conversation does not work out as hoped: "Oh, I guess I can pick up those extra shirts next week (from the dry cleaner example). It's too busy in here. -Bye."

CHAMELEON TECHNIQUE

Chameleon Technique: like the Camouflage Technique and the concept of Decoys before it, the Chameleon Technique can be helpful in early meetings and conversations. The Chameleon Technique is used for those special situations where you slightly *modify your character* (just momentarily) in order to coax a potential mate to relax and enjoy a conversation with you.

As a Chameleon, so to speak, you might pretend to be *other* than your true self if it makes it appear that the two of you have more in common. In the museum example above, you, as a Chameleon might say, "Oh, yes, I love these Picasso's *too*," as he rambles-on about a painting you actually find grotesque (but you can't admit it because you want to give him the impression you both have something in common). Hopefully, he doesn't really care that much about the painting. Manipulative? Yes. But, I guess if you meet your mate while being a bit of a Chameleon, you can always apologize for the impropriety later, when you both are doing something you *really* have in common.

If you are irresistibly charming, you may not need to work at getting a date in such a calculating manner. However, a good fisherman knows a first tug doesn't mean you've caught a fish. You may need as many fishing techniques as possible.

Is He Interested and Is She Available?

So, you did it. You smiled in a flirtatious manner, looked him right in the eye, and got his interest. Whether through personal ads, a dating service, or good old common sense and practice, you find yourself talking with a man you've just met. If he is available and interested, he will *hopefully* respond and sufficient Follow-Through can be achieved or a first date arranged.

At this point, your conversation partner is probably not imagining what a great pair the two of you will make, how sweet your children will look or what great sex you could be having. Maybe he is more concerned with the moment: how to sustain momentum in this conversation. What will he say next, and will it sound stupid, smart or funny?

Don't wait too long before you start to wonder: is this person truly available (*especially* once you begin to date one another) and is he or she really interested in you? If you gather this information early on, so much the better. But, if you are getting mixed signals about his or her interest (seems bored, doesn't respond to your phone messages, etc.), seriously consider moving on.

Availability is harder to gauge. You can waste tremendous amounts of time, energy, and money trying to become involved with people that are not available for a *romantic* and/or sexual relationship. She may be interested in talking with you and might even agree to see you again. She may be friendly and encouraging, but is not available for a relationship nor even a casual affair. She does like *talking* with you and might even enjoy being your friend.

Why not a sexual and romantic relationship? I don't know. Perhaps she is living with someone, already married or is in a monogamous relationship. Maybe she benefits from having you around for friendship, business, platonic companionship, or perhaps she enjoys the attention you give her.

Each person is ready for commitment at different points in their lives. Maybe you've gotten to know someone and you are ready to drop everything and marry. Yet, perhaps the other person is not thinking in those terms *at all.* Even at those times when it may be hardest (because you have such *a crush* on the person), remember the words my grandfather, Jesse, used to tell me on his New Hampshire dairy farm: "Don't pull a dead horse. It's much too heavy."

The most obvious telltale sign is a **wedding or engagement ring.** Is there a ring of *some substance* on the left hand ring finger? Noticing an engagement or marriage ring means that you can pretty much forget about the person in terms of your romantic life. Married men wear wedding bands less predictably than women; you may still have to find out his or her marital status through a conversation.

Certainly, you could have an affair with a married person if you want to, but that *probably* won't help you find your mate. Divorce is possible, and you *might* eventually become his or her mate. Judge each situation separately, but beware of the time-consuming trap of *not being selective.*

If encouraged: In the game of Monopoly: proceed to GO.
In the Dating Game: ask or hint for Follow-Through or a date.
If discouraged: In the game of Monopoly: go back to GO.
In the Dating Game: when you say good-bye, be polite and general.

THIS DATING GAME

21

BILL WENT TO THE MOVIES ALONE ONE FRIDAY EVENING. He was lonely, and had broken-up with a woman after a yearlong relationship, three months prior. He now felt ready to meet someone new should the opportunity present itself. It did.

He sat down in an aisle seat. To his right, an attractive woman was making her way across the row towards him. She smiled at Bill and sat two seats away from him. In a minute or so, as the theater became crowded, she pointed to the empty seat next to Bill (she rolled her eyes towards the gentleman next to her as if he was being a social problem of some sort). "Do you mind if I sit here?," she asked. Bill gestured to the seat next to him, "Sure." He did not need great skills as a conversationalist because she immediately started a conversation about the film they were about to see.

They talked easily for about fifteen minutes and then the film began. This was an unusual type of theater, one that showed foreign films and low budget, independently produced films. Such was the movie Bill and his new acquaintance, Cindy, were about to see. (We will come back to this point in a moment.)

OBSTACLES, OBSTACLES, AND MORE OBSTACLES

After the movie, the two started talking again, and walked together up the aisle towards the exit. Bill was attracted to Cindy, and he wondered if she would be interested in dining with him somewhere in the neighborhood. As they exited the theater, he asked her for a cigarette as she lit one for herself. This was a Stall Tactic and also, Bill liked to smoke. Glad to find out that Bill smoked, she exclaimed, "Great," and the two stood out in front of the cinema talking about the movie and puffing on their Marlboros.

Obstacle One

Just at that moment, a man came over to Cindy and greeted her with a kiss on the cheek. He asked how she liked the film because, as it turns out, he was the Director of the film! She said, "We liked it," referring to Bill. Bill wondered to himself, "Well, if she refers to us as 'we,' this fellow probably is not her boyfriend." On the other hand, as the man left he added, "I'll call you tomorrow," and that made Bill a little uneasy.

Obstacle Two

Then, as it often does, Murphy's Law interferes and an obstacle that proves too great to overcome appears. In Bill's case, the obstacle was unexpected: a second woman, loud and persistent, a third party whom neither Bill nor Cindy knew. Just as Bill was going to say, "Would you like to go somewhere to get something to eat?," she appeared. Apparently, the woman had been in theater, but left early to make a phone call. Now, she approached our smoking couple, bursting with curiosity and asked Cindy, "Excuse me. How did the film end? I had to make a phone call."

Obstacle Three

Well, Cindy was either too polite or oblivious to Bill's discomfort, because he found this new woman obnoxious and unwanted. She was pushy, selfish, and dominated the conversation with Cindy whom she did not even know. What was more disconcerting, as far as Bill was concerned; it did not seem to bother Cindy. She answered all of the second women's questions about the film. That also made Bill concerned. Did his new friend not care about continuing their conversation privately?

Did she really enjoy talking with this loud maniac? I mean who leaves a movie she pays to see, then likes it enough to come back and glean the ending from total strangers? Why didn't she come back and see it the next night? Perhaps Cindy was trying to show how polite she was, believing it might impress Bill. However, Bill found Cindy's apparent politeness to be an insurmountable obstacle. He was losing patience and he did not know how to handle it.

Obstacle Four

Unfortunately, even though Bill felt like asking for another cigarette, as he self-consciously moped, he grew tired. He prayed internally for the second, loud, woman to leave so that he could get on with this excellent new relationship. He tired of not knowing the few answers that plagued him. Would Cindy go out with him to a local eatery? Is she just a friendly person that talks eagerly to strange people, or is she not really interested in him or available? Bill did not stay around to find out, but he regretted it.

If Bill had not been attracted and interested in Cindy, then it would be understandable for him to say "Good night," and leave her recounting the film to her newfound lady friend. However, Bill really liked Cindy, given his first impressions, and he was lonely and unattached.

He just *felt awkward,* and he lost patience when the Obstacle Course of Love raised its head *just* when he was going to ask Cindy to continue the conversation in a more relaxed and private setting. There were too many unanswered questions, and he was feeling like a piece of baggage. He wasn't adding to the conversation, and he didn't even have a cigarette from which to blow smoke rings. He was standing uncomfortably, and the situation and uncertainty were too much for him. He interrupted, "Excuse me. Cindy, I have to go, but nice meeting you."

"Todd," Bill related the next day, "I think that she really liked me and wanted to go out with me. I think I blew it." *I had to agree with him.* Early conversations are often like an obstacle course. You'll need to navigate the problems as they arise and be patient. How often does an opportunity come along where you go into a movie theater by yourself, alone and lonely, and a potential mate just drops into the seat next to you, smiling and talking?!

WHAT COULD BILL HAVE DONE?

Bill could have recognized that Cindy had done a considerable amount of the initial work in putting them together. Since Bill did appreciate the effort Cindy had made, he could have done his best to be more patient and *roll with the punches.*

Recognizing that he had it easy up to the point of exiting the theater, he could have paid his dues by shuffling his feet, accepting self-doubt and nagging thoughts about the Director's role in Cindy's life. He could have suffered a bit and smiled at the second woman while politely contributing to the conversation (no matter how inane or irritating). Bill could have played it cooler, by controlling his own nervousness. Even if Cindy was not really interested in pursuing their friendship further, what did he have to lose by sticking around for a few more minutes especially since he had received so much encouragement?

Bill *had used* a prop to sustain momentum when he asked for a cigarette. His mistake was not asking for a second cigarette while waiting outside. While getting a light from Cindy, he might have said, "Cindy, I'm going to head over to the Merrik's Cafe for a bite to eat. Do you want to come along or meet me there in a few minutes?" That way, Cindy could have made the decision to stay and catch up with Bill later. And probably it would have been the signal *she was waiting for*; she would have said, "Oh sure. Let's go." "Bye," she'd call out, leaving the second woman with her mouth agape, still wanting to hear every detail. Or, in the worst case, Cindy might have let Bill know that she was not interested by politely declining.

These are, perhaps, strategies which a more experienced and *hungry* single person will employ in such situations. I mean, an important basis of this book is that love does not make itself available when we snap our fingers. If only it were so. We have to work for it, train and prepare for it. Again, you probably won't find your mate ready to pick like a piece of fruit growing on a vine or a tree, although Cindy did appear from nowhere.

Where is Bill Now?

Bill is not a shy individual, he just has normal hesitations and fears of rejection. A week later, Bill went to a local bar which had a casual atmosphere; people mingled, and the music was quiet enough so that you could hear your neighbor. A woman was sitting at the bar and the seat on her left was empty. The seat on her right was occupied by a man to whom she was talking. Bill casually sat in the empty seat, ordered a drink, and the other man got up, apparently to make a phonecall, so Bill and the woman started talking. The woman, Jan, flirted with Bill, and let it be known that the other man was visiting from out of town, and that she was not interested in his sexual advances (meaning: I'm still available). Bill found her to be attractive, a good conversationalist, and sexually forthcoming. There was no risk of rejection with Jan. She made it clear that she liked Bill and wanted to see him again. They exchanged phone numbers at the end of the evening, having had a long, cheerful conversation which included the out of town visitor once he returned.

Unlike Cindy, who did not flirt in an *obvious* way, Jan made it quite clear that she was interested *and* available. At the time of this writing, Bill is dating Jan, and is involved in a relationship which he finds "uninspiring." He enjoys being with her, but feels he is treading water in a relationship that does not really have a future. By the time this book reaches print, I'm certain Jan and Bill will not be dating.

AFTERMATH: DO WE LEARN?

Bill often thinks back to his meeting Cindy, and wishes that he could have dated her. He speculates, based on first impressions, that he and Cindy would have had more in common than he and Jan. Bill may, or may not, have really liked Cindy. He probably will never know.

Another question is more philosophical and/or psychoanalytic. Did Bill *really want* to go out with Cindy? *Was it meant to be?* A fatalist would conclude it was not meant to be. This is a common way of explaining various mistakes people make, and is one which I personally reject. I believe we can combat negative impulses and social bad habits with self-discipline, self-awareness, and a number of practiced techniques and learned responses. Of course, if men and women always acted in their own best interests, rationally and intelligently, I might think otherwise.

Bill could not overcome his nervous reactions, his fear of looking foolish or the risk of being rejected. Cindy had done such a good job of making herself available and proving her interest while conversing with Bill. Even so, Bill was scared-off by a few simple obstacles which he could easily have overcome. Instead, he is now involved in a relationship with Jan which he finds comfortable, but *knows* he does not wish to continue.

One obstacle will naturally follow another on the path to finding our mates. Apply discipline and technique to overcome any variety of obstacles and you will have more choices in the dating process.

ASKING, OR HINTING FOR THE DATE

22

A FIRST AND MAJOR ACHIEVEMENT IN THE MATING GAME is "getting the date." The day after meeting Cindy and one week before meeting Jan, my friend Bill lamented, "If I could only get a date, then I'd be fine." Well...that's his opinion. But, I do agree with him that getting the date takes a bit of luck, the good wishes of the person you'd like to date, *and often some skill on your part.*

My second cousin, Brian, spoke to me at length about a conversation he had with an *au pair* who worked for one of his customers. My cousin was in his mid-twenties and worked as a house painter; the *au pair* had just turned twenty. He stayed at the house after finishing his work. The client excused himself, probably so my relative and his *au pair* could create heart-shaped auras in his living room. My cousin spoke in earnest about what a good time they had talking together. He stayed for *three hours.*

The next week he asked me what he should do about the situation. I recommended the obvious, "Call her on the phone," which would have been so easy in his case because he and she had talked on and on for three hours! The stage was set. Only a week had passed since their meeting, and he was certain that she had a good time. I told him to make a friendly excuse for his calling like, "I really had a good time talking with you the other day, and I just wanted to check-in and see how you're doing (then pause, momentarily, waiting for a positive reply)." After some small talk, I told him to cheerfully offer, "Would you like to get together on your day off?" I'd wager she would have been more than happy to accept the invitation.

Instead, I was flabbergasted to hear his response: "Oh *right*! The worst thing that would happen if I asked her out for a date is that she'd say, 'Yes'. *Then what would I do?!*"

In the Aesop's Fable, "The Tortoise and the Hare," the tortoise is slower than the hare but eventually wins the race. I can only hope this might be true with my cousin who does remind me of a tortoise sometimes.

Are you negotiating a date with a Tortoise? You are if:

1. The person is not skilled in navigating a conversation.

2. The person doesn't know what he or she really wants.

3. The person is too shy or cautious when starting personal relationships.

4. The person is a short-term thinker and can't plan ahead. ("Well. I am really busy and I do have other plans this weekend, so I'll say 'no,' even though I like this person.")

5. The person does not respond to hints only because he or she is either not used to flirtatious innuendo or is naive.

If you leave it up to the Tortoise to make the decision for you, it may be a case of *No Action, No Date,* as was the case of my cousin, Brian, who did not call the *au pair.* Calling her caused him too much anxiety. Stopping by or writing a note seemed too risky to him. What if she were there? She did not call him either.

Yet, after three hours of fun conversation, when he was sure the *au pair* enjoyed herself, you'd think the *au pair* might have suggested seeing each other again. A good hint like, "Are you finished work here?," or "Will you be coming back again?," might have offered him the encouragement he needed. Of course, a true Tortoise would reply, "I'm finished with the work here," without including, "but it would be great to see you again sometime. When's your day off?"

Even though someone is shortsighted or unsophisticated, he or she may still, eventually, enter into a romantic relationship with you. If you have skills at negotiating in this early stage, a first date can generate the familiarity, interest, and excitement a Tortoise needs. Future dates will be much easier to arrange.

ASKING A PERSON IN PERSON

Body language, facial expressions, and tone of voice combined, will usually help accomplish the task of asking, or hinting for a date with more subtlety than your voice alone on the phone. A picture is worth a thousand words; there are a multitude of signals, given and taken, when you speak in person. In person or on the phone, arranging a date usually happens in two parts, the first being optional.

Part One (optional), Hinting: "It's been nice meeting you (smiling)," you remark to a person you met and had a conversation with in the supermarket. (You spoke with him or her for fifteen minutes in the aisle and again while in line to pay.) "I've never met someone *shopping* before (reviewing the past, you make it clear it was special)." This gives your conversation partner an opportunity to return the compliment and maybe he will hint that he'd like to see you again.

Part Two, Asking Outright: "Are you free for coffee or lunch sometime?" In suggesting a relatively *neutral* activity, like meeting for lunch or coffee, you indicate your interest in getting to know a person without the risk of being inappropriate. You are not asking him or her to go to a movie or the lake house for the weekend, for example. Even if the person happens to be involved with someone, he or she might not object to talking with you again, since the two of you have gotten-on so well. By keeping things indirect and ostensibly innocent, you make it easier for the other person to accept.

Two Reasons Not To Put-Off Part Two:
1) You may lose the opportunity to get to know the person better.
2) You will know, realistically, if he or she is interested or available.

DIVINING AVAILABILITY AND INTEREST

If a prospective mate passes the wedding, or engagement *ring test*, it only means the person is *probably* not married or engaged. You've got more work ahead but you can't always blurt out, "Are you available? Do you have a boyfriend/girlfriend—I don't see a ring?"

Single people have subtle ways of letting each other know of their status. One way is to increase the level of flirtation, including the frequency of questions and responses in an exchange of hints, or Soft-Lines.

Try asking where a person lives (not the exact address) and include questions like, "Is it a *big* apartment?," or "Do you live alone?" Such questions may lead to informative answers like, "No. I have a roommate." (You may wonder: a lover, or really *just* a roommate.) At some point, it becomes obvious to the other person that you are inquiring about their availability and, at the same time, implying that you are interested in them romantically.

If *living situation* questions do not produce the answer you seek, try the what-could-we-do-together(?) category of hints or Soft-Lines. These may range from, "Oh, I was going to get a cup of coffee. Would you like something to drink (I'm going anyway, so why not?)," to a more direct, "I don't know what your situation is (it's clear you are referring to their romantic 'situation'), but would you like to go to the Flower Show at the Town Hall — I'd really like to see it."

If he says, "I've already seen the Flower Show," and dampens your enthusiasm for colorful petals and fragrances, don't let it throw you. Keep the momentum going: "Well, would you like to do something else, sometime, together?" Honest and direct, this approach is often necessary, especially, if you do not have the luxury to hint, flirt, and make innuendos for an extended period of time.

By Hinting, You Imply the Following:
"I'm only hinting that we could go out, and I realize you may be involved with someone. By hinting, I'm giving you an easy way out that will save face: mine."

TIPS WHEN ASKING FOR A DATE

1. ***A Sense of Timing:*** Ask a general question rather than a specific one: "I'm really glad we met (wait, momentarily, for his or her confirmation of the same)." "Would you like to get together sometime, maybe for a cocktail (watch for enthusiasm)?" "Would you like to go to the movies with me next Saturday

night?," may be too direct and result in a rejection. It may put you and the other person on the spot, forcing him or her to turn you down due to a prior commitment or some other excuse. On the other hand, once you sense he or she might accept, you'll need to be direct and take the chance.

2. **Doing Some Research:** If there is something coming up on your social calendar, like your church is holding its annual dinner with a bingo game for members and their guests, it may be the perfect proposal to see each other again: "There's a fun church party I said I would go to. Are you free next Tuesday?" If something special is not on the horizon, then make something up. If you are not particularly thrilled to see the new film at the local cinema, pretend you are: "Have you seen the new movie at the Bijou?" *Note:* if you are unprepared, or if the two of you can't make up your minds what to do or where to meet, *the resulting predicament is a little ridiculous* assuming you both genuinely want to get together.

3. **Any Excuse To Romanticize:** Mandy had a friend, Barbara, who had a male roommate. When visiting Barbara, Mandy was quite taken by her roommate, Tim, who happened to be shy. When Barbara went away for a week on vacation, Mandy (who had permission from Barbara to do so) called and said that Barbara had borrowed a book, asking if she could stop by and get it. Tim said he did not know where the book was, but that she could come on over and look around, which she did. Mandy and Tim are now married, I kid you not. The lesson is that any little, mundane, excuse to become romantic is fine.

4. **May I Be Direct?:** Knowing that some opportunities are fleeting and that loneliness can be painful, there are times when patiently planning a date-request strategy doesn't work. Colleen had waited and waited for an appropriate man to ask her out, and she was ready to give up. She had read in a self-help book

that asking every person you know to introduce you to someone could be productive. "Exhaust your resources," the author implored. When a woman friend of Colleen's, named Jessica, suggested that Colleen might like Ed, Colleen called him on the phone. After a few minutes of conversation, she asked if he were interested in meeting her.

Note: Now, if you knew what an extraordinary and physically beautiful woman Colleen is, you would not believe me when I tell you she needed to be this resourceful in order to find her mate. She told me, and I quote in disbelief, "Men did not come to me, or call me and ask me out. I don't know why," she shook her head. This would have been a terrific fantasy-come-true for most men, and Ed was no different. Colleen told me this story while giving her husband a big hug, Ed, after they had been married for three years.

I DIDN'T COUNT ON THAT: MURPHY'S LAW

What you do not expect nor anticipate, unfortunately, can happen. That's as good a summing-up of the age-old Murphy's Law as we'll need. You may learn your opening lines very well, but if the cues you need do not materialize, will you still pose the question or hint for a date? Will it still sound appropriate to ask if he'd like to use the extra ticket to go to the opera, when he just said how much he hates classical music? Will you think on your feet and suggest an alternative? Or will you now keep your idea of getting together one evening to yourself?

Stephen met Cassandra while working at the same firm. He and she both worked part time but in different locations and with different schedules. Every once in a while they would see each other at department meetings. Stephen knew that he would see Cassandra on a certain day and he planned to ask her out. He planned to ask if she'd like to do something during the upcoming weekend. He had decided to ask for her phone number, at least. Otherwise, he reasoned, he probably would not see her for another month or so. Unfortunately, that was just the way it was since they had very few department meetings.

So when Stephen finally had a minute alone with Cassandra, and they were discussing what each liked to do with their free time, *in walks the boss*. He needed to speak with Cassandra before the meeting about her presentation. Well, words cannot describe Stephen's disappointment and frustration. He did not get the Follow-Through he needed (her phone number), and a date had not been arranged. Because he got nervous about approaching her again, he did not position himself next to Cassandra at the end of the meeting and she walked out the door with a girlfriend.

In situations like these, when you have an opportunity to be spontaneous and casual about approaching someone for a date, expect the unexpected. Stephen didn't see Cassandra again at work for quite some time. By that time, he had heard she was seeing a man, and he never did get a chance to get to know her. Unfortunately, at the time of this printing, he is still single and looking.

Think ahead, look ahead, and be prepared for interruptions. Don't waste time hinting if you suspect that an interruption may be approaching: speak up. Try to sound spontaneous and pleasant, regardless of what happens. The other person does not know, necessarily, that you are trying (sometimes desperately) to arrange a date.

Be easygoing, even if he or she seems disinterested in dating.
Protect your pride, and keep the potential friendship alive
by being diplomatic.

HINTING WITH SOFT-LINES

What's a Soft-Line? A Soft-Line is a hint or an innuendo communicated, in part, by tone of voice and body language. *A Soft-Line* may be fairly transparent at times, or obvious, but its function is to be inviting. The Soft-Line can be flirtatious, playful, and may even imply an answer in its very presentation. Nevertheless, the Soft-Line invites its listener to respond. If a Soft-Line is returned with a *Soft-Response*, then a *Soft-Line Exchange* can continue as a form of flirtation.

When Bill and Cindy met in the movie theater, as described in the last chapter, he and she might have entered into a Soft-Line Exchange but the two were interrupted by the arrival of the second woman outside the theatre. In the context of that example, if Bill had hinted invitingly, "I was going to have a bite to eat at Merrik's Cafe across the street (Soft-Line)," he would have implied, "Would you like to come along?" It may even have been inferred, "Or, if you have a better suggestion, that would be fine too." Maybe it is obvious that without her participation, Bill really doesn't give a hoot about going to Merrik's for a bite to eat. Maybe Bill would just go home if she didn't accompany him.

Maybe it will be obvious to Cindy that Bill wants, expects, and hopes that by giving her a Soft-Line that she will respond with a Soft-Line of her own: "Oh, that sounds like a good idea (Soft-Response)." Perhaps Bill would then add to her Soft-Response, "Do you want to come along and get a drink or something to eat?" She already implied that she would like to accompany him when she responded, "That sounds like a good idea." By continuing the Soft-Line Exchange, Bill is making it seem like he and Cindy have arrived at the idea together, step by step: a mutual agreement of a really good idea, a potentially *romantic* idea, in fact.

In this scenario, does Cindy really want a bite to eat? Or, does she primarily like the idea of sitting across from Bill, while neither can eat a bite because he and she are so romantically interested and/ or feeling excited and upbeat about being together?

Being versatile in the language of Soft-Lines is a learned skill, and can be very helpful when negotiating a first date.

Soft-line Exchanges

Person One: "I hear that movie is really good" (already suggesting the possibility of going to a movie together, maybe even that particular one).

Person Two: "Yes. I heard it's good too. I love movies. I'll make any excuse to go" (meaning: *just ask me*, or give me another Soft-Line).

Person One: "Oh. It would be fun to go sometime" (implying: *we*, together).

Person Two:	"Yes" (with an emphasis which leads to...)
Person One:	"Do you want to get together sometime on a Friday or Saturday and see a movie?" (Implying: *any* day would probably be good, or *any* weekend.) Person One might also add, "What nights are *you* free?" (Implying, 'Gee. I wonder if *I* have a night free next week; I'm so busy with work' — as if he or she was not available at the drop of a hat.)
Person Two:	"That would be great (as if Person Two has not been acutely aware, consciously or unconsciously, that the last five or six Soft-Lines were leading up to this)."

Flush-out opportunity, little by little, with the use of Soft-Lines. Both people are given opportunities along the way to curtail the flirtation if it becomes uncomfortable. In a Soft-Line Exchange, if both people are interested and available, flirtation will often dominate the conversation and a first date can easily be arranged.

SOFT-LINE REJECTIONS

1. That Drive Would Be Nice, Wouldn't It?

Jack was interested in Liz, but from the following exchange we can deduct that she was not interested in him. They had dated a few times, and this conversation occurred towards the end of their short relationship.

Jack:	"I need to get out of the city. The weather is so nice (hint, hint)."
Liz:	"Your car works, doesn't it? Why don't you drive to the country?"

Jack suspects that Liz is not interested in driving to the country with him, but he does not want to take the hint. He likes Liz and does not want to lose her. Instead, he wonders about her response, but gives her many more chances to turn him down, one of which follows:

Jack: "I've been working so hard these days. It would be good to get away. What about you?"

Liz: "I have a lot to do. Why don't you drive out to the beach?"

Clearly, a more positive response from Liz might have been, "Oh, I wish I could go with you, but I have so much work to do today."

2. I Was Hoping You Might...

Sean had met Kim at a dinner party at a mutual friend's home. Kim was attracted to Sean and wanted to pursue a relationship with him. Sean was not that interested in seeing Kim again, however. Riding the elevator down to the front lobby, Kim hinted at possible ways to see Sean again. She had previously mentioned an exhibit of photographs she had seen at a museum. Sean seemed interested in the photos, at least, conversationally.

Kim: "Oh, I'd really like to go see that photography exhibit at the art museum again." (Any activity will do, but since I mentioned photography earlier this evening, sure.)

Sean: "But you've already seen it." (Implying: if I were interested, don't you think I'd jump all over your Soft-Line?)

Kim: "Yeah. But it was great. You should go see it. I think I'll try to go next weekend." (Get my hint?)

Sean: "Maybe I'll get a chance, but I don't get up there often." (Please don't continue the Soft-Line Exchange as I am really not interested in seeing you romantically. Sorry.)

Taking a hint is just as much a skill as giving a hint.
An outright rejection, "No, I'm not interested in seeing you again,"
is usually not necessary. Most people can communicate,
indirectly, through innuendo.

NEGOTIATING SOFT-LINE REJECTIONS

Soft-Line Rejection #1

Person One: "Do you think you'd like to go to the race-track together sometime?"

Person Two: "Actually, I'm pretty busy."

Person One: "Well, we could talk another time and see if there is a day that was convenient. I know what you mean. There always seems to be something to do (lightly spoken with an understanding laugh)."

Person Two: "Okay (leaving it open for discussion another day)."

By keeping it open-ended, Person Two doesn't need to reject Person One's request. This not only saves face and avoids out-and-out rejection, but it is especially important if Person Two *is* open to seeing Person One again.

Soft-Line Rejection #2

Person One: "Do you think you'd like to go to a movie together on Wednesday night?"

Person Two: "Oh, I can't. Thanks. I've got a meeting at work that I'm committed to."

Person One: "Well, maybe another night this week? I don't know what your schedule is like. When are you free?"

If you immediately follow with another suggestion regarding day and time, it may be the negotiating technique you need. You might think Person Two would volunteer, "I can't tonight, but to-morrow or the next day would be great!" The fact is, that even if she wants to see you, she won't necessarily suggest an alternative time. She may feel ambivalent or socially awkward. She might be short-sighted and not consider the possibility that if she doesn't speak up, you may not ask again.

WHAT THEY DO IN TEXAS

My slow-as-molasses attorney from Texas, whom I've mentioned before, clued-me-in on one of his secrets, "Todd. When there is something you want from another person, and if they are not forthcoming, ask again, in the course of the conversation. Ask three times, each time in a slightly different way, agreeing with a point they made previously, but looking at it from a different angle. That way, a 'no,' has a chance to turn into a 'maybe' or 'yes.' "He *would* say the same thing three times.

Fine and dandy when negotiating a business deal, and fine if you have already agreed on going on a date and are discussing particulars. But if a person is simply being polite and letting you down easy, take the Soft-Line as a hint: that's the best price you can negotiate.

There are people who mean what they say, and there are other people who are unable to take a hint. If you find yourself with a person who cannot take a hint, you may need to be more direct (while still being polite), "Oh, that's a nice idea, but I'm seeing someone now (even if not true). Sorry."

Whether you are tactful, subtle, need to repeat yourself in three different ways, or if you have to ask directly, do ask. In the Dating Game, it is proper etiquette to let your suitor off-the-hook easily, assuming he or she can take a hint: "I'm busy," "I have plans," or "Sorry. I can't go," are usually effective.

TIME-TESTED PHONE TECHNIQUES

23

THE CONDUCTOR LIFTS HIS BATON AND THE INSTRUMENTA-lists begin, but they are interrupted by, "Uugggg!," the conductor shrugs, "Horrible." Most conductors are more polite, but in a typical classical symphony orchestra's rehearsal, the conductor will want to try passages over and over again until the orchestra gets it right. Union fees cost the orchestra's management a lot of money, but it's worth it on opening night when the orchestra performs the music beautifully.

When an audience is present, the conductor won't have the luxury to try sections over again to correct mistakes. Hopefully, the musi cians will feel secure enough after several rehearsals to give it their all. If a musician gets a case of the nerves, or doesn't feel good that night, the musician plays well, regardless, because he or she is a professional who has practiced.

YOUR REHEARSAL (WRITE IT DOWN)

While we are not performing with the Chicago Symphony, we are working with precious little time in a phone call, and we need to say things in a reasonably articulate manner. If you think you will feel nervous, embarrassed or inhibited, rehearse ahead of time and draft a script which you can follow. If you falter, check your notes and get back on track.

Since you cannot communicate with gestures, facial expressions, or other nuances (excepting video conference calls), practice responding to different scenarios which may arise in a phone call (Call Waiting interruptions, loud music playing in the background, or he or she sounds sleepy, etc.).

Write it down. You can sound spontaneous, even if you've re-hearsed. That's how musicians prepare for a concert, after all. If you have a patient friend, practice together. Dale Carnegie wrote in *Making Friends and Influencing People,* "I'd rather pace up and down the street for ten minutes making sure I know exactly what I want from a person, than walk into their house for a business meeting and not be sure." We're not talking about a business call in this case, but it is a similar problem.

You need to be as efficient as possible because you cannot be sure what will happen on the other end of the connection. If you don't know someone well, and the call is important, you might get performance jitters. (Will they be glad to hear from me, or even re-member who I am?) The other person may be aware that you have called to initiate a friendship and anticipate your hints or direct re-quest for a date.

What if we reach him or her at a bad time? What if someone else answers the phone, and it becomes clear he or she is romantically involved? What if the person is glad to hear from me, but does not really want to go out on a date?

Depressing? Yet, there are many, many times when making con-tact by phone is the *only* way. Your choice is to take a slight risk of being disappointed, or not to make contact at all, foregoing the possibility of being happily involved in a new and promising relationship.

FOLLOWING THE SCRIPT

If you are able to sound confident, it will be easier to save face if things progress unexpectedly. In the beginning of a phone conversa-tion, try to avoid improvising until you feel reasonably secure about talking with the other person. All details of the call need not be per-fect: Stu...stu..stu..stu.. stut-stutter if you have to, bu..bu..but-t just get the words out.

Again, write down the scenario as you imagine it will unfold. Write out the phrases and sentences you would like to use, and get to the point sooner than later. Be open to spontaneity and consider alternate scenarios (if he or she seems disinterested, wants to call you back later, etc.). In reality, you may only refer to your script in bits and pieces, but by writing it down you'll sound more at ease and the content will be as planned.

Practice aloud in order to hear your voice. Try tape-recording your lines and make sure you come across in the manner you envision. You'll need to have a face saving *exit-phrase* (or two) if your prospective mate lets you know of their engagement to marry or if there is some other excuse for not getting to know you better. Suitable for this purpose might be, "Sure, I was just asking — I thought it might be nice. Anyway, I'll see you around. Bye," or, "Well, that sounds great (whatever their excuses)—Good luck with it!" Wishing the person well ends the conversation on a positive note, and does not stress that your primary goal of the call has been rejected. Onwards and upwards!

Hopefully, all of this careful planning and worry is just that, *worry over nothing*. The call will go smoothly on its own, and you can toss out your script. However, nothing can derail your confidence more than falling on your face, while sputtering through the phone wires, "I wsaan..ted toa aask ya iiff a youd go movie wid widt me." *Devastating?* Temporarily perhaps, but completely unnecessary if you make the effort to rehearse and write-out, at least, part of your call.

You will be surprised how quickly you'll get over a minor rejection and be able to move on and call the next potential mate.

---

*   *   *

After hundreds of calls, you'd think *I'd have learned*. I met a very interesting and lovely woman named Mara at a modern dance concert. After watching some truly magnificent bodies in motion, one of them, hers, I met Mara backstage. I went to this particular concert because I had previously met the choreographer and Director of the dance company through a friend, and I wanted to test-out if she might be my Ms. Right.

However, at the reception after the concert, the company's Director did not seem to remember me. I definitely remembered her, and so I took it to be a sign of lack of interest. Rather than go home completely dejected, I easily moved into a conversation with one of the other dancers, Mara, using a compliment about her dancing as an opening line (genuinely offered).

It seemed that a group of people she knew were going out to dinner, and I recognized that I did not seem to be invited. Why should

I be? I had just happened along, and did not know anyone. So, I took this to be a cue, and said my good-byes with a smile.

Since Mara was friendly and attractive, I decided to give her a call under the pretense that I wanted to send her some music I had composed (true). The connection was that she might hear a tune to which she could choreograph a dance. I thought I would ask for information such as where and to whom I might send my recording, in the event she did not care to listen.

Feeling overconfident (I'm not sure why), I looked her up in the phonebook and made the call *spontaneously, without preparation.* Her message machine answered, which caught me off-guard. I hadn't anticipated leaving a message and I lost confidence, became nervous and began to stutter my way through one of the most unintelligible messages I had ever left on any piece of tape anywhere. Pauses in-between consonance's and vowels thrown every which way, "Hi Maara. Rhis is Todd (I exaggerate). We mat at the donce concertt the otherra night, an I..." When I hung up the receiver, I wanted to cry. Maybe Mara would not have been interested anyway, but she never returned the call after that message. I gave up on Mara.

Of course, *you* may be a very relaxed person, one who doesn't have to worry about a strength-sapping case of nerves. That's very nice. But for the rest of us, while practice may not make perfect, it can make a conversation smoother and help us prepare for the unexpected.

If he or she sounds busy when answering the phone, or the conversation does not work out as you had hoped, how will you react?

ANSWERING MACHINES

The blessings and evils of telephone answering machines are sung far and wide. Regardless, if you don't have an answering machine, I recommend you get one. You may argue that you are home certain hours of the day, and if someone really wants to get in touch with you, they will. True, *if* he or she is persistent. Fine, *if* this person is unequivocal in his or her passion (interest, dedication) to reach you.

Unfortunately, people are fickle. What if a woman to whom you gave your business card at a party last weekend gets up the nerve to call you one evening when you are not in? Will she promptly call back early the next morning, or at all, and was that a call you would have liked to received? If you have an answering machine, there is a good chance she will, at least, leave a message.

Not every caller will be persistent, but most people
are used to leaving messages on machines.

A Conundrum

Shannon was a colleague of mine who was almost impossible to reach. We both served on the Board of an arts organization, and I had tried to call her several times to discuss our next meeting, and to give her some information she had requested. I tried her several times on Saturday, Sunday evening, weekdays, and at all times of day. There was no one home and she did not have an answering machine. I was ready to give up when I spoke with someone she knew. He threw his hands in the air, "Call her late. That's the only time you'll get her in."

When I finally reached her, late one evening, I suggested that she buy an answering machine. Her response was frustrating to me: "I'm not good with machines" —A fatalist's answer: one which floats like a rock sits on top of a lake. She did not have the flexibility, desire or energy to change. Yet, I was the one that had to spend *my* time calling to reach her with information *she* had requested from me.

Shannon had separated from her husband the year before, and I knew that she was lonely. She was placing herself even farther from society by not allowing friends, relatives, and possible suitors a means by which to reach her. Even I almost gave up on calling her; I considered writing her a note instead.

Shannon requires a lot of dedication on the part of any suitor. If you asked her how she liked being single, she laughed nervously, "Well, maybe someone will come along one day." Shannon is not unlike many other men and women who do not realize they are being inconsiderate to others, and lowering their chances of going out on a date by not having an answering machine, voice mail or some other form of a message-taking device.

No, I don't work for the phone company but, yes, I believe in the efficiency of this simple technology and the dating benefits of using new, evolving communication services and technologies to come.

Keep chance, opportunity, and timing all on your side.
With an answering machine, you will rarely miss a call.

INCOMING AND OUTGOING MESSAGES

The Message A Person Hears On Your Machine: Leave a friendly, well-rehearsed and spontaneous message. Yes, people have different senses of humor, but avoid leaving asocial messages like this one: *"Rooooaaaar"* (a man imitating a lion's roar)...then, "This is Jerry's place....*Rooooaaaar*...leave a message (yelled out)." Another example to avoid: really loud music left blaring for thirty seconds without a person's voice, then a short tone is the caller's cue to say something.

The people who leave this type of message may believe it is cute, humorous, creative or perhaps the intention is to communicate displeasure towards the world like, "Don't bother me." Whatever, for someone who is single and hoping to receive a call from a prospective mate, these types of unconventional, asocial messages (often expressing anger or depression) are counterproductive. *Remember, few people actually want to be with a stick in the mud.*

Instead, think like an advertiser and consider what the other person wants to hear. Appeal to the other person who is questioning whether or not he or she wants to leave a message on an impersonal machine to begin with. Make it easy.

Leaving Your Message On Their Machine: Try to leave a friendly, upbeat message which invites a person to return your call. You may decide to hang up, preferring to speak with him or her directly, especially if you do not know the person well. Leaving a message puts the destiny of the relationship in the other person's court. Your message is another piece of information a prospective mate will analyze (consciously or unconsciously).

Three Message Tips

1. **Keep your message open-ended:** If you say, "Would you like to get a slice of pizza tomorrow?," and the potential mate does not call you back, what will your next message say: "Uh, I guess you weren't able to have the pizza, but how about roast beef tonight?" And after that?

In contrast, an open-ended message might be, "I thought maybe we could get together some time," leaving the decision, and details, open-ended.

2. **Stay flexible:** If your message says you will wait for him or her to return your call, you may wait for a long time. If you become impatient and call again, you have defeated the message you left earlier which said you would wait. To avoid this situation, allow for the possibility that you may try back later: "You can reach me at 842-9675, or I will try you again over the weekend."

3. **Leave your full name and number:** If you do not know the person well, don't assume you are the only man named Todd who has called in the last few days. Some people are very popular.

SHE WAS JUST OUT OF REACH:
I once thought it was more personal to leave my first name only, but I learned my lesson when trying to date a woman named Ida. Three weeks after Ida did not return my call, I tried her again. In the course of the conversation, it became apparent that I had called previously but did not hear from her. "Oh. Was that you? I know another Todd and I thought you were him, so I called him back." It turned out that the two of them began dating around that time. This can happen, especially, with younger, popular men and women. I do not know if we were meant for each other long-term, but on a first impression basis, she was a superlative "10" in my book, a Ford model, very bright, and I had serious regrets about losing the chance to see if we might have had a relationship.

Your message should be open-ended in case the person is out of town or too busy to get back to you. Try not to reveal any anxiety you may have about the outcome of your message(s).

CALL WAITING

One of the more helpful telephone features is Call Waiting. For the uninitiated, Call Waiting allows a second call to interrupt a first call (which you are still on) with a beep or click, and gives the ability to switch back and forth between the two calls. This can be inconveniencing, however. You may be on the phone with Joeseph when Frank calls. You hear a pleasant tone, or click, letting you know that a second person is calling. With the flick of a button, you can speak with Frank while Joseph is on hold. Joseph will not hear a word you say to Frank and vice versa.

Yet, Call Waiting is a diplomatic mess to some people. What do I do? Decide to talk with one person and risk offending the other? Inform Joe, "Well, I think I'd rather talk to Frank now (of course not), so can I call you back?"

Call Waiting has its detractors, mostly because many people are not skilled at navigating the problems it creates diplomatically. If your call is interrupted, and Jill says to you, "I've got to get this call— hold on," and proceeds to gab with the new caller for two minutes before getting back to you, yes, *that is rude*. Since that often happens with Call Waiting, many people dislike it, both on the calling *and* receiving end. However, if you follow a few guidelines, you will be able to take advantage of what Call Waiting offers.

Diplomatically Speaking:
When That Second Call Interrupts

Who is Your Priority? Tell the first caller you will take the second call, but that you will call whoever it is back later. Make it clear to the first caller, Joseph, that he is your priority: "Let me tell this person I'll call them back later — just a sec (defining the short time you will be away)."

Are You Glad to Hear From Me? When you speak with the second caller, Frank, be friendly and sound glad to hear from him. Hide your impatience about wanting to get back to Joseph. It would be rude to make Frank feel it was a mistake for him to have called.

Be Communicative: Immediately, and in a friendly way (hide your impatience), let Frank know you are on the other line and that you will call him back (ask if you can reach him in about fifteen minutes, or however long you anticipate).

Thanks for the Call: When Frank replies, "Sure. No Problem," add, "Thanks. Speak to you shortly," acknowledging the fact that he is patient and understanding.

Sorry for the Interruption: Say, "Sorry," when you get Joseph back on the line, acknowledging the interruption and his patience. Share information, if you can. Volunteer, "That was my cousin Frank," so to include Joseph and make him feel that you are not hiding anything from him (like that was really my *other* suitor). However, if it was another suitor, you probably will want to keep it to yourself and not volunteer information about the second caller, if possible.

Defining Priority: Let the second call ring and do not allow it to interrupt the first call. Sometimes you'll want the first caller to know his or her call is *really* important to you, and that you'll let the second caller try again another time: "Whoever it is will call back later," you reassure.

By being flexible and diplomatic, you'll manage repeated interruptions and miss fewer calls.

FAX ME, WILL'YA?

There is nothing like speaking with a person in person, face to face, expression to expression. Unless you can afford video conferencing equipment, the next best communication is speaking live on the phone, laugh to laugh, breath to breath, inflection to inflection. The fax machine also offers excellent possibilities for communication but, mostly, in special situations. Depending on your relationship with the person, a fax which hints at getting together and requests a response, could be humorous and charming.

If a person shares a fax machine at an office, beware that any message can be read by others and is not private. Therefore, a direct request for a date, not cloaked in a business tone or a simple request for the person to get back to you, could be embarrassing to the person you've faxed.

In General, Take a Hint

Remember, it takes two to tango. It is always the right of the other person not to return your call or wish to see you again. The question often asked is, "How many times is it appropriate for you to call or leave a message (write a friendly note, fax, accidentally bump into the person, etc.) before you start to become a thorn in their side?"

When are you coming on too strong? That is a good question. When a relationship is not already established, you have only a certain amount of *phone-capital* (patience or openness) before it's clear the other person is not interested in the idea of you two lovebirds tweedle-deeing in a tree.

Unanswered messages usually communicate a high probability that he or she does not want to answer your call.

E-Mail and Online Services

Future advances in technology will bring about new and exciting ways for singles to meet one another. The telecommunications industry is fast developing a "super highway" of interactive cable channels and video-telephone conferencing. Computer online services are expanding rapidly and so are the number and variety of dating services.

Computers now offer possibilities unheard of a few years ago, and e-mail has revolutionized communications. For the uninitiated, e-mail is the process of sending a typed message from your computer to another person's computer by accessing an ID or code. E-mail is stored at one location or another until the person accesses their ID and finds "mail" waiting to be read.

Commercial online services now offer a variety of Personal Ads. (Note: the same principles apply to online Personal Ads as those we discussed for newspaper and magazine ads.) "Chatrooms," Internet bulletin boards and "user-groups," are amongst other features which offer opportunities for singles in search of companionship. These expand the possibilities for men and women to meet one another through "live" online discussions; some topics being open and general and others quite specific.

University students, or employees of a large company, who share the same computer network, may find e-mail particularly useful in meeting individuals who live nearby and with whom they share something in common, e.g. their school or work environment. For example, my nephew, Ryan, attends a university and can easily communicate with other students on his computer screen. When a co-ed reads his message, she may or may not decide to respond with a message of her own. Ryan told me that he and one young lady had arranged to meet in person at a school hockey game.

A seductive attribute of both the Internet and commercial online services is the vastness of their reach. Thousands of people, many of them single, learn to "surf the net" or log-on to online services each day. Given our search to meet a potential Mr. or Ms. Right, however, our old nemesis, the Needle in the Haystack Syndrome, can have a nagging presence.

An array of e-mail pen pals or potential long distance relationships may not be what you originally had in mind. While you can meet other singles from the convenience of your home and PC terminal, is it helpful for you to meet someone online who lives in Florida when you reside in Michigan? While it is often possible to narrow down location by limiting telephone area codes or zip codes, it's not the easiest way to meet someone local nor is it for everyone.

By the way, if e-mail, per se, is not used as a means to meet someone new, it can be a wonderful means of communication with a person you've just met. Like a fax machine or telephone, creative use can be fun and effective if both people have access.

When communicating online, keep focused on your goal of meeting a partner for a day-to-day relationship, and remember: "the closer you travel to home...the more the odds increase you will meet someone who lives nearby."

May a Lady Ask?

Of course!....A lady should and does ask. Yet tradition, centuries old, favors the male role model of being the aggressor. Centuries of tradition encourages the feminine role of waiting for the male to take the first action, whether in the initial meeting, telephoning, or directly asking for a date. With the approach of the new millennium, new social attitudes and a wider variety of high-tech communication systems, flirtatious exchange between men and women with regard to dating will become easier, particularly for women.

There is at least one good thing that does come out of this anti-quated tradition. Men take note: ladies *expect* to be called or asked directly for a date. Women have prepared themselves to listen to a nervous man getting ready to *pop* the question of whether or not she will want to accompany him to a show or a dance since they were young girls. What power a woman has (assuming a man calls or asks) to decide "yes" or "no." If she sounds disappointed, bored, has no time today, tomorrow, or any day, then a gentleman needs to po-litely back-off.

Gosh and Gee. I wish I had a thousand dollars for every female that wanted to ask me out over the years but didn't (even if it was only five, that would be five thousand dollars). Especially during the many years I was shy, it would have been helpful to have those calls whether it was five or twenty-five. However, today, statistically, un-fortunately, it is still the man who initiates the relationship in the majority of cases, as well as the request for a date. While this is a definite disadvantage for many women, a woman can learn to excel in attracting an appropriate male, initiating communication and ask-ing for a date with a combination of charm and technique.

With both sexes, the tone of voice, inflection and timing all com-bine to communicate this message: *you would like to see the other per-son again.* "What do you usually do with your time off?," or "Maybe if you're in the area, I could show you that new computer I bought," are the types of lines which can stir the other person into action especially if he's shy. If you determine he is shy, you'll need to be more direct, "I wanted to see this new movie in town. Would you be interested in going?"

If he unexpectedly says, "Oh, I'm married," or is silent for a moment and says, "I don't know if that is a good idea," at least you'll know where you stand. You will then be able to get on with the more important task of meeting an interested and available man.

BY ALL MEANS

There aren't any rules that say you can't offer a man your phone number unsolicited. He may be happy that you did. Perhaps you'll save him the effort. Try doing it in a casual way like, "Oh (I *just* remembered), I wanted to give you my number because I'm hard to reach at work (you told him where you work). I'm really interested in that lawn mower you were talking about (he mentioned that he was selling his lawn mower, dumpster, pickup truck, whatever). Do you think I could take a look at it sometime?" (Any excuse to see him is fine.)

FLIRTATION: YOUR MAGIC FISHNET

Flirtation is one of the most powerful tools for communicating a sexual/romantic interest. Think of *flirtation* as a series of *hints* and closely related to our discussion of Soft-Lines. When talking with another person, a series of hints includes body language: smiling, moving or positioning one's body in a suggestive way. (On the phone, one flirts by *what* one says and *tone of voice*.)

One stereotypical role model is an old-fashioned image of a *southern belle*. She plays a flirtatious role, as she excels at manipulating menfolk with soft-spoken innuendo. With or without the charming accent, try imitating aspects of this, or any other role when it is useful. In order to elicit the reaction you want from your male friend, cajole, tease, or subtly manipulate him in a fun, flirtatious manner.

Both sexes should borrow, or use, whatever images of behavior that might help them succeed in the earliest stages of meeting a prospective mate. If it helps, pick a sex symbol from Hollywood's finest and imitate (subtly, of course) the tone of voice or pose he or she takes. For example, a man will often put on a macho air, talk tough, or say things with a manly flair (perhaps enacted for the occasion) which he thinks will impress a lady.

All is fair in finding your mate, as long as your partner agrees.
If you do not find a way to ask, directly or indirectly,
you may never see or hear from him or her again.

IMPROVE YOUR PHONE TECHNIQUE

1. *Time the Call Appropriately:* Do not apologize unless

you are calling very early or very late. If you start meekly with, "Hi. Did I get you at a bad time?," he or she needs to answer a question right off the bat. Instead, start out with a confident "Hello," and identify yourself. If you do sense you woke the person and that it *really* is a bad time, inquire, "Did I get you at a bad time? I can call back."

If you are on the receiving end and it's late, be sleepy but remain polite, "Oh, I'm glad to hear from you, but...could I call you back? No need to say something like, "You got me at a real bad time, I'm busy. I can't talk now." *That kind of rudeness may not deserve a call back.*

2. **Be Prepared to Get to the Point Quickly:** Do not beat around the bush. You may feel that you need to test his or her interest first, but if the conversation slackens, hint or ask directly so the purpose of your call becomes clear.

3. **Conceal Your Enthusiasm or Nervousness:** Talk with a potential mate as an equal, even if you are overwhelmed with the event. Try not to appear overly excited and keep self-doubts to yourself.

4. *Exiting a Conversation While Saving Face:* If he or she seems disinterested in getting together, take the hint gracefully and change the topic of conversation (as if nothing had happened). Refer to the pile of work you have to get through before bedtime and add, "Well...It was nice speaking with you, and if you'd like to play racketball sometime (beach ball, visit the new aviary in town, whatever), let me know."

5. *Remain Sociable Even If the Other Person Declines:* He or she may choose to decline your invitation or may never return your call. By keeping your approach open, light and positive, you can always say (if you bump into the person later), "Oh, hi! I meant to call you. How's everything going?" There is no need to be confrontational or a sore-sport about it. ("I guess *you* decided that you didn't *like* me enough to be my friend.")

6. **Be Generous When He or She Calls:** When someone

calls, recognize it took effort on his or her part, and let it be known you appreciate it. Put his mind at ease and let him know he called at a good time, "Oh, Hi, Steve, I'm glad you called. I was just thinking about you." Remember, Steve called you and he may be nervous about it. If you lavish him with a few friendly lines, you are being considerate. If you sense he would like to get together, why not be the first to bring up the idea? "The weather is so great these days. Do you feel like going to the beach?"

Keep your own anxiety about your relationship,
or lack of one, to yourself.

THE DATE OF THE CENTURY?

Your first date does not have to be the date of the century. However, it is a normal expectation that if you call, you have an idea of something you'd like to do with the other person: go to a museum, a sporting event, or perhaps there's a play or film to which you can still get tickets. Or, you have the idea to take a walk in the fine spring weather and wondered if he or she wants to come along. In fact, there's a place along the way to stop and have a cappuccino.

Being prepared with one or more possibilities gives the impression you are organized. It also diminishes any indecision regarding whether or not you two are going to see each other on a given day at a given time. *So, first, get the date set: the day and time. Then have one or two ideas for a shared activity.*

A mutually-agreed destination or activity should not be too complex. Minimize the back and forth: "I'll try to get tickets, and then I'll call you back and leave a message on your machine. You call my machine to confirm, but if I can't get tickets, I'll call a car rental place and see if we can drive twenty miles to the country if I can make a reservation at this particularly quaint restaurant."

The most important point of getting together is to determine *if you get along.* As long as you are at a place where the two of you can talk, intimately, any activity both people find acceptable will be okay. Even a loud rock concert can work fine if that's what appeals to you both. You can always talk afterwards.

Once the date has begun, be flexible, "Hey, would you rather do something else, or is this okay?" Compromise: go with the flow as needs arise. If she says the rock concert is fine, but "I wish there was a food concession because I missed dinner," offer, "We could go get something to eat during intermission. Is that too long to wait?" Place value, foremost, on communicating with the other person and making sure he or she is comfortable and having a good time.

You'll want to be charming, and that means being attentive and giving priority to the needs of the other person.

BOND OR CLOUSEAU?
HOW I MET MS. RIGHT

("Well, hey, what about the guy who wrote this book? So far, just a bunch of misguided mishaps. Did he ever meet his mate?")

24

IT HAPPENED ONE FRIDAY EVENING. THAT WAS THE NIGHT I slept peacefully and deeply, clutching my memories of that wonderful new woman in my life: Marie.. I had just met her a few hours ago. She was real, not a fantasy or some missed Vapor Factor figment caught in my imagination. She seemed to like me, and I had achieved the all important and necessary Follow-Through.

That day had started out poorly, however. You might say I was in the midst of seeking Ms. Right. I was, admittedly, somewhat zealous or well, addicted to the pursuit of — *grasping* for love as it were. I was desperately seeking Ms. Right or, if not one, then many. Fact is, I was known to more than a few friends as a *womanizer.*

I've confessed. Well, how else would I have the know-how to dream up the various techniques and observations in this book?! People do, and can, change especially once they meet Mr./Ms. Right. I *have* changed since my dating days before I met Marie, and I'm proud to say that I am now a one-woman man. But the days and evenings before I met Marie were lonely on balance, and I was still in my searching mode, emulating neither Clouseau nor Bond, but someone more like *me* and smack in the middle...

TRAPPED BETWEEN SEVERAL WOMEN, AND NO MS. RIGHT!

Years ago, before I met Marie, I was a kind of *friendly* predator, I admit. A confirmed bachelor sounds better, but it does not take into account all that my life-style entailed. Multiple relationships, short relationships, and long distance relationships existed in ways and numbers most people would not be interested in entertaining.

Just as I approached the day I would meet Ms. Right, my compulsive behavior caught up with me. I was becoming burdened by it all. The pure sensationalism of my life-style ended in one dull thud just before I met Marie. I overdosed in one confusing set of circumstances which left me ready for the psychiatrist's couch (a process which actually did change the course of my life almost as much as meeting Marie).

To describe the sensation, it was as if for several moments my brain ceased to function and my thoughts blurred together. I blanked out and, then and there, I caught my breath. Then and there, I promised myself to do something about the compulsive pattern I was trapped in. The old hamster wheel seemed to be stuck in its characteristic mode of transportation but it was getting mighty rusty.

What exactly happened? Just the night before, I had gone out on a date with one of the women I was dating at the time. I was seeing more than *four or five* women at the time, and I was just about getting ready to overload my system. Coinciding with an urgent need to find the real Ms. Right, I walked out the door and one of the strangest moments I've ever experienced struck me like a wet noodle sliding down my face.

You see, that day I had been on the phone for forty-five minutes with Angela, going over the reasons why we were breaking-up or, rather, listening to her tell me why she needed to stop seeing me. That morning I had kissed Lidia good morning as she left for work and I headed back to my apartment to do some writing. Midday, I made a call to Laura, whom I had just met the previous weekend to see if she were available to get together at some point. She was: the next evening. I made a mental note to call Susan the next day, because I felt it was due. I had a message on my machine from Marsha whom I had not seen for two weeks and she was coming to town over the weekend. Anyway, you get the idea.

Not that any one of these women thought that I was only seeing them. I did not mislead them, in general, but more often than not I kept various particulars to myself. Was any one of these nice women Ms. Right? No, and I knew it. But, I was a Master Of The Hampster Wheel That Was Rusting. I was a compulsive womanizer for a period of several years in my life. Not to the extent that you hear about

where so and so was married to three different people and led different lives. No. But, enough to drive me nutty and, I am sure, to com-
plicate and confuse the lives of the many different women I was dating during this time.

But anyway, that's over. Back to that evening, the evening before
I met Ms. Right. I walked out of my apartment and stopped in my
tracks. Yet, there was no one in the hall but me. *But who was I?*
For several bizarre moments, I could not remember where I was going or rather, I knew *where* I was going; I was going to meet one of
my girlfriends at the corner, but *which* girlfriend? Not only that, but
what had I told this person I was supposed to have done the night
before? With whom had I told this woman friend I had spent the
previous evening?

My social life was very active, and I was now confused by my
own activities. Had I lied to protect her feelings or to avoid compli-
cating my own affairs (in order to keep the relationship alive, *self-
ishly*)? Or, was this a woman with whom I shared the truth and nothing but the truth. *I could not move, and I could not remember.*

My own life-style and selfish manipulations had caught up to
me, having swirled around my brain so many times it was like pea-
nuts now being crushed in a peanut butter machine in one smashing
sensory overload: Thwwooooooooooooooooooooooop! Hit in the face
with my own foolish behavior. "Yuuuuuuuuuuuuuuuuuuuk!" And, to
think, all I truly wanted, in my own desperate way, was Ms. Right.
Where the heck was she!

DESPERATELY SEEKING WHAT'S-HER-NAME?

The combination of loneliness, my need for too many girlfriends,
and my desperate need to find Ms.Right was overwhelming —I was
caught in my own neurotic web. It was at that point in my addiction,
I decided to seek professional advice. Four years of psychotherapy
helped quite a bit. Still not perfect in all ways, but I am more considerate of others, including the woman and relationship I now cherish.

I'm only human after all, much more like that bungling Inspector Clouseau than the impeccably controlled Bond I so admire. This
story probably differs from your own. Mine was an extreme case and
my problems finally culminated and made me unhappy. That pain
and unhappiness forced me to make a decision to change, at least, to

want to change. The actual discovery of Ms. Right was the catalyst that helped *bring about that change.*

We humans tend to accept the status quo when the status quo is not too painful. Realizing bad habits — much less changing them when we are busy earning a living and assuming various responsibilities is often too much to handle. But, settling for our faults and bad habits, unfortunately keeps us trapped on the old rusting hamster wheel, churning and churning and churning.

I won't digress into a discussion of my personality or my own escapades which led through dozens and dozens of relationships with women. I'll just proceed back in time to that evening when I met Marie...

Back to That Friday Evening

Was it a romantic evening? Oh yeah. Full of sexual innuendo and flirtation? Definitely. Complete with the techniques which this book presents? Absolutely. The stuff that sexy Hollywood films are made out of? Sure. In fact, I followed the advice in this book so closely that two words sum it up nicely: *Primo Bond.*

After a great deal of effort learning how to master techniques for meeting people, and far too numerous relationships with women that did not result in marriage, I met my wife-to-be. Just like that. She came along like many other new friends or relationships had. Seemingly accidentally, sort of by Fate (with a little help).

I had felt in my heart and soul that Ms. Right was just around the corner, and I made it my priority to find her: if not today, tomorrow, next week or next month, but I felt she was close. You might say I looked for her frantically and that I often accepted various, sometimes time-consuming, detours off the path while searching.

It was a Friday evening and I had suggested to one of the women I was dating that we meet at a concert where a friend of mine was having a piece of his music performed. I was increasingly unhappy in this relationship, partly because Ellen was *married* (legally separated, but not yet divorced for reasons she described as relating to her son and financial affairs). To be fair, I had let her know that I was looking for someone to have a *complete* relationship with, and that I did not think she and I were appropriate for the relationship I was seeking, long term. Yet, we were good friends, in the strange context of our relationship.

I confide in my readers these humbling truths so you see my imperfections, more importantly, to make it clear that *you need not be perfect to succeed in meeting your mate.* You also *do not need to juggle different relationships* until they fall into place, as I did. You only need to test-out different potential relationships or partners *to the point of knowing whether or not to pursue the relationship further.* You *do* need to push yourself to meet people and to take chances which may unfortunately result in numerous, but mostly insignificant, rejections along the way.

Inauspicious Beginnings

Earlier that Friday, I had been invited to an unusual kind of social event: an opening reception for a new line of designer/architectural furniture. Hey, some people both like and pay for that kind of thing. I didn't have a problem with the fancy furniture. I was only too glad to have the opportunity to scout around a bit for Ms. Right. I liked being around people and knew that by being socially active, I would eventually meet my mate. So, I encouraged people to invite me to this event and that event, and I tried to get my name on as many mailing lists as I could. I knew there were lots of special events: sales, promotions, conferences, etc., where two people might accidentally (sort of) meet.

Well, at the furniture show, after three or four failed conversations with women (one truly absurd conversation with a group of three teenagers: me, in my mid-thirties; not one of the three showed *any* interest in talking to me), I tired of the wrought iron, brass knobs, and odd-shaped chairs. The conversations I had with one or two other women were reasonable, skillfully presented introductions and continuations. It was a party environment with about one hundred people in a large loft and showroom; the Party Phenomenon was working its magic. But, I was bored and supposed to meet Ellen at a concert uptown. "If Ms. Right is here, I've missed her," I thought, making my way down the stairs.

Just A Normal Evening Out

Anyway, I was slightly bummed-out by my lack of success, and with two glasses of wine in me, I headed for the subway (as so often in this book, I was in New York City). Now, low and behold, an attractive woman was standing on the subway platform (often that *is* the case). I heard her talking in an open and friendly manner to two policemen, making conversation about the train being late. The First Impression Factor was signaling "Okay." I liked her looks, her voice, and the fact she was so friendly. I also bet she would probably be friendly to me too.

When the police officers left, I decided to take advantage of the momentum of their conversation still in the air and extend it, as if I had been a part of it all along. "I've waited twenty minutes for these trains sometimes," shaking my head, and thinking that she must be from out of town — what else could account for such a sensitive, intelligent woman being so friendly to strangers in a New York City subway station?

It worked, and probably almost anything would have, as she was very friendly and talkative. We sat together on the train, care-free, without any need to make excuses. We talked, and by the second or third subway stop I determined that, yes, she was nice and attractive, but she was not the woman for me. The facial expressions, the content of what she was saying, and other elements in her behavior struck me as being less interesting than my first impression had gauged. No problem. (Besides, I didn't notice any *particular interest* on her part in me.)

We said good-bye and I knew, once again, that while my Ms. Right was getting closer, she was still somewhere out there ahead of me.

Music to My Ears

I met Ellen, my married friend, at the concert. She informed me that she had to leave early, at intermission, in order to go home and receive a long distance call. The audience was comprised of a fairly small group of people, maybe sixty in number (it was a semi-private affair), and I spotted more than one person whom I knew. Well, one conversation led to the next before the music started, and I waved to my good friend Oscar who had spotted me and was on his way across the room to join us.

Whooooooaaaaaaaaaaaaaaaaaaaaaaaaa (flashing lights with strobe effect), I was stunned. "Who is that woman??," I thought, staring into the crowd to my left. Not only does she look great, but what

refinement in the way she moves and talks. After the concert began, I kept checking to make sure this woman did not leave and disappear from my life.

Remember: if your Screen of Interpretation flashes green in shades of bright neon, and the word "Yes" swirls around your brain like fireworks on the Fourth of July, ask yourself, "How often does this happen?" The lingo that comics are made of floated in front of my eyes: Swish! Baaaamm! Ballooooeeeyy! The expressive emphatic of the land of comic books roared on in my brain while the musicians on stage played.

Intermission: Ellen had gone home, and there I was standing with Oscar, a Willing Decoy. Together we stood in the aisle and I quietly let him know that there was a wonderful woman in the audience. He agreed, saw my point, but wanted to talk about the music.

First Contact

Our eyes met, and our glances locked-on to each other, like laser beams. We were about twenty feet apart: she sitting, me standing, with Oscar looking elsewhere scratching the bald spot on the center of his head. She seemed to be trying to stare me down: our eyes locked for about five seconds — It seemed like forever. I pulled away. "What was that?," I gasped. Was she intentionally trying to stare me down?

I watched her interact with others for a few minutes and the concert continued. I sat patiently with Oscar, knowing that I would try to meet this woman after the concert, if at all possible. During the rest of the concert I was obsessed with the following thought, "Was she here alone or is she the girlfriend, or wife, of one of the musicians on stage?" What a depressing thought.

After the concert, there was a lot of hand shaking and people were talking with one another. I mingled a bit, but always kept an eye on the woman I wanted to meet. She seemed to be part of a small group of women, and I heard one introduce her exclaiming, "Here is the ballet teacher I told you about." "Hmmmmm," I thought. "A ballet teacher. Okay," I said to myself, "I like ballet." I waited patiently, smiling inanely as people said things to me, hoping that my smile was an appropriate response, and meanwhile edged closer and closer to this woman. Suddenly, she began to head towards the exit door along with two or three other women! I had to act quickly. Oscar was no where in sight, and would no longer be able to help out as a

Willing Decoy. I had to go it alone.

One of the most important psychological techniques in meeting people in a crowd or public space (where you do not have the luxury of being invited to a sit-down dinner party with various single people) is this: *be flexible, think on your feet, and act sooner than later.* I had smartly made the decision to discard the convention of saying good-bye to my good friend Oscar. Why? It was rude: I should have at least made eye contact, smiled from across the room as I waved good-bye. Yet, I knew I would be able to speak with him the next day, that I could apologize for my behavior and he would forgive me.

If I allowed the tang of guilt I felt to persuade me to find Oscar and say good-bye, I would probably have lost the opportunity to meet Ms. Right. Which option would you take? *It is surprising that when confronted with the unknown and the risk of going-it-alone, reason is cast aside for an action which is more comfortable though less productive.* Many people would have gone for the familiar, friendly feeling of finding (procrastinating) Oscar to say good-bye and thereby losing the opportunity to meet one's mate. Obstacles are often treacherously disguised by that which *seems to be the right thing to do.*

Being experienced and directed, and not having much alternative, I followed the group of women in a Bond-like fashion, hoping that an opportunity to begin a conversation would arise. I stayed comfortably behind, not knowing what action to take. It was legitimate for me to be leaving the concert at the same time and I fumbled with my concert program, reviewing the titles of the pieces of music I was supposed to have listened to.

Then, opportunity knocked. The three other women got into a taxi, calling out good-byes to Marie who continued to walk down the city block. Again, a less experienced person might have watched her disappear into the night, thinking, "Well, how am I supposed to catch up to her? She is seventeen feet ahead and walking at a fairly fast clip. She is, after all, in shape: a ballerina."

WATCH THOSE INTERSECTIONS!

With all of my experience, it was still the same: *Performance Anxiety.* Will I be met with interest or disdain? Is this other person available? Remotely interested? There was still a good ten feet between my bride-to-be and myself, and I knew that I had to act soon because she would be approaching an intersection ahead. (How would I know which street she would take?)

There was no Lag Time to help out. No time for procrastination. I walked quickly, outpacing her, perhaps with a kind of *loping* stride characteristic from my gym days. I took a chance and took action. I was carrying a piece of paper which had the directions to an after-concert reception. (Remember: luckily, it was a semiprivate gathering.) I figured she would have been invited as well. I approached her with a friendly smile and that Something-In-Common Bond: "Hi. Are you going to the reception?"

She smiled back, encouragingly. She seemed undecided about the reception (which I hoped meant, "My, you are quite the *loper*. Well, maybe, especially if *you're* going"). Rather than try to talk her into going to a reception (at a mutual acquaintance's apartment, which would have presented a nice environment in which to get to know one another), I immediately started talking about the concert *and* our mutual acquaintance (not someone I knew well, but I hoped familiarity would chip-away at her defenses) and, of course, the music (finally). The exchange was friendly, full of smiles, but I was very nervous about the encroaching intersection. Luckily, the light was red, and we stood at the corner while the decision was being made as to where she was going.

Just a few more seconds to work with I thought. Since she had not mentioned the reception, I offered, "Well, maybe we could get a drink first, in that Steak and Beverage across the street. Then we could figure out if we want to share a cab to the reception." It was a chance I had to take. I felt that our exchange had been a friendly one, somewhat flirtatious, and that by stressing our common bonds (the concert we had both attended, our mutual acquaintance, and our common invitation to the same reception), she might possibly agree.

The problem I faced was this: If I had said, "Well, I guess I'm going to the reception (decisive move), she might have said, "Well, it's late and I have to get up early tomorrow to go to work, so I guess I'll go home." By keeping the reception a possible goal, communicating my own indecision about going, but letting her know I would be pleased to continue our conversation, I gambled.

If she said, "Well, I'd rather get a drink at the reception," I could have said, "Yeah. That's a better idea. Shall we share a cab?" Only if she said, "No thanks. I think I better go home. Nice meeting you. Bye." Only then would I have lost her, probably because she was not interested in me or available.

There seems to be no time quite like the present.

Finally, No More Obstacles

As soon as she said, "Yes," I did not allow time for an awkward silence to develop, no bumbling thoughts of, *"Wow. She accepted, and now we're having a kind of date!,"* to tense-up the atmosphere. Rather, I continued the friendly pace of conversation, asking her questions about herself and volunteering relevant things about myself. I tried not to appear overly excited or indicate there was anything out of the ordinary going on between us (*"Zooks! She is fantastic,"* I held under my breath). It turned out that the restaurant had a nice, empty bar and we eased into our seats. The conversation seemed endless, constant. Flirtation seemed natural, not forced.

There was never any mention of going to the reception. Why? We had arrived at something much better. Into our second hour of conversation, it was getting late. She said that she'd be taking a cab home. I suggested that we share a cab since we were going the same direction, and I mentioned that I would get out first as I lived closer. Sharing a cab is more economical and so, it had a rational sounding logic behind it.

Better yet, it gave us *something else to share*: a cab ride in New York City, and it suggested that we could socialize away from the Steak and Beverage or the concert where we had, sort of, met. It also hinted that I lived alone since I did not say, "Gee, I guess my wife will be asleep. It's late." Also, I was going to be dropped-off in front of the building where I lived, and that would reinforce that I was real, not a figment of her imagination; a friendship was budding, or so I hoped.

Meanwhile, we had another fifteen minutes of fun, flirtatious conversation in the cab. As we approached my building, I made sure to say my good-byes early (rather than, "Oops. Gotta run. Wish I had gotten your number. Darn!"). "Well, this was great," I said. "I'm so glad I went to that concert, after all." This allowed her to reciprocate, which she did. It also was a smooth lead-in. I did not say, "Babe. How about doing a movie-thing with me Saturday?" Instead, I gradually hinted at a second meeting, "We should do this again some-time. Can I call you?" This allowed her to make the decision of whether or not I would be calling.

She smiled knowingly, but did not exactly give me her business card or even her phone number which I would have eagerly memo-rized. Instead, she coyly said, "I'm in the phone book. No one else has a name like mine." Hmmmm. I took that as a "Yes."

Getting out of the cab, into my apartment building and up six-teen flights on the elevator, I had but one objective in mind: to get to that phone book. Was she kidding? Is she really in the book? Or, was that a way of saying, "It was great, but I don't think I want to repeat this. I'm not available anyway." Was I going to be disappointed by some mischievous rejection?

Mind racing...I search for the phone book...turn on the light, trip over Merve, the cat. Her last name with a V. Lot 's of V's in Man-hattan. Vi...Vick. L's the letter. I need an L. Vicklare, Vicklaren, Vicklarenson. There is only one Vicklarenson. Just like she said. She meant it. Got it! Got the Follow-Through.

So Who Is Going To Pop This Balloon?

Not wanting to come on too strong, I waited a couple of days, till Monday, and called her. She knew who I was, why I was calling, and said "Sure." She agreed to get together on Saturday and she agreed right away! I was very happy. This woman, to be sure, was the clearest prospect, the most Ms. Right-like feminine being I had met in what seemed like years. I told all of my friends.

One day later, a call, a message on my machine. Polite, because she was a class-act: Wonder Woman Supreme but, nevertheless, she had decided to decline. "Todd, this is Marie. I've given it some thought, and I need to cancel our getting together Saturday. I'm very sorry. If you'd like to talk about it, you can reach me later tonight."

When Obstacles Pop-Up Like This...

UUUUggggghh! How *unpleasant* to receive that message. She changed her mind? Isn't that rude? Was this a mildly-spoken rejec-tion? But, since she invited me to call her, I did.

Calm, cool and collected, I called. She, also, was calm, "I've just broken up with a man I lived with for three years, and I really need more time before seeing other people." Oh. Is that it (Phew! — A tremendous sigh of relief. You mean, it's not me then? — ran through my mind).

"Well, I can understand that," I maturely replied. "What if we just got together for lunch. (Obviously, I was trying anything to see her again.) I have to take my stereo for repairs (true) at that Disco Repair shop in your neighborhood." "Ahhhh," Marie laughed, knowingly. "I don't think so," she chimed. "We could just be friends," I held on (hoax: I was phenomenally attracted to her)." Her reply: "Ahhh, I don't think so. Maybe you could do that, but I'm not sure I could, and I'd rather not get involved right now." Grasping at straws, I'm thinking, "Well. At least she's admitted to being attracted to me, and I'll take that as an encouraging sign."

Can't let this go, I'm almost begging her. Am I ready to say goodbye and be all alone in the world again? "Well... can I call you in a couple of months (randomly chosen time period; figured next week would be too soon)?" Pause. "Yes. That would be okay," she consented. "Okay. I'll speak to you in a couple of months." ("A couple of months?," I thought, "Who knows where and with whom I might be in two months!?")

The compromise solution was still very promising and so I marked it down on my calendar. "Call Marie Vicklareson two months *and one week* from today (so not to appear *too* eager)."

Be patient with people because often they require it.
You can only push a person so far, when the negotiation is over.

Sometimes A Little Frog Can Help Out

Time passed. She still remembered me in two months (plus one week for good measure). I still had terrific memories of her, but two months and one week is long enough that I was starting to forget what she looked like. During this waiting period, I decided to take a chance and drop her a short note which I sent to her place of work (so not to presume I could contact her at home—I did not want to break the rules too much).

I enclosed a tiny ceramic frog (the size of a thumbnail), which I had paid all of two dollars for in a gift store. It was supposed to be a good luck charm, accompanied by a printed translation in Japanese: "Keep this in your purse and all the money which leaves it will later be returned to you." I'm not sure about the fortune, but I liked the tiny frog and I thought it might be agreeable to Marie accompanied with a note saying, "Hi, Saw this good luck charm in a gift store and thought you might like it, Todd."

When I called her, she agreed to see me. We arranged to meet at a friend of mine's book party. That is, he had just published a novel, was reading a few chapters, signing copies and having a reception. A reception, after all. It seemed appropriate, perhaps not romantic, but it was a convenient meeting place near the ballet school where Marie taught. We planned to go out to dinner afterwards.

My, how the magic of our first meeting was starting to dissipate. Our first date seemed strained in so many ways. We were both disappointed. The two month waiting period was just one obstacle: the first of quite a few. Our first meeting had been so smooth, so easy and promising. Yet, even with many difficulties and problems to come, we started dating on a regular basis.

I quickly bowed out of my other relationships with women friends, and Marie and I became serious about seeing one another. After six months of dating, we lived together for a year, became engaged for a year, got married and now happily have a child. Call it good timing, luck, and/or determination on both of our parts to become mates for life: we did it.

*   *   *

Most people have their quirks, difficulties, and histories filled with some hurt and disappointment. Not all people have complicated histories or are temperamental and difficult to get along with. But, probably, most people *whom you become involved with are.* It's only human, so be prepared to be patient.

If a fundamental attraction to the person is strong,
you may want to give him or her a chance,
or two, or three, or four....

EPILOGUE

== **25**

ADIEU

WHO EVER THOUGHT PEOPLE COULD BE SO NERVOUS AND socially awkward, including me for so many years. What's there to fear in meeting and dating other people? Why does so much work need to go into it? Are there so few Mr./Ms. Rights out there? Do you need these answers? Yes, it would help to have these answers and numerous others, but your Mr./Ms. Right is probably alive and well, somewhere, even if you don't have answers to these questions.

    *   *   *

You've got a date with someone promising?! Now what? Well, I am working on the *next book*, so I won't leave you on your own for long. One date will probably not lead immediately to your mate. It will probably take many dates, many relationships: healthy, unhealthy, emotionally painless, emotionally painful but, finally, you are likely to meet your mate.

If you've read this book and are even thinking about reading my next one on dating, well, it sounds like you are quite serious about finding a mate. It sounds like you are willing, even driven to sift through a large number of people in search of the person you hope to meet.

Often we may meet a potential mate but lose him or her to one or more obstacles which then delays our goals. Often the most important obstacle is ourselves. You can work on improving yourself, or a good therapist can help. It is not a stigma or a sign of weakness to approach a psychologist or psychiatrist but, actually, it is a sign of the need and wish to be more mature in your interactions with other people.

Until we meet again, stay in practice. Be alert: your next door neighbor, the tutor in math class, or the woman who takes your ticket at the local cinema may be that very person you will want to get to know better. Take the chance that your feelings may be hurt. You may feel awkward about trying or be shy. You may not know how to deal with a situation but, in any case, begin to improve your social behavior in all possible areas in order to prepare for the arrival of Mr./Ms. Right.

SWAN SONG

My life has been no different than many lives in the primal, mating calls of the wild: sometimes a dog's life, sometimes that of a shaky king looking out over his harem worrying about the frailty of mortal lives and the perils of STD. I grew up in the trailing days of the hippie generation's plea for freedom of choice and lack of commitment. Now, my life mirrors middle American dreams of family vacations and my son Kyle's Little League baseball games and spring piano recitals.

You could say, I'm leaning back in my chair with my feet up on my desk. But I'm not pulling away from the single's life-style entirely (writing books about dating, and helping out other single people keeps me in touch). I'm feeling comfortable being committed to one woman, children running around the house, the dog and the cat. True, I'm busy. But I've got more energy to devote towards what I want to do with my life.

Now, the Sherlock Holmes hat hangs on the wall, the Inspector Clouseau cloak on the door, and the Bond sunglasses in the drawer. In the old days, I'd spend so much time trying to meet the woman of my dreams. Sure, I had lots of fun, drama and adventures, but consider me retired from that activity and onto others.

Now, often, I think about my wife with an intense feeling which is love and, in part, an appreciation for her as the human being with whom I share my life: these past years and for all those to come. At times, the intensity of my feeling overwhelms me, flush with tears, and I find a deeper understanding of what relationships are. Sure, our lives may have been more romantic at times in the early days, months and years. And compatibility ebbs and flows with the cycles of our personalities and the circumstances of our lives.

But our relationship takes on a new power with time, and that power sometimes translates into a feeling I have for Marie which is mostly love, but only part, because part is an indescribable, timeless feeling we humans have for all humanity. At these quiet times of reflection, when my thoughts rest on our sleeping child and Marie sings softly to herself nearby, it is in these moments that I am so thankful for having her to share my life, and it is in these moments when I realize that it is *this feeling which my search was all about.*

*   *   *

So ladies, if some fine fellow passes you an opening line one day, and it's "oblique" and he's got some charm, no, it won't be Yours Truly, but it may possibly be one of your co-readers of these very pages. Maybe you'll appreciate his effort, and maybe you will give him a chance. I hope so.

And gents, if a woman let's you know she's got you fixed in her focus and gives you a smile which sends a flush of blood through your veins, I doubt it will be my very beautiful wife, but don't shy away. Do your part to generate a conversation, because the two of you might be starting something that will lead to a lasting happiness.

People have solved this mating puzzle since time began, bumping their way through the Obstacle Course of Love. I only hope that this writing helps a few love-deserving folk find their mate with fewer bumps along the way

Happy Dating,

Todd Landen

Always Keep Our Best Rule in Mind:
There is no real alternative...
unless you're considering the monastic life.
For most of us, well...
that just doesn't sound like very much fun.

ALWAYS KEEP THESE RULES IN MIND

1. Many opportunities are lost because a necessary level of Follow-Through is not achieved. Ask for information which might allow you to see one another again. Carry a business card or, at least, a pen or pencil in the event you have to write down information.

2. Follow the Momentum Rule. You do not want to lose momentum in an early conversation just when you have met someone whom you'd like to talk to. He or she might not be skilled in the various techniques necessary to sustain momentum.

3. Use body language to disguise your own interest while gauging the interest of others. Props and Camouflage Technique can help create seemingly legitimate reasons for being in a certain place; you are not there solely to make conversation with a potential date.

4. Find out if the other person is available as well as interested. You'll be surprised how many people will enjoy flirting and who will maintain a friendly, platonic relationship with you, but will have no interest in taking the relationship any further.

5. Getting a first date may involve a lot of hinting or simply asking outright. Be prepared for a variety of obstacles to interfere. Rarely does a date just fall into your lap and offer you sweet kisses.

6. The intricate language of Soft-Lines, or hints, enables single people to sense-out availability and interest in others, diplo-

matically. Keep your antenna alert for signals, whether they are encouraging or discouraging.

7. *A Tortoise is defined as a shy person, not skilled in conversation, and not always sure what he or she wants. He or she probably sounds like many of the people you may meet and become interested in. Be advised that a Tortoise is not skilled at hinting, flirtation or asking for a date...but you can be.*

8. *If you are very relaxed and skilled on the telephone, fine. Most people, however, benefit from writing down the gist of what they intend to say before making the call, so to boost their confidence. Become versatile in the use of answering machines and Call Waiting; make sure you are accessible and miss as few calls as possible.*

9. *When arranging the particulars of a date, realize that the object is to converse and be comfortable (both of you). Make sure the other person is not just being polite and that, indeed, the decisions regarding place and time are mutual.*

10. *Recognize that people are capable of changing, and that many single people are somewhat desperate in their hopes and pursuit of finding a mate. Ultimately, dating behavior will be replaced by stability in a good relationship along with a deeper feeling of companionship and love.*